CW01271474

Frontispiece - 1st Edition of *Kobzar*, 1840
Engraving by Vasyl Ivanovych Shternberg

THE COMPLETE KOBZAR

The Poetry of

TARAS SHEVCHENKO

Translated from the Ukrainian
by PETER FEDYNSKY

Glagoslav Publications

KOBZAR
by Taras Shevchenko

Illustrations by Taras Shevchenko
Translated by Peter Fedynsky
Edited by Svitlana Bednazh
Cover Art by Ivan Kramskoy
Cover Design by Hilary Zarycky

Glagoslav Publications Ltd
88-90 Hatton Garden
EC1N 8PN London
United Kingdom

www.glagoslav.com

Library of Congress Cataloging-in-Publication Data
Shevchenko, Taras, 1814-1861.
Kobzar. English
Kobzar / Taras Shevchenko;
translated from the Ukrainian by Peter Fedynsky.
450 p. 15,6 X 23,4 cm
Includes index.
ISBN 978-1-909156-55-5 (pbk.)
Poetry – United States – Literature. I. Title

PG3948.S5
K613 2013 2013421026

ACKNOWLEDGEMENTS

The translator and publisher express appreciation to the following institutions in Kyiv, Ukraine for providing digital copies of Shevchenko's original art, manuscripts and photographs used in this edition:

Shevchenko Institute of Literature at The Ukrainian Academy of Sciences
http://www.ilnan.gov.ua/

Taras Shevchenko National Museum
http://museumshevchenko.org.ua/

The translator and publisher express gratitude for generous grants provided by the following donors, without whose assistance the illustrated version of this translation would not have been possible:

The Self Reliance New York Federal Credit Union
http://www.selfrelianceny.org

The Ukrainian Institute of America
http://www.ukrainianinstitute.org

The Temerty Family
Toronto, Canada

Special thanks to the Ukrainian Congress Committee of America for promoting Taras Shevchenko over the decades and most recently this translation.

The translator recognizes Editor Svitlana Bednazh for her excellent advice, long hours, and commitment to this translation. My appreciation also to Maxim Hodak, Camilla Stein and Max Mendor at Glagoslav Publications, as well as designers Hilary Zarycky and Dmytro Podolianchuk. And I am grateful to those who provided help, guidance and encouragement:

Michael Balahutrak, Oleksandr Boron, James Brooke, Roman Czajkowsky, Jurij Dobczansky, Andrew, George and Paul Fedynsky, Lesia Generaliuk, Bob Holman, Andrew Hruszkewycz, Taras Hunczak, Adrian Karatnycky, Vitaly Korotych, Bohdan Kurczak, Roman Kyzyk, Vasyl Makhno, Alexander Motyl, Michael Naydan, Sviatoslav Nowytski, Dzvinia Orlowsky, Adam Phillips, Yulia Schilenko, Dmytro Stus, Daniel Swistel, and Mykola Zhulynsky.

A KOBZAR FOR A NEW MILLENNIUM

When I was sent the first several pages of this translation of Ukrainian national bard Taras Shevchenko's *Kobzar* (*The Kobza*[i] *Player*) for perusal, I was immediately impressed both by the translator's dedication to translate the *entire* work, and by his approach — to convey the poet's verse in a modern English idiom that could be understood easily by readers of today. Shevchenko's *Kobzar,* as his collected poetry is now known, is dotted with archaisms here and there, but remains just as vibrant a work now as when it first appeared in 1840. The style is virtually as accessible to Ukrainian readers and the message of Shevchenko's poetry just as important as it was when it was written. Shevchenko combined the vernacular with folk rhythms of Ukrainian songs to capture and embody the sufferings and deepest strivings of his people. It may not be much of an exaggeration to say that today's independent Ukraine could not have been realized without Shevchenko's poetry and his presence as poet-prophet to galvanize Ukrainian identity. His prolific output includes a large volume of poetry; nearly one thousand paintings, etchings and drawings; several prose novellas; two plays; and a journal that he kept from 1857-1858.

Shevchenko's entire oeuvre in its parts and sum comprises a compendium of the trauma of the Ukrainian people under czarist oppression. It is also an indictment of all authoritarian rule. The poet chronicles both imperial czarist abuse as well as an unquenchable thirst for Ukrainian freedom, self-determination and nationhood.[ii] From the publication at the age of twenty-six of his slim but critically acclaimed volume *Kobzar,* which originally contained just eight poems, Shevchenko inspired an entire population ranging from illiterate peasants, who only heard and memorized the poems as oral literature or song, to the leaders of a small but avid band of Ukrainian intelligentsia with the agenda of nation building.

To a Ukrainian, the name Taras Shevchenko is emblematic of Ukrainianness and greatness. What Homer is to the Greeks, Mickiewicz to the Poles, or Pushkin to the Russians, Shevchenko is to Ukrainians. He is the first great Ukrainian poet to infuse his poetry with a nearly magical reverence for the Ukrainian land and its distinctive nature. He also experiences a longing nostalgia for it and, in fact, elevates Ukraine's natural features into symbols that serve to recreate Ukraine inside himself and to focus on what constitutes Ukrainian identity for all.

---

[i] The *kobza* is a Ukrainian instrument similar to a lute and a precursor to the Ukrainian *bandura.*

[ii] For a discussion of the impact of Shevchenko on Ukrainian culture, see the articles in George Luckyj, ed. *Shevchenko and the Critics: 1861-1980* (Toronto: U. of Toronto Press, 1980).

Shevchenko's own story, which is reflected in his poetry, is one that moves from his birth as a serf to liberty, and then to exile in the farthest reaches of the Russian Empire along the Aral Sea in today's Kazakhstan. Orphaned at an early age, his owner took the teenage Shevchenko from Ukraine to Warsaw, then Vilna (Vilnius in today's Lithuania), and eventually to St. Petersburg, Russia. His freedom was purchased there by Russian and Ukrainian "abolitionists" of their time, who recognized Shevchenko's talent as an artist. They included Karl Briullov, one of Europe's finest painters. Briullov's portrait of the poet Vasilii Zhukovsky raised 2500 rubles in an auction to free Shevchenko. Ironically, the winning bid was placed by the family of the Czar. Shevchenko then became one of Briullov's favorite students, but soon began writing poetry not approved by the authorities, leading to his arrest and persecution.

The poet was forced into exile as a soldier under personal orders from Czar Nicholas I not to write or paint. Shevchenko initially ignored those orders and continued his creative activities in the city of Orenburg, a frontier outpost on the border of Europe and Asia. Upon discovery by the authorities, he was sent even deeper into exile at the Novopetrovsky Fort on the desolate eastern shore of the Caspian Sea, where he wrote no poetry for seven years. He did, however, serve as an artist on military scouting missions in Central Asia and left a record of many people and places. Thanks to lobbying on his behalf by influential nobles, including members of the prominent Tolstoy family, Shevchenko was allowed to return to St. Petersburg after ten years in exile. Nonetheless, he lived in the Russian capital under the watchful eyes of czarist agents.

Ostensibly free but bound to a foreign land, Shevchenko recreates Ukraine in his thoughts, in his paintings and etchings, and in his poetry. His emphasis on the common natural features of Ukraine (the Dnipro River, the steppe, the shady groves) serve on a symbolic level to rouse the Ukrainian people, to unify them with the palpable notion of their inheritance of the Ukrainian land through a sacred history built on the bones and burial mounds of ancestors who defended and developed that land. Hence Shevchenko's strong emphasis on mounds, which represent Ukrainian historical continuity and are mentioned in the *Kobzar* more than 100 times.

The Dnipro River for Shevchenko becomes the sacred locus for his longing in exile. For him it is a living, breathing entity. We see this even in the now quite famous opening lines of his first poem, *Mad Maiden (Prychynna)*, which many Ukrainians know by heart:

> The mighty Dnipr' roars and groans,
> An angry wind resounds,
> It bends tall willows to the ground,
> It raises waves like mountains.
> A pale moon just then

Peeked through the passing clouds,
And like a boat in azure seas
It rolled and pitched across the sky.
Third roosters[iii] had not crowed,
And nowhere was a soul astir,
The owls called out across the grove,
At times an ash tree creaked.[iv]

While the nature depicted in the passage is largely generic except for the mention of the Dnipro, the poem's magical visual properties, rhythm and language anchor and elevate it in Ukrainian consciousness.

The Dnipro and the steppes become emblems for Ukraine, for which the poet longs. The mighty waterway represents vitality and power. It is also the river that joins the two distinct parts of Ukraine, the left and right banks, which to this day have different histories, political personalities and interests.

Shevchenko's reverential and powerfully emotional attitude toward the Ukrainian land and the Dnipro is embodied in what is perhaps his most famous poem, commonly referred to as *The Testament (Zapovit)*, which was written in 1845 during a dire illness:

When I die, then bury me
Atop a mound
Amid the steppe's expanse
In my beloved Ukraine,
So I may see
The great broad fields,
The Dnipro and the cliffs,
So I may hear the river roar.
When it carries hostile blood
From Ukraine into the azure sea...
I will then forsake the
Fields and hills –
I'll leave it all,
Taking wing to pray

[iii] A cock can crow at any hour, but in Ukrainian, those that do so at midnight are referred to as first roosters. Second roosters are heard at two o'clock. Third roosters mark the end of night when evil spirits must disappear. [Translator's note]

[iv] All the quotations of Shevchenko poems here are translated by Peter Fedynsky.

To God Himself... till
Then I know not God.
Bury me, rise up,
And break your chains
Then sprinkle liberty
With hostile wicked blood.
And in a great new family,
A family of the free,
Forget not to remember me
With a kind and gentle word.

The poem has been set to music by several composers and is considered a powerful anthem that animates the Ukrainian spirit. Ukraine's trauma as an imperial colony is presented on an individual as well as collective level and often focuses on women. For example, in *Mad Maiden,* a young girl loses her mind over fears that her beloved has died in battle, and then falls prey to nymphs that take her life during the witching hour. He returns only to die of grief on seeing her lifeless body. Similarities in the plot to Shakespeare's *Romeo and Juliet* are unmistakable. In Shevchenko's poem, fate, somehow, or a curse, stands in the way of the union of the lovers in this world. In the long poem *Kateryna,* the heroine fails to heed the *Kobzar's* cautionary words not to fall in love with soldiers from Muscovy (*moskali*). She becomes pregnant and then, abandoned by her Muscovite lover, is shunned as a social outcast, leaving her with a single recourse — to drown herself in a pond. While this and other personal tragedies occur on a microcosmic level, they too are emblematic of the subservient relationship between a weaker Ukraine and a politically more powerful Russia that is played out in Shevchenko's poetry in the female/male paradigm.

Shevchenko, too, both exalts and laments Ukraine's Kozak warriors of the past in many poems such as *The Night of Taras, Ivan Pidkova,* and *The Haidamaks.* The latter, Shevchenko's longest poem, is a vivid depiction and denunciation of indiscriminate killing during a series of bloody 18th-century peasant and Kozak uprisings in Ukraine against Polish landowners, Jews and Uniate Catholics. The historical enemies of the Kozaks, and, by analogy, Ukraine, are distinctly outlined in Shevchenko's narratives: the Poles, the Golden Horde, and Muscovy. There are enemies, too, from within. There are images of glory and courage in battle as well as sadness over loss. One lesson learned from history is that unity leads to victory; disunity and the quest for unbridled revenge to failure. Violence always begets more violence in endless cycles. Shevchenko manages to create a living poetic history from an indigenous Ukrainian perspective, rather than the Empire's rendition of it from the conqueror's colonial viewpoint. That poetic history is not one of just dry facts, but an emotional and emotive one that seeks to generate a sense of common cultural heritage as well as empathy.

The collection, too, is largely about a quest for Ukrainian identity, connecting historical events that showed courage along with the shared trauma that serve to define Ukrainians as a people and nation. Shevchenko creates all this in a dynamic literary idiom that smashes the Russian Empire's imposed stereotype of Ukrainians as a rural peasantry that speaks a "dialect" of Russian, which does not lend itself to higher thought. Myriad parallels, of course, can be made between Ukraine's relationship with Russia to slavery in American history. Millions of Ukrainians were serfs, i.e., the property of other individuals during both Russian and Polish rule in Ukraine, which Shevchenko refers to as "the land that's ours — but not our own." The prominent essayist Mykola Riabchuk, in discussing the colonial context of Ukraine's history, has referred to the supposed "blackness" of the Ukrainian language as a kind of stigma and sign of inferiority to Russians of a chauvinist bent. Shevchenko's *Kobzar* establishes the maturity and high stature of the literary Ukrainian language.

One of the major themes throughout Shevchenko's poetry is that of orphanhood, which, of course, mirrors Shevchenko's own status in life without parents and without a free homeland. He depicts orphans in various contexts, including the parents in the poem *Kateryna,* who are "orphaned in old age," and the river Dnipro that would be "orphaned with the sacred mountains." The ill-fated lovers in his first poem, *Mad Maiden,* are both orphans. In the long poem *The Haidamaks,* the murder of the sexton leaves his daughter orphaned, which motivates the rage that Halaida (Vagabond) directs against his enemies. The kobzar minstrel is an orphan in the poem *The Rambler,* so too is Stepan in *The Blind Man.* To be an orphan, as Shevchenko often says in his poems, is "tough and trying."

Shevchenko also devotes considerable attention to religion. At times, he humbly praises God, and sometimes defiantly accuses the Creator of turning a blind eye to evil. The poet prefaces a number of his verses with quotations from the Bible and makes several mentions of Israel, Biblical figures and the Holy Land. He also wrote imitations of Hosea, Isaiah and Ezekiel, as well as several Psalms of David. In addition, Shevchenko paid homage to martyred Czech religious reformer Jan Hus (*Heretic*), the Blessed Virgin Mary (*Maria*), and to the first Christians (*Neophytes*). In that poem, a pagan mother watches a leopard slaughter her Christian son in the Roman Coliseum.

The arena roars a second day.
Its golden Lydian[v] sand
Is smeared with purplish red,
Turned to mud with blood.

[v] *Lydia* – A Roman province in Asia Minor known for gold deposits.

And the Nazarenes of Syracuse
Have not yet stepped
Inside the Coliseum.
On the third day, they as well
Were led into the slaughterhouse
By guards with swords unsheathed.
The arena roared just like a beast.
And into the arena proudly stepped your son,
With a psalm upon his lips.

One, too, needs to address the fact that some of Shevchenko's poetry on occasion has been criticized for its treatment of Jews. They happened to be historically allied with the Poles, and thus enemies of the Kozaks, during the haidamak uprisings and earlier in the time of Hetman Bohdan Khmelnytsky, a 17th century Ukrainian leader considered a hero by many Ukrainians, but detested by Jews and also disparaged by Shevchenko as a fool who lost Ukraine's independence in his ill-fated 1654 Pereyaslav Treaty with Russia. The poet at times gratuitously mentions Jews and particularly paints less than flattering pictures of tavern keepers, many of whom happened to be Jewish in Shevchenko's day, largely because that was one of the few professions permitted for Jews by the Russian Empire that exiled them beyond the Pale of Settlement to the fringes of the empire.[vi] Yet on a personal level there is a documented instance in 1846 when Shevchenko ran into a burning home to help salvage the belongings of its Jewish owner in the Ukrainian town of Pryluky. The poet then berated others for not helping their neighbor in distress.[vii] And Shevchenko joined several other leading Ukrainian intellectuals to sign a public letter in 1858 that Canadian scholar Myroslav Shkandrij observes is "...one of the first public protests against anti-Semitism in the Russian empire."[viii] Shkandrij indicates that "Shevchenko's attitude toward Jews has been the subject of some ill-informed controversy"[ix] and argues for a more nuanced reading of his works in that regard. Shevchenko's basic humanity encouraged sympathy for all the downtrodden and oppressed. This humanity was recognized by Zionist leader

---

[vi] By edict in 1791 Catherine II (the Great) forced Jews to live in a region outside of Greater Russia called the Pale of Settlement that are now located in present-day Latvia, Lithuania, Belarus, Poland, and Ukraine.

[vii] As noted by Myroslav Shkandrij, *Jews in Ukrainian Literature: Representation and Identity* (New Haven: Yale UP, 2009): 22.

[viii] *Ibid.*, 20. For a more in depth discussion of the subject regarding Shevchenko and his relationship toward Jews, I would recommend the "Taras Shevchenko" rubric on pages 19-30 in Myroslav Shkandrij's book. For the most comprehensive biography of Shevchenko that discusses the Jewish question in detail in his works and life, see Ivan Dziuba, *Taras Shevchenko. Zhyttya i tvorchist'*, 2nd ed. (Kyiv: KM-Academy Publishing House, 2008). It is available only in Ukrainian at this time.

[ix] *Ibid.*, 19.

Ze'ev Jabotinsky, who wrote that Shevchenko gave his people and the entire world brilliant and unshakable proof that the Ukrainian soul is capable of flying at the highest reaches of cultural innovation.[x] The poet's capacity for empathy also played a large role in his close friendship in the winter of 1858-59 with African-American Shakespearean actor Ira Aldridge, with whom he shared a personal history of prejudice and oppression.[xi]

Shevchenko died of heart failure in St. Petersburg on March 10, 1861, forty-seven years and a day after his birth. He lived as a free man for merely thirteen of those years. Though monuments to him have been erected throughout Ukraine and the world, he has been largely unknown in the English-speaking world. It is a great tribute to Shevchenko and his stature that numerous Russian notables such as Fyodor Dostoevsky, Ivan Turgenev, Nikolai Nekrasov, and Mikhail Saltykov-Shchedrin attended his first funeral in the Russian capital on March 13, 1861. Nekrasov, a Russian poet, who like Shevchenko often depicted the downtrodden and those who suffer in society, penned a poem *On the Death of Shevchenko,* which outlines the myriad sufferings in the life of his friend whom he calls a "remarkable man." By May of that year, Ukrainian friends honored the wish Shevchenko expressed in his *Testament* for his final resting place to be "atop a mound amid the steppe's expanse in beloved Ukraine" and had his body transported to Kaniv, Ukraine where it was reburied on a hill overlooking the Dnipro River.

On a personal level, several of the poems in Shevchenko's collection express the poet's own doubts, as well as his anguish and loneliness in the wilderness far away from his homeland. Just as Moses was allowed only to see and not to step foot in the Promised Land, Shevchenko, a prophet for the Ukrainian people, never realized his dreams of living in a free and independent Ukraine. But like Moses, he was granted a vision of his deepest desires for his people that he could see from afar in his heart, in his poetry, and in his dreams.

Michael M. Naydan
Woskob Family Professor of Ukrainian Studies
The Pennsylvania State University

[x] Volodymyr Zhabotynsky, "Nauka z Shevchenkovoho iiuvileiu" in *Vybrani statti z national'noho pytannia,* Trans. Israel Kleiner (New York and Munich: Suchasnist, 1983), p. 78.

[xi] For a discussion in English of that friendship, see Demetrius M. Corbett, "Taras Shevchenko and Ira Aldridge: The Story of Friendship between the Great Ukrainian Poet and the Great Negro Tragedian," *The Journal of Negro Education.* 33, 2 (Spring, 1964): 143-150.

TRANSLATOR'S INTRODUCTION

It is a rare literary translation between any two languages that does not involve a compromise between aesthetics and meaning. Preservation of the former often comes at the expense of the latter and vice versa. This dilemma is particularly acute with Shevchenko's *Kobzar*. Its eloquence is so light and effortless that it is extremely difficult to convey even in other Slavic languages. Shevchenko's friend and first Russian translator, Aleksey Pleshcheyev, wrote to novelist Fyodor Dostoyevsky: "I recently translated Shevchenko's poem, *The Hireling*. I don't know how the translation came out, but the original is a wonderfully poetic thing. It's hard to translate. It becomes unsophisticated. It's incredible."[xii] It is all the more difficult to translate Shevchenko into a Germanic language such as English, which does not share many of the linguistic mechanisms of Ukrainian, particularly diminutives for nouns and even adverbs. Shevchenko uses them routinely to underscore sympathy or sarcasm. Some of his words are neologisms derived from Church Slavonic, whose flavor is impossible to convey in English without resorting to archaic vocabulary. Shevchenko also relies heavily on syntactical inversion, which is endlessly flexible in Ukrainian. For example, the inverted word order for the phrase "*Мої там сльози пролились*," from the poem, *If You Gentlemen but Knew*, sounds loftier than what one might ordinarily say. There are 24 combinations of those words in Ukrainian, all of which make sense. Not so in English. Keeping the original word order in English, i.e. "My there tears shed," would be gibberish. In addition, Shevchenko often uses the passive voice to underscore his emphasis on fate, which victimized millions of Ukrainians through their accident of birth into serfdom. English tends toward the active voice.

I have opted for a translation that focuses on Shevchenko's content, which is as compelling as his poems are lyrical. His poems are alternately frightening, funny, despairing, hopeful, sacred and sacrilegious, but always illuminating and entertaining. They serve not only as a guide to long submerged, even prohibited elements of Ukrainian history, geography, personalities and folklore, but also to universal themes of love, envy, oppression and freedom. In addition, Shevchenko's poems represent considerable courage, because he took on Russia's imperial regime at a time when few dared to challenge it. The world should know that. And English-speakers who trace their heritage to Ukraine should realize that the bard of their ancestral homeland is more diverse and interesting than the cursory introduction they received on Saturdays in Ukrainian School. Shevchenko skewers autocrats, chauvinists, sell-outs, and fools. He muses about religion, fate, friendship and solitude; and charms the reader with tender tales of love and devotion. He laments the

[xii] Volodymyr Melnychenko, *Taras Shevchenko: Moye perebuvannia v Moskvi* (Moscow: Olma Media Group, 2007): 365.

loss of Ukrainian independence and garroting of its language and culture, but raises the promise of national revival and social justice. He also employs metaphors, word pictures, and history to expose the blunt force realities and pathologies of serfdom and national oppression — the invaders, drunks, bastards, unwed mothers, marauders, rapists, murderers, poseurs, thieves, and the injustice those characters represent.

The Kobzar is not without dissonance. A selective reading will provide fodder for anyone seeking evidence of xenophobia or religious controversy ranging from atheism to anti-Catholicism. Shevchenko also makes occasional use of stereotypes and pejoratives against Russians, Poles and Jews, which could offend some readers. As translator, I found the poet's lines about Jews to be especially grating, but I can no more dismiss him than I could such venerable writers as Shakespeare, Dostoyevsky, Dickens, T.S. Eliot and many others accused of literary anti-Semitism. I note, however, that Shevchenko places many of his dubious statements about Jews into the mouths of characters who are drunk or demented. But he is direct in his criticism of Ukrainian leaders who betrayed their nation. Indeed, the poet rebukes his own people for apathy. With regard to Russia, Shevchenko condemns that country's autocracy, not its people. Accordingly, he depicts Russian writer Mikhail Lermontov as a "blessed angel," and he sketched a portrait of Alexander Herzen, referring to the influential Russian political thinker as an apostle. The poet penned a separate verse, *To the Poles,* in a call for friendship between the peoples of Poland and Ukraine. When it counted, Shevchenko showed courage by getting into the fray soon after exile in a public support for Jews, which Professor Michael Naydan notes in his introduction to this translation. So the despair and enmity in Shevchenko's poetry is descriptive, not prescriptive, and *The Kobzar,* taken as a whole, is forgiving and redemptive. In essence, he is saying, "such is life… but let's do better." His longest poem, *Haidamaks,* for example, is a chilling catalog of bloodshed in a 1768 Ukrainian peasant uprising against Polish nobles, Jews and Ukrainian Catholics. In a postscript to the poem that he refers to as a preface, Shevchenko writes, "Let the sons and grandchildren know that their parents were mistaken. Let them again be brothers with their enemies." Thus the poet resolves the dissonance and should ultimately be understood as an individual who knowingly sacrificed his well-being in a fervent commitment, evident in *The Kobzar,* to the liberty of his fellow Ukrainians and their peaceful coexistence with former foes. And just as hope saw him through a decade of banishment to a bleak corner of the world, so too Shevchenko believed that Ukrainians will not wait in vain for their own "[George] Washington with his new and righteous law."

Shevchenko was a keen observer of human affairs. Unfortunately, many of the things he wrote about in the mid-19th century, I reported as a Moscow-based journalist in the 21st. The fatherless children and unwed mothers in his poetry, for example, were victims of rape by overlords who committed the most heinous of crimes against their serfs, including murder, with impunity. Then as now, the elites of Ukraine often escape justice if someone they assault or kill is not a member of the ruling class. This is also true in Russia. All too often, journalists are murdered; pedestrians are run down by speeding politicians or their children; property is seized by the rich and powerful; justice is rigged in their favor. And drunks? According to the World Health Organization, Ukraine has the sixth highest per-capita adult alcohol consumption rate in the world and the highest among adolescents. Unaccountable rulers? *Mazhory* is the Ukrainian word for unruly children of public officials who escape prosecution for brutal beatings and deadly car accidents; Serfdom? Ukrainians in rural areas today are virtual hostages to land they own on paper, but are forbidden to sell. Serfs? Hundreds of thousands of Ukrainian girls have been trafficked as sex slaves. The belittling of Ukrainian culture? Senior Ukrainian government officials have referred to their own language as "useless," or have dismissed entire Ukrainian-speaking regions of the country as not being genuinely Ukrainian. Trampling of property rights? The word *raider* has entered the Ukrainian and Russian languages as a term for well-connected groups that seize buildings and businesses by force and bureaucratic machinations. Chechens? *The Caucasus,* Shevchenko's 1845 poem about the bloody Russian conquest of the the mountainous region could almost have been written yesterday. Ukrainian vs. Ukrainian? Ukraine's Red Army veterans who fought for Soviet power are pitted against their countrymen who struggled for independence in the Ukrainian Insurgent Army. Elites feeding at the public trough? Kyiv abounds with palatial estates and $500,000 automobiles. The Holodomor? Shevchenko's poem *The Princess* anticipates 20th century tyrants who planned and profited from the genocidal starvation of Ukrainian peasants. Therefore a comparison of Shevchenko and today's news reports along with a reading of earlier narratives about the Russian Empire by the Marquis de Custine of France and 16th century British diplomat Giles Fletcher, among others, suggests that the difference between the past and present in that part of the world is one of degree, not kind.

Though Shevchenko wrote about Ukraine, he did so mostly in Russia, where he spent the greater part of his life. The first book I read when I arrived in Moscow for a three-year assignment as Voice of America Bureau Chief was a compelling biography of the poet entitled, *Taras Shevchenko – My Sojourn in Moscow.* It was written by Volodymyr Melnychenko, the director of the Ukrainian Cultural Center in the Russian capital. The book was not only a vivid account of Shevchenko's brief visits to the city, but a Baedeker that allowed me to trace the poet's steps in local streets and to appreciate him as a human being who saw friends, sipped tea, took ill, bought art supplies, and listened to Beethoven's music. I also lived and worked just a brief walk from his monument on the Moscow River opposite the Russian White House. Thus the poet became a routine, if unseen presence in my life.

It seems that what is happening in contemporary Russia and Ukraine has been happening throughout history — the powerful exploit the weak, whether the former are called boyars, *starshyna,* commissars or *siloviki* and the latter *kholopy,* serfs, peasants, or *lokhs.* They are like hermit crabs that succeed one another in the same shell. Shevchenko suggests it has long been so. Poems such as *The Princess*, *The Blind Woman*, and *Petey* call attention to injustices still being perpetrated by authorities. *Neophytes*, a poem about the first Christians, anticipated dictator Josef Stalin and any authoritarian ruler elevated by satraps to the level of God. *Dream*, the satire that resulted in Shevchenko's ten-year banishment, outlines the strict power vertical headed by the czar. The pecking order differs little today, running from the Russian president through his ministers, bureaucrats, pliant legislators, their relatives in the lucrative notary business on down to migrants from former Russian imperial holdings in Central Asia who sweep the country's farmers' markets.

All of the authoritarian injustice of Russia, the Kremlin's continued sway over Ukraine, and the decency of ordinary people in both countries weighed on my mind when I took a long walk in Moscow in early June 2010 with only three weeks left in my tenure. As I crossed the Novo-Arbatsky Bridge over the Moscow River, I looked at Shevchenko's monument, knowing I may never see it again. At that moment, an unmistakable feeling swept across my chest that told me to translate *The Kobzar*.

It is sad to say that mine is the first ever complete English version of Shevchenko's poetry collection. That is not to claim special credit or to disparage his previous translators, whose work I admire and often referred to. It is instead grudging recognition of the Kremlin's remarkable ability not only to have inhibited Ukrainian intellectual activity, but to have kept a country as large as Ukraine invisible to the outside world. It did so through prolonged enslavement, isolation and the slaughter of Ukrainians by the millions; through the murder, character assassination, exile or coopting of the country's leaders; through selective revisions of history to deny Ukrainians their past, as well as czarist bans against the literary use of Ukrainian, and Soviet pressure to muzzle the language. Ukrainians who managed to flee oppression were dispersed around the globe, rendered mute and effectively disconnected from one another and their homeland. Such relentless pressures are the hallmarks of genocide, which made it exceedingly difficult for Ukrainians to multiply, establish a common identity and to find a place of their own on the world stage as a Slavic people no less worthy of independent statehood than Poles, Czechs, Bulgarians, Serbs or Russians for that matter.

Similar pressure came close to preventing the publication of even this translation. That it has seen the light of day is a testament to my father's courage and devotion to his family. He left Ukraine in August 1939 with his fiancée, my mother. World War II, which broke out less than a month later, pinned him down in Krakow, Poland for a few years. My mother then returned with her newborn, my oldest brother, to her village in Western Ukraine, where NKVD agents came looking for my father when Soviets occupied the region. There is no doubt they came to execute him, because that is what they did to his brother, to my mother's brother-in-law, and many other Ukrainian patriots and intellectuals. In 1946, my father crossed the newly descended Iron Curtain from Vienna with a series of forged travel documents, jumped from a train near my mother's village, and smuggled her and my eldest brother back to Austria. It was an audacious life or death gamble. Sitting next to them was another NKVD agent who was traveling to Austria's Soviet Zone. But he kept silent. There were a few such people in the NKVD. When they had successfully crossed the border, he said, "Attaboy! He smuggled out his family." Had that agent betrayed them, I would not have been born five years later in Pennsylvania; there would have been no education in American schools, or my parents' uncompromising requirement that I speak Ukrainian… and no translation of Shevchenko.

Some critics might say my rendition of *The Kobzar* adheres slavishly to the original. That is by design. The closest to a complete translation of Shevchenko's verse was the 1964 effort by Canadians Watson Kirkconnell and Constantine Andrusyshyn, and I do not believe the 200th anniversary of the poet's birth should go by in 2014 without making his message accessible in English. I hope other translators will take the next step to share Shevchenko's intricate meter and rhyme.

Though all but two of *The Kobzar's* poems are in Ukrainian, its meaning is also relevant to Russia, where authoritarian rulers have denied liberty to Russians themselves. This includes the renowned writer Fyodor Dostoyevsky, who came within minutes of execution by a czarist firing squad; Russia's greatest poet, Alexander Pushkin, and Soviet-era giant Alexander Solzhenitsyn were exiled. Many others were also persecuted simply for writing, which prevented contemporaries from acting on and benefitting from their compelling insights and information. Oppressed cultural figures in Russia and Ukraine have traditionally been placed on pedestals only when the truths they illuminated no longer threatened members of the authoritarian establishment. Shevchenko was himself co-opted and tamed during the Soviet era through selective interpretation of his poetry.

The Kobzar abounds with patriotic references to Ukrainian history, geography and culture, many aspects of which have long been ignored, disparaged, twisted or prohibited by Russian and Soviet censors and propagandists. Shevchenko's remarkable ability to weave universal stories of justice and love around those references in expressive verse defies the imperial narrative of a common eternal bond between Ukrainians and Russians, and attests to the separate national, social and cultural identity of each.

As the personification of Ukraine, Shevchenko has major significance for all of Europe. His vision of Ukrainian independence and social justice pits the promise of democratic values and mutual respect against the prospect of continued authoritarianism that has long daunted ordinary citizens of Ukraine and Russia, and negatively impacted the peoples of Europe. It is my hope that this translation will help acquaint the reader with Taras Shevchenko's unflinching depictions of tyranny and his bright vision of liberty and justice for all.

SHEVCHENKO: THE ARTIST AS POET AND POET AS ARTIST

Taras Shevchenko's consistent and multifaceted depictions of a nation are without precedent. They are the product of a generous, dynamic and patriotic soul, who demonstrated in sweeping and eloquent terms that the Ukrainian nation exists.

Shevchenko's hand was guided by a melding of Romanticism and the spirit of his age, which shaped his ideas of nationhood and methods of realizing them. His studies at the St. Petersburg Academy of Arts coincided with democratic ferment and social unrest in mid-19th century Europe. The artistic movement away from academism had begun even earlier. Thomas Gainsborough and George Morland, for example, depicted ordinary life in the English countryside, and Jean-Baptiste-Siméon Chardin illustrated kitchen maids, villages and children in France. They and other artists showed in the tradition of 17th century Dutch art that there is poetry even in poverty and the daily life of common people. In literature, rustic themes were popularized in Shevchenko's time by such writers as George Sand in France, Józef Ignacy Kraszewski in Poland and Ivan Turgenev in Russia.

Such themes were consistent with Shevchenko's creative pursuits, which he expressed using both word and image to formulate Ukrainian-centric ideas, as well as to identify and understand the individual. Elevation of the small person is evident from Shevchenko's first watercolors to his later dramatic poems with which he championed the downtrodden and persecuted. ("I'll exalt those mute and lowly slaves! And beside them as a sentry I will place the word.") He revitalized them with his word and by the example of his own life. Shevchenko worked selflessly so that any Ukrainian could realize his or her power to gain national independence and social justice through awareness of their ethnic and cultural milieu, their landscape and history.

When reading Shevchenko, one must always remember the correlation between the writer and painter. A visual image sets the tone for most of his poetry. The eye, not the word, is always first, notwithstanding his renown as a poetic genius. The eye is his main instrument. It is always active, energetic and ready to transmit information. It dictates the form and selects winning ways of reaching the reader. The eye also creates emphases capable of generating a powerful stream of emotions and associations. The visual apparatus of any person has an impressive ability to see the invisible; to visualize any kind of sensory input, which is why the poet-artist so readily guides the imagination and shares unanticipated perspectives with others. Shevchenko impresses with an ability to fuse different ages, civilizations and levels of culture. He presents various circumstances, personalities and objects on a large and timeless scale. Rome, Egypt, Judea and Siberia are part of humanity's continuum, which Shevchenko organically adapts to the Ukrainian dimension with such poems as *Maria, Czars, and Neophytes.*

The eye, the painter's "operating system," functioned automatically in Shevchenko's literary work. Troubling visual impressions from his travels around Ukraine from 1843 to 1845 that are partially recorded in his albums of drawings and watercolors, fundamentally changed the poet's perceptions, and are programmed as bitterness and tragedy in his *Three Years* series of poems. It was that which the perceptive eye of the artist *saw* that provoked a protest against slavery in dozens of poems, including *The Caucasus, Plundered Mound* and *To Hohol (Gogol).* In essence, the artist created the poet-rebel, infusing the latter's sensitive being with sharp eyes and the ability to discern discrete segments of reality. Examples are plein-air paintings, which Shevchenko painted in mid-September 1845 that depict the ruins of Bohdan Khmelnytsky's residence and the Illin Church built by the 17th century Ukrainian Kozak Hetman. The abandoned ruins, symbols of Ukraine's erstwhile might, so moved the poet that by the beginning of October he wrote his programmatic *Great Vault,* which is inseparable from his watercolors in Subotiv, where the ruins were located. The paintings and historic synthesis of the poem serve as an alarm, a soul's *cri de coeur* over the fate of a people that lost their autonomy after the 1654 Treaty of Pereyaslav, which Khmelnytsky signed with Russia. In a series of similar plein-air paintings in Pereyaslav in August 1845, Shevchenko painted several churches and penned poetic invectives that accused Ukrainian hetmans of surrendering Ukrainian interests. The visual symbols of the *Church of the Protectress in Pereyaslav,* including a dead-end, a bog and pig, are unmistakable, as is the title page of the *Three Years* series. Shevchenko recalled those images 14 years later in the scathing poem, *If you, the drunken Bohdan.*

Shevchenko painted expressive images with words, depicting the luxuriant landscapes of Ukraine as a kind of Eden with heavenly fields, blossoming orchards, verdant groves, and radiantly white homes that serve as symbols of Ukrainian spirituality and tradition. He both draws "a little white home" amid willows by the water, and conjures up the poetic image of a cloudscape with "small white houses peeking, like children in white shirts." The simple elegance, radiance and a kind of pleasant magnetism of the Ukrainian home are .accentuated by lush green surroundings, which the poet paints as if with a brush. He lovingly "lists" the general categories of greenery: the deep forest, groves and orchards. He writes not so much about a generic tree, but specifically about the ash, oak, sycamore, willow, poplar, or guelder rose. Shevchenko's trees are also anthropomorphic: "...a verdant oak, like a Kozak, steps out from the grove to dance beneath the hill," "...oak trees from the hetmans' days stand tall and proud like wizened elders," "...willows even leaned to hear her talk." Elsewhere, trees are like playful girls, "There's a little row of poplars standing neatly by the common, as if the girls of Ohlav went to tend a flock of sheep."

Rich landscapes with streams and ponds are set in relief against ravines, valleys and mounds, and then dotted with occasional bell towers and church cupolas. Biedermeier scenes of a family dinner, of children at play in the manner of William Collins and Ludwig Richter round out the Ukrainian idyll. As Shevchenko put it, "Eden pulses in our hearts."

In opposition to the idyllic, Shevchenko frames light against darkness in his refrain that "we created hell in paradise," which leads him to portray images of poverty, suffering and violence against ordinary people. He evokes not only the social tragedy in paradise — ravaged villages, abandoned homes, overgrown trails and orchards, and orphans — but he also depicts startling images of rebellion. Polar opposites of the idyllic are painted with words in such poems as *Haidamaks, Hamaliya and Night of Taras,* which are iconic representations of Kozaks and the armed struggle of Ukrainians against bondage. The poetry becomes exceptionally effective through the use of principles extrapolated from art. Ominous images of the wind, storms and light emerge from verbal pictures of popular uprisings, as when the moon in *Haidamaks* laments that his illumination will not be needed during the bloody haidamak uprising of 1768: "Infernos will instead heat and light Ukraine." Using momentum from art, the poet releases internal tension through accent and contrast lighting. To his depiction of Russia and St. Petersburg, "...the earth grows dark," "...a heavy fog above darkens like a cloud," Shevchenko also adds the expressive touch of fireworks at dusk, "Fires flared, lighting all around." The poet describes storms as a painter who shows things affected by the wind: "...[It] bends tall willows to the ground," "...bends the poplar in the field," "winds have swept the yellowed leaves," "...his long gray whiskers and old tuft disheveled by the wind."

Shevchenko visited many Ukrainian villages, which he paints literally and figuratively, as for example, in *The Princess.*

> A village in our dear Ukraine –
> As pretty as an Easter egg.
> Ringed by woods of green.
> Blooming orchards, whitened homes,
> And on the hill's a palace.
> It all seems like a wonder.
> All around are broad-leafed poplars,
> There are woods, and woods, a field
> And hills of blue beyond the Dnipro.

The visual is enhanced by the magical sound of his words, which allowed him to create a picture in the mind's eye of a nation with its own unique history and traditions. Having presented it visually, he quickened the pulse of Ukraine and refined it with color and dynamism.

Though many scholars have said Shevchenko the artist is a pale imitation of Shevchenko the poet, his literary themes are nonetheless derived from art. An artist, as

German Romantic painter Caspar David Friedrich put it, draws not only what he sees in front of him, but what he sees in himself. Shevchenko's art professor, Karl Briullov, demanded that his students observe with spiritual vision. This allows the artist to penetrate and to recreate the substance of things. While Shevchenko painted flawlessly with words, he needed to draw in order to realize and understand his ideas.

In exile, having comprehended Russia's imperial strategy, he became even more adamant about awakening the slumbering Ukrainian nation. His constant appeals to Ukrainians for self-awareness, sub-themes of such poems as *The Great Vault, Caucasus, Heretic, My Fraternal Missive, Chyhyryn,* and *Psalms of David,* were reiterated in the politically-charged *Prodigal Son* series of images. He extrapolated from The Bible to depict the state of his people, presenting the stages of its historic development, colonial dependence, strategic mistakes, sufferings, and penitence. Key periods in the life of the nation — its historic choice and internal conflict — are shown through one individual, the prodigal son. He represents the Ukrainian people, in particular, its middle echelon. They undergo difficult trials, which have not ended, because the father's forgiveness is absent, and the people must first reject their decision to perform menial tasks for a foreign country, realize their own cabal, and appreciate the catastrophe of spiritual collapse.

Shevchenko's prodigal son appears in several iterations. The first is the Biblical and spiritual aspect of a strong, attractive people and their political and spiritual leaders, who wield considerable wealth endowed by their Father (God). But the son is wasteful and squanders everything. This is the image of the Ukrainian gentry and agreements made by Kozak hetmans; an image of the Kozaks' proud spirit that was sold for "a pot of lentil soup." In contrast to the Biblical hero, neither the youngster in the animal shed, nor cemetery appreciates his tragedy, which Shevchenko drives home in the poem, *My Fraternal Missive.* The absence of self-awareness led to the loss of a specific Ukrainian Christian identity (*Among Thieves*). What inexorably follows is punishment for meandering without nationhood (*Running the Gauntlet*); the prodigal son is then deprived of his language (*Punishment with Muzzle*). The painful question of which punishment is the worst is written in the eyes of the shackled hero (*In Prison*). It is directed at all Ukrainians who fail to see their yoke, but are nevertheless capable of rebirth. Shevchenko's leitmotiv of national awakening both in verse and illustrations is not accidental. Shevchenko believed in his people and knew them implicitly. He documents their altruism and empathy and shows them to be gifted with wisdom, curiosity and aesthetics, so that even their utilitarian implements became objects of art. He depicts hardworking, genial, meek and patient individuals. The men are generally slow, somber and quiet; the women lyrical, lively and talkative. Shevchenko's women are also expressive, enchanted with the world, spiritually fulfilled, sincere and devoted to their lovers and children. If the poet sings praises of their faithfulness, the artist underscores it with the tender and trusting ovals of women's faces in portraits of Princess Yelizaveta

Keykuatova, Hanna Zakrevska, Maria Maksymovych and others. In exile, he imparted such character to the women of Kazakhstan with *Samaritan* and *Prayer for the Deceased.* The artist's subtle psychological approach was evident in the portrait of Repnin's children, and in others: the demanding Platon Zakrevsky, the ironic intellectual Panteleimon Kulish, and kind-hearted Anton Lagoda.

Tribunal and *Friends* are appealing because of their depictions of individuals and also of their iconic portrayal of distinctive Ukrainian characteristics. In addition, Shevchenko created a gallery of Russian portraits, including aristocrat Fyodor Tolstoy, actor Mikhail Shchepkin, and various military leaders. He also drew likenesses of Polish, Italian, French and German personalities in St. Petersburg, as well as Ira Aldridge, the renowned African-American Shakespearian actor. As an artist on Russian military scouting missions in Central Asia, Shevchenko left abundant documentation of life and nature that are referenced to this day by historians, ethnographers and geologists in Kazakhstan.

Shevchenko's self-portraits cannot be casually dismissed. One thing remained constant in the metamorphosis of his face from an inspired and determined art student in 1840, to a smiling dandy in 1845, and then to an indignant exile and tragic figure late in life: an inquisitive gaze. It is the appearance of a deep and independent intellect, which had the courage to ask confounding eternal questions and to seek answers to them. Shevchenko's individualism and rebellion against authority were accompanied by determination that people should not fall into despair, but should instead work to their utmost ability. Shevchenko's poetry was not about dreams, but action regardless of circumstances.

The restoration of the human spirit is evident in Shevchenko's depictions of *Robinson Crusoe, Milo of Croton, Saint Sebastian* and *The Dying Gladiator*. Despite destructive blows in each case, the spirit does not die, but instead confirms "the image of God," and becomes indestructible.

Shevchenko had a fondness for the sky, the frontier between earthly material existence and the spiritual world. This is evident in many watercolors, where two-thirds of the image are frequently devoted to the sky and clouds. They correspond with such poetic references as, "...God's azure sky", "...the holy heavens smiled," "...we hear God amid the heavens." The sky, the clouds and lofty heights were the realm of the artist's imagination and ideas, which he frequently associated with the soul, "...like the endless stretch of azure sky, so too the soul exists with no beginning and no end," "...his muse frolics in the clouds above beside the world's edge, like a gray-blue eagle, with expansive wings that beat against the sky so blue." He also materializes an emotional state: "...the joyous sun was hiding in the happy clouds of spring," "...the sun beamed, the sky was cloudless." In exile, the soaring and diagonal clouds evident in his landscapes indicate a longing for freedom and Ukraine. It is a symbolic path of return to his lost paradise: "...my beautiful, my lush and wealthy land."

Unlike the English poet William Blake, Shevchenko did not see the sky as an abstract, but as a space with clear geographic coordinates. Art allowed Shevchenko to express himself in a less linear manner than literature. It gave him an unlimited field for association, symbolism and experimentation. As an artist and self-made man, he was on the cutting edge. Having come of age at the crossroads of academic, Romantic and Realist art, Shevchenko also borrowed artistic elements from Ukrainian iconography and Ukrainian baroque. Preserving the code of different cultural epochs, he created his own system and style of images.

Shevchenko's ability to perceive reality through the aesthetic of art allowed him to live as a creative, active and thoughtful individual. Social change and the pursuit of existential freedom was his mission as both a poet and painter. And at the junction of two artistic systems, the verbal and iconic, he created a personal code that is entirely original in world culture. Shevchenko differs from other poet-artists, such as Théophile Gautier, Dante Gabriel Rossetti and Victor Hugo, in his non-standard approach to problems of plasticity and in variable use of artistic language. In addition, his literary and artistic work is filled with bold conceptualism, symbolism and allegories in support of his effort as a champion of the Ukrainian nation. Notably, he is being read more deeply and attentively today in a world that has progressed by several generations. Although the dynamics, as well as the ethical and aesthetic sensibilities of this world differ from those of the 19th century, Ukrainians are coming closer to an understanding of Shevchenko's program for national and individual self-awareness.

Lesia Generaliuk
Doctor of Philological Studies, Art Critic
Taras Shevchenko Literary Institute
The Academy of Sciences of Ukraine
Kyiv, Ukraine

To my parents, Alexander and Alexandra Fedynsky

KOBZAR

MAD MAIDEN

The mighty Dnipr'[1] roars and groans,
An angry wind resounds,
It bends tall willows to the ground,
It raises waves like mountains.
A pale moon just then
Peeked through the passing clouds,
And like a boat in azure seas
It rolled and pitched across the sky.
Third roosters[2] had not crowed
And nowhere was a soul astir,
The owls called out across the grove,
At times an ash tree creaked.

At that hour on a hill
Beside the water
Near a darkened grove
A pale something goes a wandering.
Perhaps a nymph[3] out
Searching for its mother,
Or perhaps it lingers for a Kozak[4]
To delight and tickle.
But no, it's not a nymph,
It is a girl wandering.
She knows not
What she does (she's mad),
For that is what the seer did
To ease her aching heart;
That she might sleep
And walk at midnight,
To seek her youthful Kozak lover
Who left the year before
With promises of swift return.
But alas, he's likely dead!
No nankeen[5] to
Close his Kozak eyes,
No maiden's tears
To cleanse his fair and handsome face:
An eagle on a foreign field
Gouged his hazel eyes,
His fair body eaten by a pack of wolves —
It was the fate he met.
For naught the girl's nightly watch.
The dark-browed lover won't return
Nor will he greet her once again.
He won't undo her long, long braid
Nor tie her wedding scarf.
The orphaned Kozak will not rest in bed
But rather in a grave.

It was the fate she met... O why, good Lord!
She's a youngster, why Your punishment?
Because she dearly loved his Kozak eyes?..
Forgive the orphan!
Whom will she now love?
Without her father and dear mother,
She's all alone,
Like a bird astray in distant lands.
Grant her fortune — she's so young
And will be scorned by strangers.
Is the lovebird to blame
If she's fond of her lovebird?
Is the lovebird to blame

---

[1] *Dnipr'* — Shevchenko's contraction of Dnipro, the Ukrainian name for the river commonly rendered in English from the Russian as Dnieper. This translation uses Dnipro or its contraction.

[2] *Third roosters* — A cock can crow at any hour, but in Ukrainian, those that do so at midnight are referred to as first roosters. Second roosters are heard at two o'clock. Third roosters mark the end of night when evil spirits must disappear.

[3] *Nymph* — In Ukrainian mythology, a river spirit that preys on the unsuspecting, whom they tickle to death.

[4] *Kozak* — The Ukrainian transliteration of Cossack. It generally refers to Zaporizhian Kozaks, a powerful military force from the 16th to the 18th centuries, consisting mostly of Ukrainians seeking to escape serfdom. Zaporizhians were forcibly disbanded Russian Empress Catherine.

[5] *Nankeen* — A red silk burial cloth imported from China. Russia later produced such fabric from cotton.

If he's killed by a hawk?
It's saddened, it coos
And strays o'er the world,
Flying and searching, thinking — it's lost.
The fortunate lovebird flies high in the sky,
Taking wing to the Lord —
To ask of her sweetheart.
But whom can the orphan petition,
Who will respond and who is to know
Where her sweetheart now quarters:
In a dark distant forest?
Or the swift-moving Danube
Where he waters his horse?
Loves he another, and has he forgotten
The dark-brow he loved?
If only she had the wings of an eagle,
She'd find her sweet darling
Beyond the blue sea;
He'd live for her love
And she'd strangle the other,
And should he be dead,
She'd join him in death.
A heart does not love to share with a third,
Nor can it abide what God has decreed:
It cares not for life nor does it want sorrow.
"Sorrow," it's said, allows one to grieve.
O my good Lord! Such is Your will!
And such is her fortune, such is her fate!

Onward she walks,
Not a word from her lips.
The mighty Dnipr' fell silent:
The wind blew away all the dark clouds,
And lay down to rest alongside the sea.
The moon shines so brightly
From heaven above;
O'er waters, o'er forests,
Amid silence all 'round.
Then all of a sudden —
Small children, each laughing,
Emerge from the Dnipr'.
"Let's get warm! The sun has now set." —
Each little one shouted. (Stark naked;
Their braids trimmed with sedge,
'Cause they're girls.)

. . . .

"All here? — calls the mother —
Let's look for our dinner.
We'll play, we will dance,
And a ditty we'll sing:
Aw! Aw!
I've a soul of straw!
My mother gave me birth
But buried me unchristened.
O sweet little moon,
Our moon oh so dear,
Come join us for dinner:
In the reeds we've a Kozak,
In the reeds and the sedge,
A ring made of silver graces his hand;
Young, dark-browed,
Found him yesterday in the grove nearby.
Shine longer on the meadow
So we can have our fill of dancing.
Shed more light,
While witches soar,
Before the roosters crow...
Over yonder something walks!
Look, it's doing something by the oak.
Aw! Aw!
I've a soul of straw!
My mother gave me birth
But buried me unchristened."

The unchristened ones all cackled...
Then the grove responded;
Screams, yells.
As if butchered by the Horde.
Like madmen,
Toward the oak they fly... Hush.
The unchristened ones calm down,
They look — a glimmer.
Something's crawling up the trunk
Toward the highest branch.
It's that very girl
Who wandered while asleep:

Thus the seer
Drove the girl to madness!
She reached the top
And stopped there on a branch…
Her heart is racked with pain!
She looked each way
And climbed back down.
The nymphs gathered 'round the oak
In silent expectation;
They took the poor dear,
To delight and tickle.
Enchanted by her beauty,
They stood and gazed
For quite some time…
The morning roosters:
Cock-a-doodle-doo! —
They slipped into the water.

The lark warbled
On his upward flight;
The cuckoo called,
Sitting on his oak tree perch;
The nightingale sang —
It echoed in the grove;
Past the hill the sky turns red;
The plowman sings.
The shady grove
Where Poles once roamed,
Stands beside the water;
Tall Kozak mounds[6] beyond the Dnipr'
Loom in shades of blue;
A rustle spread throughout the grove;
Thick vines whisper.
And beneath the oak the girl sleeps
Beside a well-worn path.
Know that she sleeps well
And does not hear the cuckoo's call;
She reckons not the length of life…
Know that she is sound asleep.

From the grove, meanwhile,
Comes a Kozak riding;
His horse is black, its gait quite feeble.
"You're tired, my good friend!
Today, we'll rest:
Home is near,
My girl will unlatch the gate.
But perhaps she's opened it already —
Not for me, but for another…
Faster, horse, faster, horse,
Hurry faster home!"
The black steed grew wearier
But yet he tripped along, —
Around the Kozak's heart
Coiled a snake of dread.
"Here he is that old and gnarled oak…
It's she. Good Lord!
Waiting, she dozed off, you see,
O my sweetheart!"
He dismounts and runs to her:
"O my God, O God!"
He calls and kisses her… To no avail!
"Why'd they drive us both apart?"
He laughed, revved up —
And ran headfirst into the oak!

Girls go to fields for harvest,
Along the way they sing, you know,
Of how a mother bid farewell
As her son went off to war,
Of how the Tatar fought at night.
They go — and there's
A horse that's slaughtered
Beside the verdant oak.
The curious (no point denying it),
Sneak up to scare the couple;
But themselves are startled,
Finding both are dead,
So away they run in fear.

---

[6] *Mounds* — Shevchenko uses the image of the burial mound throughout the Kobzar. It connotes not only the place where ancestors rest, but also a symbol of Ukrainian historical and cultural continuity.

Her girlfriends gathered, wiping tears;
The Kozak's friends all gathered
Digging graves for both;
Priests came too with banners
To the sound of tolling bells...
The people buried them
As was just and proper.[7]
Two mounds were raised
Beside a road
That crossed a field of rye.
There's not a soul to ask
Why they both had perished.
On the Kozak's grave
They placed a spruce and sycamore,
And atop the girl's, a guelder rose.[8]
Above their graves a cuckoo weeps;
Each night a nightingale
Lands to warble;
It sings and warbles till the moonrise,
Till nymphs emerge for warmth
From the Dnipr' waters.

St. Petersburg, 1837

Nymphs, 1859

[7] *Just and proper* — Suicide was considered a grave sin. Those who took their own lives were buried outside of cemeteries, which were blessed by the church.

[8] *Guelder rose* — A tall flowering shrub that produces bright red berries. It is a national symbol of Ukraine and is mentioned throughout Shevchenko's poetry, Ukrainian folklore, art and culture. Also known as the snowball tree or European cranberrybush (*Viburnum opulus*).

A THOUGHT

Water flows into the azure sea,
But never runneth out.
A Kozak seeks his destiny,
But there's none for him to find.
The Kozak traveled far afield;
The azure sea is restless,
And restless is the Kozak heart,
But a thought intrudes:
"Where go you without asking?
For whom have you abandoned
Both your father
And your aging mother,
A young girl?
In foreign lands the people
Are not quite the same —
It's hard to live among them!
You'll have none to shed a tear with,
You'll have none to talk to."
The Kozak sits upon a distant shore,
The azure sea is restless.
He thought he'd find his destiny —
All he found was grief.
And cranes above wing homeward,
Homeward in formation.
The Kozak weeps — his beaten paths
Are thick with thorns.

St. Petersburg, 1838

A THOUGHT

Raging wind, O raging wind!
You talk with the sea.
Awaken it, and play with it,
Ask the azure sea.
It knows where my sweetheart is,
Because it carried him.
It will answer, yes,
The azure sea will answer
Where it's hidden him.
If it drowned my sweetheart,
Blow the sea apart;
I'll go find my sweetheart,
I'll go drown my sorrow,
I'll drown all my misfortune
And turn into a nymph.
I'll search among the dark, dark waves,
I'll sink down to the bottom.
I will find him, I'll embrace him
And swoon upon his heart.
Then, O wave,
Carry my darling with me
Wherever the wind may blow!
If my sweetheart's on a distant shore,
O raging wind, you know
Where he walks and what he does,
You talk with him as well.
If he's crying, I cry with him
And if not — I sing.
If my dark-browed one has died
Then I shall die as well.
So take my soul to him
To my dearest sweetheart;
Place it on his grave
As a crimson guelder rose.
It will ease the orphan's rest
In a foreign field.
As a flower above him
His beloved will grow.
As a flower and a guelder rose,
I will bloom above him,
So the foreign sun won't scorch,
So that no one treads upon him.

Evenings I will grieve for him
And mornings I will cry,
I'll dry my tears at sunrise,
They'll be seen by no one.

Raging wind, O raging wind!
You talk with the sea,
Awaken it, and play with it,
Ask the azure sea.

St. Petersburg, 1838

A THOUGHT

Life on earth is tough and trying
For an orphan without kin,
There is no place to rest.
May as well just leap
From a mountain into water.
He'd drown himself, the youngster,
To avoid a vagrant's life.

He'd drown himself — it's hard to live,
For there's no place to go.
One man's fortune wanders fields,
Reaping spikes of grain,
But mine is lazy,
Roaming overseas.
A rich man has it good,
And people know him well,
But me it seems they meet and
Somehow see me not.
A girl likes the thick-lipped well-to-do
But at me, the orphan,
She merely laughs and jeers.
Do you find me not so handsome,
Do I not look like you,
Is my love for you not true,
Did I ever laugh at you?
Love anyone your heart desires,
Love whomever you may know.
But do not mock me
Should you think of me.
And I'll go to the world's edge,
I'll find someone better
In a foreign land or die,
Shriveled like a sunbaked leaf.
The Kozak left in sorrow,
He abandoned no one.
He sought his fortune
On a foreign field,
And that is where he died.
Dying, he looked
At where the sun was beaming.
To die is tough and trying
In a foreign land…

St. Petersburg, 1838

A THOUGHT

Why my dark brows,
And why hazel eyes,
Why years of youth,
Why joys of a girl?
Those years of my youth
Are of little avail,
Eyes only shed tears,
Dark brows fade with the wind.
The heart withers,
It wanders the world
Like a bird without freedom.
What good is my beauty
If I live with no fortune?
For me it's so hard
Living orphaned on earth;
My people — they're strangers,
There's no one to talk to,
There's no one to ask,
Why the tears in my eyes;
There's no one to tell
Of what my heart yearns,
Why the heart, like a dove,
Quivers all day and by night;
Nobody asks,
And nobody knows, nor does anyone hear.
Strangers won't ask —
But why should they ask?
The orphan should cry,
Let her waste all her years!
The heart should be crying,
The eyes should be weeping
Before falling asleep,
Loudly, despondently,
So the four winds may hear,
And so blustering breezes may
Carry my cries beyond the blue sea
So my treacherous dark-hair
Might be tortured with grief!

St. Petersburg, 1838

NIGHT OF TARAS[9]

At a crossroads sits a kobzar[10]
Strumming on his kobza,
Gathered 'round are guys and gals,
Flowering like poppies.
The kobzar plays and sings,
His words recounting
How the Russkies, Horde and Poles
Fought against the Kozaks,
And how the people gathered
On a Sunday morn
To bury a young Kozak
In a verdant valley.
The kobzar plays and sings
Till even sorrow laughs...

"The Hetmanate[11] was long ago,
Alas it won't return!..

A cloud gathers past the Lyman[12]
Another drifts in from the field;
Ukraine is saddened —
Its fate is such!
It's saddened and it's crying
Like a little child.
No one tries to save it...
Kozakdom is dying;
Dying is the glory, the homeland,
And there is no place to hide.
Kozak children grow unchristened
The unwedded make illicit love,
The dead are buried without priests,
The faith is peddled to the Jews,
Church attendance is denied!
Like jackdaws[13] on a field of carrion,
Poles and Uniates[14] swoop in —
There's no one to give counsel.
Nalyvaiko[15] then responded —
There's not enough militia!
Pavliuha[16] answered —
Off he went to get more Kozaks!
Taras Triasylo countered
In a bitter show of tears:
"My destitute Ukraine,
Trampled by the Polacks!
Ukraine, O my dear Ukraine,
My dearest!
When I think of you, my homeland,
My heart can only cry...
Whither all the Kozaks
Whither their red coats?
Whither our good fortune
And whither blessed freedom?

---

[9] *Night of Taras* — Culminating night of a 1630 peasant revolt against Poland led by Taras Fedorovych, a Ukrainian hetman. He is known by the surname of Triasylo, i.e. the one who jolts or shakes others.

[10] *Kobzar* — An itinerant Ukrainian bard, often blind, who sang religious songs and national epics. Kobzars accompanied themselves with a kobza, a Ukrainian instrument similar to a lute. Russian composer Dmitri Shostakovich wrote in his memoirs that the last kobzars were summoned to a congress under Stalin and shot, thus destroying Ukraine's oral tradition.

[11] *Hetmanate* — The Ukrainian Kozak state from the mid-17th to the mid-18th centuries.

[12] *Lyman* — The Dnipro River estuary.

[13] *Jackdaw* — A type of crow *(Corvus monedula)*.

[14] *Uniate* — A Ukrainian who converted from Orthodoxy to Catholicism following the Union of Brest in 1596. Sometimes used as a derogatory term.

[15] *Severin Nalyvaiko (?-1597)* A Kozak otaman and leader of a rebellion against Poland from 1594-96.

[16] *Pavliuha* — Nickname of Pavlo Mikhnovych Bout (?-1638), hetman and leader of a peasant and Kozak uprising against Poland in 1637-38. Executed in Warsaw.

The maces, the hetmans?[17]
Where has it all gone? Set ablaze?
Did the deep blue sea submerge
Your stately mounds and mountains?...
The sea is restless, mountains mute,
And the mounds are mournful,
As the Poles rule Kozak children.
May the sea roll on,
May the mountains all stay silent,
May winds frolic o'er the fields —
Weep, Kozak children,
Such is now your destiny!"

Taras Triasylo responded
To liberate the faith.
The gray-haired eagle answered,
And let the Polacks know!
Mr. Triasylo responded:
"Enough stewing!
Let's go, my men and brothers,
Let's go fight the Poles!"

Triasylo fights not just three days
Nor a mere three nights.
Fields were decked with corpses
From the Lyman
North to the Trubailo.[18]
The Kozak was exhausted,
He was deeply worried.
And the rotten Koniecpolski[19]
Was oh so very pleased.
He called together nobles
And the treats were all on him.
Taras summoned all the Kozaks
To ask for their advice.

"Otamans,[20] my friends,
My brothers and my children!
Give me some advice,
For what are we to do?
Our enemies the Poles revel
In our suffering."
"Let them have their banquet,
Let them toast to their good health!
Let the bastards banquet
Till the sun sets for the day,
And mother-night will give advice —
The Kozak will track down the Pole."

The sun set beyond the hill,
And stars dressed up the sky.
Then the Kozaks, like a cloud,
Surrounded all the Poles.
When the moon took front and center,
A cannon opened fire.
The noble Poles and lords awoke —
Finding not a place to turn!
The noble Poles and lords awoke,
But could not rise from bed.
The sun had set
And the Polish lords and nobles
Were all mown down and dead.

The Alta,[21] like a bloody serpent,
Carries news for ravens
To fly in from fields
To eat the noble Poles and lords.
In flew ravens
To arouse the high and mighty,
So too did the Kozaks meet
In prayer to the Lord.

---

17 *Hetman* — The title of a Ukrainian Kozak leader.

18 *Trubailo* — A left bank tributary of the Dnipro River.

19 *Stanislav Koniecpolski (ca. 1590-1646)* — A Polish nobleman and military commander. He suffered defeat in 1630 near Pereyaslav at the hands of Ukrainian rebel leader Taras Triasylo.

20 *Otaman* — A Kozak leader.

21 *Alta* — A tributary of the Trubailo.

The black ravens cawed,
Gouging out the Polish eyes.
And the Kozaks
Sang about the night
Of Taras and all the Kozaks,
The bloody night of glory
That had laid the Poles to rest.

A mound looms
Above the river on an empty field,
Green grass is growing
Where the blood of Kozaks flowed.
A raven sits atop the mound
Cawing out of hunger...
A Kozak recollects the Hetmanate,
He remembers it and cries!

Once we ruled, but will no more!
We'll ne'er forget that Kozak glory!.."
The kobzar then turns sad and silent:
The hands somehow refuse to play.
All around the guys and gals
Wipe away their tears.
The kobzar ambles down the street —
Out of sorrow how he plays!
The guys around bent low to listen,
And he declares,
"It's like this, my children.
You stay put here by the hearth,
I'll take my sorrow to a tavern
And there I'll find my wife.
I'll find my wife, I'll buy a round
And crack some jokes about our foes."

St. Petersburg, November 6, 1838

Kozak Banquet, 1838

IN EVERLASTING MEMORY OF KOTLIAREVSKY[22]

The sun above is warm.
Down into a valley
Blows a wind across a field.
It bends a willow and a guelder rose
Growing by the waterside.
It rocks a single nest
Inside that guelder rose.
Where's the nightingale?
Don't ask, who knows?
Mention grief — it matters not...
It's vanished... Gone...
Mention good — the heart wilts,
Why did good not last?
As I look and I recall:
At twilight it would warble
On that guelder rose —
None passed it without stopping.
The man of wealth and fortune
Was like a mother to its child,
Cleaning, caring
And not passing up the guelder rose.
Or the orphan who wakes up for work
Before the break of dawn,
Goes by and listens
As if mom and dad
Were asking him and chatting, —
The heart beats, it's pleasant...
God's good world seems like Easter,
And people are like people!
Or the girl who awaits her sweetheart
Each and every day.
She withers as an orphan,
Knowing not where she could go,
She takes the road to look
And cry beneath the willow.
To hear the nightingale warble
Makes her tears dry up.
She listens up and smiles,
She'll go along the twilit grove
As if she's spoken with her sweetheart,
And the bird, you know, sings on.
The song is fine and steady
Like a prayer to the Lord,
Until a bandit hits the road
With a knife stashed in his boot. —
An echo rolls across the grove
It rolls and then there's silence — why warble?
It won't stop the reckless bandit's soul,
It'll only waste its voice,
And not impart a thing of good.
Let him rampage, till he dies himself,
Till the raven caws misfortune.
The valley will be sleeping.
The nightingale atop the guelder rose
Will doze a bit himself.
The wind will blow throughout the valley —
The echo bounces past the grove,
The echo dances, it's God's language.
Poor wretches will awake for work,
Cows will move along the grove,
Girls will come to fetch the water,
The sun will gaze —
It's heaven, say no more.
The willow laughs, all over it's a festival!
The bandit, evil bandit will shed tears.
At first that's how it was — but look now:
The sun above is warm.
Down into a valley
Blows a wind across a field.
It bends a willow and a guelder rose
Growing by the waterside.
It rocks a single nest

22 *Ivan Petrovych Kotliarevsky (1769-1838)* — Writer, poet and playwright. He is considered the father of modern Ukrainian literature. His parody of Virgil's *Aeneid* was the first literary work written in the Ukrainian vernacular. This poem is Shevchenko's response to Kotliarevsky's death.

Inside that guelder rose.
Where's the nightingale?
Don't ask, it does not know.
Recently, just recently in our Ukraine
Thus warbled our old Kotliarevsky;
He's now silent, the poor fellow,
And he's orphaned
All the seas and mountains
That he was first to wander,
Where the vagabond dragged
His crew along,[23] —
All is gone and all is sad
Just like the ruins of Troy.
All is sad — just glory
Beams with sunlight,
The kobzar will not die,
For glory hails him forever.
You will, dear father, reign
As long as there are people;
Till the sun shines in the sky,
You'll never be forgotten!
O righteous soul, accept my language
Though it's not so smart,
But please accept it, welcome it,
For it is quite sincere.
Do not leave it orphaned
As you did the groves.
Come to me to share a single word at least,
And sing to me about Ukraine.
Let the heart smile in a foreign land,
Smile if but once, seeing how
Your words alone brought every
Kozak glory into the meager orphan's house.
Come gray eagle, for I'm alone,
An orphan in this world
And in a foreign land.
I look upon the deep, broad sea,
I'd sail to the other shore —
But they'll grant no boat for me.
I recall Aeneas, I recall my kin,
I recall and cry just like a little child.
And waves drift,
Crashing on the other shore.
Perhaps, I'm dim and fail to see,
A cruel fate perhaps
Cries upon that shore,
An orphan will be ridiculed
By people everywhere.
Let them laugh, for the sea there is alive,
The sun, the moon shine brighter there,
There the wind converses
With a mound amid the steppe,
And I'd be not alone if I were right beside.
O righteous soul, accept my language
Though it's not so smart,
But please accept and welcome it,
For it is quite sincere.
Don't leave it orphaned
As you did the groves,
Come to me to share
At least a single word,
And sing to me about Ukraine.

St. Petersburg, November-December 1838

23 *Where the vagabond dragged...* — Reference to Aeneas and the Trojans.

KATERYNA

To Vasilii Andreyevich Zhukovsky[24]
In Memory of April 22, 1838[25]

I

Fall in love, you dark-browed girls,
But not with Muscovites.[26]
For Muscovites are strangers,
They will do you wrong.
A Muscovite loves jokingly,
And jokingly he'll leave you,
He'll return to Muscovy
And leave the girl to perish...
Were she all alone,
It could still be nothing,
But there's the aging mother,
Who gave her birth in God's good world,
And she must also perish.
The heart withers, singing,
When it knows the reason why;
But people will not see the heart,
They'll say instead — you're lazy!
Fall in love, you dark-browed girls,
But not with Muscovites.
For Muscovites are strangers,
They make a mockery of you.

Kateryna heeded not
Her father or her mother,
With a Muscovite she fell in love,
Persuaded by her heart.
She gave the young man all her love
And in an orchard strolled with him,
Until her destiny and she were ruined
Within that very grove.

Mother calls for dinner,
But the daughter does not hear;
Where she banters with the Muscovite
Is where she'll spend the night.
It wasn't just a couple nights that
She sweetly kissed his hazel eyes,
Before news went 'round the village
And turned into disgrace.
But let those people speak their minds;
She's in love and does not hear
The anguish that had stolen in.
Bad news came —
The bugle sounded for a march,
And off to Turkey[27] went the soldier.
They covered Katie,
Though she noticed not;
She's indifferent to her covered braid:[28]

For a sweetheart, like a song,
Pining is a pleasure.
The dark-browed one has promised
To return to Katie
If he does not die.
And then Kateryna will herself
Become a Muscovite,
All her grief will be forgotten.
For now, let people say whatever.

---

[24] *Vasilii Andreyevich Zhukovsky (1783-1852)* — Russian poet and prolific translator. A tutor of the future Czar Alexander II. A portrait of Zhukovsky was auctioned to buy Shevchenko's freedom.

[25] *April 22, 1838* — The day Shevchenko's freedom was purchased.

[26] *Muscovite (Москаль)* — Term for a soldier and also a pejorative Ukrainian term for a Russian. Both connotations are used in the poem *Kateryna.* Elsewhere in *The Kobzar,* it mostly refers to soldiers.

[27] *Off to Turkey* — Reference to the Russo-Turkish War of 1828-29.

[28] *Covered braid* — The braid in Ukrainian culture was a symbol of maidenhood. Covering the braid was a sign of disgrace for bearing an illegitimate child.

Kateryna's not concerned —
She wipes her tears,
Because the girls on the street
Sing their songs without her.
Kateryna's not concerned —
She'll cleanse herself with tears,
She'll take some pails,
And fill them up at midnight
So that foes won't see;
She'll step up to the well,
And stand beneath the guelder rose
To sing the song of *Greg.*[29]
She sings, recites
Till the guelder rose starts weeping.
She returned — delighted,
There'd been no one out to see her.
Kateryna's not concerned
Nor does she have an inkling —
Peering out the window
In her new babushka.
Kateryna gazes.
Half a year passed by,
A queasy feeling gripped her heart,
She felt a stabbing in her side.
Kateryna's feeling ill,
She barely, barely breathes...
Recovering, she rocks
Her baby by the hearth.
The women-folk ring malice,
Heaping scorn upon her mother,
That the Muscovites return
To spend the night with her:
"You've got a dark-browed daughter,
But she's not alone.
In the nook beside the hearth
She's bringing up a Russian's son.
She got herself a dark-browed boy,
Perhaps you taught her how..."
To hell with all you busybodies,
May misery defeat you
As it has the mother,
Who bore a son to mock you all.

Kateryna, O my sweetheart!
Hardship is your future!
Where on earth are you to go
With a little orphan child?
Who will care and who will greet you
Without your darling in this life?
Mother, father — strangers both,
Living with them is so hard!

Kateryna's well again,
She draws the window open,
Looks out upon the street
And rocks her baby child;
She looks — he's gone, gone...
Will ever he come back?
She'd go cry inside the orchard,
But people would be watching.
The sun sets — Kateryna,
Son in arms,
Walks around the orchard,
Glancing to and fro:
"Here I waited for the drill to end
Here I talked with him,
And there... and there...
My son, my son!"
She did not finish saying.

Sweet and sour cherry trees
Turn the orchard green.
As she did at first,
So she came again.
She came, but does not sing
Like she sang before,

[29] *Greg* — Reference to *Oy ne khody Hrytsju*, a Ukrainian folk song. An American adaptation, *Yes, My Darling Daughter*, was a hit in the early 1940s with performances by Dinah Shore, Benny Goodman, Glenn Miller and others.

Of how she waited for the dashing soldier
In the cherry grove.
The dark-brow does not sing,
She curses her own fate.
In the meantime petty foes
Do exactly as they please —
They forge malice.
What is she to do?
Were the dark-browed lover here
He'd know how to stop it…
But the dark-browed lover's far away
He neither sees nor hears
How enemies make fun of her,
And how his girl cries.
Perhaps the dark-browed lover's dead
Somewhere past the Danube;
But maybe he's in Muscovy
Loving yet another!
No, the dark-browed lover isn't dead,
For he's alive and well…
Where'll he find such pretty eyes
And such a dark-browed beauty?
There is no peer to Kateryna
Not in Muscovy, the world's end,
Nor any distant shore;
Yet she was born to grief!..
The mother knew to give her daughter
Hazel eyes and pretty brows,
But did not know to grant her
Providence and joy.
A fair face without good fortune
Is like a lonely field flower:
Scorched by sunlight, swayed by winds
Or picked by passersby at will.
Wash your pretty face with tears
Because the Muscovites returned,
Taking other roads.

II

The father's sitting at the table's edge
His head is in his hands,
He does not see the good Lord's world:
He's heavily perturbed.
Beside him sits the mother
On a little bench,
Barely-barely through her tears
She asks the daughter this:
"What, a wedding, my dear daughter?
Where's your groom?
Where are all the candles, maids,
The elders and best man?
In Muscovy, my daughter!
Go and find them all,
But don't tell gentle people
That you have a mother.
Cursed was the hour
That I gave you birth!
Had I known, I would have
Drowned you before sunrise,
You'd have been handed to a viper.
Now you're given — to a Muscovite…
O my daughter, dearest daughter!
My little rosy blossom!
I loved you and I raised you
Like a birdie, like a fragrant berry
And it came to grief. My daughter,
What is it that you've done?
What gratitude!.. Be off to Moscow,
Find your in-law mother.
You failed to hear my missives,
Listen now to hers.
Go dear daughter, find her,
Find her, greet her,
Be happy in the midst of strangers,
Don't come back to us!
Don't come back, my dearest daughter,
From the far-off land!
And who will rest my weary head
When you're no longer here?
Who will weep for me
If not the child I bore?
Who will plant a guelder rose
In the soil above my grave?
And who without you is to serve
The memory of my sinful soul?
O my daughter, dearest daughter,

O my dearest child!
Go away from us..."
She barely-barely
Gave a blessing:
"God be with you!" — And as if dead
She crumpled to the floor...
The aged father then spoke up:
"What keeps you, my poor dear?"
Kateryna wailed,
And, plop, she fell down at his feet:
"Forgive me, my dear father,
For all that I have done!
Forgive me, dove,
My falcon, oh, so dear!"
"May God forgive you,
And may good people do as well;
Say a prayer to the Lord and go —
It will be easier on me."

She barely rose and bowed,
Leaving home without a word;
The father and the mother
Orphaned in old age.
She proceeded to the cherry orchard,
And prayed to God above,
She took soil from beneath a tree
And rubbed it on her cross,
"I'll not return!," she said,
"I'll be buried far away by strangers
In an alien land;
And this speck of dirt will lie upon me
Telling strangers of my fate and grief...
But best be quiet, dear!
Where I'm buried matters not,
Just so people don't malign me.
You'll not say... But here's the one to say
That I'm his mother!
O my good and gracious Lord!..
My grief!
Where am I to hide?
Alone I'll hide, my child,
Beneath the water,
And you'll expiate my sin with people
As an orphan, as a bastard."

Crying, Kateryna wandered
Through the village;
A kerchief on her head,
A child in her arms.
With an aching heart she left the village;
Looking back, she nodded,
Letting loose a mournful cry.
Like a poplar, she stood amid a field
Beside a beaten path;
Her tears rolled down like dewdrops
Before the break of dawn.
Behind those tears, those bitter tears
She could not see the world,
But rather drew her child close,
Kissing him and crying.
The child, like an angel,
Knows absolutely nothing,
Searching for her bosom are his tiny hands.
The sun set,
Behind the grove the sky turns red;
She wiped her tears, she turned and left...
Only dreaming.
For some time after in the village
They talked a lot about it,
But such things no longer reached
The father and the mother...

That's what people do in life to people!
They tie this one, hack up that one,
And another kills himself...
For what? Lord knows.
The world, you see, is broad,
But there's no haven for the lonely.
Fate graces one with endless land
And for another leaves a burial plot.
Whither are the people,
Whither are the good
Sought by the heart for life and love?
Vanished, vanished!

There is good fortune in this world
But who exactly knows it?
There is freedom in this world

But who exactly has it?
There are people in this world
That shine in gold and silver,
And though it seems they rule,
Good fortune they know not —
Neither liberty nor fortune!
Wearily and grievously
They don their fancy overcoats,
But to cry — they're too ashamed.
Take the silver, take the gold, be rich,
And I will take the tears —
To pour away the grief;
I will drown misfortune
With fine and streaming tears,
I'll trample my oppression barefoot!
Only then will I be happy,
Only then will I be wealthy
When my heart is free to dance.

III

Owls screech, the grove's asleep
Beneath the twinkling stars,
Marmots dance beside the road
Amid some amaranth weeds.
Decent people are asleep,
Each grown weary for a reason:
One through fortune, one through tears,
All's enveloped by the night,
The darkness blankets everyone,
As would a mother all her children.
And where did night embrace Kat'ryna,
In a forest, in a house?
Or is it on a field beside a hay stack,
That she diverts her son,
Or is she in a grove beneath a log
On guard against a wolf?
Would that no one had such
Dark enticing brows,
If their price is so much grief.
And what's ahead?
There'll be trouble, yes indeed!
She'll come by shifting sands
And strangers;
She'll come by howling winter...
Will he that knows and meets
Kateryna also greet her son?
With such a man the dark-brow
Would forget the roads,
The sands, the grief;
Like a mother, he will greet her,
Like a brother, he will chat....

We'll see, we'll hear...
But now — I'll rest
And in a while I'll inquire
About the road to Muscovy.
A long road, my good fellows,
Oh, I know it, yes I do!
It chills the heart when I recall it.
I traversed it once
So I needn't walk it twice!..
I'd share the tale of that woe,
But would they all believe it?
They'd say "that so-and-so is lying!"
(But of course not to your face.)
"He's just messing with the language
And also people's heads."
You're right, it's true, good people!
But why know that
I'll pour my eyes out with you?
What's the use?
Everyone has worries
Of their own aplenty.
But enough of this!..
Meanwhile, just pass some flint
To light tobacco, so at home,
You know, they won't be worried.
To tell tales of woe
Will conjure up a nasty dream!
To hell with that!
Better that I ponder
Where my Kateryna's taken to
With little Ivan.

Beyond Kyiv, beyond the Dnipro
By a shady grove,

Some chumaks[30] on a road
Sing about the screech owl.[31]
Along that road a young lass goes,
It must be from a pilgrimage.
Why so sad, why so down,
Why the teary eyes?
With patches on her peasant coat,
A sack slung 'cross her back,
One hand grips a cane,
The other bears her sleeping child.
She met the chumaks,
Child concealed,
Asking, "Where, good people,
Is the road to Muscovy?"
"To Muscovy? It's the one you're on.
Going far, young lady?"
"All the way to Moscow.
For the love of Christ,
Give me something for the road!"
Taking half-a-kopeck piece,
She quivers, for it's hard to do!..
So why do it? For the child?
She is indeed its mother.
Teary-eyed she took the road,
In Brovary[32] she rested
And spent the bitter coin
To buy her son some ginger-bread.
Long and far the poor dear walked,
Asking as she went;
And there were times she spent a night
Sleeping with her son
Beneath a hedge or fence...

Look what use came of those hazel eyes:
To cry them out
Beneath some stranger's fence!
So, take heed, repent young maidens
Lest it comes to searching for a Muscovite,
Lest it comes to search like Katrya...
Afterwards, don't ask why people curse,
Or why to you
Their homes are closed at night.
Don't ask, O dark-browed girls,
For people do not know;
Whom God shall punish here on Earth,
People too will punish...
People bend like willows,
Wherever winds may blow.
The sun shines on an orphan
(Shines, but does not warm) —
If only people had the power,
They'd block the sun itself,
So it would not shine upon the orphan,
Would not dry her tears.
And why, dear God!
Why adrift upon this world?
What is it that she did to people,
What is it that they want?
For her to cry!.. My dear!
Do not cry Kateryna,
Do not show your tears to people,
Suffer till your death!
And so your face won't whither
With its dark and pretty brows,
Go before the break of dawn
Into the deep dark forest
To bathe yourself in tears.
Having bathed yourself —
They will not see,
And so they will not laugh;
Thus the heart will rest,
As long as tears pour down.
The tragedy, dear girls, is such, you see.
The Muscovite dropped Kateryna jokingly.
Misfortune does not see
With whom it's fit to jest,

---

30 *Chumak* — A merchant and trader who carted goods to and from Ukraine before railroads. The chumaks were venerated in Ukrainian folklore and culture. They could be known today as truckers.

31 *Song about a screech owl* — Reference to the Ukrainian song, *Oj sydyt puhach v stepu na mohyli.*

32 *Brovary* — An old Ukrainian town, now a suburb of Kyiv.

And though people see,
People feel no sorrow:
"Go ahead, — they say — let the lazy girl die,
If she lost her self-respect."
Respect yourselves, my dears,
Even in the darkest hour
So it does not come
To searching for a Muscovite.

Oh where does Kateryna wander?
Overnighting by a fence,
Rising bright and early,
She hastened on to Muscovy;
Then — winter fell at once.
A blizzard whistles 'cross the field,
On trods Kateryna
In her skimpy woven shoes —
Oh, how wretched her despair
Dressed in but a peasant coat.
Kateryna hobbles on;
She looks —
Something glimmers up ahead
It seems, some Muscovites…
Trouble!.. The heart grows faint
She flew ahead, she met
And asked "Is not my dark-haired Ivan
With you?" And they, in Russian,
"This we do not know."
And, of course, like Muscovites
They jest and joke around:
"Atta babe! Our guys rock!
Just who they won't bamboozle!"
Kateryna looked:
"I see you're quite some people!
Don't cry, my son, my trouble!
What will be will be.
I'll go farther — I've walked more…
Perhaps I'll meet him yet;
I'll give you up, my dove,
Then I'll die myself."
The snowstorm roars and groans
It rolls and rages o'er the field;
Standing there,
Kateryna gives her tears their freedom.
The snowstorm tired out,
Here and there it yawned;
Kateryna would have cried some more
But her tears had all run out.
She gazed upon her child —
Bathed in tears,
He was like a crimson flower
Moist with morning dew.
Kateryna smiled,
A heavy smile it was:
Around the heart — like a serpent
Blackness had returned.
She looked around without a word;
She saw the woods were growing dark;
And beside those woods,
Beside the road,
It seems a hut emerged.
"Let' go, my son, it's getting dark;
Perhaps they'll take us in,
And if not, we'll pass the night outside.
We'll pass the night beside the house,
My son, my dearest Ivan!
And where are you to rest at night
When I'm no longer here?
You'll spend your time, my son,
With all the dogs outside!
Dogs are mean and they will bite,
But won't deceive you with a word,
They'll not jeer you with a story…
To eat and drink with dogs…
My weary head!
What am I to do?

The orphaned dog has his own fate,
That orphan gets a kindly word on earth;
He's beaten, cursed ansd chained
But no one gets a laugh
By asking of his mother;
Little Ivan, though, will soon be asked,
They'll not wait until he talks.
At whom do street dogs bark?
At one who sits alone,

Exposed and hungry by a fence?
Who guides a blind and worthless bum?
The dark-haired bastards…
His only fortune — his dark brows.
But even those he cannot sport
Without another's envy.

IV

Beneath a peak along a valley,
Oak trees from the hetmans' days
Stand tall and proud like wizened elders.
The valley's dammed, willows queued,
The pond's imprisoned under ice.
And an ice-hole — to fetch water…
The sun reddens like a child's hoop,
And blazes through a cloud.
The wind picks up; it blows —
Then there's nothing: it's a whiteout…
It swept throughout the woods.

The snowstorm roars and whistles,
Howling through the woods.
Like a sea, the white, white field
Was enveloped all in snow.
The woodsman left his home
Taking measure of the woods,
Ain't nothing doin'! It's so bad,
The world's obscured.
"What a blizzard!
Forget the woods,
Best that I head home…
But wait, what's there?
Oh, there's plenty of them!
The bad snowstorm's spread them,
As if it they had a purpose.
Hey man! Just look
How white they are!"
"What, Muscovites?.." —
"Where are any Muscovites?"
"What's your problem? Take a break!"
"Where are the Muscovites, the dears?"
"Why look, right there."
Off flew Kateryna
And did not even dress.
"Muscovy, it seems,
Has made a solid mark on her!
For all she does at night
Is cry out for the Muscovite."
Across the stumps and drifts
She flies, barely breathing as she goes.
She stopped barefoot on the road
Wiped her sleeve across her brow.
The Muscovites rode out to meet her
All as one on horseback.
"O my trouble, O my fate!"
Toward them… When she looks —
The officer rides up front.
"My dearest Ivan!
My beloved heart!
Where is it that you've lingered?"
She steps toward him…
Grabs the stirrup…
He looks
And spurs the horse in both his sides.
"Why do you run?
Have you forgotten Kateryna?
Do you not recognize?
Look, my dear
Take a look at me —
I'm Kateryna, your beloved.
Why spur your horse away?"
Faster does he bid his mount
As if he does not see.
"Take heed, my dear!
Look — I am not crying.
Did you not recognize me, O Ivan?
Look my sweetheart,
It is I, dear God, Kateryna!"
"Let go, you fool!
Take this crazy one away!"
"O my God! Ivan!
Are you another who forsakes me?
But you gave your promises to me!"
"Take her away! Don't just stand there!"
"Who? Me? Take me away?
Oh why, say why, my dove?

To whom will you give away your Katie
Who saw you in the orchard grove
And bore for you a son?
O daddy, O my brother!
Don't you as well reject me!
I'll become your servant...
Love another if you wish...
Love the whole wide world...
I'll forget we ever loved,
That I had a child with you,
And became an unwed mother...
An unwed mother... oh, what shame!
And the reason why I'm dying!
Drop me, disregard me
But don't ever leave your son.
You won't leave him? O my dearest,
Do not run from me...
I'll bring your son to you."
She released the stirrup
And headed for the house. Returning,
She carries him his son.
Unswaddled, all in tears
Just a poor and little child.
"Here it is, just take a look!
And where are you? In hiding?
Run away!.. and gone!.. The son, the son
Abandoned by his father!
O my dear Lord!.. O child of mine!
Where am I to go with you?
Muscovites! My dears!
Take me with you, please;
Don't reject it, my beloved:
It's an orphan child;
Take it, give it
To an officer as a son.
Take him, or I'll leave him,
Just like his father left him, —
At least misfortune did not do so!
It was in sin that mother bore you
Into this God's world;
Grow and be the people's laughing stock!"
She laid him on the road.
"Stay to look for daddy,
For I have searched already."
Like one possessed
She darted to the woods!
The child remained,
The poor dear cries... For Muscovites
It's all the same; they passed.
It's just as well; but in a lousy turn
The woodsmen heard him cry.

Shoeless, Katie runs around the woods,
She runs and shouts;
She curses her dear Ivan,
At turns she cries and pleads.
She emerges at the forest edge;
And takes a look around,
Then toward the valley... running...
Stopping on the pond without a word.
"Take my soul, dear God,
And you — my body!"
Splash, into the water!..
Beneath the ice a rumble spread.

Dark-browed Kateryna
Found what she was seeking.
The wind blew across the pond,
Not a trace was left.

It's not the wind, it's not the rage
That breaks the mighty oak,
It's not trouble, nor much hardship
When a wedded mother dies;
The children aren't quite orphaned
When they've buried their dear mother —
They are left with good repute
And a tomb remains as well.
Whenever evil people mock the orphan;
It can cry its eyes out on the tomb —
Its little heart can rest.
But what remains for him,
For him upon this world,
Whose father's never seen him,
And whose mother left him?
What's the bastard left with?

Who will talk with him?
Neither family, nor a home;
Roads, sands, anguish...
A lovely noble face, dark brows...
What for? To be recognized!
Her beauty graced him unobscured...
Had it only faded!

V

The kobzar went to Kyiv
And sat down for some rest;
Bags wrapped
Around his guide-boy's neck,
The little child beside him
Snoozing in the sun.
Meanwhile, the old kobzar
Sings of Jesus Christ,
And he who walks or rides
Does not pass him by:
This one leaves a bread roll,
That one leaves some cash;
Some give to the old man,
Girls leave half-a-kopeck
With his little bagboy.
They'll gaze upon
The dark-browed kid —
All shoeless and uncovered,
"He's got — they say — dark brows,
But fortune he has none."

On the road to Kyiv
Six horses draw a Berlin coach.[33]
Inside the coach a lady
With a lord and all their kin.
Ending up beside the beggars —
The dust begins to settle.
Little Ivan runs, he's beckoned from
The window by a waving hand.
Little Ivan gets some money
And the lady's all enchanted.
The lord glanced...
He turned away...
The villain recognized, he did,
Those hazel eyes and brows so black...
The father recognized his son
But will not take him in.
The lady asks, what is his name?
"Ivan." — "O how sweet!"
The coach moved on,
Leaving Ivan in the dust...
They counted what they got.
The wretches rose,
Said a prayer with the rising sun,
And went about their way.

St. Petersburg, End of 1838 – Early 1839

Sketch for Kateryna, 1842

---

[33] *Berlin coach* — A fashionable, fast and covered traveling carriage with a leather suspension.

THE RAMBLER[34]

The Rambler, old and blind —
Is there anyone who knows him not?
He wanders all about
Playing on his kobza.[35]
People know the one who plays
And they thank him for it:
He dispels their longing,
Though he roves the world aimlessly.
The poor soul spends his days and nights
Living by a fence;
There's no home for him on earth;
Misfortune jokes
Around his aging head,
But he's indifferent...
He'll sit, and sing:
The Kozak in a Stormy Meadow!
He'll sing and then recall
That he was orphaned long ago,
He'll brood, he'll worry,
Sitting by the fence.

That's the Rambler,
Old and strange!
He'll sing about the turncoat *Chaliy*[36]
And riff about the *Turtledove;*
With the pasture girls —
It's *Greg* or *springtime tunes.*
In the tavern with the guys —
The Serb, The Barmaid are his numbers,
At weddings for the newlyweds
(With an evil in-law mother) —
He'll sing of poplars or cruel fate,
And then — *The Meadow;*
At the market — *Lazarus*
So they may know,
He'll sing in heavy heaving tones
Of how the Sich[37] was ruined.
That's The Rambler,
Old and strange!
He'll sing, he'll laugh
And end it all with tears.

The wind blows gently,
Dancing o'er the field.
The kobzar sits atop a mound,
Strumming on his kobza.
Around him spreads the steppe,
It's like a sea of boundless blue:
Beyond that mound are still more mounds,
Those others though are hazy.
His long gray whiskers and old tuft
Disheveled by the wind;
It grows still and listens
To what the kobzar sings.
Of how his heart likes laughter,
Of how his blind eyes cry...
It listens and picks up a bit...
The old man hid
Atop a mound amid the steppe,
So no one there would see,
So the wind could carry lyrics
Far across the field,
So people would not hear,
For it's the word of God,
It's his heart freely talking to the Lord,
It's his heart chirruping the Savior's glory,

---

[34] *Rambler* — A loose translation of the Ukrainian word "perebendia," which refers to a rambling and capricious joker or oddball.

[35] See glossary or fn. 10

[36] *Sava Chaliy (? —1741)* — A Kozak officer who participated in the haidamak uprising against Poland but switched sides. He was executed by haidamak rebels.

[37] *Sich* — Fortified Kozak stronghold on an island in the Dnipro rapids near the modern city of Zaporizhia. Russian Empress Catherine II ordered its destruction in 1775.

And his muse frolics in the clouds above
Beside the world's edge.
It's like a gray-blue eagle,
With expansive wings
That beat against the sky so blue.
He'll rest beneath the sun and ask,
Where it spends the night,
How it rises in the morning;
He'll listen to the sea
To find out what it's saying,
He'll ask the darkened mountain:
Why are you so silent?
Again he reaches for the sky,
Because there's grief on earth,
Because for all its breadth
There's not a nook
For him who knows and hears
All there is to know:
Of what the sea declares,
Of where the sun lays down to rest —
Here on earth no one admits him;
He's alone among them,
Like the sun so tall,
People know him,
For he too walks the earth;
But if they heard that he, alone,
Sings atop a mound,
Conversing with the sea —
They'd ridicule God's word,
They'd pronounce the man a fool,
And drive him from their midst.
Begone, they'd say, go dance atop the sea.

Thou art good, my kobzar,
You do well, dear father,
To head out for the mound
Just to sing and talk!
Go right ahead, my dove,
Before your heart lies down to rest,
And sing your songs,
So others may not hear.
And lest they shun you,
Humor them, my brother!
When a rich lord bids you jump,
Jump as he commands:
That is why he's rich.
That's the Rambler,
Old and strange!
He sings a wedding song
But ends it on a minor key.

St. Petersburg, 1839

THE POPLAR

A wind howls above the grove,
It dances o'er the field,
Beside the road it bends a poplar
To the ground below.
Its tall bearing, its broad leaf
Turning green in vain.
A field stretches far and wide,
Like the sea, it shines with blue.
A chumak wanders by,
He stops and bows his head.
A shepherd in the morning,
Flute in hand,
Sits atop a mound,
He looks — his heart aches:
Nothing, nowhere, not a blade of grass.
Alone, alone, like an orphan
In a foreign land, dying.

Who nurtured it so lithe and slim
To perish in the steppe?
Pay attention — I'll tell all.
Listen up, my girls!

A dark-browed girl was smitten,
Smitten with a Kozak.
She fell in love — but could not stop him:
He went away — and perished…
Had she known he'd leave her —
She would not have loved him;
Had she known he'd perish —
She would not have let him go;
Had she known — she would not
Have filled her pail so late,
She would not have stood
Till midnight with her sweetheart
By the willow.
Had she only known!..
This too is a curse —
To know ahead
What waits for you on earth…
Best not to know, dear girls!
Do not ask about your fate!..
The heart alone knows
Whom to love.
Let it wither till you're buried,
It won't be long, my dark-browed ones!
Your lovely hazel eyes
And pretty rosy faces —
They're not for long, dear girls!
They last till noon and then they wither
The dark brows fade away.
So live and love,
Your heart knows what to do.

A nightingale twitters
In a meadow on a guelder rose,
A Kozak sings
And strolls along the valley.
He sings until his dark-browed beauty
Emerges from her house,
And he'll ask her,
If her mother did not beat her.
They stand, embrace —
The nightingale sings.
They'll listen, go their ways
Both of them quite happy…
It's a scene that no one sees,
Nor will anyone inquire:
"Where'd you go, what did you do?"

She knows herself…
She lived, she loved,
Her heart grew faint —
The heart felt trouble,
But knew not how to say it.
And did not — left alone,
She grieves by day and grieves by night
Like a lovebird lost without its lovebird,
And no one there can hear her…

On the meadow by the water
The nightingale twitters not.
The dark-browed girl does not sing,
Standing by the willow.
She does not sing —
And like an orphan roams the world:
Without the sweetheart,
Her parents seem like total strangers,
The sun without her sweetheart shines —
But laughs much like a foe,
Without her sweetheart all's a grave…
Yet the heart still beats.

One year passed and then another —
Still no Kozak;
She withers like a flower;
Mother does not ask:
"What makes you wilt, my daughter?"
The old one did not ask,
But quietly sought to match her
With a gray old rich man.
"Go, my daughter, — says the mother, —
Don't waste your years in maidenhood!
He is rich and unattached —
You'll live the life of lords."
"I want no life of lords,
Nor, mama, will I go for him!
Use the wedding scarves I got
To lower my coffin in a grave.

Allow the priests to chant
And let the bridesmaids cry,
Reclining in a coffin's better, mama,
Than to look at him."

The old mother did not listen,
She did what she knew how —
The dark-browed girl watched,
And wordlessly she withered,
She went late at night to see a seer,
To divine her fortune,
How much longer in this world
Must she live alone?..
Granny, dear,
My heart, O caring one,
I want to hear the honest truth,
Where's my dearest sweetheart?
Is he alive and is he well,
Does he still love me true?
Did he forget and did he leave me?
Tell me, where's my dearest?
I'll sail to the world's edge
If that is he where he's at.
Granny, dearest!
Tell me, 'cause you know...
My mother wants to give my hand
To an old guy I don't want.
To love him, O my dear,
Is something you can't teach your heart!
I'd go and drown myself —
But it's a shame to lose your soul...
If my dark-browed one no longer lives,
Make it so, my dove,
That I'll not ever go back home...
It's hard for me, it's hard!
The old guy waits there
With the matchmakers...
Tell me, please, my fate."
"Okay, my child, rest a bit.
Do my bidding.
I too was once a maiden —
I knew such heartbreak well;
It passed — I learned:
I'm here to help the people.
Your fate, my child!
I've known it for a couple years,
That's why yesteryear I got a potion.
The old one went and from a shelf
She got an inky vial.
"Here's for you, my wonder.
Go to the well;
Before the roosters crow,
Douse yourself with water
Then drink a bit of potion —
It'll heal all the troubles.
Drink — and really run;
Whatever screams behind you,
Don't look back, until you stop
At the place you bid farewell.
Rest a while; and when
The moon rides high above,
Drink again; should he not come —
A third drink is required.
The first will make you like
You were that year.
With the second —
A horse amid the steppe
Will raise and stomp his hoof, —
If your Kozak's living,
He'll come to you at once.
And the third time, O my child!
Ask not what will be...
Another thing, you hear,
Don't cross yourself —
For everything will sink in water...
Now go, go see the beauty
Of your yesteryear."

She took the potion, bowing:
"Thank you, grannie!"
She left the house — to go, or not?
"No! I'll return no longer!"
She arrived... washed, drank
And broke into a quiet smile.
She took the second drink, the third
And never turned around.

She flew, as if on wings,
And fell amid the steppe,
She fell, she rose, she cried
And… and sang:

"Swim, swim, my little swan!
Along the sea so blue —
Grow, grow, my little poplar!
Upward, ever upward,
Grow lithe and tall
To reach the very clouds,
Ask the Lord if I will live
To ever see a mate, or not?
Grow, grow, and peer far
Beyond the sea so blue.
On the distant shore — my fortune,
On this one — my misfortune.
My dark-browed darling yonder
Sings and dances somewhere,
While I cry, and waste my years,
Expecting his return.
Tell him, O my heart!
That people laugh.
Tell him I will die
Should he not return!
My own mother wants
That I be buried…
But who is to caress her head?
Who will care, who will ask
And who will help in her old age?
O my mother!.. O my fate!..
Dear Lord, O God!
Look yonder, poplar!
If he's gone — you'll cry,
Early, before sunrise
Lest anybody see…
Grow tall, my poplar dear
Always upward, ever upward;
Swim, swim my little swan!
Along the sea so blue."

Thus cried and sang
The dark-browed girl…
And in a wondrous turn
She became a poplar in the field.

A wind howls above the grove,
It dances o'er the field,
Beside the road it bends a poplar
To the ground below.

St. Petersburg, 1839

TO OSNOVIANENKO[38]

Rapids rage; the moon is rising
As it's always risen…
There's no more Sich, and gone is he,
Who ruled it all!
There's no more Sich;
The cattails ask the Dnipro:
"What became of all our children,
Where are they carousing?"
A seagull squawks in flight
As if crying for its children;
The sun beams, the wind blows
O'er the Kozak steppe.
Throughout the steppe are mounds,
Mounds that stand and mourn;

---

38 *Hryhoriy Fedorovych Kvitka-Osnovianenko (1778-1843)* — Ukrainian writer, cultural and civic figure. He is known as the father of Ukrainian prose.

They ask the raging wind:
"Where do our men rule?
Where's the place they rule and revel?
Where is it that you tarry?
Come back! Look —
Now the rye bows low,
Where once your horses grazed,
Where feather-grass once swished,
Where the blood of Poles and Tatars
Formed a crimson sea...
Come back." — "They won't!" —
So said the azure sea. —
They won't come back,
They're gone forever!"
The sea is right, the blue one has it right!
Their fate is such:
There's no return for those awaited,
There's no return for freedom.
There's no return for Kozaks,
The hetmans won't rise up.
They will not wrap Ukraine
With all their crimson mantles!
She's in tatters, crying,
Orphaned high above the Dnipro;
It's tough and trying for an orphan,
But it's something no one sees...
No one save the enemy, who laughs...
Go ahead and laugh, fierce foe!
Just not too much, for all things pass —
Glory will not perish;
It won't perish, but will tell
What happened in this world,
Of justice and injustice
And whose children we remain.
Our idea and our song
Will neither die nor perish...
And that, good people, is our glory,
The glory of Ukraine!
No gold, no stone,[39]
Nor cunning speech
But loud and true,
Just like the word of God.
Is it not so, our father otaman?
Do I not sing the truth?
Alas, were it only so. What can I say?
I have not what it takes.
There is, moreover — Muscovy,
Strangers all around...
"Don't indulge them," — you might say,
And what of it?
They'll ridicule the psalm
That I'll pour out with my tears;
They'll ridicule... It's hard, father,
To live among the foes!
I too perhaps would fight
If only there was strength;
I'd sing — once I had a voice,
But it's beholden to the past.
So heavy is the anguish.
O my father, O my friend!
I ramble through the snow
And to myself I sing:
The Kozak in a Stormy Meadow!
I won't cut it anymore. And you, my father,
As well you know,
People have respect for you,
You're gifted with a voice;
Sing to them, beloved,
About the Sich, about the mounds,
When they formed each one,
And who was put to rest in them.
About old times, about the wonder
That once was and slipped away...
Strike up a tune, kind sir,
So they may hear all 'round the world
Of what transpired in Ukraine,
Of Kozak glory
And why it flourished in this world!

[39] *No gold, no stone* — This is interpreted as meaning Ukrainian glory is a spiritual notion that does not need gold or stone monuments to be remembered.

Strike up a tune, kind sir,
Let me cry,
Let me see Ukraine again,
Let me hear that sea just one more time,
And how a girl sings *Greg*
Beside a willow tree.
Permit my heart to smile again
In this alien land,
Before it rests in foreign soil
In a foreign coffin.

St. Petersburg, October-December 1839

IVAN PIDKOVA[40]

I

There was a time — cannons roared
Throughout Ukraine;
There was a time — Zaporizhians[41]
Knew how to command.
They ruled, they garnered
Liberty and glory;
It's all gone — what remains
Are only mounds amid the fields.
Those mounds are tall and in them
Rests a pale Kozak's body
Veiled in nankeen cloth.
Those mounds are tall,
Blackened silhouettes like mountains.
Furtively they speak of freedom
With winds that blow across the field.
The witness to grandfathers' glory
Converses with the wind,
The grandson, scythe in hand,
Walks into the dew
With songs about them on his lips.

There was an age — that trouble
Pranced about Ukraine,
Grief quaffed honeymead
Like rebels in a tavern.
There was a time
When living in Ukraine was good...
Let's recall it! Perhaps the
Heart will rest a bit.

II

A black cloud covers sun and sky
From the Lyman and beyond.
The azure sea is like a beast,
It wails and it moans.
The Dnipro delta flooded.
"Hey, fellas,
Man the longboats.
The sea's stuck up a tune —
It's time we went and romped."

The Zaporizhians all poured forth —
They wrapped the Lyman
With their longboats.
"Roll on, blue sea!" — they sang,
The waves turned white with foam.
Ringed by waves like mountains:
No earth below, no sky above.
The heart grows faint,
Just what the Kozaks need.
They sail along and sing;

40 *Ivan Pidkova (Ioan Potcoavă ?-1578)* — A Moldovan who became a Zaporizhian Kozak leader and fought against Turks, Tatars and Poles. He was captured by Poles and beheaded in Lviv. His name in Ukrainian means "horseshoe," perhaps because he was said to have the strength to bend horseshoes with his hands.

41 *Zaporizhians* — Ukrainian Kozaks who lived beyond the Dnipro River rapids in Central Ukraine.

A cormorant flies above…
Up front the otaman
Leads as best he can.
Along the boat he walks,
His pipe just smoldering in his mouth.
Looking to and fro —
Where to go for work?
Curling long black whiskers,
Reaching by his ear
He raised his hat —
The boats stopped still.
"May the enemy die!
It's not to Sinope,[42] otamans
And young men,
But to Carihrad[43] and to the sultan
That we'll pay our visit."
"Good, our fearless leader" —
It resounded all around.
"Thank you!"
He donned his hat.
Again the azure sea begins to boil;
Again along the boat
The otaman strolls silently,
Peering at the waves.

St. Petersburg, 1839

Sketch of Kozak, 1841

My thoughts, my thoughts,
Troubled is my life with you!
Why've you stood on paper
In a sad array?..
Why's the wind not scattered you
Like dust across the steppe?
Why's trouble not consoled you
As it would its child?..
For trouble has, as if by jest,
Brought you here into this world,
Tears have watered you…
Why did they not engulf you,
Not sweep you out to sea,
Or wash you far afield?
People would not ask what hurts,
Nor why I curse my fate,
Or why I roam the world? "Doing nothing" —
They'd not say derisively.

O my blossoms, O my children!
Why have I so loved you,
Why have I so cared for you?

---

[42] *Sinope* — A Turkish port city on the Black Sea.

[43] *Carihrad* — Variation on Czarhorod, the former Ukrainian name for Istanbul (Carigrad in other Slavic languages). Derived from the words czar (Caesar) and hrad (city).

Will a single heart in this wide world
Cry for you as I?.. Perhaps, I've guessed…
Perhaps I'll come across a girlish
Heart and hazel eyes,
That will cry about these thoughts.
I do not wish for more…
A single tear from hazel eyes —
And I'll become the lord of lords!..
My thoughts, my thoughts,
Troubled is my life with you!

For the sake of pretty hazel eyes
And engaging dark, dark brows
The heart raced on and laughed,
Pouring out a string of words,
It poured them out as best it could
For the sake of moonless nights,
For an emerald cherry grove
And a girl's favor…
For steppes and mounds,
That dot Ukraine,
The heart grew faint;
In foreign lands it would not sing…
Amid the snows, amid the woods,
It wanted not to summon
The advice of sceptered Kozaks
Bearing maces…
Let Kozak souls
Wander all throughout Ukraine —
It is from end to end
A happy, boundless land…
Like that bygone freedom,
The Dnipro's wide — a sea,
The steppe and steppe,
The pounding rapids,
All the mounds are mountains.
Kozak freedom pranced there,
It's where they all were born.
It sowed the fields with noblemen
And members of the Tatar Horde.
It sowed the fields with corpses
Till it turned repugnant…
Then it laid down for a rest…
Meanwhile, a mound arose,
A black eagle flies above it,[44]
A sentry on the watch.
Good people hear the kobzars
Singing songs about the mound,
The blind wretches sing of how it was,
Because they're smart and witty…
And I, and I know only how to cry,
I've only tears for dear Ukraine…
But words — I've none…
As for trouble… Oh, be gone!
Who really knows no trouble!..
Especially he who watches people
With all his heart and soul —
His life in this world's just pure hell,
And in the next…

Grief
Won't summon me good fortune,
If I've so little of it.
Let hard times persist three days —
I'll then bury them,
I'll inter the vicious serpent
Right beside my heart,
So foes won't see
Trouble's laughter deep within…
May my thoughts, just like a raven
Fly around and caw,
Secretly the heart will chirp
And cry just like a nightingale —
People will not see
And therefore will not laugh…
Please don't dry my tears,
Let them be to stream.
Every day and every night
They irrigate a foreign field,
Until, until… they bury me

[44] *Black eagle* — Reference to the two-headed Russian eagle.

And cover my eyes
With foreign sand…
So it is… But what to do?
Grief won't help.
Whoever envies the poor orphan —
Punish him, O God!
My thoughts, my thoughts,
O my blossoms, O my children!
I've raised you
And I've nurtured you —
Now where am I to send you?
To Ukraine, my children!
Go to our Ukraine
As orphans under fences,
While I stay here to die.
There you'll find an earnest heart
And a kindly word,
There you'll find the honest truth,
And maybe even glory…

Welcome them, my mother!
O my dear Ukraine!
Welcome all my foolish children
As if they were your own.

St. Petersburg, January-Early March 1839

TO N. MARKEVYCH[45]

Bandurist,[46] O gray eagle
You've got it good my brother,
You have wings and you have power
And there's time to fly.
Now you fly to our Ukraine,
They await you there.
I'd fly after you,
But who would welcome me?
Here I'm foreign and alone
And in Ukraine, my dear one,
I'm an orphan just like here.
The heart pounds, it longs, but why?
I'm alone there.
All alone… Ah, Ukraine!
The boundless steppes!
The boisterous breeze will blow,
He'll speak up like a brother,
There's freedom in that open field,
There the blue sea praises God,
It dispels the longing,
Mounds amid the steppe converse there
With the blustering wind,
They converse in sadness
And here is what they say:
"It was — it's gone
Never to return."
I'd fly, I'd listen
And I'd cry with them.
But fate, alas, has clipped my wings
Among a foreign people.

St. Petersburg, May 9, 1840

[45] *Mykola (Nikolai) Andriyovych Markevych (1804-60)* — Ukrainian historian, poet, ethnographer and amateur musician. Friend of Shevchenko.

[46] *Bandurist* — A musician who plays the bandura, a plucked Ukrainian string instrument with 30 to 68 strings.

TRIBUTE TO SHTERNBERG[47]

You'll travel far
You'll see a lot;
You'll look around, you will be sad —
Remember me, my brother!

St. Petersburg, May-June 1840

HAIDAMAKS[48]

To Vasyl Ivanovych Hryhorovych[49]
In Memory of April 22, 1838[50]

All is passing, all is fleeting — forever without end.
Whither goes it ? Whence?
Neither fool nor wise man knows.
Living... Dying... One thing blossoms,
One thing wilts... It wilts for all eternity...
And winds have swept the yellowed leaves.
But the sun will rise as always,
And red stars that always drifted
Will later drift as well, and you, the pale moon
Will rise to dance upon the azure sky.
You'll rise to gaze upon the trough and well,
Upon the endless sea, and you'll shine,
As you once did in Babylon above its Hanging Gardens,[51]
And will above our sons and all their twists of fate.
You're eternal, limitless!.. I love to speak with you,
As if you were a sibling,
And to sing the thoughts to you that you whispered unto me.

---

47 *Vasyl Ivanovych Shternberg (1818-45)* — Friend of Shevchenko at the St. Petersburg Academy of Arts. This poem was considered of dubious origin until confirmed in 2003 with the discovery of a rare early *Kobzar*.

48 *Haidamaks* — Participants in bloody 18th century Kozak and peasant rebellions against Polish nobility, Jesuits, Uniate Catholics and Jews. The main haidamak uprisings occurred in 1734, 1750 and 1768.

49 *Vasyl Ivanovych Hryhorovych* (1786-1865) — Art historian and professor at the St. Petersburg Academy of Arts. Hryhorovych was among the Ukrainians who played a role in winning Shevchenko's freedom.

50 *April 22, 1838* — The day Shevchenko's freedom was purchased.

51 *Hanging Gardens of Babylon* — One of the Seven Wonders of the Ancient World.

Advise me once again, what am I to do with sorrow?
I'm not alone, I'm not an orphan —
I have children, but what to do with them?
Bury them with me? That's a sin, for they've a living soul!
Perhaps its lot upon this world may ease
If someone reads the tear-stained words
That is once spewed out so earnestly,
That it so furtively cried over.
No, I'll bury nothing, for there's that living soul.
Like the endless stretch of azure sky,
So too the soul exists with no beginning and no end.
But where is it to go? Empty words!
May someone on this world recall it —
It's hard to leave this world for the man of ill-repute.
Remember, girls — you must remember!
It loved you, O my rosy blossoms,
And it loved to serenade your fate.
Rest, my children, till the sunrise,
And I'll ponder where to get a chief.

My sons, O haidamaks!
The world is broad, it's free —
Go my sons, go frolicking,
Go searching for your fate.
My sons, my little ones,
O my unknowing children,
Who will welcome you in earnest
With no mother in this world?
My sons! My eagles!
Fly to our Ukraine
Though grief will meet you there,
It won't be in a foreign land.
There'll be a kindly soul,
Who will not let you die,
But here... but here... It's hard, my children!
When they let you in a home,
Having greeted you, they'll laugh,
For such, you see, are people:
They're all literate and published,
But they even scorn the sun:
"That's not the spot, — they'll say — to rise,
It doesn't shine quite right,
Here is how, — they'll say — it should all be done..."

What are you to do?
You must listen, for indeed perhaps,
It doesn't rise quite as it should,
So have read the literati...
They're smart and say no more!
And what have they to say of you?
I know your glory!
They'll sneer and scorn a bit,
And throw you down beneath a bench.
"You go ahead, — they'll say — and rest,
Until the father rises
And tells us in our language
About his glorious hetmans.
As is, some fool spins tales
In dead language[52]
Of some Yarema he parades before us,
Dressed in peasant shoes. A fool! A fool!
He was beaten, never taught.
From Kozakdom through hetmans' rule
Only towering mounds remain —
Nothing else is left,
And even they are plundered;
And he wants that others listen
To the singing of some beggars.
Useless work, good fellow:
If money's what you want
Or that wonder known as glory,
Then sing about Matriosha
Sing about Parasha and our joy,
About sultans,[53] spurs and parquet floors —
That's where glory's at! Instead he sings,
The Lively Sea so Blue,
Though himself he cries, and behind him
Stand his people dressed in dowdy coats!.."
True, O wise ones!
Thanks for the advice.
A warm sheepskin coat, just too bad
It wasn't sewn for me,
And your wise word is

---

52 *Dead language* — Shevchenko ridicules the contempt of some Russian literary critics toward use of Ukrainian in his 1840 edition of the *Kobzar.* They considered Ukrainian a dead language and Russian the key to success.

53 *Sultan* — Plumage on an officer's cap.

Lined with lies.
Pardon me... holler as you please,
I'll not listen to a word
And won't summon you to me:
You are wise —
And I'm a fool; all alone
In my own home
I will sing and cry,
Just like a little child.
I'll sing — the sea is lively,
Gentle breezes blow,
The steppe grows dark, the mound
Converses with the wind.
I'll sing — the towering mound
Is plundered,
The steppe's expanse is covered
By Zaporizhians to the sea.
Otamans on black stallions
Prance before the scepters...
Among the cattails
Angry rapids moan and roar,
They sing a song of something dreadful.
I'll listen, worry,
Then I'll ask the ancient ones:
"Why so sad, old folks?"
"Unhappy times, dear son!
The Dnipro's angry at us,
Ukraine is shedding tears..."
And I weep as well. Meanwhile,
The otamans trot forward in exquisite rows,
Centurions with lords and hetmans —
All decked out in gold.
They came inside my little home,
Sat beside me,
Talking, telling tales of Ukraine.
Of how they built the Sich,
Of how Kozaks on their longboats
Passed the Dnipro rapids,
Of how they frolicked on the azure one,
How they warmed themselves down in Scutari[54]
And how, having smoked their pipes

[54] *Scutari* — Today's Uskudar, a suburb of Istanbul on the Anatolian side of the Bosporus.

In Poland's blazing fires,
They came back home to banquet in Ukraine.
"Play on kobzar, hey, barkeeper, pour some more!"
The Kozaks roared.
The barkeeper knows what's what and pours
Without another thought;
The kobzar hit it, and the Kozaks —
Why all of Khortytsia[55] is buckling —
Together all break out
In whirling dances and the hopak;[56]
The jug is passed and passed again
Until it all dries out.
"Dance, sir, take off your coat,
Dance, wind, across the field,
"Play on kobzar, hey, barkeeper, pour some more!
Until our fate stands upright."
Arms akimbo in a squat dance,
Young fellows with the old guys.
"That's the way to do it, kids!
Kids, you're doing well
You'll be lords one day."
Otamans at the banquet stroll about,
Conversing as if they were in council;
But the noble group could not refrain,
Their old legs stomped away.
And I look and see,
Laughing through my tears.
I watch, I laugh and wipe the tears —
I'm not alone, there's someone in this world to live with.
In my little home, like on the boundless steppe,
Kozaks dance, the longboat hums,
In my little home the azure sea plays on,
The mound grieves, the poplar whispers,
Quietly a girl sings *Greg* —
I'm not alone, I can live my years out with another.
There's my good, my money,
There's my glory,
And thanks for your advice,
For advice that's only wicked.
That dead language

[55] *Khortytsia* — One of the largest Dnipro River islands and former stronghold of the Zaporizhian Kozaks.
[56] *Hopak* — The Ukrainian national dance. It is characterized by acrobatic jumping and spinning.

Will suffice for me until I die
To pour out grief and tears.
So long, be well,
I'll go see my sons off
On a long road.
Let them go — perhaps they'll
Find an elder Kozak,
Who will greet my children
With old tears.
But enough of me. I'll say once more:
A lord I am among the lords.

And so, sitting at the table end,
I reflect and think:
Whom to ask? Who will guide them?
Outside, daylight dawns;
The moon's extinguished, the sun's ablaze,
The haidamaks are up,
They've prayed, they've dressed and
Stood up all around me.
Sadly, sadly, just like orphans,
They bowed without a word.
"Bless us, father — they say,
So long as we have strength;
Bless our search for fortune
On this vast wide world."
"Hold on... the world's no home,
And you're just little children,
Ignorant. Who's the chief
That shall go before you?
Who will lead? Trouble, O my children,
Being with you is plain trouble.
Lovingly I raised you, nurtured you,
Rather big you've grown;
You're stepping out among the people,
But out there it's now become all literate.
Sorry that I didn't teach you,
For though they beat me, beat me good,
They still taught me quite a lot.
I know the ABC's of Church Slavonic,
But still can't cut the accent marks.[57]

[57] *Accent marks* — Reference to diacritical marks used in Church Slavonic *(оксія)*.

What will they tell you?
Let's go, my sons, let's go and ask.
I have an earnest father[58]
(Though my own is gone)
He'll tell me what to do with you,
Because he knows full well,
How hard it is to roam the world
For an orphan without kin;
He is besides — an honest soul
Of Kozak roots.
He did not renounce the word
Sung once by his mother
As she wrapped her infant,
And chatted with her little babe;
He did not renounce the word
The blind old beggar sang so sadly by the fence.
He loves that ballad of the truth,
That of Kozak glory,
He loves it — let's go, my sons
To a caring council.
Had he once not met me at the darkest hour,
They'd long ago have buried me
Amid the snow in foreign land;
They'd have interred me, saying:
'Yes... some ne'er-do-well...'
To roam the world is tough and trying,
Knowing not the reason why.
It's past, may it not recur in dreams!..
Let's go, boys,
If abroad he did not let me die,
Then he'll welcome you and greet you
Like a child of his own.
And from him, having prayed,
Off you'll go into Ukraine!"
Good morning to you, father,
Bless my little children
At the threshold of your home,
And set them, if you will, on their lengthy way.

St. Petersburg, April 7, 1841

---

[58] *Earnest father* — Vasyl Ivanovych Hryhorovych, to whom the poem is dedicated.

INTRODUCTION

There was once an Aristocracy,[59]
Quite a noble lady:
She measured up to Muscovy,
The Horde, the Sultan,
And the Germans… It once was…
But what's not fleeting?
It once was, know this, that the gentry boasted,
Dancing up the day and night,
Lording even over kings…
I won't say Stefan[60]
Or Jan Sobieski[61] —
Those two were uncommon —
But others. Those sorry sights
Ruled silently.
Sejms,[62] and petty sejms roared out,
Neighbors remained silent,
Watching kings flee Poland,
Listening to fire spouted by the gentry:
"Nie pozwalam! Nie pozwalam!"[63]
The gentry howls,
And magnates burn down houses,[64]
Tempering their little swords.
Such things went on for quite a while,
Until in Warsaw the lively Poniatkowski[65]
Became ruler of the Poles.

He took control and thought he'd
Rein the gentry in a bit…
He thought but was not able!

---

59 *An Aristocracy* — Reference to Rzeczpospolita, the Polish feudal state when the country was ruled by a privileged noble class from the 16th almost through the 19th centuries.

60 *Stefan Batory (1533-86)* — Polish king, considered one of the country's greatest.

61 *Jan Sobieski* (1629-96) — Polish king and military commander who defeated the Turks in the 1683 Battle of Vienna.

62 *Sejm* — Polish legislature.

63 *Nie pozwalam* — Polish phrase for "I do not allow." A single member of the Sejm could veto any proposal by shouting the term, which became associated with anarchy.

64 *Magnates burn down houses* — Reference to licentiousness of Polish nobles.

65 *Stanislaw August Poniatkowski (1732-98)* — Before his election as Poland's last king, he was Polish ambassador to Russia and lover of Empress Catherine II. He tried to limit the nobility's veto power and conducted pro-Russian policies. Poland was partitioned during his reign.

He wanted good, as might a mother for her children,
He thought he'd strip the gentry
Of the single term "nie pozwalam!"
And later!.. Poland went ablaze,
Petty lords went rabid… Shouting:
"Word of honor, his work is useless,
A usurper, he's a hireling of the Muscovite!"
Incited by Pulaski[66] and by Pac[67]
The gentry's lands rose up
Together in a hundred confederations.[68]
The confederates scattered
Throughout Poland and Volyn,[69]
Throughout Lithuania, Moldavia
And all throughout Ukraine;
They scattered and forgot
To rescue liberty,
Then buddied up with Jews
And started to destroy.
They destroyed and murdered,
Turning churches into kindling…
Meanwhile, the haidamaks
Began to consecrate their knives.

VAGABOND

"Yarema, herst tu,[70]
You churlish son?
Go bring the mare,
Hand the missus her slippers
Bring me water,
Clean the house, lug in kindling,
Spread the feed for turkeys,
Give the geese some,
Go to the cellar, to the cow,
And hurry up, boor!.. Wait!
When you're done, run to Vilshana,[71]
The Uniate's[72] wife needs help. Don't delay."
Off Yarema went, stooping.

---

66 *Jozef Pulaski (1704-69)* — Organizer and leader of the Bar Confederation, an association of Polish nobles opposed to the reforms and pro-Russian policies of King Poniatkowski.

67 *Michal Jan Pac (1730-87)* — Member of the Bar Confederation.

68 *Confederations* — Ad hoc political and military alliances of Polish nobles that opposed royal authority. They also persecuted peasants and the Orthodox in Ukraine, which was one of the reasons for the haidamak rebellions.

69 *Volyn* — A region of Northwestern Ukraine.

70 *Herst tu* — "Listen up" in Yiddish. Akin to the German "hörst du," do you hear?

71 *Vilshana* — A small town in Central Ukraine. Shevchenko lived there in 1828 or 29 as his master's servant.

72 See glossary or fn. 14

Thus the evil Jew began the morning
By pushing 'round the Kozak.
Yarema stooped,
Because he did not know,
The wretch did not yet know
He'd sprouted wings,
That he'd reach the sky in flight,
He did not know and stooped...
O my dear God!
Living in this world's so hard,
Yet still one wants to live:
One wants to see the shining sun,
One wants to listen how the sea resounds,
How the songbird twitters,
How the longboat rushes,
Or how the dark-browed girl
Starts singing in the grove...
O my dear God, what a joy to live!

The orphan Yarema —
The impoverished orphan:
Neither brother, sister, nor anybody else!
Just the lackey of a Jew,
He grew upon a ledge;
But he doesn't curse his fate,
Doesn't bother others.
And why curse? Don't they know already
Whom to stroke and whom to torture?
Let them feast...
Their fate takes care of them,
The orphan has to get his own.
At times it happens that he softly cries,
But the reason's not an aching heart:
It may be something he recalls or sees...
And then it's back to work.
That's the way to live!
Why a father, why a mother
Or a lofty palace
When there's no heart to talk with yours?
The orphan Yarema — the wealthy orphan,
Because there's someone there to cry with,
Someone there to serenade:
There are hazel eyes —
Twinkling just like stars,
There are fair and little hands —
Swooning and embracing,
There is a one and only,
A girl's tender heart,
That cries, laughs, dies and revives again,
Like a holy spirit
That waits for him at night.
Such is my Yarema,
An orphan, oh, so wealthy.
I too was once like that.
It's gone, girls...
It's gone, dispersed,
Not a trace is left.
The heart grows faint, when I recall...
Why no trace?
Why no trace, why no welcome?
Easier it would have been
To pour out tears and grief.
People took, for they had little.
"What need has he for destiny?
Need to bury it:
Even so, he's rich..."
Rich in patches
And fine tears —
So long as they're not wiped!
Destiny, O my destiny!
Where to look for you?
Come back to me, to my little home,
Or at least appear in dreams...
I don't want to sleep.

Forgive me, good people:
Perhaps it's not appropriate,
But who will not be hindered
By accursed misery-misfortune?
Perhaps we'll meet again,
As long as o'er this world
I hobble with Yarema,
And perhaps... I don't even know.
Trouble, people, trouble all around.
There's no haven:
As they say, wherever fate decides to bend,

That's where you too need to bend —
Bend, and smile, wordlessly,
So people do not know,
What's hidden in the heart,
Lest they snub you for it.
It is their favor, after all...
May he who's blessed by fate
Have dreams, may the orphan
Never dream of it, not ever!
To express yourself is hard and dull,
But I know not how to keep my silence.
Pour forth my words and tears:
The sun's not warm enough to dry them.
I'll share my tears...
Not with a brother nor a sister —
But with a silent wall
And in a foreign land... Meanwhile —
To the tavern I'll return,
To see what's happening there.
A Yid
Trembles, bending
By his bed and night lamp,
The cuss is counting all his money.
And on the bed... O how stuffy!..
Uncovered, she tossed
Her little fair white hands...
She turns crimson
Like an orchard flower;
The blouse clings to her bosom —
It's undone... Perhaps it's stuffy
Sleeping on feather bed
All alone and young;
With no one there to talk to, —
She whispers to herself.
She's extremely gorgeous
And unbaptized!
That's the daughter, that's the father —
The very devil's pocket.
Old Khaika lies face down
On a grimy feather bed.
Where's Yarema? Having grabbed a sack
He took off for Vilshana.

THE CONFEDERATES

"Open up you damned Jew!
Or you'll be beaten... Open up!
Break down the door,
Before the old creep comes."
"Wait!
Hold on, just a minute!"
"Whip
The swine behind the ear.
You wanna joke with us, or what?"
"Me? With lords?
God forbid! Just a minute, let me rise,
Your excellencies (whispering — pigs)."
"Colonel, break it down!"
The door fell... And the whip splattered
Up and down the Jewish spine.
Here's to you, swine, here's to you, Jew,
Here's to you, the devil's son!"
Again the whip, again the whip.
And the Jew bent down:
"Please, no joking, gentlemen!"
"Good evening to this home!"
Give the cunning bastard yet another!
More!.. Enough!
Excuse us, you damned Jew!
Good evening! And where's your daughter?
"Died, gentlemen."
"You lie, Judas! Whip 'em!"
They showered lashes once again.
"O my dear gentlemen,
I swear to God, she's gone!"
"You lie, conniver!"
"If I lie,
May God punish me!"
"Not God, but we. Confess!"
"Why would I hide her if she lived?
God, may I be damned!"

"Ha, ha, ha, ha!.. The devil, gentlemen,
Sings a litany.
Cross yourself!"
"How's it done?
Indeed, I know not how."
"Watch, like this..."
The Pole crosses himself,
And Judas follows after.
"Bravo! Bravo! We christened him.
And, well, for such a miracle
A drink, your excellencies!
You listening, christened one?
A drink!"
"At once, at once!"
They roar like mad,
The Poles roar, and a rebel
Dances on the table.
"Jeszcze Polska nie zginęła!"[73] —
Some of them shout out.
"Service, Jew!"
The christened one,
Know this,
Darts from house to cellar, pouring,
And the confederates, know this,
Shout, "Hey, Jew, pour more mead!"
The Jew can't even think.
"Where are the cymbals?
Play, you mongrel!"
The tavern downright shakes —
They rip into Pecker Dances,[74]
Waltzes and Mazurkas.
The Jew glances, whispering:
"Such is noble nature!"
"Fine, enough! Now sing!"
"I swear to God, I don't know how!"
"No appeals to God, you mangy dog!"
"What's your pleasure?
The Wretched Maid?
There was once an Annie,[75]
The crippled wretch,
Appealed to God,
And prayed
About her aching feet;
She did not work her master's field
But quietly
And daintily
Chased the boys
Amid the weeds."

"Enough! Enough! That one's lousy:
Schismatics[76] sing it."
"What's your pleasure? Maybe this one?
Wait, I'll remember it...

The Jew walks a trembling
Before a Mister Theodore,
Backwards,
Forwards
Before that Mister Theodore."

"Fine, enough! Now pay!"
"You're joking sir:
Pay for what?"
"That we listened.
Don't make faces, ugly man!
We're not kidding.
Fork the money over!"
"Where am I to get it?
I have not a penny;
The gentry's favor is my wealth."
"You're lying, dog. Fess up!
Come on, gentlemen,
The whips!"
And they whistled,
Christening Leiba once again.
They thrashed and thrashed,

[73] *Jeszcze Polska nie zginęła* — From the Polish national anthem. The term means "Poland has not yet perished."
[74] *Pecker Dance* — A fast Polish dance also known as the Krakowiak.
[75] *Annie* — The original refers to the Ukrainian name, Handzia.
[76] *Schismatic* — Polish term for a non-Uniate.

So much that feathers blew…
"Honest to God, not a penny!
Devour my body!
Not a penny! Help! Save me!"
"We'll save you, alright!"
"Wait, I'll tell you something."
"We're listening, yes, we're listening,
But don't bother lying,
And croak if you so wish,
Lying will not help."
"No, in Vilshana…"
"Your money?"
"Mine!.. God forbid!
Rather, what I'm saying, in Vilshana…
Schismatics there
Are living three, four families to a home."
"This we know, 'cause we're the ones
Who ripped 'em off."
"But no, not that… forgive me…
So you may never know of hardship,
So that money comes to you in dreams…
In Vilshana in the Catholic church…
With the sexton…
And, my, his daughter Oksana!
Good God! What a fine young lady!
What a beauty!
And, oh, how many coins of gold!
Though they're not his,
But what's the difference?
It's money all the same."
"Money all the same, indeed!
Leiba speaks the truth;
But if the truth is to be certain,
Let him show the way.
Get dressed."
Off the Poles went to Vilshana.
A lone confederate too drunk to stand
Mutters cheerfully beneath a bench:
"We live, we live,
Jeszcze Polska nie zginęła!"

THE SEXTON

"In a grove, in a grove
Not a breeze is blowing;
The moon's on high
The stars are twinkling.
Come out, my sweetheart, —
I can't wait to see you;
If even for an hour, sweetie!
Come out, my dove,
We'll coo a bit,
Some sorrow we will share;
Because this night will take
Me on a distant journey.
Come out my birdie,
O my sweetheart,
While we're close we'll coo a bit…
Oh, how tough and trying!"
And thus, walking by the grove,
Yarema sings and waits with bated breath;
But Oksana's not come out.

The stars are twinkling;
The pale moon shines high above.
The willow hears the nightingale,
It peers into a well;
The bird pours out a song from a guelder rose beside the water,
As if he were aware of why the Kozak waits.
But Yarema barely, barely walks along the valley,
Neither seeing, neither hearing…
"Why good looks,
If there's no luck or fortune!
My youth will vanish all for naught.
I'm alone upon this world bereft of kith and kin
And fate — it's but a stem, a blade of grass upon an alien field.
A stem, a blade of grass is scattered by the winds:
So it is that people know not what to do with me.
Why are they avoiding me? It's that I'm an orphan.
There was a single heart, a single one in this whole world,
A single honest soul, alas, I see it too has
Has now forsaken me."
And then his tears poured out.
The poor guy cried a bit, wiping with his sleeve.
Be well, my dear. I'll either find my fortune on my distant journey,
Or my head will lie beyond the Dnipr'… But you'll not cry,
And you, my sweetheart, will not see the raven peck
The hazel Kozak eyes that you so fondly kissed!
Forget my tears, forget the orphan,
Forget your promises; find yourself another;
I'm not for you; my coat is drab
But you're a sexton's daughter.
Welcome someone better,
Take anyone you know… My fate is sealed.
Forget me, birdie, forget and do not worry.
And say a silent prayer should you ever
Hear my head has fallen on a foreign field.
Of all the people on this world
At least you alone, my sweetheart,
Say a prayer for me."
Then the poor soul shed some tears,
And rested on his staff,
Softly crying to himself…
A rustle!.. He looks:
Sneaking quietly beside the grove,
Tiptoed his Oksana.

He forgot, he ran, and they embraced.
"Sweetheart!" — Then serenity for both.
Long-long sighs of only "sweetheart" —
And again they'd both fall silent.
"Enough, my little birdie!"
"A wee bit more,
Some more... some more... my falcon!
Release my soul!.. Again... Again...
Oh, how weary I have grown!"
"Rest, my guiding star!
You've descended from the heavens!"
He spread his coat.
Like his pet she smiled, and sat.
"You too, sit right here beside me."
He sat and they embraced.
My sweetheart, O my star,
Where have you been shining?"
"I was late today:
My father came down with an illness;
I attended to him all the while..."
"With no concern for me?"
"Oh, come on, for goodness' sake!"
And tears shimmered in her eyes.
"Don't cry, honey, I'm just joking."
"Jokes!"
She smiled.
She leaned her head upon him
And seemed to fall asleep.
"You see, Oksana, I'm just joking,
But you are really crying.
Don't cry, take a look at me:
For tomorrow you won't see me.
Tomorrow I'll be far away,
Far away, Oksana...
Tomorrow evening at Chyhyryn[77]
I'll get a sacred sword.
It'll give me gold and silver,
It'll give me glory;
I'll dress you, give you shoes
I'll enthrone you like a peacock,

[77] *Chyhyryn (Chyhryn)* — A city in Central Ukraine that was the country's capital during the Kozak Hetmanate.

Or a hetman's wife,
And I'll gaze at you;
I'll gaze and gaze until I die."
"Or perhaps you'll just forget?
Getting rich, you'll go to Kyiv
With some gentry folk,
You'll find yourself a noblewoman
And forget Oksana!"
"But is there any better pick than you?"
"Perhaps there is — I do not know."
"You offend the Lord, my sweetheart:
There is none better,
Not beyond the deep blue sea
Not in heaven, nor beyond.
No one, nowhere is your better!"
"What is this you're saying?
Have some common sense!"
"It's true, my dear!"
Again and again
And for a long, long time, you see,
Amid their words and talk
They embraced and kissed
With all their loving might;
At turns they cried and vowed
Then vowed again.
Yarema told her how they'd live together,
How he'd come by gold and fortune,
After haidamaks hacked all the Poles
Now living in Ukraine,
How he'll rule,
Should he not die.
It was repugnant stuff to hear,
Verily, young girls!
"There's one for you!
Indeed it seems repugnant."
If, my dears, your mother
Or your father see
You reading of such wonders, —
Their lips would loudly cry out sin!
And then, and then... 'Nuff said,
But still, it's really something!
By the way, it's worth telling you,
How a dark-haired Kozak

Hugged his girl
And now sadly sits
Beneath a willow tree
Beside the water;
And like a dove Oksana coos and kisses;
In turns she cries and swoons,
And leans her head upon him:
"O my sweetheart, O my fortune!
O my dearest falcon. You're mine!
The willows even leaned to hear her talk.
Such talk! It's a late night tale,
My dear dark-browed ones
And it's best that I not tell you,
Or it'll haunt you in your dreams.
Let them part just as they met, —
Quite softly and quite nicely,
So that no one sees
The fine tears of the maiden
Or the Kozak's heartfelt ones.
Let them be. Perhaps they'll
Meet again upon this world... We'll see.

Meanwhile, light shines from
All the windows at the sexton's.
What goes on there?
Need to look and tell...
Best not to see,
Best not to see, and better not to tell!
Because there's shame felt for the people,
Because it hurts the heart.

Look and see: it's confederates, people,
Gathered in defense of liberty.
The damned defenders... Cursed be the mother,
And the day and hour, when she conceived,
When she gave birth to bring them here into this world!
Just look at what hell's children do
Inside the sexton's home.
A flame burns in the fireplace,
Lighting up the home.
The damned Jew sits in the corner
Shaking like a dog; the confederates
Bellow at the sexton: Want to live?

Tell us, where's the money?"
He's silent.
His hands are tethered,
They tossed him to the ground —
Nothing, not a word.
"The agony's not enough!
Get hot coals! Where's the tar?
Thrash him! That's the way! Cooling off?
Quick, go get more hot coals!
What? You gonna tell, conniver?..
He does not even moan!
Courageous bastard! Just you wait!"
They filled his bootleg with more coal...
"Pound a nail in his skull!"
Unable to withstand the holy torment,
The poor guy crumpled to the ground.
Perish, soul, without a holy penance
To absolve your sins!
"Oksana, O my daughter!" — and so he died.
The Poles pondered, standing,
But stayed determined nonetheless.
"Now what?
Gentlemen, advice! Let's think,
There's nothing more to do with him.
We'll set the church on fire!"
"Help, help someone!
All God-fearing people!" — the voice outside
Shouts with all its might.
The Poles grew limp. "Who's that?"
Oksana rushed toward the door: "Murder! murder!"
She fell face first with outstretched arms.
The officer waved his hand.
The sullen group of Poles ran like greyhounds
From the room. Alone the officer
Takes the girl who fainted...
Where are you,
Yarema, where? Look!
But he's off wandering, singing
Of Nalyvaiko's fight against the Poles.
The Poles perished; and Oksana with them perished.
Here and there across Vilshana
Dogs bark then stop in silence.
The moon grows bright; people sleep,

The sexton sleeps…
He won't awaken in the morning:
This night the just man's sleep will last forever.
The light burned, went out,
Extinguished… The dead man's body seemed to shudder.
Then sadness, oh, such sadness spread throughout the home.

HOLY DAY IN CHYHYRYN

Hetmans, hetmans, if only you'd arise,
Arise to look upon the Chyhyryn
You built and where you ruled!
How hard you'd cry, for you'd not
Recognize the paltry ruins
Of Kozaks' bygone glory.

Market squares, where the sceptered army
Blazes like a boundless sea of red,
And when his Excellency,
Mounted on his pure black steed,
Presents the hetman's mace —
The sea boils…
Boils — and surges through
The steppes and valleys;
Evil falls before them.
As for the Kozaks…
But what is there to say? It's gone;
And don't recall what's gone,
My good fellows,
Lest others hear about it.
And if perchance you should recall
What of it? You'll recall — you'll cry.
But, let's glance at least at Chyhyryn,
That onetime Kozak city.

From the woods
And through the mist
The moon floats low above,
Round-faced, crimson,
Glowing, but not shining,
As if he knew that no one
Really needs his light,
That infernos will instead
Heat and light Ukraine.
Darkness fell, and Chyhyryn
Is like a tomb.
Sad, oh, how sad.
(So it was throughout Ukraine
That knives were blessed
On the Eve of Makoviy.[78])
Everyone is quiet;
A bat flits across the market
Upon his boney wings;
A screech owl by the pasture
Pasture punctuates the hush.
But whither all the people?..
Gathered by the Tiasmyn[79]
In a darkened grove;
Old, young, poor, rich,
All united — all await
The holy day.
In a darkened grove,
In a verdant thicket
Fettered horses graze on aftergrass;
Saddled horses; black steeds ready.
Where will they be going?
Who will be their mounts?

[78] *Makoviy's Eve* — The eve of an Eastern Christian feast on August 1 that celebrates the seven Jewish Maccabean martyrs, who died protecting their faith in one God from imposition of paganism. But historians now indicate the 1768 uprising began in May.

[79] *Tiasmyn* — A right tributary of the Dnipro River that runs through the former Kozak capital, Chyhyryn.

There they are, just look.
They sprawl across the valley,
As if brooding, not a word is heard.
Those are the haidamaks.
Ukraine has sounded an alarm
And its eagles have responded;
They will dole out
Punishment to Jews and Poles;
For all the blood and arson
Haidamaks will now give hell
To Poles.

Beneath the grove are wagons
Filled with iron sustenance,
A gift provided by a lady.[80]
She knew just what to give to whom,
Not bad, she is, so let her reign;
But may she not get in the way,
If she does not hear!
Among the wagons
Not a place to stand:
Flocked like birds at nesting grounds,
Simple Kozaks and the officers
Descended there from Chyhyryn
And from all around the Smila region[81]
For a certain cause.
Kozak gentry paces,
Dressed in hooded mantles,
As one of them speaks softly,
Looking back at Chyhyryn.

FIRST OFFICER

Old man Holowaty's[82] acting up a bit.

SECOND OFFICER

Smart head on him, he sits at his estate, seems he doesn't know a thing, but if you look — Holowaty's all around. He says, "If I can't pull it off myself, I'll hand it to my son."

THIRD OFFICER

And that son is quite a doozie! I met last night with Iron Max;[83] the things he says about him is too much! He says, "He'll be a Kozak chief, that's clear, perhaps a hetman too, if that..."

SECOND OFFICER

Why Gonta?[84] And Iron Max? She herself... herself wrote Gonta: "If, — she says..."

FIRST OFFICER

Be quiet, it seems they've rung the bell!

---

80 *Gift provided by a lady* — Reference to Russian Empress Catherine the Great, who is said to have helped arm the haidamaks.

81 *Smila* — A town in Central Ukraine.

82 *Holowaty* — A composite literary figure.

83 *Iron Max* — Translator's rendering of Maksym Zalizniak (ca. 1740–?), leader of the 1768 haidamak rebellion. The root word of his surname is derived from the Ukrainian word for iron. He was captured by a Russian unit and sentenced to life at hard labor in Siberia. Russia feared the rebellion's spread.

84 *Ivan Gonta (?-1768)* — One of the leaders of the 1768 haidamak rebellion. He was captured by a Russian unit, which handed him to the Poles. After brutal torture, his body parts were nailed to gallows in 14 towns.

SECOND OFFICER

Nah, it's just the people mumbling.

FIRST OFFICER

Until Poles hear all the mumbling. Oh, the heads are old and wise; they deliberate, deliberate, and turn a plow into an awl. Wherever you can use a satchel, there's no need to have a sack. They bought some horseradish, they have to eat it, even if the eyes crawl out: they saw what they were buying — just don't let money go to waste! They think and think, not out loud, or silently; and the Poles will guess — so what you'll get is zilch! What's their meeting all about? Why don't they ring the bell? How do you stop the people, so they don't go on just murmuring? It's not ten souls, but thank God, the entire Smila region, if not all Ukraine. Over there, ya hear? They're singing.

THIRD OFFICER

Yeah, somebody's singing something; I'll go stop him.

FIRST OFFICER

Don't stop him, let 'em sing, just not too loud.

SECOND OFFICER

Oh, it's probably just Volokh![85] The old fool couldn't hold himself back: got to, and that's that.

THIRD OFFICER

What he sings is smart! Whenever you listen, it's always something different. Let's sneak over, brothers, and listen, then meanwhile they'll ring.

FIRST AND SECOND OFFICERS

Okay then? Let's go!

THIRD OFFICER

Okay, let's go.

The officers stood quietly behind an oak, and beneath the oak sits a sightless kobzar; gathered 'round are haidamaks and Zaporizhians. The kobzar softly sings with dignity.

O Volokhs, Volokhs,[86]
Few of you remain;
And you, Moldovans,
Are no longer masters;
You're servants of the Tatars,
Of the Turkish sultans,
In chains, in chains you're fettered!
But not to worry;

[85] *Volokh* — The name of a kobzar who followed the haidamaks.

[86] *Volokhs* — Ancestors of today's Moldovans.

Nicely say a prayer,
Join our brotherhood,
The brotherhood of Kozaks;
Recall Bohdan,
Our old hetman;
You'll be masters,
And like us, with knives,
With sacred knives,
And with father Max
Tonight we'll go a romping,
We'll rock the Poles,
We'll romp them hard
So hell itself will laugh,
The ground will tremble,
The sky will catch on fire...
We'll have ourselves a real good romp!

ZAPORIZHIAN

A real good romp! The old guy sings the truth, unless he's fibbing. And what sort of kobzar would he be, if not a Volokh!

KOBZAR

But I'm no Volokh; only that — I spent some time in Wallachia, and people call me Volokh, though I don't know why.

ZAPORIZHIAN

Whatever; strike up anything. How 'bout you hit a tune about our father Max.

HAIDAMAK

But not too loud, so officers won't hear.

ZAPORIZHIAN

What are your officers to us? They'll hear, they'll listen, if they've anything to listen with, and that's that. We only have a single officer — father Max; and if he hears, he'll even give a buck. Sing, God's elder, don't listen to him.

HAIDAMAK

Yeah, man, so it is; I know it for myself, and here's what's more; not lords, but sublords, or — the darkest hour is just before dawn.

ZAPORIZHIAN

Lies! Sing, you holy beggar, whatever you may know, otherwise, we'll wait forever for the bell — we'll fall asleep.

TOGETHER

That's right, we'll fall asleep; sing anything.

KOBZAR

(sings)

O the eagle soars, the gray one soars
Beneath the heavens;
Iron Max dances, father dances
Across the steppes and forests.

Oh, the eagle soars
And behind him fly the eaglets;
Iron Max dances, father dances
And behind him are the boys.
Zaporizhians those boys,
His sons, his children.
He'll ponder then he'll plan,
To beat up someone,
Belt down something,
Or to dance, and then they'll do it
Till the ground around them shakes.
He sings — they sing,
Until evil starts to cackle.
Vodka, mead and not by shot glass —
He guzzles like a rebel.
He'll lie in wait
To let no enemy or killer pass.
That's our otaman,
Our gray-winged eagle!
He fights and prances
Using all his might —
He has no home,
Nor does he have a pond or orchard…
The sea and steppe;
All around him *beaten paths,*
All around are gold and glory.
Take care, you hostile Poles,
You rabid dogs:
Iron Max is on the Black Road,[87]
Behind him are the haidamaks.

ZAPORIZHIAN

Yeah, that's it! He ripped into it, what can you say: right on and true. Good, really, good! What he wants is what he sings. Thank you, thank you.

HAIDAMAK

I didn't get something, what did he sing about the haidamaks?

ZAPORIZHIAN

What a blockhead, really! You see, here's what he sang: may the evil Poles, the rabid dogs, repent because Iron Max is taking the Black Road with the haidamaks, you see, to butcher…

HAIDAMAK

And to hang and murder! Good, honest to God, good! That's the way to do it! Really, I'd give a buck, had I not blown it boozing yesterday! Too bad! Whatever, but let the good times roll. Be so kind and front me, I'll pay it back tomorrow. Strike up anything about the haidamaks.

KOBZAR

I'm not all that keen on money. So long as someone listens, I'll sing till I go hoarse; and when I go hoarse — a shot or two of strong-stuff, and as they say, it's off again. Listen up, all you gentlemen here.

The haidamaks stayed overnight
In a verdant grove,
Their tethered horses grazed,

[87] *Black Road* — A road from the Dnipro to Lviv.

Saddled, at the ready.
The Polish petty gentry stayed o'ernight
With the Jews in buildings.
They drank, sprawled out,
And then…

THE CROWD

Quiet! It seems they've rung the bell. Hear it?.. Again… Oh!..

"They rang, they rang the bell!"
It echoed 'cross the grove.
"You all go out and pray,
And I'll wrap up the song."

The haidamaks pressed forward
Till the grove began to moan;
Chumak musclemen did not roll wagons,
But carried 'em on their strapping backs.
And again behind them the blind Volokh:
"The haidamaks stayed overnight
In a verdant grove."
He limps, he mumbles,
But his tune is out of place.
"Something different, God's elder!" —
Shout the haidamaks bearing
Wagons on their backs.
"Okay boys, take this one!
Fine! Fine! Okay, boys!
Come on guys, let's strike it up!"
The ground bends
And they also carve it
With their wagons. The kobzar plays,
And adds some silly words:
"Hop, hop, just like that!
A Kozak calls on Annie:
"Come on Annie, here's a joke for you,
Come on Annie, here's a kiss for you,
Come Annie, let's go see a priest,
We'll say a prayer to the Lord;
We've got no rye, we've got no wheat
So make the dumplings simple."
He got married, he grew worried —
There's nothing to be had;
The kids grow up with canvas clothes,
And the Kozak sings:
"It's tap-tap-tap of little feet
All throughout the house they run,
And all throughout the cellar,
Tap-tap-tap,
Boil some fish, my dear.
Tap-tap-tap, tap-tap-tap!"

"Good! Good! More! More!" —
Shout the Kozaks.

"Hop, hop, what a wonder,
The Polacks brewed a batch of beer,
We'll run the tavern
And we'll serve petty Polack gentry,
We'll serve it up to Polacks,
We'll joke around with petty lords,
Hop, hop, yes indeed!
The Kozak calls his pretty lady:
'Little lady, O my birdie!
Little lady, you're my fortune!
Don't be shy, give me your hand
And let's go out and dance;
Let people dream of anguish
But we will sing.
Yes, we will sing, and we will sit.
Little lady, O my birdie!
Little lady, you're my fortune!' "

"Again, again!"

"If it's either this way, maybe that,
If it was indeed a Kozak,

If indeed the man was young, young,
He'd move about the house at least,
He'd move.
Oh, how I wouldn't want the hassle
Of dealing with an old guy. It's either..."

"Here, here you madmen. Get a grip!
You got carried away, you see. And you,
Old dog, instead of prayers,
You're spouting all this drivel.
Devils all!" —
The otaman shouts. They finished;
And then a church is seen.
The cantor sings,
Priests swing censers,
And they sprinkle holy water;
The congregation — silent,
As if it weren't alive... Priests went amid
The wagons with the holy water;
Behind them people carried banners,
Just like blessing Easter baskets.
"Pray, my brothers, pray!" —
Thus the elder priest began. —
A sentry from the other world
Will stand by holy Chyhyryn,
Crucifixion of the holy he will not permit.
And you defend Ukraine:
Don't let a mother perish
At the hands of tyrants.
Since Konashevych [88] till this day
The blaze is not extinguished,
The imprisoned die in agony,
Naked and unshod...
Unbaptized children grow,
Kozak children; and the girls!..
Beauties of the Kozak land
Wither with the Pole,
And their braids are left uncovered
Thrashed, like mother's, with disgrace.
Hazel eyes in bondage flicker; the Kozak
Doesn't wish to break his sister's chains.
He's not ashamed of agony
Beneath the Polish yoke...
Sorrow, sorrow!
Pray, my children! The Poles bring
Last Judgment to Ukraine —
And dark mountains
Will break out in tears.
Recall the righteous hetmans:
Where are their burial mounds? Where
Lie the last remains of glorious Bohdan?
Where's a simple mound
For Hetman Ostrianytsia? [89]
Where is Nalyvaiko's? [90] There are none!
They burned the living with the dead.
Where's Bohun, [91] where's that winter?
Each winter, the Inhul River freezes over —
Bohun won't rise to pack the ice
With bodies of the gentry.
The Polack dances!
There's no Bohdan to redden
Yellow Waters [92] or the verdant Ros. [93]
The ancient Korsun [94] mourns:
There's no one who will share its grief.
And the Alta River cries: "Life is hard!
I'm draining out, drying up...

---

[88] *Petro Kononevych Konashevych-Sahaidachny (1570?-1622)* — Ukrainian hetman (1614-22). Fought successfully against Turkey and Muscovy. Developed Ukrainian civic, cultural and religious life.

[89] *Yakiv Ostrianytsia (?-1641)* — A Ukrainian hetman and leader of a Kozak rebellion against Poland in 1638. He was tortured and quartered by Poles.

[90] See glossary or fn. 15

[91] *Ivan Bohun (?-1664)* — A Ukrainian Kozak colonel and hero of the 1648-57 uprising against Poland.

[92] *Yellow Waters (Zhovti Vody)* — Site of a 1648 battle near the Zhovti Vody River in which Kozaks defeated Polish troops.

[93] *Ros* — Site of the 1648 Battle of Korsun, a Ukrainian Kozak rout of Polish troops on the Ros River.

[94] *Korsun* — A town on the Ros River in Central Ukraine.

Where's Taras?[95]
Nowhere to be heard...
Children don't take after father!"
Don't cry, my brothers: We're backed
Alike by righteous souls and the might
Of Michael the Archstrategist.[96]
The time of reckoning looms ahead.
Pray, my brothers!"
They prayed,
The Kozaks prayed in earnest,
Earnestly, like children;
In the past they did not worry,
They thought... But what transpired...
Kerchiefs on the Kozak mounds[97]
A single good, a single glory —
A kerchief's gleaming white,
But they'll strip it off as well...
And the deacon:
"May the enemy die!
Take your knives! They're blessed."
A roar resounded in the grove:
"They're blessed!"
It chills the heart!
They're blessed, they're blessed!
Die, gentry, die!
Each took one, they flashed
Throughout Ukraine.

THIRD ROOSTERS

In Ukraine, another day of torment
At the hands of rabid Poles; and another,
Then on the last and final day,
Ukraine and Chyhyryn both mourned.
And that one passed —
The Day of Makoviy,
Ukraine's great holy day.
It passed — the Pole and Jew
Got drunk on blood and vodka,
They cursed and crucified schismatics,
They cursed the lack of more to grab.
And the haidamaks waited silently
Till the villains went to sleep
With not a thought in mind
That they would never wake again.
Poles fell fast asleep,
But Judases count money
Late into the night,
They count their profits without light
So people may not see, you see.
On their gold they too then rested
And dreamed their sinful dreams.
They dream... may they dream forever!
Meanwhile, the moon floats by
To scan the sky, the stars,
The earth and sea,
And to watch the people's actions
To tell God about it in the morning.
His pale face shines throughout Ukraine,
He shines, but does he see my orphan,
Oksana from Vilshana, my orphan?
Where she's being tortured,
Where she softly moans?
Does Yarema know?
Does he know or hear?
We'll find out later, I'll not sing of that,
Not now, but of something else;
Not girls, but evil will do all the dancing.
I'll sing of the misfortune
In the land of Kozaks:
Listen, so that you may tell your children,
And that they may tell the grandkids,

[95] See glossary or fn. 9

[96] *Michael the Archstrategist* — Reference to Michael the Archangel, soldier of the Lord.

[97] *Kerchiefs on the Kozak mounds* — White pieces of cloth were often attached to crosses on Kozak graves.

How the Kozaks harshly punished gentry
Because they knew not
How to rule with virtue.

Ukraine resounded,
Long did it resound,
Blood flowed long,
It flowed and reddened
Long across the steppes.
It flowed and flowed and finally dried.
The steppes grow green;
Granddads rest,
Great mounds above them
Tinted in a shade of blue.
So what if they are lofty?
No one knows them,
No one sheds a real tear,
No one mentions them at all.
Just the breeze
Blows quietly above them,
Just the early morning dew
Will bathe them with fine tears.
The rising sun will dry them, warm them;
And the grandchildren?
It matters not to them,
They're just sowing rye.
There's many of them, but who will say,
Where is Gonta's mound,
Where was the righteous martyr buried?
Where is Iron Max, the earnest soul,
And his final resting place?
Tough! Trying! The tyrant rules,
And does not mention them.

Ukraine resounded,
Long did it resound,
Blood flowed long,
It flowed and reddened
Long across the steppes.
All day and through the night,
Anguished cries and cannon fire;
The earth moans and bends;
Sad and scary, but recall it all —
The heart breaks into a smile.

O moon so bright! From the sky above
Go hide behind a mountain,
Illumination is not needed;
It'll scare you, though you saw the Ros,
The Alta and the Seine,[98]
Where, who knows why,
A broad sea of blood was spilled.
What now? Hide behind a mountain;
Hide, my friend, lest you
Cry in your old age...

The pale moon shines sadly, sadly
In the sky above.
A Kozak rides beyond the Dnipro,
Perhaps returning
From a village gathering.
He moves sadly and unhappily,
He barely drags his feet.
Perhaps the girl doesn't like him
Perhaps because he's poor?
The girl loves him,
Though he's dressed
In patches upon patches,
He's dark-browed,
And if he does not perish
He'll be wealthy nonetheless.
Why does he proceed so sadly,
Unhappily — just on the brink of tears?
O Kozak, some hard misfortune
Is foretold.
The heart feels, but won't say
What anguish is to come.
It will pass... All around him

---

[98] *Seine* — Reference to the 1572 St. Bartholomew's Day Massacre in Paris, where Roman Catholic mobs slaughtered Protestant Huguenots. Bodies of the dead were dumped in the Seine.

People have died out, it seems.
Not a rooster, not a dog:
Just wailing wolves
Far beyond the grove somewhere,
Whatever! Yarema's riding,
But not to his Oksana,
Not to a youthful gathering
In Vilshana —
But to Cherkasy, to the evil Poles.
That's where the third rooster
Is to crow...
And there... and there... Yarema goes,
Looking at the Dnipro.

"O Dnipr', broad and strong, my Dnipr'!
You, father, have carried so much
Kozak blood to sea;
You'll carry even more, my friend!
The azure one you reddened,
Though quench him you did not;
But you'll get drunk tonight.
This night a hellish feast
Will roar throughout Ukraine;
A lot, a lot, a lot of noble blood will run.
The Kozak will revive;
So too will hetmans in their golden coats;
Fortune will awaken;
The Kozak will then sing:
'Neither Jew nor Pole,'
And in the steppes of Ukraine —
O my sweet Lord —
The mace again will glisten!"

So thought Yarema, that poor soul,
In his patched up peasant coat.
And with the blessing in his hand.
The Dnipro seemed to listen:
Broad and blue,
He picked up waves like mountains;
And in the reeds
He roars, moans, howls,
Bending willows to the ground;
Thunder roars with laughter,
Lighting rips the cloud apart.
On goes our Yarema,
Seeing not a thing;
One thought smiles
Another cries.
"Over there's Oksana, there it's happy
Even in a dowdy coat;
And here... and here... what's next?
Maybe, I'll still die."
Meanwhile, from the ravine
The rooster — cock-a-doodle-doo!
"Ah, Cherkasy!.. God of mercy!
Take me not before my time!"

RED BANQUET

They rang all bells
Throughout Ukraine;
The haidamaks then shouted:
"The gentry's dying, dying!
The gentry's dying! We'll dance
And warm the cloud a bit."
The Smila region has caught fire,
Reddening the cloud.
But Medvedivka was the first to
Heat the sky above.
Smila burns, the Smila region
Pours on blood.
Korsun burns, Kaniv burns,
Chyhyryn, Cherkasy;
The Black Road ignites,
And blood spills over to Volyn.
In Polissia,[99] Gonta feasts,
While in the Smila region,

[99] *Polissia* — A marsh region in Northern Ukraine.

Iron Max tempers his *Damask,*[100]
And in Cherkasy, Yarema tests
His metal blessing.
"That's it, that's it! Good, my children,
Murder the rabid ones! Good, boys!" —
Iron Max
Shouts in the bazaar.
A ring of hell; the haidamaks
Dance all over hell.
And Yarema — frightening to watch —
Lays down three, four at a time.
"Good son,
A plague be on their mothers!
Kill, kill: you'll end up in Paradise
Or get to be an adjutant.
Dance on, son! Come on, children!"
And the children rushed through
Attics, barns,
And cellars, everywhere;
They dispatched all, took everything.
"Enough for now, boys!
You're tired, rest up."
The streets, bazaars
Were decked with bodies,
Flowing with their blood.
"The damned aren't punished
Quite enough!
They must repeat the suffering,
So that the damned,
Unbaptized souls won't rise."
The haidamaks gathered
At the market square,
With them comes Yarema.
Iron Max calls out:
"Do you hear, young man? Come over!
Don't be scared, I won't frighten."
"I'm not scared!" Taking off his hat,
He stood as if before a master.
"Where are you from? Who are you?"
"From Vilshana, sir."
"From Vilshana, where the dogs
Snuffed out the sexton?"
"Where? Which one?"
"In Vilshana;
And they say they seized
His daughter, if perhaps you know her."
"A daughter, in Vilshana?"
"The sexton's, if you know."
"Oksana, Oksana." —
Yarema barely uttered
And to the ground he fell.
"O my! Look here… Sorry for the boy,
Mykola, give the kid some air."
He came to. "Father! brother!
Why don't I have one hundred arms?
Give me a knife, give me strength,
Give torment to the Poles, yes torment!
Awful torment, so that hell itself
Shudders and blacks out."
"Good, son, knives will all be ready
For the sacred deed.
Come with us to temper them
In the village of Lysianka."
"Let's go, let's go, otaman,
My father, my one and only brother!
I'll fly off to the world's end,
I'll get her, sir, I'll spring her out of hell…
To the ends of the world, but I won't find,
No, I won't find Oksana!"
"Perhaps, you'll find her.
What's your name?
I don't know it."
"Yarema."
"And the last name?"
"No last name!"
"Not a bastard, are you? No surname…
Enter it in the register, Mykola.
Let it be Naked,
That's what you write!"
"No, that's bad!"

100 *Damask* — A type of steel used in medieval swords.

"Well, how about Trouble?"
"That's also not quite it."
"Wait a minute,
Write Vagabond."
They did.
"Well, Vagabond,
Let's go dancing.
You'll find your fortune...
If you don't...
Let's move it, boys!"
The transport unit gave Yarema
A surplus horse to ride.
He smiled sitting on the jet black steed,
But again broke down in tears.
They traveled past the outskirts;
Cherkasy's all in flames...
"All present, children?
"All present, father."
"Move on!"
The Kozak company
Stretched along the grove
Above the Dnipro.
The kobzar Volokh rides behind them,
Hobbling-wobbling on a horsey,
Singing to the Kozaks:
"Haidamaks, haidamaks,
Iron Max is dancing."

Off they went... And Cherkasy
Burns and burns.
No one cares, no one looks back,
They laugh and spew profanity
At the cursed gentry. Some talk,
Some listen to the kobzar sing.
Iron Max up front
Pricked up both his ears;
Puffing on his pipe, he rides along
Without a word to anyone,
The mute Yarema close behind.
A green grove,
Darkened woods,
The mighty Dnipro and high hills,
The sky, the stars, virtue, people
And also awful agony —
All is lost, everything! Like a *dead man,*
He knows nothing, he sees nothing.
It's hard for him,
So hard, but he does not cry.
He does not cry:
A fierce and greedy serpent
Drinks his tears, grips his soul
And rips his heart apart.
"O my tears, my fine tears!
You'll wash away the grief:
Wash it away... it's hard! An ordeal!
It would take the blue, blue sea,
And the Dnipr'
To wash away the anguish,
And the Dnipr' would run dry.
Will it all destroy my soul?
Oksana, Oksana!
Where are you, where? Look,
You're my one and only,
Look upon Yarema.
Where are you? Perhaps she's dying,
Perhaps she's cursing her cruel fate,
Cursing, dying,
Or maybe she's in chains
Expiring in some master's dungeon?
Perhaps she recalls Yarema
And recalls Vilshana.
She calls out: "My sweetheart,
Please embrace Oksana!
Let's embrace, my falcon!
We will swoon forever.
Let the Poles torment us. —
We'll not feel it!.." The wind
Blows and blusters from way beyond
The Lyman,
It bends the poplar in the field —
So too the girl bends wherever
Fate decides to tilt her.
She gets sad, she'll worry.
She'll forget... and maybe...
The very lady in an overcoat;
And the Pole... God, O God!

Damn my soul to hell,
Pour a sea of suffering,
Dole out punishment upon me,
Just spare my heart the treatment
Of anguish such as this: It'll burst
If even it was made of stone.
O my fate! My heart!
Oksana, Oksana!
Where've you gone,
Where have you vanished?"

And his tears gushed out:
Fine-fine tears came pouring.
Where'd they come from!
And Iron Max speaks up
To tell the haidamaks to stop:
"Into the woods, boys! Dawn is breaking,
And the horses are exhausted:
We'll graze them." And quietly
They holed up in the woods.

THUMPING GROVE[101]

The sun rose; Ukraine in places
Burned or smoldered,
And elsewhere gentry fainted,
Having locked themselves in buildings.
Gallows all throughout the villages;
Corpses hanging —
Of only elders, then the lesser nobles —
Piled upon piles.
On streets, at crossroads
Dogs and crows
Gnaw at gentry, peck their eyes;
No one stops them.
There's no one
Who could do so anyway:
All that's left are kids and dogs —
Taking oven-forks along,
Even women joined the haidamaks.

Such was the horror that
Occurred throughout Ukraine!
Worse than hell... And what for,
Why are people dying?
Kids are kids,
Their fathers notwithstanding
Best to live in brotherhood.

But no, they knew not how,
And didn't want to,
There's a need to split,
A need for blood, a brother's blood,
Because of envy that the *brother*
Has a barn and field
As well as happiness at home!
"We'll kill the brother! Burn his house!"
They said it, and it happened.
It seems that would be all;
No, in added punishment
Orphans stayed to suffer life alone.
Bred in tears, they then grew up;
Weary hands became unbound —
Then blood for blood,
And hurt for hurt!
It pains the heart, when you recall:
Children of old Slavs
Got drunk on blood. And who's to blame?
Latin priests and Jesuits.

The haidamaks wandered
Through the woods and valleys,
With Vagabond behind them
Still pouring out fine tears.

---

101 *Thumping Grove (Гупалівщина)* — A small forest in the village Budyshcha where haidamak leader Maksym Zalizniak shook Poles from hiding places in trees. They are said to have thumped when they hit the ground.

They passed Voronivka, and
Verbivka; in Vilshana
They arrived. "Should I ask,
Ask about Oksana? I won't so
They'll not know just what I'm dying for."
Meanwhile, the haidamaks pass through
Vilshana too. He asks a boy:
"So, they killed the sexton?"
"No, sir; father said they
Burned him, those Poles lying over there,
And they also seized Oksana.
The sexton, he was buried yesterday
In the graveyard over yonder."
He did not hear the end... "Carry me,
My horse!" And he dropped the reins.
"Why did I not die the day before I knew!"
And should I even die today, I'll get up
From my coffin to torment all those Poles.
O my sweetheart! Oksana, Oksana!
Where are you?
He fell silent, brooded,
Gaited forward.
Fighting grief is tough and trying
For the wretched soul.
With the others he caught up.
They're already passing
Borovyk's hamlet.[102]
The tavern and the barn still smolder
And Leiba's nowhere to be seen,
So Yarema smiled,
Smiled heavily.
Just a couple days before
This is where, yes here,
That he bowed before the Jew,
And today... It was even sad
That all that trouble passed.
The haidamaks above the valley
Turned off the beaten path.
They're pressuring a teen.
A boy in peasant garb,
All in patches, feet in leather wrapping;
A sack slung 'cross his back.
"Hey, beggar-boy! Listen up!"
"I'm no beggar, sir!
I'm, you see, a haidamak."
"And a lousy one at that!
Where ya from?"
"From Kyrylivka."
"Do you know of Budyshch
And the lake nearby?"
"I know the lake, it's over yonder;
Take this valley then you're there."
"And did ya see the Poles today?"
"Nowhere, not a one;
There were plenty yesterday.
We couldn't bless the wreaths:
Damned Polacks wouldn't let us.
Instead we beat 'em,
Me and dad, who used his sacred knife;
Mom was sick
Though otherwise
She'da surely joined us."
"Good, young man.
Here's something for ya, friend,
This little ducat, just don't lose it."
He took the gold piece,
Looked it over: "Thank you, sir!"
"Okay, boys, let's hit the road!
And are you listening? No noise.
Vagabond, follow me!
There's a lake along this valley
With a forest by the hill,
And in that forest is our treasure.
When we get there, we'll surround it,
Tell that to the boys.
Perhaps some filth remains,
Guarding all the hollows."
They came,
And 'round the forest took positions;
They looked — there's no one...

102 *Borovyk's hamlet* — A hamlet between Vilshana and the town of Zvenyhorod. It is known today as the village of Borovykove in the Cherkasy region.

"Helluva of a lot of 'em here!
My, what pears have ripened!
Knock 'em down, boys!
Faster! Faster! That's it, that's right!" —
And the confederates poured down,
All half-rotten pears.
They knocked 'em down,
Picked up the harvest;
The Kozak's weren't half bad,
They found the hollows,
Took the treasure,
Emptied Polack pockets for good measure,
Then came punishment in Lysianka,
Where they dragged the scoundrels.

BANQUET IN LYSIANKA

Darkness fell. All around Lysianka
Everything lit up:
Iron Max and Gonta
Began to smoke their pipes.
Oh, how dreadfully they smoked!
Not a soul in hell
Knows how to smoke that way.
Waters of the Rotten Tikych[103]
Flow red with blood of Jews and nobles;
Blazing up above it are
Both humble home and mansion;
It's as if fate is punishing
Both the haves and have-nots.
And in the marketplace
Stand Iron Max and Gonta,
Shouting, "Punish Polacks!
Punish Polacks,
So they all repent!"
And the children punish.
There's moaning and there's crying.
One pleads,
Another curses;
That one prays, confessing sins
Before his brother,
Who has since been killed.
They show no mercy,
Inflicting only zealous punishment,
Like ferocious death,
They pay no heed to age or beauty
Of the noble or the Jewish maiden.
The blood runs off into the waters,
Neither crippled,
Nor the aged
Nor the little child spared —
None was able to appeal
The hour of their evil fate.
All were killed, one beside another;
Not a noble or a Jewish soul remained.
And the flames spread twofold
Lapping at the clouds.
And Vagabond, take note, cries out,
"Punish Polacks, punishment!"
Like a madman, he slices up the dead,
He hangs the dead and burns them.
"Gimme Polacks, gimme Jews!
There aren't enough for me.
Gimme Polacks,
Gimme villains' blood to pour.
There's a sea of blood...
The sea's not big enough...
Oksana! Oksana!
Where are you?" — he shouts and
Hides amid the flames, amid the blaze.
Meanwhile, haidamaks lined
The marketplace with tables,
They set them up,
Bring whatever food they find
To dine while there's still light.
"Let's party!" — they all shouted.
They dine amid the glow of hell.

---

[103] *Rotten Tikych (Hnyliy Tikych)* — A small river in the Dnipro highlands of Central Ukraine.

Noble guests hang from the rafters,
Their corpses blackened by the flames.
The rafters burn, the nobles fall.
"Drink up, children! Drink! Pour!
Perhaps we'll meet more lords like these
To have another dance."
And Iron Max the rebel
Swallows in a single gulp.
"For your damned corpses,
Your damned souls
I gladly drink again! Drink up, children!
Let's drink, my brother Gonta!
We'll drink, my friend, we'll dance
Together like a couple.
And where's Volokh? Just sing to us,
Old kobzar, not about our forebears
Because we're no worse than they
At inflicting Poles with torment.
And skip the grief,
Which we neither knew, nor know.
Strike up a happy tune, old man,
Make the ground break up, —
About the widowed lass
And all about her sorrow.

(The kobzar plays and sings)

From one village to another
There's dancing and good music:
I sold a chicken and an egg —
I got a pair of shoes.
Now I'll go a dancin'
From this village to another:
Neither cow, nor bull
Just the house is left.
I'll give away or sell the house
To my child's godfather.
I'll buy or make a
Counter right beside a fence;
I'll trade and tend to liquor
By the little shot glass,
I'll dance and party with the bachelors.
O you, my children,
O my little dears,
Don't worry, take a look
At how your mother dances.
Myself I'll be a servant
And I'll send the kids to school,
But my little red shoes
I'll take, yes, I'll take out for a spin!

"Good! Good! Now the dances,
Now the dances, kobzar!"
The blind man hit it —
They hopped and sprang
To dance at the bazaar.
The ground sways. "Go, Gonta, go!"
"Go, brother Max!
We'll keep on striking, pal,
Before we have to die!"

"Don't be surprised, girls,
That my clothes are worn;
Because my father made things easy
And I take after him."

"Good, brother, I swear to God!"
"Now, it's your turn, Max!"
"Just you wait!"

"Do as I do:
Love a daughter, anybody's —
A priest's, a cantor's
Or peasant's pretty one."

Everybody's dancing, but Vagabond
Hears not and neither does he see.
He's sitting at the table's end,
Crying like baby.
What's the use, you see?
The red mantle laced with gold
Surely has its glory,
But it's all without Oksana;
There is no one to share fortune with,
There's no one to sing songs with.
Alone, alone, the orphan has to perish.
And this, and this he does not know

That his Oksana's
On the other shore of Tikych
In a mansion with the lords,
With those very ones that
Slaughtered her dear father.
The beasts now hide behind some walls
And watch the Jews expire in pain,
Your brothers! And Oksana peers out
Through a window
At Lysianka's glowing light.
"Where is my Yarema?" —
She ponders. She knows not,
That he's quite near her,
In Lysianka, dressed not in peasant garb —
But in a crimson overcoat,
Sitting, thinking all alone:
"Where is my Oksana?
Where does she,
My confined sweet dove, shed tears?"
It's hard for him.
From the valley
Someone steals
In a hooded Kozak mantle.
"Who are you?" —
Asks Vagabond.
"I'm Mr. Gonta's messenger.
Let him party,
I'll just wait."
"No, you won't await him,
Jewish dog!"
"God forbid, what kind of Jew am I!
You see? A haidamak!
Here's a kopeck...[104] take a look...
How could you not know?"
"I know, I know," —
As he reaches for his bootleg
To draw the blessed one.
"Fess up, you damned Jew,
Where is my Oksana?"
Then he took a swing.
"God, have mercy!..
In the mansion... with the lords
Decked out in gold..."
"Help out then!
Help out, you scourge!"
"Okay, okay... My, Yarema,
You're persistent!
I'll go help right now:
Money breaks down walls.
I'll tell the Poles — instead of Pac..."
"Okay, okay! I know.
Go faster!"
"At once, at once!
Amuse Gonta for a couple hours,
And then whatever.
Go and dance...
Where shall I then take her?"
"To Lebedyn!
To Lebedyn — you hear!"
"I hear, I hear."
Vagabond went to
Dance with Gonta.
And Iron Max picks up a kobza:
"Go dance, kobzar, I'll play."
Springing
'Round the market, the blind one
Rips his leather wrappings,
Singing as he goes:

"There's parsnip, parsnip in the garden;
Am I not your Kozak, Kozak?
Don't I love you, love you?
Won't I buy you fancy shoes?
I'll buy, I'll buy,
My dark-browed beauty,
Just for you I'll buy,
I'll buy that wonder.
I'll walk, my sweetheart,
I, my sweetheart,
Will forever love you."
"Oh, hop, dance the hopak!
She began to love the Kozak,

[104] *Kopeck* — The coin was used as a way of haidamaks to identify one another.

Though he's old and red-haired —
Such is lousy fate.
You go worry, fate,
And you, old man,
Go fetch the water,
And I — well, to the tavern.
I'll drink a shot, I'll drink a second
I'll drink a third one
For some pleasure,
A fifth and sixth
And then it's over.
The old hag went a dancing
Followed by a sparrow,
Bending-twisting...
The sparrow's quite a fellow!
The old red-hair calls the hag,
And she just flips the bird:
'You got married, Satan,
Go make money for some millet;
You gotta feed the kids,
You gotta dress the kids.
And I'll give birth to more.
And you, old man, don't sin
Go rock the baby by the hearth,
Just be silent, don't you breathe.'"

"When I was young and righteous,
I hung an apron on the shutters;
Whosoever comes around —
Does not pass it by,
There's a nod, perhaps a wink.
As I embroider using silk,
Through the window pane I peek:
Simon, Ivan,
Get your fancy duds,
Let's go dancing,
Then we'll sit and sing."
"Chase the chicken to a barrel,
And the chicks into a fishnet.

. . . .
. . . .
Hey... ace!
Daddy bends the trace
Mama pulls the hame;[105]
"And you, our daughter tie it."

"Some more? Enough?"
"More, More!
A bad one even!
The legs will carry anyway."

"Oh, add the parts
And chop the mushrooms:
The old man and his old lady
Got it good together, —
Both of them are happy.

Oh, add the parts
And chop the parsley:
. . . .
. . . .
Oh, add the parts
And chop horseradish:
Pour the water, water,
Find the ford across the water..."

"Enough! enough! — screams Gonta —
Enough, the flames are dying out.
More light, children!.. And where's Leiba,
Why is he not here?
Find him, string him up.
Use a hog's noose!
Go to it, children!
The Kozaks' torch[106] is going out."
And the Vagabond: "Otaman!
Let's go dancing, father!
Look — it's burning; at the bazaar
It's lit, and level.

---

105 *Trace and hame* — A trace is strap connected to a draft animal. The hame is a curved piece on the animal's collar to which the trace connects.

106 *Kozaks' torch (каганець)* — Figurative use of the word torch to mean conflagration.

We'll dance. Play kobzar!"
"I don't want to dance!
Fire, children! Tar, oakum!
Give me cannons;
Open fire at the hideaways!
They think I merely jest!"
The haidamaks all roared:
"Good, father! We hear you!"
They surged across the dam,
All shouting, each one singing.
And Vagabond yells out: "Father!
Stop!.. I'm losing it!
Wait, don't kill:
My Oksana's there.
Just an hour, O my elders!
I will save her!"
"Okay, okay!.. Max,
Give a holler, have 'em light the fuses.
She'll become a Polish saint…
And you, young bird,
You'll find yourself another."
He looked around —
Vagabond was gone.
The hills roared —
And the mansion
With the Poles
Is dancing near the clouds.
What remained was lit by hell…
"Where's Vagabond?" — shouts Max.
There was no trace
And as long as all the boys
Kept dancing,
Yarema crept with Leiba
To the mansion to the very cellar;
Yarema grabbed Oksana half alive
And flew to Lebedyn.

LEBEDYN[107]

"I'm an orphan from Vilshana,
I'm an orphan, grannie.
Poles brutalized my father,
And I… I'm scared,
I'm scared to mention, my dear grannie…
They took me with them,
But don't ask, grandma,
What became of me.
I prayed, I cried,
My heart was ripped apart,
Tears dried out, the soul expired…
Oh, if I knew I'd see him one more time,
That I'd see him yet again, —
I'd have suffered two times,
Three times more
For just a single word!
Forgive me, my dear!
Perhaps, I sinned,
God perhaps rebukes me just for that,
That I fell in love,
That I loved his lanky stature
And his hazel eyes —
I loved as I knew how,
Just as the heart desired.
In captivity I prayed
Not for myself, not for my father —
Nor for grandma, but for him,
For my sweetheart's fortune.
Rebuke me, God! Your truth
Is something I must bear.
Sad to say: I thought of
Snuffing out my soul.
If not for him, perhaps… perhaps
I would have done so.
It was hard! I thought:
"O my dear Lord!
He's an orphan —
Who will welcome him
Without me?
Who, like me, will ask him

107 *Lebedyn* — An Orthodox nunnery in Central Ukraine near Chyhyryn.

Of fortune and misfortune?
Who, like me, will hug him?
Who will bare their soul?
Who will say kind words
To the needy orphan?"
I thought this way, grandma,
And the heart began to laugh:
"I'm an orphan: I've no mother,
I've no father,
And he alone upon this world,
He's the only one who loves me;
And if he hears I killed myself,
He'll end it all himself."
So I thought, prayed,
Waited and peered out for him:
"He's gone, he'll never come,
I'm left here all alone..."
And she cried. A nun,
Standing right beside her, worried.
"Grandma,
Tell me, where am I?"
"In Lebedyn, my little bird,
Don't get up: you're ill."
"In Lebedyn! Has it been long?"
"Why no, just two days."
"Two days?.. Wait, wait...
The fire above the water...
The Jew, the mansion, Maidanivka...
They call him Vagabond..."
"He calls himself Vagabond, Yarema,
The one who brought you here..."
"Where is he, where?
I know not now!.."
"In a week he promised that
He'd come for you."
"In a week! A week!
O my blessed paradise!
Grannie, the trying time is over!
That Vagabond — he's my Yarema!..
They know him
All throughout Ukraine.
I saw the villages on fire;
I saw the Polish tyrants
Shaking and collapsing
At Vagabond's mere mention.
They know, they know
Who he is and where he's from,
And who he's looking for!..
He looked for me and found me,
He's my gray-winged eagle!
Come fly to me my falcon,
O my precious dove!
Oh, the world's a joy,
How joyous it's become!
In a week, grandma...
Three days left.
Oh, how long!..
"Mama, rake the coals, coals,
For your daughter you'll be sorry, sorry...
Oh, the world's a joy!
And you, grannie, are you happy?"
"With you,
My birdie, I am happy."
"Why do you not sing?"
"I've sung what's mine to sing..."
The vesper bells rang out;
Oksana stayed.
The nun, having prayed,
Hobbled off to church.
A week later in Lebedyn
They sang in church:
Rejoice Isaiah![108] They wed Yarema
In the morning;
By evening, my Yarema,
(What a regular guy!),
Lest he anger the otaman,
Left behind Oksana:
To finish off the Poles;
He holds his reception
With Iron Max amid the
Fires of the Uman region.[109]
She keeps a lookout —

---

108 *Rejoice Isaiah* — Sung at church weddings.

109 *Uman region* — The area around the Central Ukrainian city of Uman on the right bank of the Dnipro.

She looks to see if he's not coming
With the bridegrooms —
To take her from the cell
To a house upon a hill.

Don't worry, keep your hopes up,
Say your prayers to the Lord.
And now for me, it's Uman
That I need to look at.

GONTA IN UMAN

The haidamaks boasted
On their way to Uman:
"Hey good fellas,
We'll rip up silk to wrap
Our leggings."

Days go by, the summer passes,
And Ukraine, take note, still blazes;
In villages cry naked children —
No parents. Yellowed leaves
Rustling in the grove;
Clouds frolic; the sun's asleep;
Human speech is nowhere heard;
Just a beast wails in the village,
Gnawing on the corpses.
They've not interred the Poles,
But fed them to the wolves,
Until the gnawed remains were
Buried under drifting snow…
A blizzard did not stop
Any of the hellish torment:
Poles froze, and Kozaks
Warmed themselves beside infernos.
Spring arose,
It woke the slumbering black earth,
Adorning it with primrose,
Wrapping it with periwinkle;
There's a skylark in the field,
In the grove a nightingale.
The earth, bedecked by spring,
Is welcomed in the morning…
In a word, it's paradise! But for whom?
For people. And people?
They don't even care to glance at it,
And if they glance —
They'll just condemn.
Blood is needed to embellish,
Fire to illuminate:
Not much sun, not much periwinkle
And a lot of clouds.
Hell does not suffice!.. People,
O dear people!
Will you ever count your blessings?
Strange, strange people!

Springtime didn't stop the blood
Nor the human anger.
Hard to look at; to just recall —
So it was in Troy.
So will it be again.
The haidamaks
Frolic and they punish;
Anywhere they go —
The earth is burned
And steeped in blood.
Iron Max acquired a son
Known throughout Ukraine.
Though Yarema's not his natural son,
He's earnest nonetheless.
Max butchers, but Yarema
Butchers not — he rages:
With knife in hand, he spends his
Days and nights by fires.
He shows no mercy,

Missing no one nowhere;
It's payback for the sexton,
For the sacred father;
For Oksana. He swoons
Just thinking of Oksana.
And Max: "Frolic, son,
Till fortune rises up!
We'll frolic!"
They frolicked —
The Poles lay dead
In piles and piles
From Kyiv to Uman.

At midnight, like a cloud,
The haidamaks surrounded Uman;
By the break of dawn
They set the town ablaze;
They set the fires, shouting:
"Punish Polacks once again!"
Across the marketplace
Dropped Polish Narodowi[110] horsemen;
Little children dropped
And so did ailing invalids.
Pandemonium and uproar.
At the marketplace,
Like in a bloody sea,
Stand Gonta and the zealous Iron Max.
Both together shout: "Good, children!
That's the way to kill the damned!"
And lo, the haidamaks escort a Jesuit
Along with two young boys:
"Gonta, Gonta!
They're your kids.
You butcher us — so butcher them:
They're Catholics.
Why've you stopped? Why not butcher?
While they're small, kill them too,
'Cause they'll grow to butcher you ..."
"Kill the dog! And the puppies
With my blade I'll butcher.
Call the public. Confess:
What, you're Catholics?"
"Catholics... because our mother ..."
"O my great Lord!
Quiet! quiet! I know, I know!"
The public gathered.
"My children — they're Catholics...
Esteemed gentlemen,
Let there be no treason,
Let there be no talk!
I took an oath and sacred knife
So I may kill the Catholic.
My sons, my sons!
Why aren't you grown up?
Why do you not butcher Poles?.."
"We'll butcher, daddy!"
"No, you won't! No, you won't!
Damn the mother,
That damned Catholic,
Who gave birth to you!
Why did she not drown you
Before the break of dawn?
That much less of sin there'd be:
You'd have died non-Catholics;
And today, my sons,
I'm distressed to be with you!
Kiss me sons,
For it's not I who kills you,
But my sacred oath."
He swung the knife —
The kids were gone![111]
The butchered ones collapsed.
"Daddy! — they mumbled. —
Daddy, daddy... we're not Poles!
We're..." — and they fell silent.
"Should we bury them?"
"No need!
They're Catholics.
My sons, my sons!
Why aren't you grown up?

110 *Narodowi* — Reference to Polish dragoons known as the Kawalerja Narodowa, or People's Cavalry.
111 *Kids were gone* — This scene is a literary invention. Gonta's real wife and children were exiled to Siberia.

Why have you not carved the enemy?
Why have you not killed your mother,
The damned Catholic
That gave you birth?..
Let's go, brothers!"
He took Max,
They went along the marketplace,
Both began to shout:
"Punish Polacks, punish!"
And they punished: awfully, awfully
Uman burned.
Nowhere did a single mansion
Or a Polish church remain.
All perished. The horror that
Took place in Uman
Never happened anywhere.
The Basilian school where Gonta's
Children studied
Is being ruined by Gonta:
"You consumed my children! —
He shouts, he rages, —
You consumed the little ones,
Not having taught them any good!..
Knock the walls down!"
The haidamaks
Knocked the walls down —
They knocked them down,
And bashed the priests against the stones,
The students, yet alive,
Were laid to rest in water wells.
They killed the Poles till late at night;
Not a soul remained. And Gonta shouts:
"Cannibals, where are you?
Where are you concealed?
You've consumed my children —
My life is hard to live!
It's hard for me to cry!
There's no one I can talk with!
My darling sons, my dark-browed boys,
Where are you now hidden?
It's blood I need, more blood!
Noble blood, because I want to drink,
I want to watch it blacken,
I want to get my fill...
Why does the wind not blow,
Why won't it blow some Poles my way?..
My life is hard to live!
It's hard for me to cry!
O righteous stars,
Go hide behind a cloud;
I did not engage you,
I slashed my little children!..
Oh, the grief, my grief!
Where will I find refuge?"
That's how Gonta shouted,
As he ran all over Uman.
Then amid the blood the Kozaks
Set up tables in the market square:
They scrounged some things,
They brought the food
And sat down for some dinner.
Final retribution,
Now a final dinner!
"Dance, my sons!
Drink while drinking's to be had,
Break while there are things to break! —
So shouts Iron Max. Hey, big guy,
Play us anything, bend the ground,
Let my Kozaks dance!"
And the kobzar hit it:

"My father's quite a barman,
And a cobbler;
My mother is a spinner
And quite a go-between;
My brothers they're all falcons,
From the grove
They brought a cow
And necklaces to boot.
And I'm just me, Christine,
I wear a pretty necklace,
My shirt has needlework
Resembling lovely leaves,
And to match the outfit,
I've got a set of boots.
The cow I go to in the morning

I give the cow a lot to drink,
I then milk it
And hang out,
I hang out with the boys."

"Hop, hop, after dinner,
Listen children, close the doors,
And you, old lady, don't you worry
Just come snuggle up to me!"

Everyone is dancing.
But where's Gonta?
Why is he not dancing?
Why is he not drinking
With all the other Kozaks?
And why is he not singing?
He's gone; right now, singing
Isn't likely what he's into.
And who
Is walking past the market
In a black and hooded mantle?
He stopped; uncovering a pile of
Polish dead: he's searching.
Leaning over, he slings two small
Corpses 'cross his back
And in the market square,
Stepping over bodies,
He hides amid the flames
Behind the Polish church.
Just who is this?
Gonta, grief-stricken,
Carries his children to be buried,
To cover them with earth,
So the little Kozak bodies
Aren't consumed by dogs.
Along the darkened streets
Where fires have died down,
Gonta lugged his children,
So that no one sees
Where he is to bury them,
Or that Gonta cries.
He took them to a field
Some distance from the road;
He draws the sacred one,
And uses it to dig a hole.
Uman burns,
It lights up Gonta's work,
And lights the children's faces.
They seem asleep, just fully dressed.
What's the horror in the children?
Why does it seem that Gonta steals
Or hides a secret treasure?
He trembles even. From Uman
One can barely hear — fellow
Haidamaks are calling:
It's as if Gonta does not hear,
He builds his sons a home
Deep beneath the steppe.
And he built it. He takes his sons,
Lays them in their deep dark home,
And doesn't look, but seems to hear:
"Daddy, we're not Poles!"
He lay both down;
From his trouser pocket
He draws a nankeen cloth;
He kissed the dead boys on the eyes,
Crosses them,
And with the crimson cloth
He veils their Kozak heads.
He lifts the cloth,
And looks once more...
His crying's hard and heavy:
My sons, my sons!
Look at that Ukraine:
You and I are dying for her.
And who will bury me?
Just who will shed a tear for me
In a foreign field?
O destiny, my destiny!
My unlucky destiny!
What is it you have done?
Why'd you give me children?
Why did you not kill me?
Better they had buried me,
But now I bury them."
He kissed, he crossed,

And veiled them, and now he fills
Their grave:
Rest, my sons, in this deep dwelling!
The bitch, your mother,
Didn't get new linen.
Rest, my children,
Without basil, without rue,
And plead, ask that God
Punish me on earth
For what I've done to you,
For this great sin of mine.
Forgive me, sons! I forgive
That you are Catholics."
He tamped the soil, replaced the sod
So none would see
Where Gonta's children
Lay their little Kozak heads.
"Rest in peace, and wait,
I will soon be with you.
I cut short your years,
And I will get the same.
They will kill me too…
If they'd only do it soon.
But who will bury me?
The haidamaks! I'll go once more,
One more time I'll frolic!

Gonta left, stooped over;
He goes, he stumbles,
Fires light his way; Gonta looks,
He looks — and smiles.
Dreadful, dreadful was that smile,
As he gazed upon the steppe.
He wiped his eyes… a mere sketch
Within the smoke, he vanished.

EPILOGUE

It's long since past, when I once
Roamed in burlap as a little orphan child
Across that Ukraine
Where Iron Max and Gonta frolicked,
Sacred blades in hand.
It's long since past when on the road
Once strode by haidamaks,
I too walked and cried,
And searched for people
Who would teach me virtue.
I now recall, sadly I recall
The passing of the anguish,
All the youthful anguish! Were it to return,
I'd trade my present fortune for it.
I recall the anguish, the boundless steppes,
My father and my old granddad… [112]
Granddad still cavorts,
But father's passed away.
At times, on Sundays, having closed
The Book of Saints,
Having joined the neighbor
To down a shot of liquor,
Dad would ask my grandpa
To tell stories of Koliyivshchyna,[113]
Of what had happened then.
How Iron Max and Gonta
Punished all the Poles.
A century sparkled in his eyes like stars,

---

[112] *Granddad* — Shevchenko's grandfather, Ivan Andriyovych Shevchenko (1761-1849), witnessed the haidamak uprising as a boy and shared stories of it with the poet. The grandfather outlived the poet's father.

[113] *Koliyivshchyna* — 1768 haidamak uprising, the last and bloodiest of the three major 18th century Kozak and peasant rebellions against Polish nobles, Jesuits, Ukrainian Catholics and Jews. The term is derived from the Ukrainian word for impaling.

As laughing word poured after word:
How the Poles expired,
And how Smila burned.
Fear and sorrow rendered neighbors mute.
I, the little child, more than once
Shed tears of sadness for the sexton.
No one saw the little child crying in a corner.
Thank you, granddad, that you saved
Those Kozak glories in your wise old head:
I've now shared them with the grandkids.

Forgive me, gentle people,
That I tell of Kozak glory
In such a random manner
With no reference to books.
That's how granddad told it,
The best of health to him!
And I take his lead. The old man
Did not know that learned people
Would come to read those things.
Forgive me granddad —
Let them curse: meanwhile
To my verses I'll return
And bring them to conclusion.
I'll conclude — then rest,
And will look if only in my dreams
At that Ukraine, where haidamaks
Roamed with sacred knives, —
On those roads I measured
With my little feet.
The haidamaks frolicked,
It was quite a frolic:
Not quite a year, they doused Ukraine
With noble blood
And then they all fell silent —
They chipped their knives.
Gonta's gone;
Neither cross nor mound
Upon his grave.
Raging winds have spread
The ashes of the haidamak,
And there's no one who may pray for him,
No one who may cry.

A sole blood brother's left
On this entire world,
And having heard how
Hellish children
Tortured his good brother,
Iron Max broke down in tears, something
He had never done; he didn't wipe them,
The wretch had simply died.
Anguish crushed him in a foreign field,
It lay him in a foreign land:
Such was his fate!
Sadly, oh so sadly the haidamaks
Buried the force of iron;
They raised a lofty mound,
Cried, and then dispersed
To whence they all had hailed.

Only my Yarema leaned upon his staff,
And lingered for some while.
"Rest, father, in a foreign field,
For in your own there is no room,
Nor is there room for freedom...
Sleep, Kozak, earnest soul!
May someone yet recall you."

The poor wretch, wiping tears,
Embarked upon the steppe,
He looked back a long, long time,
Till all was lost from sight.
A silhouetted mound
Remained alone amid the steppe.

Haidamaks in Ukraine sowed rye,
But weren't the ones to reap it.
What are we to do?
There's no truth, it did not grow;

Injustice is what thrives...
Haidamaks dispersed
To any place that each had known:
One went home,
Another picked the forest
With a knife stashed in his bootleg

To finish off the Jews. Such renown
Has lasted to this day.
They, meanwhile, ruined the Sich of old:
One fled for the Kuban,
Another 'cross the Danube,
All that's left are rapids
Roaring and resounding in the steppe:
"They interred our children,
And break us up as well."
They roar and roar, they always will.
People passed them by;
Ukraine forever,
Forever she has gone to sleep.
Since that time, the rye turns green:
There's no sound of crying,
There's no roar of cannons,
Just the blowing wind,
Bending willows in the grove,
And in the field, feather-grass.
All is silent. So be it;
The will of God is such.

Only sometimes in the evening,
Along the grove above the Dnipro,
Walk some aging haidamaks,
Singing as they go:

"Our Vagbond's home is on a hill,
Roll on blue sea! Good, blue sea!
O Vagabond, good will come to pass!"

St. Petersburg, April-November 1841

NOTES[114]

1. *The Encyclopedic Lexicon,* Volume 5. The Bar Confederation and *History of the Polish Monarchy,* J. S. Bandtkie, Volume 2.
2. Vilshana or Olshana, a town in the Zvenyhorod District of Kyiv Province; the Borovyk hamlet and a tavern were located between Zvenyhorod and Vilshana, where Yarema the Bastard, later Vagabond, was a Jew's hireling. (Related by old people.)
3. Poles referred to non-Uniates as schismatics.
4. This is what people who saw the Confederates say; and no wonder, because this was a prideful aristocracy, without discipline; no desire to work, but eating is a must.
5. An anachronism: Poles tortured and killed the sexton in winter, not summer.
6. A kobzar followed the haidamaks; they called him the Blind Volokh (Related by grandfather.)
7. Pavlo Nalyvaiko was burned alive in Warsaw, Ivan Ostranytsia and 30 Kozak officers were quartered after terrible suffering and their bodies were dispersed throughout Ukraine. Zinoviy Bohdan and his son Tymofiy were buried in Subotiv near Chyhyryn; Czarniecki, the Polish crowned Hetman, not having taken Chyhyryn, burned their dead bodies out of anger (Heorhiy Konynsky.)
8. Colonel Bohun drowned the Poles in the Inhul River. Zinoviy Bohdan [Khmelnytsky] slaughtered some 40,000 Poles on the Ros River in Korsun. Taras Triasylo slaughtered Poles on the Alta; the night this happened is referred to as the Bloody, or Night of Taras. (Bantysh-Kamensky)
9. This is how old people speak about the feast in Chyhyryn.
10. *The Nights of Taras* and of *St. Bartholemew* are worthy of one another to the disgrace of the Roman tiara.

---

114 *Notes* — Shevchenko published these notes in his initial editions of *Haidamaks.* He removed them in the 1860 edition of *The Kobzar,* the last in his lifetime.

11. *Third roosters* — a signal; they say Zalizniak's captain, not having waited for the third rooster, burned Medvedivka. It is a town between Chyhyryn and Zvenyhorod.
12. *The Black Road* began on the Dnipro between confluences of the Sokorivka and Nosachivka and ran along the Zaporizhian steppes, through the voidvodships of Kyiv, Podilia, and Volyn to Red Rus and Lviv. It was called black because Tatars used it to raid Poland and their herds trampled the grass.
13. Until the Union (of Brest), Kozaks and Poles lived in peace, and were it not for the Jesuits, perhaps they may not have slaughtered one another; The Jesuit papal legate, Possevino, initiated the Union in Ukraine.
14. *Kyrylivka*, or *Kuryłówka* is a village in the Zvenyhorod District. The chervonets coin that Zalizniak gave the boy is still in the possession of his son. I saw it myself.
15. In the village of Budyshcha, not far from Kyrylivka, there is a lake in a valley. Above that lake is a small forest referred to as The Thumping Grove (Hupalivshchyna), because that is where Zalizniak shook Poles from the trees. The cellars where noble treasure was hidden are still evident, except they are ruined.
16. *Lysianka* is a town in the Zvenyhorod District above the Rotten Tikych River. Gonta and Zalizniak gathered here and destroyed an old building supposedly built by Bohdan [Khmelnytsky].
17. *Maidanivka* is a village not far from Lysianka.
18. *Lebedyn* is a nunnery between Chyhyryn and Zvenyhorod.
19. *Uman* is a district city in Kyiv Province.
20. The People's Cavalry *[Kawalerja Narodowa]* was the name of Polish dragoons. At the time, there were 3,000 of them in Uman, all killed by the haidamaks.
21. Gonta killed his children in Uman because their mother, a Catholic, helped Jesuits convert them to Catholicism. Mladanovych, a friend of Gonta's sons, saw them die. He also saw how Gonta drowned pupils of the Basilian school in a well. He wrote much about the haidamaks, but nothing was published.
22. Gonta was betrayed, captured and horribly tortured. They brought him in shackles to a Polish camp near the Baltic Sea with his tongue and right arm cut off. B., a Polish general, ordered this so that Gonta would not say anything about him. The executioners then stripped him just the way his mother gave birth and placed him on hot iron spikes. Then they removed 12 strips of skin from his back. Gonta rolled his eyes and looked at B., who waved his hand and they cut him up in fours, dispersed his body and nailed it for display on crossroads. Zalizniak, having heard how terribly Gonta was tortured, cried, took sick and died. Haidamaks buried him in the steppe above the Dniester and dispersed.
23. Thieves, rogues or haidamaks are what the haidamaks remained after the Kolyivshchyna. That is how they are known today.

PREFACE

After the text — a preface. It could do without, but you see: Everything I have seen printed, — only seen, since I've read very little, — always has a preface, and I have none. If I did not publish my *Haidamaks*, then no preface would be needed. But now that I'm circulating it among people, it needs to be done properly, so they don't laugh at the ragamuffins and say: "Look at him! Were the grandfathers and fathers more stupid he, because they did not even publish a grammar book without a preface?" Thus, indeed, and thus, forgive, but a preface is required. So how to compose it like all prefaces are composed, without any offense or truth? Slay me, but I don't know how; praise would be shameful and there is no desire to disparage. Thus let us begin at the very beginning of the book: It is pleasant to watch the blind kobzar sitting with a boy beneath a fence, and pleasant to listen to him sing a ballad about things that happened long ago, and how Poles fought with Kozaks; pleasant... but nonetheless you'll say: "Thank God it's over," — especially when you recall that we are children of the same mother, that we are all Slavs. It pains the heart, but the story must be told: Let the sons and grandchildren know that their parents were mistaken. Let them again be brothers with their enemies. From sea to sea, may rye and wheat, like gold, forever cover undivided Slavic land. I relate that which happened in Ukraine in 1768 as I heard it from old people; I did not read any publications or critiques, because apparently there are none. Vagabond is half-invented, but the death of the sexton in Vilshana is true, because there are still people who knew him. I do not present Gonta and Iron Max, the otamans of the bloody deed, as they really were, — I do not vouch for their portrait. Whenever my grandpa (best of health to him) begins to relate what he heard but did not see himself, he first says: "If the old people lie, then I lie with them."

GENTLEMEN SUBSCRIBERS!

"We see, we see that he deceived and still wants to beg off with a lie!" That's what you'll instinctively think when you read my *Haidamaks.* Gentlemen of the community! I listen and what emerges is a babel. One says, — "There's a need," another says, "There's no need," and a third says nothing. I thought, "What in the world to do?" By God, I do not lie. Here's the thing! I thought and very much wanted to nicely print your Kozak names in rows; there already were 20 or 30 of them. I took and nicely squandered the money needed to pay for a sheet, and to you I write this note. It would be nothing if it were only that. What only happens in the course of life! Everything happens in the long run. But here's the trouble for my troubles! There are also gentlemen who were ashamed to print the name of their honorable family (Kyrpa-Hnuchkosheyenko-v) in a peasant book. Indeed, it's true!

T. Shevchenko

The wind converses with the grove,
It whispers to the sedge,
A boat floats down the Danube
Alone upon the water.
The boat, filled with water, floats,
No one tries to stop it.
But who's to stop it — it has no
Fisherman on earth.
The boat floated to the sea so blue.
The sea arose, swelled
And picked up waves like mountains —
Even splinters were not left.

The way is not that long —
Just like the boat
That floats to sea —
The orphan ends up in a foreign land
And there he lives in anguish.
Good people pick on him
Like cold and lapping waves.
They watch the orphan cry.
But ask them later,
Where's the orphan, —
They neither heard nor saw.

St. Petersburg, 1841

Forest Edge, 1845-47

MARYANNE THE NUN

To Oksana K......ko[115]
In memory of what happened long ago

In the grove a wind
Bends the willow and the poplar,
It breaks the oak and tumbles
Tumbleweeds across the field.
Such is fate: it breaks that one,
It bends this one;
Me, it tumbles, and where it stops,
Fate itself knows not —
In which land they will bury me,
Where I'll bend, and sleep forever.
If there's no kind fate, no destiny
And no one to abandon, then
No one will recall,
Nor even say in jest:
"May he rest in peace, it was
His fate to sleep so early."
Is it not true, Oksana? O long-lost dark-browed girl!
You won't recall that orphan
Dressed in peasant garb, at times, so happy
When he saw the wonder — of your beauty.
Whom you taught
Not using words
To use the eyes, the soul and heart to speak.
With whom you smiled, cried and worried,
To whom you loved to sing the song called *Peter.*
You'll not recall. Oksana! Oksana!
I still cry, and I still worry,
Pouring out my tears for that Maryanne of mine,
I look at you, and pray for you.
Remember, after all, Oksana, O long-lost dark-browed girl,
And adorn Sister Maryanne with primrose,
Give a happy smile at times for Peter,
And just for fun remember how it was.

St. Petersburg, November 22, 1841

[115] *Oksana Stepanivna Kovalenko (1817–?)* — An orphan, village neighbor and childhood friend of Shevchenko.

I

Sunday at the pasture,
Girls danced,
Joked with boys,
And some sang songs —
Of evening parties;
Of how mama beat her daughter
To stop those meetings with a Kozak.
Usual stuff, girls...
They sing of what's familiar,
Each of what she knows...
And lo, an old kobzar
Comes hobbling to the village
With a boy in tow.
In the old man's hands are boots,
Across his back
A patched up sack; and the child!
Wretched child!
Ragged; it barely, barely
Drags its weary little feet...
(Certainly Kateryna's son.)[116]
The girls watch...
"The kobzar's coming!
The kobzar's coming!"
Each one quickly dropped the boys,
And ran to meet the sightless man!
"Grandpa, darling, sweetie,
Play us any tune.
I'll give you half a kopeck." —
"I will give sweet cherries."
"Anything that's needed, —
That is what we'll give you...
You will rest,
And we will dance...
Play us anything..."
"I hear you, dearies, yes, I hear you.
Thank you, blossoms,
For the word of kindness.
I'd play for you, but look,
No gear... no gear.
I was at the market yesterday,
The kobza broke...
It got smashed up... — "Are there strings?"
"Only three remain."
"So play at least with three."
"Using three... O my girls!"
I once played on only one,
But can't do it anymore...
Wait, my dears,
I'll rest a bit.
Let's sit down, my boy." They sat.
He untied his sack,
Removed the kobza,
And twice he hit the broken strings.
"What should I play for you? Wait...
Have you heard of Sister Maryanne? —
"No, we haven't."
"Listen, girls
And repent...
Long ago there was a mother,
And a father too, though he passed away;
She was left a widow,
Not very young at that,
With oxen,
And with carts,
And a little daughter.
The daughter Maryanne matured,
And grew into a nice young lady, —
Hazel-eyed and tall,
Fit for any hetman.
Mom began to think
How to match her with a lord.
Not with the lord
Did Maryanne go dancing.
Not with the lord who's
Mustachioed, old and paunchy.
But every blessed evening
She talked, she joked,
Embraced and swooned
With Peter in the grove or meadow...

---

116 *Kateryna's son* — Reference to Ivan from the earlier poem, *Kateryna.*

At times she smiled, cried,
Or just fell silent…
"Why, sweetheart, do you cry?" —
Asks Peter.
She looks, and smiles:
"I myself don't really know…"
"Perhaps, you think I'll leave you?
No, my darling,
I'll come see you, I will love you
Till the day I die!.."
"Did it happen in this world
That true lovers ever parted,
Not betrothed and yet alive?
No, it's never been, my dove.
You have heard of what they sing…
They're fictions of the kobzars,
Because they're blind and do not know,
Because they do not see
The black enticing brows,
The hazel eyes,
The Kozak's lanky stature,
Or the girl's supple grace;
That there are braids, long braids,
And a Kozak's handsome locks…
That even in my silent grave I'll smile
And respond to Peter's talk;
I'll tell him:
"O my gray-winged eagle,
I love you in this
World like I loved you in the other."
Thus, my sweetheart, we'll embrace,
This is how I'll kiss you,
Let them bury us together…
I'll die… I'll feel nothing.
I'll not feel it." They embraced,
They hugged and swooned…
This is how they loved!
In tight embrace
They hoped to reach the other world;
They got together every evening,
And mother did not know,
Where did Maryanne spend midnight
And with whom did she converse?
"She's still little, just a child,
She doesn't know a thing."
Old mama guessed,
But didn't guess it all,
She forgot to realize that she
Herself was once a maiden.
Mama guessed: Maryanne — she's but a child,
Who doesn't know
How one should live on earth.
She thought — neither people nor the coffin
Will keep her split from Peter…
She knew exactly how to love.
She thought kobzars just sing songs,
Because the blind do not see hazel eyes;
That the minstrels only frighten maidens…
Yes, they frighten, girls,
Frighten with the truth!
And I too frighten you,
Because I know that anguish.
May no one in the world know —
That which I have come to know…
It's over, girls!
The heart has not dozed off,
You — I've not forgotten.
I love you still,
As a mother would her children,
I'll sing to you until I sleep.
And then, my dears, when I expire,
Remember me and my Maryanne;
From the other world, my dears,
I'll share a smile with you.
I'll smile." And he began to cry.
The girls watched,
And did not ask him why the tears.
But why ask?
It's over, gone. Of assistance
Was the maidens' kind
And earnest word…
"Forgive me… —
Wiping his blind eyes. —
Forgive me, dears,
Unwittingly I worry.
So, you see, every evening Maryanne

Talked with the pauper Peter,
But mother did not know,
And wondered what it was
That had gotten into Maryanne.
Was it not the evil eye?
She sits to sew —
But her sewing's not quite right;
Instead of singing *Greg*, she broods
And out comes *Peter.*
Talking in her sleep at times,
She gives her pillow kisses...
Mother laughed at first,
Thinking — it's a joke,
But then she sees it's not a joke at all,
And says: "Maryanne!
You should await the matchmakers,
Perhaps even from the wealthy lord!
Knock on wood, you're all grown up,
And you have been a maiden;
I'm now thinking that, you see..."
She forced it out.
"That it's time for marriage, when that..."
"And with whom, mama!?"
"The one who strikes my fancy is the one
I'll give your hand to."
Maryanne begins to sing:
"Mama, give my hand away,
But don't give it to an old guy,
Give my hand, my heart,
Please let it be to someone young.
Let the old man wander,
Let him earn more money.
But the young one loves me,
He's not searching for his fortune.
He's not searching, he's not wandering
Across some foreign steppes:
He has his oxen, his own cart,
And with the guys,
He's like a poppy blossom
That buds and blooms amid the flowers,
He has a field, he has freedom,
Though he has no fortune.
His fortune and his fate
Are my dark brows,
My long lashes, hazel eyes
And my gentle word.
Mama, give my hand away,
But don't give it to an old guy,
Give my hand, my heart,
Please let it be to someone young."

"My daughter, Maryanne,
I'll give you to a lord,
To an old and wealthy man
To the Captain Ivan."
"I'll die, beloved mama,
If I'm to marry Captain Ivan."
"You'll not die, you'll be a lady,
You'll also feed your children."
"I will be a servant,
I'll step out among the people,
But with the Captain I'll not partner."
"You, my daughter Maryanne,
Will marry Captain Ivan."
Poor Maryanne
Broke down in tears and sobbed.
"With an old man... with a rich man...
With the Captain Ivan..."
She talked about it to herself,
And later spoke out loud:
"I, mama, have not grown,
I've not yet been a maiden.
Because you didn't let me
Reap the rye,
Gather flax,
And hang out mornings at the well,
Nor did you let me go to parties
Where girls joke and sing with boys,
And where they also
Whisper things about me,
About the dark-browed beauty:
"She's the daughter of a wealthy dad
From a line of nobles."
It's hard for me. It's hard, mama!
Why did you give me beauty?
Why did you paint my brows,

And give me hazel eyes?
You gave everything, but happiness,
You don't want to give me happiness!
Why'd you feed me?
Why'd you care for me?
Before I came to know of heartbreak,
Why did you not bury me?"
The old mother did not listen,
And turned in for the night.
And with her tears poor Maryanne
Barely left the house.

II

"Hop, hop,
No, I did not drink,
I was at a wedding.
I didn't get back home
And dropped in by the neighbor.
At the neighbor's
Before lunchtime
In the cellar I had slept.

From the cellar to a cellar
We twirled amid the peas
In the shack and in the open,
A twosome with a bachelor.
We joked around,
We misbehaved
And spoiled all the peas.

Hop, hop, not alone
I gave my pal a bit to drink
And brought him to my home.
Tom did not see this.
Tom, we'll sleep here
In this house,
Tom's not even home.

Damn you, Tom!
At home I will not sleep.
I'll see a pal,
It's Al I'll see,
In the shack in piles of hay.
Well, she had some drinks!
But our girl, our girl
Was quite proper!
Her apron reddens;
She's the child of honest kin."

Like a horde came wedding guests,
A singing bunch of drunks;
Maryanne saw it through a woven fence.
Not having finished looking,
She fell and had a hard, hard cry.
Such was the anguish, all because
Her love was true. Years upon this world,
My children, are hard to live alone,
It's harder still, my blossoms,
To love another not your equal.
Look at me: I cried my eyes out.
I don't miss them, I'm not sorry.
There's not a thing to look at:
Those maiden eyes…
That once… that once…
Thoughts and sorrow,
Is all I had and have,
And with currency like that
It's hard to live on earth.
I sleep beneath a fence,
And banter with the wind,
People are embarrassed
To let me in their homes
And to say a word of welcome
To an old and feeble man.
Cut short, O God, the years of youth
Of one who's fate is not to love.
It's easier, my dears,
To be blanketed with earth,
Than to see a rich old man
Giving kisses with his money,
Getting married with her…
O God! My God! May Your will be done,
Destroy my body, wreck my soul."
The kobzar cried, he cried
With his sightless eyes.
The girls were surprised:

Death, closing in behind his back,
And he, all blind and gray,
Still cries about the past.
Don't be surprised, my girls,
At the elder Kozak's earnest tears.
They're not morning dew
On knotweed by the road,
And they're not the tender tears you shed.
He got his fill of crying.
He strums the broken
Threesome on his kobza.
"Maryanne cried till evening
In the darkened forest;
Peter came, she told him all
That she had heard from mother
And she knew herself.
She did not refrain, and told
How drunken wedding guests
Walked, singing down the street.
"Maryanne! Maryanne!
Why are you not poor! Why am I not rich!
Why have I no stable
Filled with jet black horses!
Mother would not ask
Where you go a dancing,
Nor with whom you hang around.
You yourself would ask your heart;
You'd set it free to love at will,
I'd hide you far away! Far away!
So that no one knew, no one saw
Where happiness resides,
My fate, my happiness,
You, my Maryanne.
Why aren't you in peasant garb,
Why have I no overcoat?"
And like a child, Maryanne
Without a mother, cries.
Peter stands beside her,
Seeing nothing —
Only tears shed by his Maryanne;
And a maiden's tears by day
Cause anguish,
What then
If they're shed at night as well?
"Don't cry, my sweetheart,
I've got vigor, I've got will,
Love me darling, O my sweetheart,
I will find my fortune.
Beyond tall mountains,
Past broad steppes,
In a foreign field,
One way or another,
I will find my fortune!
I'll not return in peasant garb,
But rather as a captain.
You'll hold Peter in your arms
Not in the weeds — but in a church.
We'll embrace, I'll kiss you,
Go on people, be astonished!
And you'll be standing there,
Just blushing..."
"When is this to be?"
"Soon, soon, my darling,
Just say a prayer to the Lord.
Go home, go sleep.
I'll stand beside the road
Amid the steppe to say a prayer
To the bright-eyed stars,
So when I'm gone
And you are lonely
They will care for you."
"Will you leave me yet tonight?
Right now, perhaps?.." — "I'm joking.
Right now —
Neither Muscovites, nor Tatars —
Fight against Ukraine."
"But I heard the Poles are coming."
"Then they're joking.
Let's part, my sweetheart,
Before first light of dawn.
Again you're crying, why?"
"I myself don't know."

St. Petersburg, 1841

THE DROWNED MAIDEN

The wind's not dancing in the forest —
At nighttime it's at rest; once awake —
It whispers to the sedge:
Who's this, who's this on this side
That's combing her long braid?
Who's this?..
Who's this, who's this on this side
That's ripping out her braid?
Who's this, who's this?" —
It asks quietly, wafting,
Dozing off, till the edges
Of the sky turn red.

"Who's this, who's this?" — a question
All you curious girls may ask.
That's the daughter on this side,
On the other — it's her mother.

This all took place quite long ago
In our land, in our Ukraine.
In a village was a widow
Living in a small new house,
A fair face, hazel eyes,
Tall stature,
In a fancy overcoat;
From front to back, a lady all around.
Knock on wood, she's also young,
And chasing the young gal,
A widow, mind you,
Was a horde of Kozaks. The Kozaks
Chased her till she shamelessly gave birth
To a baby daughter.
She gave birth, but did not care;
She left the baby to be nurtured
In some different village:
That's the mom she was!..
Listen up, there's more!
People fed the baby daughter,
While the widow
Drank and danced on Sundays,
And on workdays
With married men and bachelors,
Until she met some trouble,
Till she wasn't quite herself;
Unaware that youth had passed...
Trouble, trouble! As the mother withers,
So her daughter blossoms,
And begins to grow... She grew up,
Tall and supple like a poplar,
A hazel-eyed young beauty
Everyone called Hanna.
"I'm not scared of Hanna!" —
Sang the mother;
And Kozaks cling to Hanna
Like hopvines in a field.
Especially that curly-headed fisherman,
A lively guy who swoons and wilts
When he meets the dark-browed Hanna.
Old mama saw,
And spoke with rage:
"Just look, you're a shoeless little bastard,
Filthy and unkempt!
You've grown up, you're now a maiden,
And go dancing with the boys...
Just you wait, I'll show you!..
Have you no respect for me?
No, my dearie!"
She gnashed her teeth in anger.
There's a mother for you!..
Where's the woman's heart?
A mother's heart?.. What trouble,
What a pity, girls!
To have tall and supple stature,
But to have no heart.
Tall stature bends,
Eye-brows fade,
It all happens imperceptibly;
And cackling people will
Recall your years of youth,
To say you are — a ne'er-do-well!
Hanna cried profusely
And did not really know

Why her mother mocks,
Curses and rebukes her child,
Shamelessly condemning her
As a little bastard.
She beat her and oppressed her
But all to no avail:
Hanna merely blossomed
Like a poppy in the garden;
Like a guelder rose beside a valley
In the morning dew,
Thus did Hanna's rosy tint
Become awash in tears.
"She's bewitched!.. Look out!
The livid mother whispers. —
Need to get some poison,
The old witch is who I need to find!"
She found the witch,
Got the poison,
And fed that poison to her daughter
Before the break of dawn.
To no avail.... The mother
Curses both the time and hour
That she brought her unloved daughter
Into this world of ours.
"I'm hot; let's go, my daughter,
To cool off in the pond."
"Let's go, mama."
Hanna stripped,
She stripped along the shore
And sprawled upon her bright white shirt;
The curly-headed fisherman
Stands swooning on the other side...
And I too... But enough of that!
It's embarrassing... I won't mention it.
Like a child she diverts herself
With a guelder rose,
She limbers up her agile body
And warms it in the sun.
Mother looks upon her,
Falling silent in her anger;
Turning yellow, turning blue;
Disheveled, barefoot,
Foaming at the mouth; as if mad,
She rips her braids out.
She then throws herself at Hanna,
Clawing at her braids.
"What gives, mommie? Mommie!
The wave parted,
Bubbled, sighed —
And covered both of them.
The curly-headed fisherman
Jumped full force in the water;
He swims and slices through blue waves,
He swims, he swims...
He swam right there!
He dives, emerges —
But Hanna had already drowned.
He brings her up,
Carries her to shore,
Then from her mother's rigid fingers
He pulls out Hanna's braids.
"My sweetheart! My fortune!
Open up your hazel eyes!
Look! Smile!
You won't!.. You won't!.."
Crying, he collapses by her,
He opens, kisses
Eyes now dead. "Look!..
She hears nothing, nothing!"
There she lies, fair arms
Spread out upon the sand;
Behind her the old cruel mother;
Eyes bulging from the brow
From all the awful torment,
She propped her old blue arms
In the yellow sand.
The fisherman sat long and cried:
"I have no kin, no fortune
In this world —
Let's go live beneath the water!"
He lifted her, and kissed her...
The wave sighed,
Opened, closed,
Not a trace remained...
Since then the pristine pond,
Is overgrown with sedge;

Girls don't swim there,
They skirt around along the hill;
Glimpsing it, they
Cross themselves and say it's haunted...
All around it's oh so sad...
At night, my girls, the mother rises
From the water
To sit upon the other shore;
Ghastly, blue, unkempt,
In a soaking shirt,
Wordlessly she gazes over to this shore,
Tearing out her braids...
A blue wave, meanwhile,
Carries Hanna forth.

She quivers, naked
And sits upon the sand...
And the fisherman emerges,
Green kelp draped upon his shirt;
He'll kiss the eyes —
And slip back in the water:
He's ashamed to see
The maiden's agile naked body...
And no one knows the nightly wonders
That transpire in the forest,
The wind merely whispers to the sedge:
Who's this, who's this sitting sadly
By the water,
Combing such long braids?

St. Petersburg, December 8, 1841

In Lykhvyn, 1859

THE BLIND WOMAN

(A Poem)
(From the Russian)

"As I weep,"[117]
Who is there for me to summon
That would share my pain, my longing,
Whom am I to serenade
With my lovely native song
In a distant foreign land?
I'll expire, poor, in bondage…
With silent walls around me,
I share the pain and longing
For my onetime freedom, onetime fortune.
O sacred winds, if you could hasten
To the bosom of my native land
With my lament of sorrow,
With the clank of rusted chains,
And then repeat the sounds
In that peaceful shrine,
Where my father and my mother
Caressed and gave me love.
As for brotherhood! A sinful family
Would sell a brother to a foreign tribe
Like a ram for slaughter
Just for gold derived from
Herds, from wine or holy oil.
O God, God of all Judea,
Blessed Maker of the earth,
Punish not my evil kin,
Endow me rather with humility!"

Such was the song sung quietly
By a poor blind woman,
Seized by heartfelt sorrow;
She sat beside a lordly manor
Beside an open gate.
But through it no one leaves
Nor comes, they've long
Since left the lordly mansion,
The vast courtyard overgrown,
The village left to vanish
Along with patriarchal modesty
And fathers' sacred glory —
All forgotten.
Silence rules the village,
No one comes to visit.
Renown will not revive it.
Sitting by the gate, as if
In a graveyard, the grieving
Sightless woman sings
A quiet doleful psalm.
She sings, and the daughter
Of my luckless woman
Leaned her tawny head
Upon her mother's lap,
And not aware of any grief,
Her sleep was pure simplicity.
She's gorgeous
In attire of crushing poverty;
Midday in my fair Ukraine
Gilded, loved and nurtured
Its beautiful young child.
Will days of rapture fly in vain above her,
And not sweeten all her yearning
With its bright-lit joy?
She's beautiful; the mother — crippled,
Who will lead her?
A time will come, a time to love,
But the evil heart of man
Will not spare her love.
. . . .
. . . . Innocent is
Oksana's sleep. The mother's blind,
Singing dolefully and softly,
On guard for every rustle.
And if the wind flies by
And stirs a fallen leaf,

---

117 *"As I weep…"* — Lyrics based on the Biblical story of Joseph who was sold into slavery by his brothers.

She goes numb, she trembles,
And presses to her heart uneasily
Her one and only child,
Her one and only comfort.
The sightless woman sees in memory
Delights of long ago
And of her wistful youth.
She knew people from experience…
They won't spare her
Even by this forlorn fence,
They're prepared to lacerate
Her poor decrepit hands,
They don't hear the sobs of parting,
A mother's love for them is foreign.
They claim — the law is such:
"A beautiful young orphan
Should not grovel in the dust
Nor be fed with alms;
We will dress her all in gold,
We'll move her to a lofty mansion
And her beauty we will worship,
We'll open up a world of sights,
And other passions of a finer world,
And then… and then…"
And your idol,
Goddess of your worship,
Got high on frankincense
And was smothered by the smoke;
And your wisdom shunned
All promises; that idol
So magnanimously tossed her bits of gold,
Eclipsed her sparkling eyes,
And lo, she's debauched in mud,
For the glory of your shabby days,
Drinking from a cup before
A crowd of drunken rabble . . . . . .
And washes down the heart's abrasions.
You're not to blame, she is!
You gave everything that should be given
To a sordid concubine.
But have you restored the maiden's dreams,
Have you revived the blessing
Of her innocent belief?
The innocence of her love,
The joy of quiet rapture,
And her undefiled blood,
Have you restored these too?
You couldn't!
Come, come, O sinful children
Of the earth!
Did you delight her with the hugs
A dear and kindred child knows,
And the love with which the wretch
Of heartfelt sorrow
Could pour herself into this world
And learn the mysteries of life?
With your debauched impoverished blood
You could not replicate for her
The delights of virgin love,
You left her on her own
To drag her days out
In the earthly desert;
And she'll not get a message from afar
With soothing words about her only son.
In the final dreadful hour of death,
It will be a stranger's children who will
Slake her thirst.
And it will be a stranger's grudging children
Who bear her to a lonely grave.
But if by fate it's fated
That a kinfolk's hand
Should close her lifeless eyes,
Her grave will then be rigid,
Her eternal linen rough!
Shamefully and wordlessly
Her little child will roam the earth,
And beside a gate on the sunny holiday
She'll take an Easter egg
And recall her mother
With rebuke and tears.

O autumn noon, bright noon
In that dear and native land,
Where my years first blossomed,
Where they flowed in such futility
And impoverished misfortune.

O autumn noon, bright noon
Let me greet you with these foreign sounds
Like a lovely loving friend from youth!
You're just as quiet, just as dear,
You're not aware of time, but I...
I've not become what was before,
And the path of lonely being,
And my heavy burden
Have changed me very dreadfully.
I solved the mystery of life,
I revealed the heart of man,
And I suffer not as once I did,
And neither do I love: I'm — an invalid!
In the snows of foreign lands
I've forever frozen
The throbbing of my heart.
And only sounds from our Ukraine
Perturb the heart at times,
Like an echo of a guiltless memory.
In those sounds I find my spring,
My cheerless times of leisure,
And I pine in them
And with them lose myself,
Like a balm of dew.
I treat the heart's grave wounds
And share with my Ukraine
An unaffected tear.
But all is deaf
In my distant native paradise!
In vain I raise my voice,
From the grove I get no echo
Of my dark-browed Kozak girl.
All there is asleep. A void
Defiled the heart of man,
And I am mocked and left forever,
I am — a lonely orphan!

The fading autumn noon
Lit the empty fields,
And the withered falling leaf
Sadly whispered sorrow
About this life to man.
At such a time my cripple,
My wretched sightless woman,
And her dreamboat daughter —
She slept, the mother sat,
Singing softly, sad and softly,
Of how Joseph sang about his kin,
As he sat imprisoned long ago in Egypt.
And in the firmament above
Cranes flew southward in formation
From the oakwood forests of Ukraine.
Why should she too not fly,
Like a bird so free,
To a better clime, to fly
And sing more happily?
What secret has confined her
To a place of gloomy silence?
As yet, her heart's own depths
She's not revealed,
Not even to her daughter;
She merely sang and mourned,
But the sounds
Of her child's own words
Awoke in her a quiet joy,
Perhaps of bygone shining days.
Are the gate and poplar
That sadly whisper back and forth,
Witnesses to former fortune,
Or is her witness just a
Dried out oak stump,
Covered with some wilted ivy,
That time, it seems, forgot?
All is silent!
She sings, she mourns,
And deep within her soul she weeps,
As if to sing last rights
For days gone by, of youth,
Of former sacred joys.
And those sounds sprang from
Her needy heart,
Reflecting amply of her earthly being.
For the hundredth time she finished
A muted psalm of bondage,
She drooped her tawny head,
Sighed heavily and said:

"O song, song, song of grief,
You're conjoined with me.
In the rough seas of my life
You're the only tranquil current.
Crying day and night,
It's you I sing and sing
And it's you, my melancholy,
That I send off to a distant land.
But the raging wind, the light-wing,
That once flew so joyfully,
Now blows so quietly, so sadly,
As if he's lost a friend,
As if people taught him
To pay no heed to me,
And he failed to convey you,
My melancholy song,
To that distant land!
Not seeing you,
Knowing not the day in my lonely pain,
How could I have slighted you?
Whatever have I done to you? I loved,
I prayed to the Heavenly Creator
For your sinful deeds,
I prayed, I wept… And
In my melancholy, in my grief
You, like lions thirsting blood,
Rebuked and ripped my heart,
Spoiled my blood with venom,
And for the prayers, for the love,
You tagged my own dear child,
My daughter,
With a heavy word,
And labeled me with laughter
As a blind and useless woman!
I forgave you, I forgot,
I did not take your glory,
I fed my child with alms."
And she filled with tears,
Bitter, bitter tears.
She weeps, and Oksana
Opened her dark eyes:
The mother's grieving tears
Cut short the girl's dream;
With a smile she closed
Her dark black lashes.
"What a stupid, funny dream,
And so real…"
And bashfully she blushed,
Herself not knowing why.
"How cold, and you still cry!
It'll soon be evening, why
Not tell me of your grief?
And I would cry with you,
But otherwise…"
And pouring forth were tears,
Tears of beauty's innocence.
"And you too have cried…
Forgive me for not speaking
With you of the wounds
That hurt my heart.
I'll stop weeping soon,
My heavy tear won't
Break your gorgeous dream.
And of my luckless fate
You'll not learn from me.
You'll be told by evil people,
They will spare you not.
And there will be ample, ample grief.
And the grief won't freely vanish.
It will sour the heart with emptiness,
It will take your love away,
It will take the very best.
Don't cry, Oksana!"
And crying, she consoles Oksana:
"Cry not, my child, sleep,
You start to weep too early.
Your time for spring will come,
You'll learn the secret of my tears;
You'll shed your own,
All alone you'll shed them,
A homeless orphan all alone,
And it will be my fault
That you'll not want to share…"
"And with you? Do I not love you!
Oh, even grief I love with you,
I'll share all with you.

I'll not take my heartfelt tear
To strangers — I'll bring it
To your bosom. Just don't cry,
Share with me your heavy grief,
Do not weep alone, open up to me,
It will all be better. Listen!
I'll tell you what I saw
In the dream I had.
A thicket, dense,
It seems a forest, and we
Both randomly meander.
Then it's dark, then it's light,
Then I look — and you are gone,
And I grew tired — of running, crying,
So I sat and wept.
Suddenly — a village,
A big street, very big,
And I walk along that street,
I'm so sad, the grief is great,
I then trip and fall;
It's hard for me, my chest is heavy,
People watch and laugh,
I took ill, but to look at people
It seems I was afraid.
An otaman then shouts:
"I'm here for you!" Frightened,
I took off... I ran... I fell.
His son is standing sadly by the water
And gently waves his hand at me.
So I came to him,
He grabbed me with his arms.
"Why have you lived not in the woods,
Why did you grow not in a field?"
He spoke in words like these —
"I'm not allowed to love you,
Nor may I marry you:
They will always laugh at us;
Without you, though, my life is dull,
I'll drown myself instead," he said
And gave me such a kiss!
Not one like yours... I then awoke.
A strange dream, or what?
Its portent should be bad.
Or perhaps not bad at all —
Do you not know?
It's awful how I want to know.
Why is it that you sigh again?
Or you're afraid perhaps
To share its meaning with me.
Oh, tell me, please!
What to do? If it's bad —
We'll escape into the forest,
We'll both live together,
And it will be a pleasure
For me to grieve with you.
How 'bout it? You'll tell?"
"Yes, the sightless woman sighed and said,
I should tell you all.
I'm tired, tired of unrelenting tears.
You are now fifteen.
Your dream is ominous, an awful dream!
You'll meet a rueful welcome
To your spring, your hapless spring.
Recall me not, forgive,
And share your grief
In freedom and expansive spaces,
With the doleful wind,
Just as I have grieved and mourned,
Entrusting all my daily woes
Only to the wind;
But for me he feels no sorrow,
He won't even dry my tears,
Of which there are so many
That they erode the heart.
Oksana, hear me out
And in a tragic hour
With an unmalicious soul,
Say a prayer for him and me
To the Blessed Virgin.
All people live with lies,
Don't pay them any heed!
They'll besmirch my fortune
With an evil tale,
And they'll laugh at you.
And you won't know the truth;
You'll command a trial

For your mother —
And you know the bitterness of tears
When you know you're not at fault.
Learn it all: I'll tell you of my life,
I'll not conceal joys and sorrows,
May it be for you a lesson!

My kin I did not know,
I grew up in a foster home.
A good family of strangers
Loved me as their own.
As I grew I heard
That my real mother, dying,
Asked them not to leave me
Even as she left me, a little baby child.
But who she was, what they called her,
I later could not learn.
And I grew just fine, I grew;
Me they called an orphan,
Then dubbed me as a beauty,
They loved me, cherished me,
And even tried to marry me! But I…
Oh, to know my fate!
Among people I took pride
With my gift of beauty.
My liberty,
My maiden's liberty, I guarded.
And how harshly people recompensed!
I did not weave my braid for long —
They covered it.[118] That is how it was.
In spring, the aging lord had died,
By summertime the young lordling
Came into the village.
The handsome man from Muscovy
Brought for me his evil charms;
And I loved the merriment,
And Makoviy's Day I'll not forget
Until I reach the grave.
The shining sun,
The sunset… then the night!..

My child! My daughter!
Blame not me, the hapless.
I brought shame and sorrow,
I cursed the awful day of Makoviy,
And the day of birth!
We were in the field, reaping rye;
Having finished, we went home,
My friends all sang and danced,
And like an empress I led all,
With a loosened braid,
And a garland weaved of rye and wheat.
The young lordling met us.
None adored me like he did.
I quivered, softly walked,
While he watched and smiled,
Oh, I was so happy!
My heart was filled
With such sweet dreams…
On the third day… O my solace!
Why did you abandon me?
On the third day… and I
Was in the mansion like
A lady at a feast.
My wealth did not last long.
I awoke one early winter morn —
All was empty. And the servants…
May they be judged by God!
With a smirk they turned me out
And locked the door behind me.
I sat down here beside this stump,
And cried a long, long time…
I later took the barely beaten
Path into the village I'd forgotten,
And there I met a fate most bitter:
They would not let me in a house,
All the people laughed at me
And with a plain black scarf
They wrapped my silken braid,
And I left the village for another,
Crying on a different road.

118 See glossary or fn. 28

O Oksana! In a tailored silken coat
Or in a plain gray peasant's jacket,
People all are cruel.
I walked to many villages,
But sorrow went before me.
I cried bitterly, I prayed,
And still people laughed at me.
An unwed mother, a fool they called me,
Even beggars shunned me.
In all of dear Ukraine
There was for me no place.
I feared not sleeping in a deep dark forest
Or an open field:
There in liberty with no witness
I could freely sing and cry.
For a song, albeit sad,
Relieves the pain and sorrow.
Thanks be to a needy single woman,
Sightless just as I,
Who taught me how to sing a song,
And I sing it, crying,
And will sing it till I die.
My child! My Oksana!
Soon I will stop crying.
Remember well my song
And sing it, just as I,
It will ease the aching heart.
A gorgeous spring ensued,
Birds twittered, all awoke,
And laughter filled the air —
I alone had failed to smile
At the blessed spring.
It had brought me tears.
I fell ill along the road,
And somehow made it to a hamlet…
And at the meager hamlet
You first saw the Lord's creation.
Oh, how abundant are the joys of God
For our tears and for our troubles!
Your first sound… But no,
I cannot bear it…
No… Kiss me, Oksana!
I can't express that sacred bliss
Granted just to mothers
To feel within their souls.
It exceeds all human happiness.
And how hapless and deprived
Is a childless woman…
My happiness returned with you,
I reveled in the spring,
Again I loved the flowers,
Again I treasured flowers.
I awoke at sunrise.
You slept upon my bosom.
At times, unseen by none,
I'll sneak into the woods,
I'll find a flower
And sit with you beside that flower.
You sleep softly, and it blossoms,
And I took pride in you
Beside the blooming flower.
At times, I'll pinch
A rosy, glowing petal
And place it oh so quietly
Upon your little cheek… I'll place it,
Then with my tears I wash you.
You were rosier than a flower
And glowed brighter than the morning star.
Such was the goodness that the Lord created
In all the rosy blossoms
And in your pretty face.
But… no matter how I charmed you,
No matter how I sang to you,
Not matter how I played with you,
Misfortune trailed me close behind.
I could not pride myself in you;
I had none to share
Your youthful beauty with.
You babbled "mama,"
A better word I did not know,
Just as now you do not know.
I could not take you through the village,
Yet I felt no shame —
Let the people stare,
If that is what they wish!
I exchanged the shame for love.

I feared showing you
How children play together,
I feared seeing how a
Child hugged its weary father.
Time thus passed; you grew,
And it was pleasant to behold
How you began to walk.
But for the sins of youth
The Lord has deemed
That I will bear much bitter sorrow
Till I reach the grave.
The world began to dim...
O my dear God!
I stand beside the grave,
Grant to me Your wisdom
To see God's lovely world,
As I depart the sinful earth,
And to glance at least
Upon the place where I will sleep,
Where I will sleep forever!
. . . .

I then lost my sight. A stream of tears,
Earnest prayers — nothing,
Nothing moved the Lord Creator,
And all that once amused the soul,
Seemed locked up in a grave.
What happened then I do not know,
If people laughed or not.
Recalling all my troubles,
I'm only sorry that God's world
Did not vanish
In the haven of my youth;
I'd have then known nothing:
Not my sweet curtailed fortune,
Nor even my own heart.
Clinging to my endless sorrow
Is yet another bitter sorrow.
You're nice, Oksana,
This I know, and I'm sorry —
That your ugly dream
Came to you so soon."

OKSANA

Does it
Portend for us some evil?

BLIND WOMAN

It strikes more fear in me
Than my many troubles,
And for you it's more alarming still.
You'll succumb to people too
Just as I succumbed. You don't know
That soon among them
You will meet a snake,
An awful, awful snake!
And you'll closely follow it,
You'll leave me with my worries,
Just as I forgot and left
The folks who fed and raised me.

OKSANA

Did you not know of what would be,
That wicked people yearned to laugh,
That he's an evil man,
That he'll abandon you?
Mommy, mommy,
You said things that frighten so.
And where is he, my evil father?
You said I'd see him here.
I sit here many years with you —
And still he does not come.
He'll not come, he left,
He loved you not, it seems.
Why is it that you loved him?
Let's leave this village,
I'm now frightened.

Blind Woman

O Oksana!
Where will we hide from people?
Where will I hide your youth?
But he'll come, and then,
I'll die in peace.

The unsighted woman hushed.
Oksana, in her youthful sadness,
Placed her tawny head
Upon her mother's lap.
"Sleep, — she said, — Oksana!
I'll sing a quiet song,
I'll sing your favorite song,
How brothers sold a brother
To a strange and far-off land."
She caressed and gently kissed her,
Reading softly from the Book of Psalms:

"May the Holy Virgin guard you
From wicked tribulations,
From the storms of life!
May your dreams be sweet,
Like the pristine melodies
Of sainted angels up in heaven.

May the tempter dare not enter
The loving temple of the heart,
And may the guardian angel
Lead you past a thorny path
To the lap of Paradise.

May the Blessed Virgin guard you,
From any evil miseries,
From any hostile snares,
May the Blessed Virgin
Grant Her cover most divine
To you my child, my beloved!"

In the morning young Oksana,
Like a misty autumn dawn,
Sat pale and sad
At the anguished sightless woman's feet
And grieved with all her wholesome soul.
The blind one sang the same old song,
With the same old troubled heart.
The days don't quickly flow for them.
The sun does not shine brightly.
Springtime came, and as before,
The empty courtyard came alive,
Teeming with vitality.
The lordling came for relaxation,
The anguished pair was split.
Oksana's locked inside a house,
The sightless one was given clothes,
Told to leave,
And strictly ordered not to loiter
Beside the noble's manor.
And the wretch was happy
That things turned out as she had dreamed.
"Now, — the sightless woman thought, —
Now my dear Oksana
Is protected from ill weather,
That will make her happy."
She left the village,
The rekindled village,
Her favorite song upon her lips,
And praying to the Queen of Heaven,
That She may guard her daughter well.

. . . .

Oksana sadly sits
In an ornate sunny room,
Dressed in velvet, gold brocade,
But admiring not the image
That she sees in giant mirrors.
Months follow all the days.
As befits a lady, all for her is ready,
With a servant at the door.
The lordling too brings sweets to her,
He gives her pearls and diamonds
And on his knees he pleads
That he not be called a lord or father.

. . . .

Why all this?! She cried…
The nightingale sang of spring,

Though he chirped not as before,
When he sang before the morning star,
Before the village stirred,
And when the small Oksana
Made a shelter from some weeds
To shade her loving mother
From the burning sun,
And when she went to bathe
Into the valley
To then adorn herself with
Rue and periwinkle
And to meet by chance
A handsome dark-haired Kozak.
A grievous evening was then made
More grievous by the night.
It was hard on her,
She sat there feeling sorry
For her penury of yore.
And she hears a song
Drifting from beyond the gate,
It's sung softly, sadly
By a once familiar voice:

"A river flowed across a field,
Eagles drank the water.
Growing with her mother
Was a lovely daughter,
Whom the Kozaks loved.
They all loved her, they all saw her,
They sought her hand in marriage,
But one among them disappeared.
Where, they looked,
And no one knows.
He settled in a shady home
Beyond the quiet Danube."

Silently Oksana trembled,
Every sound brought forth a dream.
"He's not forgotten, — whispered she, —
He'll not leave an orphan..."
From her heart with every sound
Leapt dark and mournful yearning,
She saw herself already
In a Kozak's loving arms.
Already past the orchard, past the gate,
In a field already... there's freedom...
There is paradise...

. . . .

"Hold him! Hold him!
Catch him! Shoot!" —
Boomed the lordling's husky voice.
And a shot rang out across the field.
"They killed him!! — cried Oksana. —
They killed him!! And he loved me so.
He loved me!!"
Seeming lifeless, she collapsed.
It was not a dream. The singer
Was a Kozak, a free and dashing
Haidamak. Oksana waited long
For the true love of her heart,
But the wait was all in vain.
The pleasant sound did not repeat.
It did not whisper hope again,
He was merely dreamt,
And dreamt again
To upset her youthful mind
With that fruitless reverie...

"O birds, my sisters all so free,
Fly off to the distant country,
Where my dark-eyed sweetheart lives,
Where my mother sits beside a road.
Her hands, her feet all racked in pain,
And yet I curse my fate,
Awaiting freedom from some field."

Thus in winter sang the poor Oksana
Beside a window in the parlor.
Confinement bleached her rosy cheeks,
Her linen cleansed with tears.
"Here, perhaps, — she whispered, —
My mother once awoke in winter,
And I... her child... and I..."
She shuddered falling silent.
Darkness loomed across the field.
From the mist arose a bloody crimson moon.

Oksana glanced with trepidation
And feared the bloody light,
Then quickly left the surly window,
Saying not a word.
. . . .
The hounds all barked,
The horns all blared,
From the gate spilled noise and laughter —
From the field the hunt returned,
And the lord advances toward the martyr,
Shamelessly besotted.
. . . .
The poor unsighted woman knew nothing
Of her daughter's plight,
Stumbling, as a stranger guided her
Among unfriendly people.
She went to Kyiv and Pochayiv,[119]
To plead with blessed saints,
Also hoping that a prayer
Would ease her suffering soul.
She furtively returned in winter
To the village of her hardship.
The heart ached of something dire,
Forewarning in a secret tongue
Of grievous and ill-fated news.
With fear and sorrow in her heart
She softly sneaks along
An old familiar path.
There's grave-like silence all around.
A cheerless pale moon
Shined from high above,
Illuminating the snowy blanket
On the lifeless, sinful earth.
Then in the distance suddenly
Was the awful sight of fire.
The poor and sightless woman walks,
Seeing not our evils nor our sanctions,
And arriving at the gate
That she had left in spring. O God!
What does she hear? Crackling, crashing,
Screaming, shouting and a drawn-out din,
Then her face was struck by heat.

She trembles. Not far away
She hears a voice... My God!
Whose voice is it that you recognized?
Recognized... it's chilling... it's Oksana!
At the spot where they both sat
For many years and grieved,
She sits again, unhappy,
Gaunt and barely clothed,
Rocking like a babe in arms
A large and bloody knife.
And she whispers frightfully:
"Be still, my child, be still,
While the bread rolls bake
We'll partake of mead,
We'll recall the lord."

(She sings)

"The lord and master keeps two fancy coats,
The third one is a peasant's,
  Yet early morn
  The lord was murdered,
Murdered in his grove.
He was killed by haidamaks,
They divvied up his coats:
This one gets a fancy coat,
That one gets a fancy coat,
And the third one gets the peasant's.
And the lord was left without
His peasant coat,
Buried in the cold white snow.
  Right on, haidamaks!"

BLIND WOMAN
Oksana, where are you?

---

119 *Pochayiv* — A large Orthodox monastery and Christian pilgrimage site in the Ternopil Region of Western Ukraine.

OKSANA

O be quiet!
Let me lull my baby boy!

(She sings)

"Hush-a-bye, hush-a-bye, my little child,
From a field to a dreamy forest,
I will bring you freedom,
I will bring you fortune.

Hush-a-bye, hush-a-bye, my little child,
I will go a hiking
In a steamy pinewood forest
To pick a pail of berries.

Hush-a-bye, hush-a-bye, my little child,
Beside a beaten path
They'll break your little arms
And your feet so fair.
Hush-a-bye, hush-a-bye, my little child,
Dark brows and hazel eyes
Turn pale
In an oaken casket.

Sleep, my child, sleep,
May you sleep forever,
I'll go to the fair alone,
From the Jew
I'll get some blood
To restore your health."

Ah, he fell asleep! Take him now.
Oo! How black he is… just look!

BLIND WOMAN

Oksana! Where are you?
What is wrong with you?

OKSANA

(Walks up quickly to her.)
And where are you going? Look,
What a happy banquet for the lord!
The lord, however, won't be feasting —
I laid him down to sleep.
Only you were absent.
I set the fire, let's go dancing.

(Sings and slowly dances)

"Hey, hey, there's no trouble!
Tears are also water,
Tears extinguish sorrow,
And I'm sorry for the sorrow,
I'm sorry for my grief,
Sorry for my friend,
My dark and gloomy melancholy…"

My… my… But no, not that…
It is now so happy, bright,
But, it seems, bowed down in sorrow.

(Sings and dances.)

"I sowed weeds expecting grief,
But the valley bloomed with guelder rose.
As for me, the beauty,
Viper earrings in my ears
Dangle down my back and hiss.
The Kozak truly loved,
The Kozak gave a gift of earrings.
Mother rested in a grave,
And I, you know,
Just went and went
Along an open road.
And behind me, always after me,
Reapers came in threes, in fours
Cutting weeds and singing…"

BLIND WOMAN

My poor Oksana, pray,
Pray to God, you sing
Such awful songs!

OKSANA

And do you, mama, want to laugh?
For many years you laughed,
I giggled, mama —
We can cry at least one night.

BLIND WOMAN

My child, O my daughter!
Take pause, my Oksana,
You've been scoffing.

OKSANA

Who? Me?
I've not scoffed! Look!
Watch the rafters fall.
Ha!.. ha!.. ha!.. He-he-he-he!
Let's go dancing, he's not here,
He'll not stand between us.

(Sings and Dances)

"There's sedge beside a road,
And pears amid a swamp,
I was smitten by a Kozak,
I gave away my soul.
But the Kozak,
Even so,
Loved me not
And strangled me,
Then hid me in the cold dank ground.
In a darkened cold dank house
A black witch lay down
With me to sleep.
She laughed, embraced,
Ate and gnawed at me.
She lit a fire,
Sang, danced, jumped and shouted:
Fire, fire, fire!
Coming through the valley,
All converged around the fire,
We reveled
And we laughed:
Ha-ha-ha, tra-la-la-la,
Not a stake remained,
Nothing but the resin
Of the devil's candle!
Across the valley walks a lamb.
Go not into the forest, Kozak,
Do not take the beaten path, Ivan,
Do not carry any gifts
For the lurking serpent,
For the black and slithering viper.
An evil sorceress
Will erase your handsome brows
And burn your hazel eyes."

BLIND WOMAN

Come to your senses,
O my daughter, my Oksana!
You sing of only evil.
Let's go to the village:
It's now dreadful here.

OKSANA

Let's go to the village, I feel stuffy here.
I dance barefoot, like on embers,
Upon the crimson snow,
Let's go to the village,
Where we'll spend the night.
And who will let us in to sleep?
The people are afraid of us, you know.
We'll caress instead the wolves
Roaming in the forest,
Since people lie that wolves are bad,
Wolves are fond of us — that's right!
Remember, you once told me...
I've forgotten all... My Kozak,
My hazel-eyed... I loved him,
And he, a Kozak, loved me back.
In the dark of night
He went into the verdant orchard,
Where I strolled about.
Oh, it was so much fun!
When he, caressing, kissed me,
Whispering sweet nothings!
You kissed me not like he
My dear and precious did,
My sweetheart, my beloved!
. . . .
You said that he's not evil,
But he, your lord, is ruthless,
Your lord the tyrant killed him,
Because I loved him so.
Because he loved me truly,
The villain shackled him in irons.
I spoke nothing of it, even not to you.
He vanished, without a trace he vanished,
Like my vanished maiden's beauty.
And you heard of wonders...
He was an otaman of the haidamaks
And this knife he gave to me.
He came...

BLIND WOMAN

Guide me!
Let's go faster!

OKSANA

Guide you where?
Toward the swamp? The woods?
Wait! Wait!
I'll guide you toward the village,
Where all is overgrown by weeds,
Where graves and crosses
Stand instead of houses,
Where my sweetheart had moved in
To a parlor dark and dank.

BLIND WOMAN

Let's go quickly. God be with you!
Cross yourself!

OKSANA

I crossed myself,
Cried bitterly and prayed,
But God rejected all my crosses,
And my heartfelt prayers.
Yes, He rejected. And do you recall?
No you don't recall, you forgot.
And I remember that you taught me,
A little youngster, to suck blood,
And to also read *Our Father.*

Blind Woman
My God, Oksana, pray,
You speak dreadfully!

Oksana
Yes, yes.
I speak dreadfully, what of it!
You did not fear to sit
Beneath a fence at night
And you sat there twenty years —
Let's go sit there once again.
Let's go, mama, we will sing,
Before the people waken.
We'll sing of how the Kozak
Prepared to fight the Horde,
And how he left his girl,
And how he loved another.
After all, it's fun —
To leave in flames a leaf of lovage
In a foreign land.

(Sings quietly)

"Float, O boat, float beyond the Danube,
Beyond the Danube I, the youth, will dance
With young departed Kozaks,
With departed Kozaks."
A pox, a pox, a pox on me!
Let's go quickly. No, wait!
I lost my shoes somewhere.
And the shoes are quite expensive,
Yet they burned my feet, but nonetheless
I do not miss them, and barefoot
We will reach the grave...

(Sings)

"A little birdie flitted
'Cross the meadow to the forest,
It lost a feather
In the Danube.
Float, O feather, float,
Let the water take you..."
I was silent, always silent,
As he whispered and he kissed me.
He promised necklaces with ducats.
You said not to take them; why?
They surely could be used for choking.
But, you know what? Let's go bathing
In the river, we'll drown,
We'll then be pikes in water.
And in a meadow birds have freedom,
And flying makes them happy,
But I'm so happy in captivity
To lose my maidenhood.
Am I some sort of sinner,
Is it poison that I cook?
No, you know, I'm not a sinner,
I trusted everyone, and all,
But who trusted in my faith?
Now it's not the same. It's flying, flying!
No, you, the cursed, won't fly away,
I will strangle you! Wait —
A crimson viper! A crimson viper!
It will fall to pieces later...
Ha! ha! he!!!..

Then, like vengeance in the flesh
She flew off with loosened braid,
Knife in hand and screaming,
And with a final shriek
She vanished in the flames.
Again, a piercing scream.
The sightless woman shuddered
Then gently crossed herself,
Whispering, "Amen, amen, amen!"
Drawn-out din replaced the screams,
A wall came down,
The din resounded,
Falling silent in the callous valley,
As if deep within a frigid soul.
The blazing fire raged,
The poor and sightless woman stood

Amid the smoke and snowy cinders
Waiting for Oksana.
Unwittingly and quivering she softly
Sang a dirge.[120]
In vain the sightless woman waited
For her dear Oksana;
She left the burning village,
Singing her beloved psalm:
"As I weep,
Who is there for me to summon
That would share my pain, my longing,
Whom am I to serenade
With my lovely native song
In a distant foreign land?"

St. Petersburg, First Part of 1842

Blind Woman with Daughter, 1842

120 *Dirge* — Reference to *With the Saints Give Rest (So sviatymy upokoi)*, a so-called kontakion, or memorial hymn honoring a saint.

HAMALIYA[121]

"O there's nothing, neither wind, nor wave
From our Ukraine!
Do councils counsel there
On how to raid the Turk?
We hear nothing in this foreign land.
Blow, O wind, blow across the sea
From the Great Ukrainian Meadow,[122]
Dry our tears, mute our chains,
Blow away our longing.
Rise, O azure sea, rise beneath the longboats
Bearing Kozaks, as their hats
Peek through the waves,
And bring them to this shore to free us.
O God, dear God, if even not to free us,
Bring them here from our Ukraine,
We'll hear the glory, Kozak glory,
We'll hear it and we'll die."

That's how Kozaks in Scutari[123] sang,
The poor souls sang and tears poured down,
Kozak tears to ease their longing.
The Bosporus even shuddered,
For he'd not heard of Kozaks crying.
The broad expanse then groaned,
The gray bull shook his hide,
And on his ribs he sent a wave,
Roaring, far across the azure sea.
What the Bosporus roared,
The sea roared even louder,
And rushed the message to the Lyman,
And the Lyman passed the word
Of anguish to the Dnipro River.

Our strapping grandpa
Roared with laughter,
Foam ran down his whiskers.
"Are you asleep, do you hear,
My brother Meadow?
Sister Khortytsia?"[124]
Khortytsia shouted
With the Meadow: "I hear, I hear!"
And longboats cloaked the Dnipro,
As Kozaks sang a song:

"There's a lavish house
Among the Turks upon the distant shore.
Roll on, blue sea, say hey!
Roar, crush the cliffs,
We're going for a visit.

The Turk has dollars in his pockets,
In his pockets he's got ducets,
It's not pockets we will empty.
We go to butcher, burn
And to free our brothers.

Janissaries[125] in the land of Turks,
A pasha on a throne
Hey, ho, enemies!
We all travel light!
Ours is freedom, ours is glory!"

As they sail, they sing,
The sea hearkens to the wind.
Up front is Hamaliya

---

121 *Hamaliya* — A composite literary figure invented by Shevchenko.

122 *Great Ukrainian Meadow (Velykiy luh)* — Grassy lowland that stretched along the left bank of the Dnipro. It ran near the Zaporizhian Sich, the Kozak island stronghold in the Dnipro Rapids. The Rapids and Meadow were largely submerged during the Soviet period by hydroelectric dams.

123 See glossary or fn. 54

124 See glossary or fn. 55

125 *Janissary* – A Christian from the Balkans or Ukraine taken from parents at a young age, converted to Islam and raised to serve in an elite Ottoman military unit.

Leading all the longboats.
Hamaliya, the heart grows faint:
The sea's gone mad,
But will not frighten! And they
Hid behind the waves —
Behind the mountains.

Byzantium dozes in a harem —
In a paradise.
Scutari dozes too; the Bosporus gurgles
As if mad, moaning some, then wailing;
He feels like waking up Byzantium.
"Don't awaken him, Bosporus:
You'll have trouble;
I'll fill your pale ribs with sand,
I'll bury you in silt! — roars the azure sea. —
Don't you know the guests
I carry to the Sultan?"
Thus the sea prevailed
(It loved the mustached daring Slavs).
The Bosporus had second thoughts.
The land of Turks dozed on.
Dozing in a harem was a lazy sultan.
Only in Scutari, in a crypt,
Poor Kozaks did not doze.
What are they awaiting?
In their native way
They plead in shackles unto God,
As waves roar and break
Upon the other shore.

"O dear God of our Ukraine!
Don't allow free Kozaks
To perish fettered in an alien land,
It's shameful here, it's shameful there —
To rise up from a foreign coffin,
To attend Your righteous judgment,
To come with hands in iron,
To stand with all in chains as Kozaks..."
"Beat and butcher!"
Kill the heathen-infidel!"
They shout beyond the wall. Who's that?
Hamaliya, the heart grows faint:
Scutari's going mad!
"Butcher! Beat!" Hamaliya
Shouts upon the fortress.

Scutari roars with cannon fire,
Enemies rage and yell,
The Kozaks are intrepid —
Lifeless janissaries rolled.
Hamaliya romps around Scutari —
In hell itself he dances,
He himself destroys the jail,
Breaks through all the chains.
"Fly free, gray birds,
Go claim your spoils
At the market square!"
The falcons shuddered,
For it's been a long, long time
Since they heard
That Christian language.
And the night had shuddered too:
The old mum had
Never seen a Kozak payback.
Fear not, behold the Kozak banquet.
It's dark all over like a weekday,
But it's quite a feast.
It's not thieves that dine
With Hamaliya wordlessly on lard
Without some shish-kebab.
"We'll make light!"
Scutari blazes to the clouds
Along with masts of warships.
Byzantium stirred,
Popped its eyes, clenched its teeth
And set its sails to help.

Byzantium roars and rages,
It takes the beach in hand;
It took it, shrieked and stood —
Silenced by the bloody knives.
Scutari burns like hell,
Blood flows through the market,
Filling up the Bosporus.
Like blackbirds in a grove,

The daring Kozaks fly.
No one in this world escapes them!
Fire's fury does not burn the furious.
They then destroy the walls, and carry
To their waiting longboats
Gold and silver by the hatful.
Scutari burns, the work winds down,
The boys come gather,
Lighting pipes from the inferno,
Boarding all the longboats —
And off they sailed,
Slicing waves like crimson mountains.
Along they sail, as if from home,
And it seems they're frolicking,
And, of course they're Zaporizhians,
So they sing a song:

"Our otaman Hamaliya,
Is a mighty otaman,
He took the boys
To frolic out at sea,
To frolic out at sea,
To win glory,
And to free his brothers
From a Turkish prison.
Oh, Hamaliya came,
He came down to Scutari,
Where Zaporizhian brothers
Sit awaiting punishment.
Oh, but Hamaliya shouted:
"Brothers, we will live,
We'll live, drink wine,
Beat the jannisary,
And we'll cover Kozak homes
With kilims made of velvet!"
The Kozaks flew to reap the rye,
They reaped the rye, they stacked it,
And sang their song together:
"Glory be to you, otaman Hamaliya,
Across the world you're great,
You're great across the world,
And all throughout Ukraine,
Because you did not let the brethren
Perish in a foreign land!"

Along they sail; sailing aft
Is the mighty Hamaliya:
Like an eagle caring for his eaglets.
From the Dardanelles blows a wind,
But Byzantium won't give chase:
She's afraid that Monk[126]
Could light Galata[127] once again,
Or that Hetman Ivan Pidkova
Could call the sea for yet another feast.
Along they sail, the waves turn red,
Backlit by the sun;
The sea ahead is calm,
It gurgles and it hums.
Hamaliya, the wind blows...
Just ahead, the sea is ours!..
And behind the waves they hid —
Behind the crimson mountains.

St. Petersburg, October – Early November, 1842

126 *Monk* — Reference to Hetman Petro Kononevych Konashevych-Sahaidachny (1570?-1622), who fought successfully against Turkey and Muscovy. He died of wounds suffered in battle and was laid to rest at a monastery in Kyiv.

127 *Galata* — A neighborhood of Istanbul located on the Golden Horn.

FUNERAL FEAST

To Princess Barbara Nikolavyevna Repnina in Memory of November 9, 1843[128]
(From the Russian)

DEDICATION

A soul with brilliant purpose
Should suffer, love, endure;
The gift of God, the inspiration,
Should be bathed in tears.
That word for you is clear!..
For you I laid down gladly
All my worldly fetters,
And I solemnly poured tears again
Into the sounds you hear.
Your good angel blessed me
With undying wings
And awakened dreams of paradise
With soft and subtle words.

Yahotyn, November 11, 1843

Seeing ye have purified your souls in obeying the truth through the Spirit unto unfeigned love of the brethren, see that ye love one another with a pure heart fervently: Being born again, not of corruptible seed, but of incorruptible, by the word of God, which liveth and abideth forever. For all flesh is as grass, and all the glory of man as the flower of grass. The grass withereth, and the flower thereof falleth away: But the word of the Lord endureth forever. And this is the word which by the gospel is preached unto you.

First Epistle of Peter 1: Verses 22-25

Twelve place settings round a table,
Twelve wine goblets standing tall;
Times goes by,
Yet no one comes. Perhaps
The friends forgot each other
They've not forgotten — at the chosen time,
They gathered and fulfilled a vow,
Singing *Eternal Memory*[129] as one,
Holding a funeral feast —
And all parted once again.
There were twelve; all were young,
Attractive, strong; in the year just past
They laid to rest their finest friend
And on that day planned yearly wakes,
Till they ascend to meet with him.
"Joyful brotherhood! The unity of love

---

128 *Barbara Nikolavyevna Repnina (1808-91)* — Russian princess, writer and very close friend of Shevchenko. She was known to love the poet, promoted his career and petitioned authorities to ease his exile. He drew two portraits of her. November 9, 1843 commemorates the day she gave him her handwritten copy of his poem, *The Blind Woman.*

129 *Eternal Memory (Vichnaya pamyat)* — A funeral hymn and tribute to the deceased.

You faithfully respected on this sinful earth;
Gather, friends, as today you gathered,
Gather long and sing a song
Of freedom on this world of slavery!"

Blessed is your path so short,
O impoverished, unknown visitor!

With wondrous power of the Lord
You begot celestial fire,
The fire of love in people's hearts.
A blessed soul!
Even with your life so brief
You sanctified God's freedom;
Amid the vale of slavery
You silently proclaimed all of freedom's joy.
When a brother craved a brother's blood —
You inspired love in strangers.
With a towering word you showed
People freedom in their brotherhood:
You rang the bell for peace on earth;
And you, departing, blessed
Love's spirit and free thought!
O chosen soul, why
So brief your stay with us?
Here it was so hard for you, so crowded!
Though you loved this prison,
You, so pure,
Looked mournfully upon conceited people.
But the timeless King of kings
Was an angel short;
And you're in heaven
Standing by the throne of God
In eternal glory,
Gazing at this dark and evil world of ours
With melancholy innocence.
I stand in awe before you,
I look with silent trembling;
With a grieving soul I pray,
I pray as if before an angel!
Descend and heal me!
Instill, inspire a mind gone cold
With but a few pristine and sunny thoughts;
For at least a single instant,
Illuminate the heart's dark dungeon,
Disperse the gloom of stubborn notions.
Truthfully, with quiet words,
Tell me of your earthly blessings,
Teach me how to rule
The haughty hearts of others,
Teach me how to rule my own,
Now debauched and wicked...
Share with me the secret teaching
Of loving prideful people
And of short and humble speech
To allay the people's butchers,
I'll then herald a prophetic hymn,
Spread truth amid the depths
And fearlessly I'll lift
My fading eyes toward heaven.
And in the hour of my final pain,
Send me faithful friends
To set my cold and dying hands,
And to selflessly shed unction
From their friendly eyes.
I'll bless my grief,
I'll kindly grin at death,
And expecting life forever
I'll rise toward you in heaven.

Blessed is your path so short,
O visitor so unsung and wonderful!

He grew up in a needy, unknown family;
As an orphan
He encountered hardship early;
He took on ill rebukes
To get his daily bread...
In his heart a serpent gnawed a wound...
His youthful dream vanished
Like a frightened dove;
Like a thief, impatiently, melancholy lurked
Within his broken heart,
With voracious lips
It sucked his blood so innocent...
The soul strained, the soul wept,

Asking for its freedom… Reason burned,
Pride boiled in the blood…
He quivered. He grew numb…
His hand, contracting, trembled…
Oh, if he could grasp
With his embittered hand the globe
And all its earthly vipers;
To grasp, to crush, to cast off into hell!..
He'd be happy, he'd be glad.
He cackled like an angry demon,
And for an awful instant,
The world blazed in every corner;
In a frenzy he grew numb, he cried,
The soul was anguished in an awful dream;
The soul was deadened, but all around,
The earth, the Lord's creation,
Expecting spring,
Was blooming and exulting
In a verdant vestment.
The soul was cheerfully awakening,
And it awoke… He fell in tears
And kissed the ground,
Like the bosom of his mother!..

He's again the pristine angel
Come from Paradise above,
Though to all on earth he is a stranger.
He glanced toward heaven: "Oh, how bright,
How superbly beautiful!
Oh, how free I'll be up there!.."
And his eyes in wondrous semi-sleep
Fix upon the vault of heaven,
And in its endless depth
He revels with his simple soul.

At a broad and sacred altitude,
Alone and like a white kerchief,
A small bright cloud
Drifts off in the distance.
"O cloudlet, cloudlet, who carries
You so smoothly and so high?
What are you anyway?
Why dress so lavishly and dearly?
Where were you sent, by whom?.."
And in the bright-lit sky,
The cloudlet quietly dissipated.
His dejected gaze he lowered
To the darkened forest…
"And where's the world's edge,
The edge of heaven
And the ends of planet earth?.."
He took a deep, deep breath,
Not a child's breath, then he let it out;
As if he buried hope within
His lonesome heart.

Who lacks faith — lacks hope!
Hope is God, and faith is light.

"Don't go out, my beacon!
Penetrate the hazy soul,
Fortify me with your strength,
And brighten with celestial light
The thorny cheerless path.
Bestow the spirit with Your shrine,
Fill it with a sacred muse,
And I'll proclaim the gift,
The gift decreed by You!.."

Hope he did not bury,
Like a dove divine, the spirit rose,
Casting light upon the murky heart,
Upon the vale of life;
He went in search of life and fortune,
Already passing by his native field,
His village now concealed…
He somehow suddenly felt sorrow,
And a tear broke through his lashes,
The heart was tight and torn.
We somehow feel sorrow
For our years gone by,
And there is also something
In our native land…
And he, a pauper, is a stranger
Here and everywhere. Our planet
End to end, our lovely world,

This paradise on earth,
Are for him completely foreign.
Silently he fell
And kissed the earth
Like he would his mother's bosom,
Then crying, softly and despondently,
He said a prayer for the road...
And with a free and steadfast gait
He left... And disappeared behind a hill.
Oh, the tears he shed
Beyond the border of his native land,
Wandering as a pauper orphan!
What an awful price he paid
To make his mind aware,
To sustain his virgin heart.

To endure the trials of a grueling life
Without small-minded blame,
To plumb the depths of passion,
To truly understand the lives of people,
To read all black pages,
To see each illicit deed...
And to sustain an eagle's flight,
And to keep the dove's heart pure!
Behold the man!..[130] To live without a roof,
(Even the sun won't warm an orphan),
To know people — and to love!
To sympathize not spitefully
With their reproachful deeds,
Not blaspheming in the dark,
Like the king of reason.
Poor and wretched,
To appease the mighty fool
For the sake of daily bread.
To think, to feel, to live!..
There's the awful, blessed drama!..
He lived through it, crying,
He did not ponder daily exploits
Like lessons from a novel;
He bared none of his heart's anguish,
Nor any of a thousand nightmares,
Nor did he allow a haze of the Byronic;
He did not deride his friends
As a paltry crowd;
He did not censure pomp and power,
Like N, he's a cautious crier,
And he who ponders without end
The thoughts of Kant, Galileo,
And the cosmopolitan man of wisdom,
But judges people without mercy,
Sparing not his closest kin;
That's a false prophet!
His judgments —
Half-baked thoughts and semi-nonsense!..

Pondering life's meaning,
And God's great and final judgment,
In a mood of contemplation
He raised his teary gaze
At nature's sacred beauty.
"How all things are in harmony!" —
He whispered
And recalled his native land;
He prayed for all things living
To the God of truth and justice,
And with a gentle thought
He pondered deeds of peoples
And the deeds of his own land,
Then cried quite bitterly...
"O blessed! Blessed land of mine!
How will I help you, crying?
You are chained, so too am I.
Telling tyrants
The great word of God's freedom —
They'll not understand!
They'll stone to death the prophet
On his native gorgeous field!
They'll wipe away the lofty mounds
And denounce them with a word of evil!
They killed and crushed you,

---

130 *Behold the man* — Reference to John 19:5. "Then came Jesus forth, wearing the crown of thorns, and the purple robe. And Pilate saith unto them, Behold the man!"

And forbid the exaltation
Of all Your splendid deeds!
O God! Just and mighty,
You have miraculous power.
Bring about celestial glory
And create a sacred wonder:
Command the dead to rise,
Bless with Your all-mighty word
A new and solemn deed,
For redemption of the earth,
An earth profaned, forgotten,
An earth once happy,
And watered since
With blood most pure."
Like clouds, the thoughts dispersed,
And tears poured down like rain!..

Blessed in this world is he, who
With a hungry brother
Freely shares some table scraps,
And can check the evil man
With a firm command!
Free and blessed!..
Yet he who looks not with his eye,
But with his soul at people's intrigues,
And can only cry alone in anguish —
O righteous God, take his eyes away!..
Your mountains and your seas,
All of nature's beauty
Will not purge his grief,
They'll not deliver freedom.
And he, martyr of a life so brief, saw all.
He felt and lived.
Having come to know the people,
He loved them all,
And grieved for them in private.
They came to love him too, *[131]
And he called them brothers;
He found friends, drawing them
With mystic power and enchantment;
Pensive among young friends, at times…
Like a wizard other times, a young prophet,
Unexpectedly astounding friends
With resounding, living words;
He blessed and fortified
Their bond of friendship.
He said the common good
Should be served through love,
To stand for people
With a noble valor and to slaughter evil.
The gala that is life, he said,
A great gala and God's gift,
Should itself be tested
And be gifted to the motherland.
He spoke of tender passion,
He spoke softly, sadly
Then fell silent..!
He left the table
In rebellious anguish
To shed some bitter tears.
The martyr shared with no one
A mystic sadness and deep sorrow
That happened not by chance.
With all their soul,
Friends loved him like their kin;
But he was always heartsick
With a cryptic sorrow,
And with free speech
He burned passionately among them.
But with guests
And marble backs
Glimmering amid a thousand flames,[132]
He sighed somewhat heavily,
Flying with his somber thoughts
To his native land, his lovely land,
To where no one waited for him,
Where none recalled his name
Or his humble fate.

---

131 * — Like a flower that blossomed in their swamp. *Note by Taras Shevchenko.*

132 … *amid a thousand flames* — Reference to a ball, where the light from candelabras reflected off the backs of women who wore fashionable gowns with open backs.

And he thought:
"What's my purpose here?
And what am I to do among them?
They all drink and dance,
They're all kinfolk among kin,
They're equals among equals,
And I!.." Quietly he leaves,
Walking home in thought;
No one leaves the home to greet him;
No one waits, all over he's alone...
Weariness and melancholy!..
On the joyous Easter holiday
He bears a century of sorrow.
He withers, withers, like blade of field grass,
Wearied in a foreign land with sorrow;
Silently he withers... What anguish
Burns within his heart so deeply?
"Woe is me, O woe! Why did I
Abandon all the joy of innocence
And my native land?
Why did I wander off, what have I achieved?
The joys of learning?
I curse them, curse them all!
For me they're maggots
That have drained my mind
And severed me from quiet joy.
With whom am I to share
My sorrow and my love?
To whom will I display
The wounds that tear my heart?
Here I have no mate,
Among them I'm a pauper,
Just a temp, a common laborer;
What will my dreams present a girl?
Love, ah, love alone!
She'd have enough to last three lifetimes,
Even for eternity!
I'd make her melt in my embrace!
Oh, how tenderly, how tenderly I'd love!"
And large tears, like sparks,
Threaded down the pale cheeks,
Moistening the frail chest, then drying.
"Oh, give me rest, smash my skull
And rip my chest, —
There are maggots there and vipers, —
Grant freedom! Let me fall asleep,
Fall asleep, quietly, forever!"

The hapless orphan suffered
Disconnected from his happy homeland,
Waiting so impatiently for it all to end.
His favorite dream —
To be useful to his homeland, —
Like a flower, to wilt together with it!
He suffered. Life's emptiness
Loomed ahead like an open grave:
With little feeling of fraternity,
There was no warmth from friends —
The soaring soul hungered for
The rays of sun from heaven.
The fire of love that God ignited
In a bashful woman's dove-like heart,
Where the eagle's soaring flight
Could stop and join the flame of love,
Of love so innocent;
Whom could he give refuge to
In the parlors
Of the heart and mind,
How can the helpless dove
Be sheltered from life's hardship;
And languishing, to rest the weary head
Upon the youthful breasts;
And, seizing up and crying,
To rest for but a minute
On life's bosom and on Eden's.
To drown the mind and soul
In her eyes and dreaminess,
And to melt the heart within a heart,
And to sink in self-forgetfulness.

But none would love requite;
None would be a pair;
The heart wept, ached
And faded out in emptiness.
Something of a future
Opened in his grievous dream,

And in the boundless heights
The holy heavens smiled.
He melted softly, silently,
Like a burning candle's wax.
And a mist veiled
The pensive eyes.
Glancing bashfully at times toward him,
A beauty worried furtively,
Long admiring him in secret.
And perhaps many maidens'
Hearts pined away for him,
But with secret will and higher power
A single path unto the grave
Is paved with jagged rocks.
Overcome, his bosom hurt,
The eyes grew dim, behind the cross
The border of eternity loomed darkly
In a gloomy void.
He lies quietly on the death bed
As the world grows dim.
His companions mournful counsel
Concerns his feeble soul.
Faithful friends by turns spent
A night beside their friend;
On any evening his lovely family gathered.
They gathered 'round the deathbed
On the final evening,
Staying till the early hours.
The eyes were being closed by dawn,
Cheerless friends were bowed by sleep,
When he suddenly enlivened
All their grievous dreams
With a learned flame
Of his recent fiery speeches;
And the friends cheered up
Their friend, saying he'll be
Singing once again among them
In a week, perhaps eight days.
"A new tune I'll not sing for you
About the glory of my homeland.
Compose instead a dour psalm
About a crowd of people's butchers;
And recall your friend, your predecessor,
With a hymn of freedom.
And for sins... his sins
Pray heartily to God...
And sing for me, my friends,
Peace to Thee be with the Saints!"

Around him stood the friends.
As he departed, they shed tears
Like children... quietly he sighed,
He sighed, sighed... And was no more!
The world lost a prophet,
And glory lost a son.

Come morn, friends
Sadly carried him to church
In an oaken casket.
Crying, they consigned
Their friend's remains
Unto the earth from which he came;
And placed a laurel wreath upon his grave
That they had washed
With tears of friendship;
Then quietly and dolefully they sang
Peace to Thee be with the Saints.

Friends that evening gathered
In a tavern at a round and common table;
Twelve of them sat quietly and ruefully:
Their hearts all ached as one.
Gloomy friends at a gloomy funeral feast!..
And I conducted such a feast.

They resolved together
To set the table yearly
On the day their friend departed;
So their friend beyond the grave
Would never be forgotten.
They gathered on the anniversaries
To recall their friend.
Many were no longer seen:
With every passing year
Places at the table thinned,
Death bereaved the friends of friends —

For many years there's now but one.
A single man, old and solemn,
Takes his place beside an empty table.
Sadly, he alone recalls
The pain and joy of younger years.
He sits long, quietly and cheerlessly.
He waits: is there not a single brother
Still among the living?
Alone and quietly,
He takes the road back home…
Quietly a door now opened
To the room where settings languish
On a round and empty table,
And the brother entered,
Forlorn and stooped by time!..
He surveyed the table sadly
With an empty gaze
And spoke his mind
In an affable rebuke:
"Lazybones! You see how
They fulfill their sacred
Law of brotherhood!
Today they did not come,
As if they left to sail the seas! —
Quietly he wipes his tears,
Sitting at the round fraternal table. —
If only one had come!"
The old man sits. And waits…

An hour passes, two go by,
It's time the old man
Should go home.
The old man rises: "They have,
Indeed, betrayed! Listen, —
Now speaking to the servant —
Drink some wine, my brother.
In any case, I can't; what's
Past is gone, —
Pray for their repose;
It's time that I head home!"
And again the tears rolled down.
The servant drank the wine,
But wondered.
"Give me, please, my hat…
It's such a bore to go back home!.." —
And quietly he left.

In a year on the appointed day,
The round and empty table was
Set again for twelve,
Twelve long-stemmed glasses
Graced the table.

The day arrives,
But no one comes,
They are forever
And forevermore forgotten.

Yahotyn, November 11-27, 1843

THE PLUNDERED MOUND

Placid earth, O my dear land,
O my dear Ukraine,
Why have you been plundered?
What is it, mama, that you're dying for?
Did you not pray to God
Before the break of dawn,
Did you not teach tradition

To your young uncertain children?
"I prayed, I worried,
Day and night I did not rest,
Caring for my little children
And teaching them our customs.
My blossoms,
My good children grew.
I too once reigned upon this world,
I reigned… O Bohdan![133]
O foolish son!
Look now upon your mother,
Upon your dear Ukraine,
Who sang of her misfortune
As she rocked you in the cradle,
Who awaited freedom
As she sang and cried.
O Bohdan, my dear Bohdan,
Had I known, I'd have
Choked you in the cradle,
Closed your eyes beside my heart.
My steppes are sold
To Jews and Germans,[134]
My sons do foreign work
In distant foreign lands.
The Dnipro, my dear brother,
Running dry, abandons me,
And the mounds so dear to me
Are plundered by the Muscovite…
Let him plunder, dig them up
What he seeks is not his own,
And meanwhile, let the turncoats grow
To help the Muscovite keep house,
And to strip the tattered shirt
From off their mother's back.
Help them, brutes,
To rack your mother."

---

133 *Bohdan* — Reference to Hetman Bohdan Khmelnytsky, who signed the controversial 1654 Pereyaslav Treaty. As a result, Ukraine came under Russian domination.

134 *Steppes sold* — Reference to German colonization of Ukraine after destruction of the Kozak Sich and Jewish colonization in the early 19th century.

The plundered mound
Is dug in quarters.
What is it they were looking for?
What did the old folks hide? —
Ah, if only,
If only they would find what's hidden,
Children would not weep, nor would mother worry.

Berezan, October 9, 1843

Chyhyryn, O Chyhyryn[135]
All upon this world expires,
So too your sacred glory.
It drifts upon cold winds
Like a fleeting speck of dust,
Disappearing in a cloud.
Years fly by above the earth,
The Dnipro's running dry,
Mounds, lofty mounds, erode —
Of your glory… and of you,
Old feeble one,
No one says a word,
No one even points.
Where did you once stand?
Why did you once stand?
Out of spite they will not say!!

Why did we battle with the Poles?
Why did we engage
The hordes in slaughter?
Why did we spear the ribs of Muscovites??
With ruddy blood
We watered what we sowed,
And raked the earth with swords.
What sprouted on that field??!
Rue's what sprouted… rue…
Our very freedom's poison.
And I, an outcast, on your ruins
Shed my tears in vain; Ukraine's asleep,
Choked by weeds, it blooms with mold,
In pools of mud her heart's composting.
She's let vipers breed in chilly hollows,
And in the steppe
Relinquished hopes of children.
And hope…
The wind scattered it across the field,
A wave took it out to sea.

Let the wind disperse it all
Upon its endless wing,
Let the heart weep, may it summon
Sacred truth on earth.

Chyhyryn, my only friend,
O Chyhyryn, as you slept
You lost the steppes, the forests
And Ukraine.
Sleep till sunrise,
Swathed with Jews,
Until those youngsters,
Hetmans, have matured.
Having said my prayers,
I too would fall asleep…
But my cursed thoughts

135 See glossary or fn. 77

Burst forth to set the soul ablaze,
To tear the heart apart.
Don't tear, my thoughts, don't burn,
I'll perhaps regain
My sad ill-fated truth,
And my quiet word.
Perhaps from it,
I'll forge anew a colter
And a plowshare to fit the
Worn out plow.
Then on to heavy tilling...
Perhaps I'll till that fallow field,
And on that field...
I'll sow my tears,
My earnest tears.
Perhaps, they'll sprout, growing
Two-edged knives,
To scrape the hard and filthy
Rotten heart...
And they'll drain the puss,
Then transfer vital blood,
Pure and sacred Kozak blood!!!

Maybe... maybe... but rue
Will be among those knives
And periwinkle too will spread —
And the forgotten word,
My sad and quiet word,
God-fearing,
Will be recalled — and a maiden's
Timid heart will throb
Just like a darling,
And she'll remember me...
My word, my tears,
O my paradise, my paradise!

Sleep, Chyhyryn, let children
Of the foe expire,
Sleep, hetman, till
Truth arises in this world.

Moscow, February 19, 1844

Gifts for Chyhyryn in 1649, 1844

THE OWL

In a verdant grove
A mother bore a son,
She gave him hazel eyes
And also dark black brows.
She swaddled him in nankeen cloth,
Imploring every saint,
So that all the holy beings
Would grace him
With a blessed fate.
"May the Holy Mother
Grant you bliss,
And everything your mother can't."
She fetched water before dawn,
Bathing him in periwinkle,
She rocked him till the midnight hour,
Singing till first light:

"Rock-a-bye baby, sweet lullaby,
The cuckoo was asked,
It cuckooed an answer.
It told the truth.
I'll live to a hundred
I'll feed you as well,
I'll parade in costly overcoats,
And I will take command.
You'll be grown, my son,
In five and two score years,
Living like a prince's child,
Tall and slender as an ash tree,
Limber, robust,
Well-off, happy,
And not single.
I'll find your equal,
Beyond the azure sea if needed.
She may be a merchant's daughter,
She may be a captain's
But she'll be a lady, son.
In an overcoat of green,
Dressed in bright red shoes
She'll strut proudly like a peacock
All around the parlor
And when she talks with you,
Your home will be like Paradise!
And I'll be sitting in a comfy corner
Just watching both of you.

O son, my son,
My child,
There's no one in this world that's better,
Nowhere in Ukraine!
There's no one better, nor will there ever be.
Marvel, people!
Not a one is better!.. As for fortune...
Fortune he'll acquire."

O cuckoo, little birdie,
Why did you cuckoo,
Why did you cuckoo up
So many years,
A hundred years for her?
Is there such a thing on earth
As deferential fate?
Oh, if only... Mom would know
To summon freedom for her children
And kinder fate from German lands,
But alas... Cruel fate
Is a thing encountered everywhere,
On the road and off,
Wherever there are people.

The mother loved her son,
As if he were a forest flower,
She loved... but meanwhile,
The father dies.
She's suddenly a widow
Though young
And not alone... but still it's tough...
With her grief and boredom
She went to ask the neighbors
For advice on how to cope...
They deemed it best that
She find work as a servant somewhere.

She wasted and she faded,
Left her home and went to serve...
She did not skirt the awful exploits.
Day and night she labored,
And she paid her soul tax...[136]
She bought her son an overcoat
For three kopas[137] that she earned.
So he, a widow's child,
Could also go to school.

O destiny, O destiny
A widow's lousy fate,
Is it in a field or forest
That you, a tattered gypsy,
Frolic with some tramps?
Water for a rich man
Flows uphill to reach his house.
But a poor man on a valley bottom
Has to dig a well.
The rich man's children grow —
Willows in a valley,
But the widow's got just one,
And he's a blade of grass.

The widow waited out her fate,
The maturing of that son.
He's literate, he's handsome —
A flower of a child!
She reigned as if she lived
Behind a door with God.
Girls made eyes
And gave him kerchiefs.
A rich girl fell in love —
But she kissed him not.
Her embroidery was sewn with silk —
Though she did not offer it.
Hardship crept from overseas
Right up to the widow's home
And then it sneaked inside...
Boys were clamped with shackles
And taken down the beaten paths
To be drafted in the army.
The widow followed other moms,
All awash in tears.
    A sentry guarded every bivouac,
    So the aging widow
    Could not enter any camp.
After coming to the draft board
They began to trim the hair.
They're all puny, they're all small,
They're the kids of rich folks.
That one's crippled, speech-impaired,
That one can't stand up.
This one's humpbacked, this one's rich
And those four share a home.
They're all no good, they all go back,
Fate is each one's mother.
    But the widow has one son
    And he's the one who measures up.

She left home again,
The dwelling of her son,
She went to be a live-in,
To get a loaf of stale bread,
Lugging water for a Jew,
Because the baptized won't accept her:
"She's become — they say, — too old,
She'll ail...." A chewed-off piece of bread
Is what they'd hand her through the window
For the sake of Christ... Forbid, O God,
That it should come to this.
Forbid, O God, that one should ask
A rich man for a drink.
She earned a kopeck at a time,
Saving fifty made a kopa.
She wrote a letter to her son,

---

136 *Soul tax* — A Russian imperial tax introduced by Peter I and levied on each man in a household based on a census. Because a census was infrequent, many widows were forced to pay for dead husbands.

137 *Kopa* — A unit of measurement that equaled 60 of certain items such as boards or sheaves of wheat. In monetary terms, 50 kopeck coins equaled one kopa.

And sent it to the army —
It eased the pain a bit. One year passes,
Two years pass, then a fourth
And still a tenth,
Without a word or even rumor.
No word; what to do?
She needs to take a sack
And go... to provoke the dogs,
Knocking door to door.
She took her sack, walked the village,
Sat down on the pasture, never to return,
Spending day and night beside the cattle gate.
Summer after summer passes.
She withered, became crippled,
Recognized by none.
And who's to recognize a needy cripple?
She sits there looking at the field and road.
The sun rises, the sun sets,
And it sets again,
All the while, there's no sign,
No sign of her soldier son.

Reeds beside the pond
Swish and sway toward evening.
The mother puts off dinnertime
To await her son till morning.
Sedge whispers in the evening
All around the pond.
A girl awaits her Kozak
In a twilit [grove].
The wind blows above the pond
Bending all the willows.

The mother cries alone at home,
The girl does so in the forest.
The dark-browed beauty
Shed some tears and then
Began to sing.
The mother shed some tears
And then began to weep.
She prayed and wept,
Cursing all on earth.
Oh, how difficult you are,
Hapless children of a mother!

Lifting crippled aging hands to God,
She cursed her fate,
And pleaded for her son.
She'd walk away in grief
With all her silent worries,
And through her tears she watched,
She watched that long, long road.
Day and night she watched
And then began to ask:
"Did no one hear, did no one see
My son, my son the soldier-Muscovite?.."
No one heard, nor even *saw.*
She sits, not entering the village,
She no longer asks or cries.
Gone insane!
She disciplines a little brick,
Scolding it and feeding it
As if it were a child,
Calling it her son,
While through her tears
She secretly and quietly
Sings a little song:

"A viper set the house on fire,
To cook some kasha[138] for the children,
It folded leather leggings,
And the Muscovites flew off.
Gray geese by fours
Converge on nesting grounds,
To nesting grounds
They fly by fours —
Honk-honk! —
On the mound there is an eagle,
Late at night upon the mound
It gouges out a Kozak's eyes,
And a maiden in a shady grove
Waits for him to leave the army.

138 *Kasha* — A type of porridge in Eastern Europe usually made from buckwheat.

By day she rummaged
Through the rubbish,
Gathering shards of pottery,
She prattled on and on
That she hid those shards
As gifts for her only son.
And at night she walks the village
All disheveled, head uncovered —
Singing, making creepy sounds.
People cursed... because, you see,
She would not let them sleep,
And she trampled
On the weeds and nettles that grew
Beside their fences.
By day, the children, sticks in hand,
Chased the widow down the streets,
They laughed and mocked her,
Calling her *The Owl.*

St. Petersburg, May 6, 1844

Woman in Sarafan & Other Sketches, 1841-42

A MAIDEN'S NIGHTS

Hazel eyes were dried
By all the maiden's nights.
Sister Maryanne

The thick braid undone
  Reaches to the waist,
Lavish breasts revealed —
  Like cresting waves at sea,
Hazel eyes have sown —
  All the stars at night,
Fair hands stretch out —
  They'd embrace
Another, but instead
They clutch a pillow,
Stiffened, rendered still,
Then unfolding with her tears.

"Why my braid and beauty,
Dovelike eyes,
And why my supple figure…
If there is no faithful partner?
There's no one here to love,
Nor to share my heart with…
O my heart! My heart!
It's hard for you to beat alone.
Whom to live with,
Whom, cruel world,
Tell me… What need have I
For glory… glory?
I want to love, I want to live
By way of heart, not beauty!
What's more, I'm envied
As a proud and wicked person.
Wicked people censure,
But little do they know,
What I've hidden in my heart…
Let them censure,
It's their sin… Dear God,
Why don't You wish to
Shorten Your dark nights,
Nights so hard on me!..
Because by day I'm not alone —
I have the field to converse with,
I converse and in that field
I thus forget misfortune,
But late at night…"
          She fell silent,
Tears poured down…
Fair hands stretched out —
They clutched a pillow.

St. Petersburg, May 18, 1844

DREAM

A Comedy

The spirit of truth; whom the world cannot receive, because it seeth him not, neither knoweth him.

John, Chapter 14, Verse 17

Each one has his destiny
And an open road,
The one lays bricks, the other ruins,
That one with a greedy eye
Scans the edges of the world
To see if there's a country he can
Seize and bring into his coffin.[139]
That one throws down aces
To con the in-law in his house,
Yet another stealing in a corner
Sharpens knives to kill his brother.
And that one, God-fearing,
Soft and sober, sneaks up like a cat,
To await your adverse hour
And to drive his claws into your liver, —
And don't plead: neither wife
Nor children can implore on your behalf.
And that one, munificent and magnificent,
Is always building churches,[140]
He so loves the fatherland,
Showing it concern,
But he drains
The country's blood like water!..
And the common man is silent,
Just staring at it all!
Like lambs. "That's okay, — he says, —
Perhaps, it's meant to be."
It's meant to be! Because there is
No Lord in heaven!
And you collapse under the yoke
Pleading for some earthly Paradise?
There is none! None at all!
Take pause. Don't waste your effort.
Everyone on earth —
Little princes, little paupers —
All of them are Adam's children.
That one... that one too...
What to make of me then?
Here's what, good people:
I frolic and I banquet
On Sundays and on weekdays.
And you're bored! You feel sorry!
By God, I do not hear.
And don't shout!
The blood I drink is mine,
It's not the people's blood!

And so, coming from
A late night banquet,
Walking drunk along a fence,
I pondered as I went
Until I stumbled home.
My children do not shout
And my wife's not one to curse,
So it's peaceful like in Paradise,
God's blissfulness is everywhere —
In the heart, and in the home.
And so I laid myself to bed.
Once a drunk man falls asleep,
Fire cannons if you will —

[139] *His coffin* — An allusion to Czar Nicholas I, who waged war in the Caucasus. He also used force to put down a Polish uprising in 1830-31.

[140] *Building churches* — Many churches were built during the reign of Nicholas I.

He won't even twitch his mustache.
And a dream, a wondrous one
Is what I dreamed —
The soberest of men would drink
And a stingy Yid would give a hryvna,[141]
To glimpse the wonders of that dream.
Oh what the hell, as much as two!
I look: It seems an owl[142]
Flies along the meadows,
Banks and thickets,
And along deep valleys,
Gulleys,
And broad steppes.
And I go after, flying after,
Taking leave of earth:

"Farewell, O world, farewell, O earth,
O surly land,
My sufferings, my furies,
I'll bury in a cloud.
And you, O my Ukraine,
You ill-fated widow,
I'll fly down for talks with you
From a cloud above.
For sad and quiet talks,
For some counsel with you.
At midnight I'll come down
As abundant dew.
We'll counsel, grieve a bit,
Until the sun comes up,
Until your little children
Rise against the foe.
Farewell, my mother,
Impoverished widow,
Feed your children; the living truth
Is with the Lord our God."

We fly. I look, it's dawning,
The sky's aglow along its edge,
A nightingale in a darkened grove
Greets the rising sun.
A gentle breeze is blowing,
Steppes and fields are dreamy,
Between valleys and the ponds
Willows cast themselves in green.
Abundant orchards bend,
Random poplars stand like sentries
Conversing with the field.
And all of it's just so, the entire land
Is green, it's bathed in drops of dew,
As it's been bathed since ancient times
To meet the rising sun...[143]
For this there's no beginning,
And there is no end!
No one can improve it,
Nor can anyone destroy it...
All of it's just so... Oh, why so sad,
My soul?
O my hapless soul,
Why the useless crying,
What is it that you pity?
Do you not see,
Do you not hear the people crying?
Glance over, take a look; and I'll fly high,
So high beyond the dark blue clouds;
There you'll find no rulers,
There you'll find no sanctions,
Human laughter, human crying
You'll not hear up there.[144]
Glance over. In the paradise you're leaving,
They'll rip the patched up tatters
From a cripple's back,
They'll rip them with the skin,

---

141 *Hryvna* — A unit of Ukrainian currency.

142 *Owl* — Shevchenko frequently used the image of the owl to convey gloom and despair.

143 *Rising sun* — An image from Ecclesiastes Chapter 1, Verse 4: "The sun also ariseth, and the sun goeth down, and hasteth to his place where he arose."

144 *Human crying you'll not hear up there* — Reference to Revelations Chapter 21, Verse 4: "And God shall wipe away all tears from their eyes; and there shall be no more death, neither sorrow, nor crying, neither shall there be any more pain: for the former things are passed away."

Because there's nothing
Else with which to dress
The feet of little princes;
And for the soul tax[145] over there
They crucify a widow,
And forge irons for her only son,
Only child, and her only hope!
They give him to the army![146]
Because, you see, he's just too much!
And that fence right there
Is where a child dies
Hungry and distended,
While its mother harvests
Wheat in serfdom.
And over there, you see?
Eyes! Eyes!
What good are you?
Why did you not dry out in youth,
Or dissolve in your own tears?
An unwed mother holds her bastard
Limping there along the fence,
Shunned by dad, shunned by mom,
Denied a welcome by all strangers!
Shunned as well by beggars!!
And the lordling, callow and oblivious,
Is with his twentieth woman,
Drinking souls away!

Does God see our tears and anguish
From up above the clouds?
Perhaps He does and helps
As much as ancient mountains
Showered with the blood of humans!..
O my poor soul!
Being with you is plain trouble.
We'll partake of poison
And rest upon a floe.
We'll send our muse to God above
And ask Him
How much longer
Tyrants are to reign on earth??
Fly away, my thoughts, fly away, my anguish,
Take the troubles and the evil with you,
They're your comrades —
You grew up with them,
You loved them, and their heavy hands
Were those that swaddled you.
Take them, fly and release a horde
Across the sky.
Let it blacken, redden,
Carry flames upon the breeze,
Let the dragon's vomit
Shroud the earth again with corpses.
And without you I will find a place
Where I can hide my heart,
And meanwhile, I'll seek paradise
Along the world's edge.

I fly again above the earth,
Again I say farewell to it.
It's hard to leave one's mother
In a roofless home,
It's harder still to watch
The tears and patches.

I fly, I fly, winds blow
And up ahead is white, white snow,
All around are pinewood forests, bogs,
A fog, a fog and emptiness.
Not a sound from people, nor a
Trace of any human's fearsome foot.
And enemies, non-enemies, forgive,
I'll not be coming for a visit!
Get drunk, and feast —
I'll no longer hear,
I will spend my nights alone
Amid the snows forever.
And I'll rest
Until you find a country
Not awash with tears and blood...

---

145 See glossary or fn. 136

146 *Give to the army* — Overlords could deliver a serf considered to be a troublemaker to the army.

I'll rest...
Then I listen —
Shackles clank
Beneath the ground... I look...
O you awful people!
Where'd you come from?
What is your endeavor?
What is it that you seek
Deep beneath the ground?
No, it's not likely
That I'll even hide in heaven!..
Why such punishment,
Why my torment?
What have I done to anyone?
Whose heavy hands have forged
The soul within the body,
Set the heart on fire
And released one's thoughts
With a jackdaw's power??
Why I suffer, I know not,
But I suffer mightily!
When I will atone,
When I'll live to see the end
I cannot tell and do not know!!

The desert has begun to stir.
As if the dead arise for truth
From the narrow confines of a coffin
To face the Final Judgment.
It's not the dead, it's not the murdered
Who are seeking justice!
No, they're people, living people
Cast in shackles made of iron.
They carry gold from pits
To stuff the mug of the insatiable!..
They're convicts.
Why? That...
The Almighty knows... And perhaps,
Even He does not quite see.

There's the place a branded thief
Drags along his shackles;
And yonder clenching teeth
Is a tortured robber,
Who seeks to waste
A pal not quite beaten unto death.
And among those villains,
Clad in chains,
Is a universal czar![147] A czar of freedom,
A czar who's wedded to a brand!
At hard labor and in pain he does not beg
Nor does he cry or moan!
Once the heart is warmed by goodness
Years will never cool it!

Where are your thoughts, your rosy blossoms,
Your well-kept, well-loved, dauntless children,
To whom, my friend,
Have you conveyed them?
Or have you, perchance,
Concealed them in your heart forever?
Oh, don't conceal, my brother!
Disperse them, spread them,
They will sprout, they'll grow,
And will reach the people!

More hardship? Or enough?
Enough, enough, because it's cold,
Frost invigorates the mind.

Again I fly. The earth grows dark.
The mind nods off, the heart grows weary.
I look: homes above the roads
And cities with a hundred churches,
And in those cities soldiers like
A flock of cranes are drilled; they drill,
Well-fed, with shoes and shackles...
I look farther:
In a valley, in a hole it seems,
A city glimmers on a swamp;

[147] *Universal czar* — Composite image of a freedom fighter punished by exile and hard labor. Many were physically branded.

A heavy fog above darkens like a cloud...
I fly near —
The city has no bounds.
Could be Turkish,
Could be German,
Could be that it's Muscovite.
Churches, palaces
And paunchy lords,
But not a single home.

Dusk set in... Fires flared,[148]
Lighting all around,
And even scaring me... "Hurrah! Hurrah!
Hurrah!" — they shouted.
"Tsk-tsk, you fools! Collect yourselves
Why so happy!
Why your fervor?" — "What a khokhol![149]
Doesn't know of the parade.
We've got ourselves a spectacle!
He himself [150] will stroll today!"
"And where's that doll?"
"There, you see — the palace."
I elbow in; until a countryman
Adorned with buttons made of zinc,
Thank you much, declares:
"How'd you get here?"
"From Ukraine." — "So how is it
You can't speak like locals?" —
"Why no, — I say, —
I can, but just don't want to." —
"What a weirdo!
I know all the entrances,
I'm a servant here, and if you wish
I'll try to get you in. But we, you know,
Are quite enlightened, you should
Spare some fifty kopecks."
Be off, you vile scrivener... Again I made
Myself unseen and pushed into the palace.
O my God Almighty!!
So here's paradise! Bootlickers
All decked out in excess gold;
And there he is, so tall and angry,
Making his official entry.
At his side, the poor czarina,
Like a dried out mushroom,
Skinny, leggy,
And the wretch, for added grief,
Has a wobbly head. [151]
So that's the famous goddess!
Woe be with you.
And I, a fool, not having seen
You, doll, not even once,
Believed your *dull-faced* scribblers.
What a fool! And experienced at that,
I took the Russky at his word; so read,
And try to trust their writing.
Behind the gods — the upper crust
All in gold and silver,
All like fattened hogs
With bloated faces, paunchy bellies!..
They even sweat and crowd
To stand closer to the *very ones*:
Perhaps they'll hit someone
Or grace them with a big fat zilch;
If even half a zilch,
Or even just a bit, so long as
It's delivered smack into their snouts.
And everyone stood in a row,
It seems they could not speak —
Not a peep. The czar is chattering;
And that marvel the czarina,
Jumps around and revels

148 *Fires flared* — Reference to fireworks.

149 *Khokhol* — Pejorative Russian term for a Ukrainian.

150 *He himself* — Reference to Czar Nicholas I.

151 *Wobbly head* — This depiction of the czarina as a dried mushroom with a wobbly head offended Nicholas I, resulting in the poet's decade-long internal exile. The czar personally prohibited the poet from writing or drawing. The depiction, however, was accurate. Shevchenko may have seen her personally, heard about her from his art professor, Karl Briullov, or read a very similar description by French aristocrat, Marquis de Custine.

Like a stork amid some birds.
For quite a little while
The two of them thus sauntered
Like a pair of puffed up owls.
They shared some quiet words —
From afar they can't be heard —
About the fatherland, it seems,
About some new *insignia,*[152]
And still newer drills!..
The czarina then sat down
Quietly on a stool.
I look and see the czar approach
The eldest in the crowd...
He proceeds to whack him
Right across the mug!..
The poor fellow took the licking;
And punched the belly of a smaller guy —
It echoed!.. And that guy
Hit a smaller ace right
Between his shoulders;
A smaller one gets hit in turn
Who plows into a little guy.
He then hits the petty ones, and the paltry
Ones beyond the door
Lunge into the streets,
To mix it up with all remaining Orthodox,
And they proclaim;
And scream; and they shout as well:
"Our padre's having lots of fun,
Hurrah!.. hurrah!.. hurrah! a-a-a..."
I broke out laughing, 'nuff said;
But I too took a solid hit. By dawn
All people were asleep,
Just here and there some Orthodox
Still moaned around street corners
And, moaning, they implored the Lord
On behalf of padre.
Tears and laughter! And so I went
To see the town.
The night there seemed like day. I look:
Palaces and palaces
Above the quiet river;
Up and down the riverbank
All is laced with stone. I marvel
As if mesmerized!
How did such a wonder happen
In what was once a bog?.. Much human
Blood was shed here —
All without a knife.
On the other shore's a fortress
And a belfry[153] like a sharpened awl
That's even stunning to behold.
There are also clocks that toll.
I then return —
A horse comes flying, its hooves
Breaking up the bluff![154]
Sitting bareback is a rider
In a peasant overcoat —
That's not a peasant coat,
And he's also hatless,
His head wrapped in a leaf of sorts.
The horse rears up and gallops —
He's just beside the river,
He'll just... just... jump right over it.
And he extends his hand,
As if to subjugate the world.
Who exactly is this?
And so I read what's carved into the bluff:
In honor of *the first — the second*[155]
Placed this wonder.
Now I know:
This is *the first,* who crucified Ukraine,

---

152 *Insignia* — Nicholas was known to meddle in trifling details, even insignia on military uniforms.

153 *Fortress and belfry* — References to the Petropavlovsky Fortress and Saints Peter and Paul Cathedral, which has a pointed bell tower. The fort was built for defense against Sweden, but then turned into a prison for perceived enemies of the czar.

154 *Breaking up the bluff* — Reference to the base of Peter the Great's monument in St. Petersburg.

155 *The first–the second* — The monument plaque refers to Peter the First and Catherine the Second.

And *the second* is the one
Who finished off the orphan widow.
Tyrants! Tyrants! Cannibals!
Both ate their fill,
And stole a lot;
And what is it that they took with them
To the world beyond?
It was very, very hard for me,
As if I'd read the history of Ukraine.
I stand, and freeze...
Meanwhile, there's some sad
And quiet, quiet singing
From something that's unseen:

"Regiments from the town of Hlukhiv[156]
Advanced with spades against a line,[157]
And I the acting hetman[158]
Was sent with Kozaks to the capital!
O our God the merciful!
O you wicked czar,
Czar accursed and evil,
You devil unassuaged!
What is it that you've done to Kozaks?
You filled the bogs
With gallant bones;
You built a capital
On tortured corpses!
And in a dark, dark dungeon,
You chained me, an independent hetman,
And starved me unto death.
O czar! O czar!
Even God can't make us part.
Shackles bind you to me for all eternity.
It's hard for me beside the Neva.[159]
Perhaps far-off Ukraine exists no more.
I'd fly off, I'd take a look,
But God permits me not.
Maybe Moscow's burned the land,
Drained the Dnipro
In the sea so blue,
And dug up all the lofty mounds —
Our glory. Dear God,
Have mercy, O dear God."
And the something then fell silent; I look:
A white cloud shrouds the leaden sky.
And deep within,
It seems a forest creature howls.
It's not a cloud — but a small white bird
Descended in a cloud
That sobs above that czar of brass:
"We too are shackled to you, cannibal,
You viper!
At the Final Judgment we'll shield
The Lord above from your greedy eyes.
You drove us from Ukraine,
Unclothed, unfed and butchered us
In a snowy foreign land;
And from our hides
You made yourself a purple mantle
Sewn with hardened veins,
Then built yourself a capital
In a brand new robe. Look:
Palaces and churches!
Rejoice, you vicious tyrant.
Damned! You're damned!

They flew away, dispersed,
The sun began to rise,

---

156 *Hlukhiv* — The capital of the Kozak Hetmanate. It was located near Russia according to Czar Peter's order to watch Kozak movements following destruction of the previous capital, Baturyn, in 1709.

157 *Advanced with spades* — Peter the First ordered Ukrainian Kozaks to work on the construction of St. Petersburg under terrible conditions. Hundreds of thousands perished from overwork, inadequate food and poor sanitary conditions.

158 *Acting hetman* — Pavlo Polubotok (ca. 1660-1724), Hetman of Left-Bank Ukraine who sought greater Ukrainian autonomy in the empire. Accused of treason, he was imprisoned in the Petropavlovsky Fortress, where he died.

159 *Neva* — The river flowing through St. Petersburg.

And I stood there wondering,
It was almost scary.
The poor began to stir,
And hurry off to work,
And soldiers at the crossroads
Had begun their drills.
Sleepy girls scurried
Along edges of the streets,
Though not from home, but homeward!
Mother had them work all night
To earn a piece of bread.
And I stand there, stooped,
Just pondering and thinking,
How hard people toil to earn
That daily bread of theirs.
Then pencil-pushers made their way
To write in senate offices,
To sign and thus to cheat
A father and a brother.
Here and there among them
Are Ukrainian girls.
They cut loose in Russian,
Laughing at and cursing parents
For not teaching them to yak in German —
So now they're ink-stained bureaucrats!
Leaches! Leaches! Perhaps, father sold
To Jews his last remaining cow
For you to learn
The language of the Muscovites.
Ukraine! Ukraine!
These are all your children,
All your youthful blossoms,
And all are drenched in ink.
They're steeped in Moscow's henbane [160]
In a German greenhouse!..
Cry, Ukraine!
O you childless widow!

Let's go to the czar to see
What's happening in his palace. I come:
The paunchy nobles
Stand there in a row; sniffing, snoring,
All puffed up like turkeys,
Looking at the door askance.
And lo, it opened.
He barely, barely drags his feet,
Like a grizzly crawling from his den.
He's all bloated, even blue
Damned in distress
From too much booze.
He shouts at all the paunchiest —
Then each and every paunchy noble
Fell into the ground!
He bulged his bug-eyes from his brow —
All those left began to tremble;
Like a madman
He berates the lesser nobles —
And they collapse into the ground;
He then lays into some petty folks —
They too disappear!
He turns upon the servants —
And the servants disappear;
Then the soldiers — the soldiers
Moaned and crumpled to the ground.
I look to see what's next,
What my teddy bear will do!
He just stands there, the poor guy
Sunk his head. What happened to
This grizzly's nature?
Like a kitten, he's quite strange.
It even made me laugh.
He heard, he snarled —
I got scared and then woke up...
That's the wonder that I dreamed.
It was something quite absurd!.. Such
Things are only dreamed by holy fools
Or drunks. Don't be astonished,
Dear and loving brothers,
I did not tell you what I saw,
But only what I dreamed.

St. Petersburg, July 8, 1844

160 *Henbane* — A potentially fatal plant *(Hyoscyamus niger)* that causes seizures and hallucinations.

She didn't stroll on Sundays
But earned money for some silk.
She stitched a kerchief,
And sang as she embroidered.

"O my little kerchief
You're inwrought
And embroidered,
I'll finish you with golden lace,
I'll give you as a gift,
I'll be rewarded with his kiss,
O my pretty kerchief.
All will be amazed come morning
That an orphan has
A pretty, inwrought kerchief.
I'll undo my braid,
And saunter with my mate.
O my fortune,
You're my mommie."

Thus she stitched,
Peering through the window,
Checking for the oxen's bellow,
Waiting for the chumak's homestretch.
A chumak comes
With someone's goods
From way beyond the Lyman.
Driving someone else's oxen,
This is what the fellow sings:
"O my fate, my fate,
Why aren't you like someone else's?
Do I drink, do I carouse,
Do I lack the strength,
Don't I know what road to take
To reach you through the steppe?
Don't I send
My gifts to you?
I have gifts —
They're my hazel eyes.
The rich have bought
My youthful strength,
Perhaps without me they've betrothed
My girl to another man...
Teach me, O my fate,
Teach me how to dance."

Then the poor wretch cried,
Trekking through the steppe.
An old gray owl cried out
Upon a mound amid the steppe.
The chumaks worried,
Their concern ran very deep.
"Allow a stop, otaman,
At the nearest village,
And we'll take our comrade
For communion in a church."
They confessed, took communion
And even asked a seer —
In vain... down the road they went,
An ailing man in tow.
Perhaps it was the work
That crushed his
Youthful vigor,
Or perhaps relentless boredom
Knocked him off his feet.
Perhaps people did
The young man wrong,
So from the river Don
They carted him back home.
He begged the Lord to see his girl...
Or at least his village.
He failed... Laid to rest,
No one even cried for him!

All those gathered placed a cross
Above the orphan
And dispersed... like a blade of grass,
Like a leaf upon the drifting water,
A Kozak left this world,
Taking all things with him.
But where's that
Colorful embroidered kerchief,
Where's that happy
Girl-child?!

The wind unfurls a kerchief
Upon a recent cross,
And a girl undoes her braid
To become a nun.

St. Petersburg, October 18, 1844

Why is it so hard for me, so tedious,
Why my weeping heart,
Why its sobs and cries
As if it were a hungry child? O my trying heart,
What is it that you want, why is it that you ache?
Is it food, or is it drink, or perhaps some sleep?
Fall asleep, my heart, fall asleep forever,
Broken and uncovered — and all the crazy people,
Let them be insane… close your eyes, my heart.

St. Petersburg, November 13, 1844

Tell me what's in store for me,
O sorcerer,
My gray-haired friend.
You have sealed the heart,
But I am still afraid.
I remain afraid to ruin
A burned out empty home,
I'm afraid, my friend,
To inter the heart.
Hope will perhaps return,
With the fresh and healing water
Of a tiny tear.
From far away it may return
To spend a winter in that dwelling,
And at least to whiten just the insides
Of that burned out home.
It'll stoke a fire, heat
And light the home…
Perhaps my thoughts, my children
Will awaken once again.
Perhaps, I'll pray again,
And share some tears with all my children,
Perhaps again I'll see the rays of truth,
If even in my dreams…
Rise up, my brother, even fool me,
But tell me what to do:
To pray, to worry,
Or to smash the skull??!

St. Petersburg, December 13, 1844

TO HOHOL (GOGOL) [161]

Behind a swarm of thoughts
Another thought escapes,
The first one grips the heart, the second rips,
A third one softly cries within the heart itself,
Unseen perhaps by God.
With whom am I to share it,
Who will welcome the expression,
And who will guess the noble word?
All are deaf — shackled,
Bowed... indifferent...
You are laughing, I am crying,
My distinguished friend.
And what will all the crying yield?
Hemlock, brother...
The roar of freedom's cannons
Won't resound throughout Ukraine.
The father will not slay his son, his child,
For honor, fame, and brotherhood,
For the freedom of Ukraine.
He won't slay — he'll nurture him instead,
Then sell him off for slaughter to a Muscovite.
It is, you see, a widow's mite
To the throne and fatherland
And a fee for German masters.
Let it be, my brother. We will
Laugh and cry.

St. Petersburg, December 30, 1844

Envy not the rich man,
He knows neither
Love nor kindness —
These are things he leases.
Envy not the mighty,
For he makes use of force.
Envy not the famous,

[161] *Hohol* — Writer Nikolai Gogol (1809-52) was Ukrainian. He is known in Ukrainian as Mykola Hohol.

Because he knows
That people love not him,
But his hard-won fame,
A delight paid for in tears.
And when the young embrace,
All is peaceful pleasure,
Like paradise, — but look:
Misfortune stirs.
Envy therefore no one,
Look around yourself,
There's no paradise
On earth's expanse,
Nor is there one in heaven.

Myrhorod, October 4, 1845

Marry not a wealthy woman,
She will drive you from the house,
Marry not a lowly woman,
You'll not sleep at night.
Marry liberty instead,
Marry Kozak destiny;
What will be will be
And if it's bare, it's bare.
You won't be pestered,
Nor amused —
Why it hurts and where it hurts,
No one will inquire.
They say perhaps it's best to share
A tear with someone else;
Don't indulge: it's easier to cry
When there's no one there to see.

Myrhorod, October 4, 1845

THE HERETIC

To Safarik[162]

Evil neighbors set a neighbor's
Nice new house on fire;
They warmed up
And went to sleep,
But forgot to rake the ashes
And disperse them with the wind.
At the crossroads lay the ashes
And in those ashes glows an ember
Of an even greater fire.
It glows, does not expire,
It awaits ignition,
Biding time like an avenger
Until a dreadful hour. The ember glowed,
It glowed and waited at the crossroads,
Starting slowly to expire.

Thus it was the Germans
Torched a once great house.
They thus split a family,
The family of the Slavs,
Letting loose with little sound
The vicious viper of domestic strife.

Blood that flowed in rivers
Doused the conflagration.
And then Germans
Divvied up the charred remains
And the little orphans.
The Slavic children grew in shackles,
And forgot in bondage
That they exist on earth!
But the spark of brotherhood
Glowed amid the ruin,
It glowed, awaiting hard assuring hands.
The wait concluded... Maturing
Deep within the ashes
Was a fire with a noble daring heart,
With a daring eagle eye!
And you, the sage, set alight
The torch of truth, of freedom...

The great family of Slavs
You counted[163]
In its darkness and its bondage,
Missing not a member,
Though you counted corpses,
Not the living Slavs.
Then upon great heaps
And on the universal crossroads
You became an Ezekiel,[164]
And — O wonder! The dead arose,
Their eyes were opened,
And brother embraced brother
Speaking words of quiet love
For all eternity!
Then all the Slavic rivers
Drained into a single sea.

Glory be to you, O sage,
You, the Czech, the Slav!
You did not permit our truth
To sink in German depths.
Your sea is new and Slavic!
It will soon be full,
And a boat with broad, expansive sails
And a solid rudder
Will set sail on a sea of liberty,
Upon its swelling waves.

---

162 *Pavel Jozef Safarik (1797-1861)* — Slovak and Czech poet, linguist. He opposed Russia as leader of Slavic peoples, promoting instead Pan-Slavism that treated all Slavs as equals. His father was a Protestant clergyman.

163 *You counted* — Safarik published a map of the Slavic peoples.

164 *Ezekiel* — Biblical Hebrew prophet who revives the dead in the Book of Ezekiel, Chapter 37. Shevchenko thus recognizes Safarik's role in Slavic cultural revival.

Glory be to you, Safarik,
For all eternity!
That you combined the Slavic rivers
Into a single sea!

Also welcome in your glory
My poor ode and contribution
About the sainted Czech,
The celebrated martyr,
About the famous Hus.[165]
Accept it, father. And I'll quietly
Pray to God,
That all Slavs become good brothers,
And sons born by the sun of truth,
And heretics,
Like the great heretic of Constance![166]
They'll grant the world the gift
Of eternal peace and glory!

November 22, 1845 in Pereyaslav

The stone which the builders refused
is become the head stone of the corner.
This is the Lord's doing;
it is marvelous in our eyes.

Psalm 117 (118): Verse 22-23

"All around are lies and bondage,
Tortured people all are silent.
And upon the apostolic throne
Sits a well-fed monk.
He squanders human blood
And rents out Paradise!
O our Lord in heaven!
Your Judgment is in vain
And so too is Your kingdom.
Thieves and cannibals
Have overwhelmed the truth,
They've ridiculed Your glory,
And Your Truth and power.
The earth cries out in shackles,
Like a mother for its child.
There's no one who will break the chains,
Who will clearly stand
For Gospel truth,
And for all the unwashed people!
There's no one! O God! O God!
Will there never be?
No, the time will come
For great celestial punishment.
The three crowns upon the proud tiara[167]
Will most certainly collapse!
They'll collapse! Bless, O Lord
The unfirm hands for
Vengeance and for suffering!"

Thus in his righteous cell,
Jan Hus considered how
To break the bonds of of hell!..
To show the wonder,
Sacred wonder, to unseeing eyes!
"I shall overcome... God is with me!..
It will happen!"
And so the good Jan Hus went off
To pray inside of Bethlehem Chapel.[168]

---

165 *Jan Hus (1369-1415)* — Czech priest and religious reformer who predated Martin Luther. Hus was burned at the stake for heresy against Catholic doctrine.

166 *Constance* — German city on the Rhine, where a Roman Catholic council condemned and executed Hus.

167 *Tiara* — Reference to the papal tiara, a crown worn by Roman Catholic popes.

168 *Bethlehem Chapel* — Chapel in Prague where Jan Hus was a preacher.

"In the name of Christ the Lord,
Crucified on wood for us,
And of all the holy saints,
Especially Paul and Peter,
With this papal bull
We do absolve all sins
Of God's servant..."
"Of the same woman who
Two days ago
Walked the streets of Prague;
Of the one, who staggered drunk
Through all the taverns, barns, and cellars,
And cloister passageways!
That same one who earned enough
To buy a *papal bull*[169] —
She is now a saint!.. O God! O God!
You're the power!
You're the glory! Look upon the people,
Ease the retribution
From Your shining Paradise.
Why do they perish? Why punish
All Your own and the obedient,
Why punish decent children?
Why did you close their decent eyes,
And fetter open minds
With shackles of a dreadful night!..
Awaken, people, day has come!
Stretch your arms and clear your eyes.
Rise up, Czechs, stand as upright people,
Not as a friars' joke!
Robbers, tyrants in tiaras
Flooded everything, took everything,
Like Tatars raiding Muscovy,
And handed us, the blind, their dogmas!..
Blood, infernos,
All the evils of the world, wars, feuds
And an endless chain of hellish torment.
And Rome is full of bastards!
That's their dogma and their glory.
Such glory is apparent...
And now the conclave has resolved:
He who died not having any holy bull —
It's straight to hell;
He who doubles payment for a bull
Gains entry into Paradise,
You can even knife your brother,
Just leave the Pope and monks alone!
The end of ends!
The robber stealing from a robber,
In a church no less. Vipers! Vipers!
Have you had your fill
Of human blood, or not?..
It's not for me a simple man,
Great Lord, to judge
The deeds of Your great will.
Absent guilt, You impose on none
The ravages of evil.

I pray, O Lord, have mercy on us,
You, O sacred power,
Tie my tongue for blasphemy,
But heal the world's sores.
Don't let evildoers mock
Your timeless glory,
And us, the simple people!.."

As Hus prayed he cried,
Bitter were his tears. People
Kept their silence, wondering:
What's he doing, who is it that he dares
To lift his hand against?

"Look here, folks: Here's the bull,
The one I read..." And he showed it
To the people. They all shuddered:
Jan Hus has ripped a papal bull!!
An echo rolled from Bethlehem Chapel
To the center of the universe,[170]
Ho-hoing all along the way.
Monks seek cover... Like punishment

169 *Bull* — A formal papal document with a seal.
170 *Center of the universe* — The Vatican.

The echo bounced
Around the conclave —
Tipping the tiara!

Monks hissed inside the Vatican,
Like a den of vipers,
Hissing too is Avignon,[171]
Along with Roman monks,
Antipapists also hiss,
Even walls begin to shake
Because of all the hissing. Cardinals,
Like vipers, coil 'round the tiara.
And furtively, like cats, they gnaw
Each other for a mouse…
And why not?
A lot of skin and so much meat inside!
Even walls began to shudder, when
Reminded that in Prague,
Geese began to honk[172]
And they fly to fight with eagles…
The conclave called a session
After coming to its senses.
They decreed with unanimity
To stand against the rebel Hus.
And to call together
All the ravens for a council
In the town of Constance!
And to guard from
Top to bottom, making sure
That no gray bird
Escapes into the Slavic field.
Like the jackdaws on a field —
Monks descended
On the town of Constance;
Steppes and roads were filled,
As if by locusts,
By barons, dukes and herzogs,
By huntsmen, heralds,
Troubadours (kobzars),
And also tavern keepers,
And the army, like a serpent,
Slithered on the road.
Following the herzogs
Came the Germans;
Some with falcons on their arms,
Some by foot, on horses
Or on donkeys —
It was even teeming.
All hurried for the hunt,
Like serpents to their nesting grounds!
O Czech! Where's your soul??
Look what powers have converged —
As if to fight the Saracens[173]
Or the great *Attila!*[174]

A dull roar washes over Prague;
The emperor,[175] and Vyacheslav[176]
And the thousand-headed Diet
Are together cursed aloud! They
Don't want to let Jan Hus
Into the town of Constance!
"God lives! My soul's alive!
My brothers, I've no fear of death!
I'll prove the vipers wrong,
I'll pull their unquenched fangs…"
And the Czechs escorted Hus
As would children lead their father…
They rang the morning bells
Throughout the town of Constance.
The cardinals,

171 *Avignon* — City in Southern France that was home to antipopes during the time of Hus.

172 *Geese began to honk* — A word play on Hus' name, which means goose in several Slavic languages.

173 *Saracens* — In Roman times, nomadic tribes around Arabia. By the Crusades, it came to mean Arab or Muslim.

174 *Attila (?-453)* — Leader of the Huns, who terrorized Europe.

175 *Emperor* — Sigismund I (1368-1437), the Holy Roman Emperor who gave Jan Hus safe passage to appear at the Council of Constance. But safe passage was revoked and Hus was executed.

176 *Vyacheslav* — Bohemian King Wencelaus IV (1361-1419), brother of Sigismund.

All smooth and red,
Converged like bulls into a pen,
There were also rows of prelates.
And three popes, and all the barons
And the wedded heads of state;
They gathered, like a group of Judases,
Holding an impious court
With Jesus in the dock.
Quarrels, noise,
Sometimes roaring,
Sometimes moaning.
Like a camped out horde,
Or a group of Jews in school…
Then suddenly all fell silent!..

Like a cedar on a field in Lebanon,[177]
They brought Jan Hus in shackles
To appear before them!
With eagle eyes
He scanned the sinful.
They shook, turned pale
Gazing at the martyr silently.
"Why me —
Have you called me for a challenge?
Should my shackles be considered??"
"Quiet, haughty Czech…"
They hissed like vipers,
Roared like beasts.
"Heretic! You, sir, are a heretic!
You sow discord!
You fan strife,
You don't accept
The sacred will!" — "A word."
"You are damned by God!
Heretic! You, sir, are a heretic!
Roared the prelates. —
You're a troublemaker!.." — "A word."
"You are damned by all!"

Hus stared at all the popes
And walked out of the chamber!..
"We won! We won!.."
They all seemed in a frenzy.
"Auto da fe! Auto da fe!.."[178]
As a group they shouted.

All the monks and barons
Banqueted throughout the night…
All drank, and drunken,
They cursed Hus
Until the bells rang out,
Until the daylight dawned…
All the monks
Go out to pray
For the sake of rebel Hus.
Beyond the hill the sun's ablaze.
And the sun would like to see
What it is that they'll inflict
Upon this righteous one?!

All the bells rang out
And they led Hus, shackled
To Golgotha,[179]
But he did not flinch…
Before the fire; he stood upon it
And recites a prayer.
"O Lord all merciful,
What is it that I've done to people?
Your people!
What is it that they try me for?
Why do they seek to crucify?
People! Decent people!
Pray!.. O innocents —
This too will befall you!
Pray! Wild beasts in sheepskin
Have come and bared their claws…
Neither mountains, neither walls

---

177 *Lebanon cedar* — A majestic tree *(Cedrus libani)* in the Mediterranean region.

178 *Auto da fe* — Medieval Portuguese and Spanish term meaning act of faith. It was used during the Inquisition to pronounce sentences followed by the burning of accused heretics at the stake.

179 *Golgotha* — Hill where Jesus was crucified. Also a place of suffering.

Will do a thing to hide them.
A crimson sea of blood will spill!
The blood of all your children.
Woe! O woe!
There they are! In white cassocks.
And angry eyes...
Now it's blood..." — "Burn! Burn!.."
"Blood! It's blood they want!
Your blood!.." And smoke
Concealed the righteous one.
"Pray! Pray!
Have mercy, Lord,
Forgive them, for they know not!.."
Then silence!
Like dogs, the monks
Stood 'round the fire.
They feared that he might slither
As a viper from the fire
And might suspend himself
From a crown or a tiara.

The fire went out, a wind picked up
And scattered all the ashes.
And simple folk *did see*
A red viper slink on that tiara.
The monks all left
And sang *Te Deum,*[180]
They dispersed
Among their dining halls,
Eating cloistered day and night,
Till all of them got bloated.
Czechs gathered as a tight-knit family,
From the pyre they took some earth
And with it went to Prague.
Thus was Hus condemned by monks,
Who burned him...
But the word of God
They did not burn,
Nor did they guess an eagle,[181]
Not a goose,
Would fly down from a cloud
To peck apart the high tiara.
To them it's all the same,
They've dispersed
Like just so many ravens
From that bloody feast.

The monks and barons
Sprawled out in their dwellings
Having no idea —
They feast and every now and then
They'll even sing *Te Deum.*
They've done it all... But wait!
There above the head old Zizka[182]
From the town of Tabor has flashed
A ruler's mace.

Maryinske, October 10, 1845

180 *Te Deum* — A Christian hymn of praise for God.

181 *Eagle* — Reference to Protestant reformer Martin Luther.

182 *Jan Zizka (c. 1360-1424)* — A Czech general and Hussite leader, who never lost a battle. He fought the Teutonic Knights and participated in the decisive 1410 Battle of Grunwald that shifted the balance of power in Eastern Europe.

THE BLIND MAN

A Poem

My youthful thoughts,
My buried children,
Do not fly to fill my void
From the world beyond.
They left me orphaned and alone
With you, my heart, my star,
My paradise and serenity!
No one knows my paradise,
You yourself don't know it,
You who hovers over me,
A star above the grove.
I look, I look,
As you, my star,
Descend to the horizon,
Speaking softly,
You will smile, you'll look —
I look and do not see…
I awaken — the heart cries,
And eyes begin to weep.

Thank you, little star! My
Hazy day is passing; it's twilight,
And death above my head is rattling
Its scythe. They'll bury me,
And there a chilly wind will
Scatter any trace of me. All is fleeting.
You'll read perchance
My muse poured out in earnest tears,
And you'll say in quiet, quiet phrases:
"I loved, I loved him,
But he did not know…"
O my star, shine
Upon my grave.
And I'll fly around the world beyond,
To sing of you, my heart, in heaven.

That one roams beyond the seas,
He sails the world,
Seeking fortune he can't find —
Nor is there any to be found!
It seems dead. Another chases destiny
Using all his might, he nearly, nearly
Reaches it, and ka-boom
Into the grave!
And a third one, like a beggar,
Has no home or field,
Just a sack, and from that sack
Peeks fortune —
Like a little baby; and he
Curses it and damns it
And pawns it to a Jew —
No, he won't abandon it.
Like a burr, he grasps
His patched lapels
And gathers spikes of grain
Upon a foreign field.
Over there are sheaves,
Over yonder — stacks.
And there in creaky quarters
Sits our orphan,
Seeming quite at home.
Such is destiny,
Do not bother searching for it:
Whom it fancies, it will find,
It will find them in the cradle.

So it was around midday, a Sunday,
It was even Pentacost,
That an aging Kozak
In a bright white shirt
Sat beside a house,
A bandura[183] in his hands.
"This way, that way,
It should be, and a pity it would be.
No, it will be necessary, let him wander
Through the world at least a couple years.

183 *Bandura* — Ukraine's national musical instrument. It typically has between 30 and 68 strings.

On his own he'll search for his,
Just as I once searched. Yaryna!
Where's Stepan?" —
"There he is, he's standing
By the fence, as if he was embedded."
"But I do not see! Just come right here;
Go now, both of you!..
Alright, kids, try this!" —
And he hit the strings.
The old man plays,
Yaryna dances with Stepan!
The old man plays, he sings along,
Tapping with his feet:

"If I'd encounter double trouble,
And my husband's mom was calm,
If my husband was a young man,
Who did not love another.
Oh, hop, click, click!
With a pair of bright red shoes
And a trio of musicians, —
I'd love my husband always
Till the end of time."
"Oh, hop, he came to see her,
Built a house, and they got married,
He lit a fire in the oven
And cooked the evening meal."

"Hey, kids, like this, kids!"
And the oldster raised himself.
See him thump and see him hit it —
He danced with arms akimbo.

"Is it so or is it not,
Some parsnip grew a lot.
Cut some parsley
For the broth —
Oh, how tasty it will be,
Yes it's so, indeed it's so
That a Kozak once got married,
He left his home
He left his room
And took off for the valley."

"No, it's not the same,
My former strength is all worn out,
I'm tired; it's your doing
To have stirred me up,
Oh, confound you!
Look what years have done!
No, I'm no longer fit,
It's all passed me by. The only dancing left
They say, is to get piece of bread
And to make some lunch.
Just sit. Stepan, you were little when
They killed your father, Ivan, during
Rule of the Aristocrats;
You had yet to crawl..." —
"So I'm not a son, dad,
Not a son of yours?.."
"Why no, you're not my son;
Just hold on a bit.
Then your mother died,
And you were left alone; and I tell my wife,
The late Maryna: 'You know what!
We'll take the infant for our child.' —
Namely you. 'Good,' — she says.
Then we paired you with Yaryna,
The two of you together...
So you see? You're of age,
Yaryna is maturing...
Need to ask the people!
And get few things done!
What say you to that?" — "I don't know,
Because I thought that..."
"That Yaryna is your sister?
She's not...
It's just that if you love each other,
She can be your wife.
But first things first!
Need to look
How others live.
If they plow,
If they sow on unplowed fields
And simply take the harvest,
Then winnow unthrashed grain.
How they grind, and how they eat —

All that must be known.
So here's the plan, my partner:
For a year or two
You need to work for others;
Then we'll see what comes.
Because he who knows
Not how to earn
Will know not how to live.
What do you think, my man?
And if you want to know, my son,
Where best to deal with trouble,
You should live upon the Sich,
And if the Lord will help you out,
You'll get your fill of every bread,
Just as I got mine.
I still feel stuffed, when I recall it!..
If you earn, you'll bring it,
Should you not earn,
You'll live and learn,
My good son;
You'll find out Kozak customs,
And you'll see the world —
It won't be like the *Brotherhood*,[184]
Instead you'll read a *living alphabet*
That's written on the sea.
You'll say a young man's prayers
To the Lord,
You won't mumble them like monks.
So it is, my son.
We'll say a prayer to the Lord
And saddle up the dun —
Then you'll hit the road!
Let's just go and have some lunch.
Yaryna, what have you prepared?" —
"It's ready, dad."
"So it is, my son!"

No food, no drink, the heart is still,
And eyes don't see, the head feels numb,
He seems not there, it's like he's dead,
Instead of bread, he grabs a ladle;
Yaryna watches, softly laughing:
"What's come over him?
Neither food, nor drink,
There's nothing that he wants!
Has he not fallen sick?
Brother Stepan! What ails you?" —
She asked him with her eyes.
The old one is indifferent,
As if he does not see.
"To reap, or not to reap,
There's still a need to sow," —
The old man banters,
To himself it seems. —
"Let's all get up,
Perhaps I'll mosey over
For the evening service.
And you, Stepan, will go to sleep,
Because you'll need to get up early
To saddle up the horse."

"O Stepan, my dearie!
Why is it that you cry?
Smile a bit at me.
Don't you see I weep as well?..
He's mad at God knows whom
And doesn't talk to me.
I'll cry and run away,
By God... you'll see.
Say something, my Stepan!
Perhaps you're really ill?
I'll get some herbs,
I'll run to call the seer,
Perhaps it's from the evil eye?"
"No, Yaryna, my dear heart,
O my glowing blossom!
O Yaryna, to you I'm not a brother!
And tomorrow I will leave...
You and father as a pair of orphans...
I'll die just anywhere,
And you won't mention me,
You'll just forget your brother..." —

184 *Brotherhood* — Likely reference to the Kyiv-Brotherhood school founded in 1615 at the Epiphany Monastery.

"Cross yourself! By God, it is
The evil eye.
Not a sister! Who then am I?
O my God, my world,
What is to be done?.. Father's gone,
He is not well, and may yet even die!..
O my God! And he's indifferent,
As if he's mocking me.
Don't you know they'll bury
Me along with you and daddy!"
"No, Yaryna, I won't die,
But tomorrow I will leave you...
I'll come back...
I'll be back next year from Zaporizhia,[185]
No longer as your brother,
But for wedding scarves...
You'll offer them?"
"Enough talk of wedding elders!
He has the nerve to joke!.." "It's no joke,
Yaryna, so help me God..." —
"So it's true you'll
Go away from dad
And me come morning?..
No, you're joking.
Tell me, please, Stepan!
Am I truly not your sister?.."
"No, my love!
My dear heart!" — "O my God,
Why did I not know?
I would not have loved you
Nor would I have kissed you.
Oh, oh, what shame! Go away from me.
Leave my hands alone!
You are not my brother!
You are not my brother!
O my torment! Torment!"

Then Yaryna cried just
Like a little child,
And through her tears she said:
"He'll leave!.. He'll leave!.."
Stepan leaned just like a sycamore
Beside the water.
Earnest Kozak tears
Boiled inside his heart!
They burned like hell...
In turns Yaryna
Curses, pleads, falls silent...
She'll give a kiss,
And wails again!
Twilight caught them unawares.
The father came upon
The sister and the brother,
Embracing as if bound together.

Daylight dawned and Yaryna
Cries... cries...
Stepan is at the well
Already watering his horse.
She took some pails and ran there too,
Supposedly for water...
Meanwhile, from the shed,
Father brings a Zaporizhian weapon,
He examines it, rejoices,
And tries it out for size... as if
The oldster was rejuvenated!
And he wept... "My weapon!
O my golden weapon!
My youthful years,
My youthful strength!
Perform, my faithful weapon,
For valor that's still young!
Perform for him as earnestly,
As you did for me!.."

As Yaryna hands the weapon,
Stepan saddles up the horse, his friend,
And dons a Kozak overcoat.
His sword is serpent-like,
His spear a sharpened rod,

185 *Zaporizhia* — The territory of the Ukrainian Kozak state. Its fortified capital, the Zaporizhian Sich, was located on Khortytsia Island in the Dnipro River rapids.

And across his back he slung
A gun that measured seven palms.
She fainted at the sight,
And the old man cried
When he saw atop the horse
A rider that was such a fine young *lad.*

Yaryna takes the reins
To lead the horse,
And cries along the way.
The father walks beside,
And instructs his son.
How to function in the army,
How to honor elders,
To respect the brotherhood,
And not to hide in camp.
"May God protect you!" —
The old man said, stopping
At the village edge,
And the three of them
Together all began to cry.
Stepan whistled, then dust
Rose up along the road.
"Do not linger
Come back soon, my son!.." —
Said the old man weeping.
Yaryna, like a valley spruce,
Bent down without a sound;
She merely wipes her tears,
And looks on down the road.
Something flickers in the dust
Then vanishes again.
It seems a hat across the field,
It rolls, it's silhouetted...
It hides... and like a gnat
It barely... barely... glimmers,
It then disappeared. Yaryna
Stood there for a long, long time to see
If perhaps the insect won't return.
It did not; she bent down,
And cried again...
The old father followed suit,
And they went back home.

Days pass by, the summer passes,
The season turns to autumn, yellowed
Leaves are rustling; the old father
Sits beside the house
Not unlike a dead man;
Illness grips Yaryna,
His only child wants to leave him;
With whom to live what years are left?
With whom to cap his life?
He recalled his young Stepan,
He recalled his feeble age,
He recalled and cried, that's what
The old gray orphan did.
Like a patch upon a patch,
The years sewed pain upon his heart.
"All on earth is in Your hands.
Your will is sacred!
What shall be shall be —
Such is my fate!"

Spring adorns the earth
With primrose, rue and periwinkle;
Like a girl in a verdant grove.
And the sun rose higher in the sky,
It stopped, and eyed the earth
As would a fiancé his bride.
And Yaryna left the house
To take a look at God's good world,
But she barely walked...
She'll smile,
She'll go and stop,
Observe, and wonder
Oh so quietly and dearly,
As if born just yesterday...
And the raging anguish...
It returned into her very heart
And obscured the earth.
Yaryna wilted like a
Blade of mowed down grass;
Tears rolled forth like
Like morning dew on flowers.
The old father stood beside her,
Leaning over like an oak.

In the great Kyiv
She prayed to all the saints;
She took Communion thrice
At the Mezhyhirsky Savior.[186]
In Pochayiv[187] at the sacred monastery
She wept and prayed
That her Stepan, his fate,
Would at least appear to her in dreams!..
No dreams. She returned.
White winter once again had
Whitened everything.
Spring again took
On the crimson cast of primrose;
Yet again Yaryna left the house
To wonder at the world.
And not to supplicate the saints —
But to ask a seer.

The seer saw,
Conjured up the evil eye,
And for three coins
She molded fate
From melted wax on water.
"There, you see, a saddled horse
With its shaking head.
Riding is a Kozak,
And there's a bearded grandpa walking.
That's money.
See, his nose is dripping.
If the rider deems to wipe;
Indeed he wipes.
Look — he hides behind a mound,
Where he counts the money.
Again he's on the road,
Squinting, bags in hand.
That, you see, is apprehension,
So he won't be met, perchance,
By Tatars or the Poles..."
Thus Yaryna left
And went back home quite happy.

A third, a fourth,
And now a fifth year passes —
Not a short year. And Stepan
Remains away, away.
In the valley past the hill
All the routes and footpaths
That were trod to see the seer,
Are now overgrown with grass.
And Yaryna now undoes her braid
To become a nun;
The old father falls beside her, pleading,
To wait a year, a summer,
Until Saint Peter's[188] or at least
The Pentacost. They waited, and
With loveroot and with greenery,
Dressed in bright white shirts,
They sat beside the house on Sunday
Like a pair of orphans.
There they sat, they grieved
And listened — behind the gate
Is something playing, it's like a kobza
Along with quiet singing.

"Early Sunday morning
The blue, blue sea rolled on,
Comrades of the Kozak chief
Requested at a council:
"Give your blessing, otaman,
To launch the chaikas,[189]
To frolic past the Isle of Tender,[190]
And to find the Turk."

---

186 *Mezhyhirsky Savior* — Church at the Mezhyhirsky Monastery in Kyiv. It was destroyed in 1934 by Bolsheviks. The area was turned into a closed resort for Communist Party elites. President Viktor Yanukovych claimed it as a presidential estate.

187 See glossary or fn. 119

188 *St. Peter's* — Reference to the Feast of Saints Peter and Paul on June 29 (July 12 on the Julian calendar).

189 *Chaika* — A dugout boat with sails and oars used in battle by Zaporizhian Kozaks.

190 *Tender* — A cape on the Black Sea near the Dnipro delta. It was once an island.

They launched the chaikas and the baidaks,[191]
Equipping them with cannons,
And set sail from the Dnipro's mouth.
In the darkness of the night,
Upon the azure sea,
They began to sink just beyond the Tender,
And perish.
One boat sinks,
Another bobs,
A Kozak waved his hand and shouted
To his brethren from an azure wave:
"May God help you, brothers!"
And in that azure wave he sinks
And dies.
Just three ill-fated chaikas
Were not sunk beneath the sea,
Among them the otaman's, thank God,
And that of Stepan, the young orphan.
The sea, instead, drove them
Without oars or rudder to captivity
In the land of Turks and Muslims.
And then the Turkish janissaries
Caught the orphan Stepan,
A Kozak duly registered,[192]
And they caught the youthful otaman.
They opened fire with cannons,
Forging shackles,
Throwing captives in a prison tower,
Then subjecting them to hard, hard labor.
O our Savior, our miraculous
Mezhyhirsky Savior!
Don't let even fiercest foes
Fall into such harsh and hard captivity
As in the land of Turks.
Their shackles weigh three heavy poods,[193]
And otamans get four.
They never see or know God's light of day,
They break up rocks beneath the ground,
They perish having not confessed their sins,
They die.
In this captivity the orphan Stepan thought
About his dear Ukraine,
About his old and unrelated father,
About his jet-black horse,
And his sister Yaryna.
He cries, he weeps,
He lifts his hands to God,
Then breaks his chains
And runs for liberty, for freedom...
The Turkish janissaries
Caught him on the third of many fields,
They tied him to a stake,
And burned away his eyes
Using glowing iron rods,
Then they fastened him
With shackles,
Threw him in a dungeon,
And sealed it up with bricks."

And thus beneath a fence
A kobzar still quite young
Stood and sang about a captive.
Behind the fence Yaryna listened —
And not hearing how it ends, she fell.
"O Stepan! My dear Stepan! —
She wept and screamed. —
My dear Stepan, my little sweetheart,
Where is it that you tarried?
Daddy! Daddy! It's our Stepan!
Come, look."
The father comes, he gazes,
And barely recognizes Stepan;
That's what shackles did to him.
"O my hapless son,
My good and decent child!
Where on earth have you been roaming,

191 *Baidak* — Large sea-going boat.

192 *Registered Kozaks* — Kozak units officially registered with the Polish-Lithuanian Commonwealth army. First force was created in 1572 under Polish King Sigismund II Augustus.

193 *Pood* — An old unit of weight used in Belarus, Russia and Ukraine. It equaled 36.11 pounds or 16.38 kilograms.

My one and only son?"
The old one cries, embraces,
And my blind one cries
With his sightless eyes,
As if he'd seen the sun.
They take him by the arms,
And lead him to the house,
And Yaryna greets him,
As if he really was her brother.
She washed his head,
And washed his feet.
And in his thin white shirt
She sat him by the table.
She fed him, filled his glass,
And laid him down
To sleep upon a feather bed…
Then she and father tiptoed
From the house.

"No, my father, there's no need,
There's no need, Yaryna!
Look: I perished,
Forever I have perished.
Why waste your youthful years
Living with a cripple… No, Yaryna,
People will make fun,
And the sacred Lord will punish
And will banish fortune
From this happy home
To a stranger's field.
No, Yaryna, God won't leave you,
You will find a mate,
And I'll go to Zaporizhia.
I won't die there,
For they love me…" — "No, Stepan,
You're my child,
And you'll be punished by the Lord,
If you ever leave me."
"Stay, my dear Stepan!
If you do not wish to marry,
We will be just who we are.
I'm your sister,
You're my brother,
And the both of us are children
Of our aged father. Don't go,
O my dearest Stevie,
Don't leave us once again.
You'll not leave us?.." — "No, Yaryna…"
And Stepan remained;
The old man rejoiced
Just like a little child,
And even grabbed a kobza;
He so wished to jump and dance
Using all his might…
All three of them sat down
On the earth beside the house.
"Tell us now, Stepan,
About your great misfortune.
Because I too once sauntered
In a Turkish prison."

"And I, already blind,
Was released with other Kozaks
To go again into the world.
The group of comrades took me
As they headed for the Sich,[194]
Going through the Balkans,
Dashing on free legs
Toward our dear Ukraine.
And on the placid Danube
We were met by Kozak brothers
Who turned us toward the Sich.
And as they cried they told us
How the Sich was ruined,
How Muscovites took the gold,
The silver and the candlesticks
From Our Lady the Protectress.[195]
How the Kozaks fled at night

---

[194] *Sich* — Reference to the Trans-Danube Sich (1776-1828), established after Russia destroyed the Zaporizhian Sich in 1775.

[195] *Our Lady the Protectress* — Reference to an icon of the Blessed Virgin Mary.

To start a new encampment
By the Danube's quiet waters.
How the empress walked with Scraggly[196]
Through the city of Kyiv
And reduced the Mezhyhirsky Savior
To a flaming ruin.
How she sailed the Dnipro
In a golden galleon,
To watch that fire spread
With a subtle, quiet smile.
And how the Zaporizhian steppe
Was divvied up by Germans.
How she enslaved free people[197]
For degenerates and bastards.
How Kyrill and his officers
Dusted wigs with powder,
Then licked slippers of the empress
Like a bunch of dogs.
That's the way it was, dad! I'm lucky
That I have no eyes,
That I don't see the world
Or know what's happening in it.
Poles were here — they seized all,
Drinking up the blood!..
And the Muscovites forged chains
To bind God's lovely world!
That's the way it is! It's hard, dad,
To leave your home
And beg non-Christian infidels
Just to be a neighbor.
Now, they say, Holowaty[198]
Gathers those left over
And exhorts them to the Kuban,
Thus alarming the Circassian.[199]
Godspeed to him,
And what comes of it —
The good Lord only knows. We'll hear
What people say about it!.."
Thus the two of them conversed
Till midnight every day,
As Yaryna kept the house.
They recalled Zaporizhia,
Kozak glory,
And sang of Sava Chaliy,[200]
About the half-smart Bohdan,
And his lazy son,
About the martyr Gonta,
And the famous Max.
Yaryna listened...
And pleaded with the saints.
Her pleas bore fruit... after Lent
She and Stepan joined in wedlock.

So this is my entire muse.
Be not astonished, people.
What has passed
Shall never be again.
My tears have passed,
My old abraded heart
Neither races, neither cries,
And the eyes no longer
See the quiet home
In this forgotten land,
Nor the quiet valley
Or the shady grove,
Nor do they see the girl

---

196 *Scraggly* — Grigori Alexandrovich Potemkin (1739-91), senior Russian political and military leader. He advised Catherine II to destroy the Kozak Sich. Kozaks called him Scraggly Greg (Hryts Nechesa) because he wore a wig.

197 *Enslaved free people* — Catherine II instituted serfdom in Ukraine by decree in May 1783. Serfs became the property of what Shevchenko called degenerates and bastards, a reference to Catherine's own illegitimate son, Paul.

198 *Antin Holowaty (1744-97)* — Ukrainian military leader. He helped organize the Black Sea Kozaks and resettled them from the Dniester to the Kuban.

199 *Circassian* — Member of an ancient indigenous ethnic group in the North Caucasus.

200 See glossary or fn. 36

And the little child,
I do not see the happy one:
All is crying, all is dying.
I'd be glad to hide,
But where, I do not know.
Lies abound wherever I look,
Everywhere they curse the Lord.
The heart dries and withers,
And the tears freeze over...
I, alone, am weary,
On this lonely road.
That is how it is! Be not astonished
That like a crow I caw:
A cloud has veiled the sun,
And I do not see the world.
Barely, barely at the midnight hour
I peek out with my heart
And send into the world
My frail muse
To seek vital healing water.
At times, indeed, it brings some,
To sprinkle in the house,
It lights a flame that's true,
Then quietly and sadly
It speaks about a wedding —
Turning next to woe.
Of the sightless orphan
My tale nears its end,
But how to finish it
The muse itself knows not.
Because there's never been a wonder
Of a woman that was happy
With a husband who was blind!
But such a wonder happened!
A year and then another passes
Since their marriage, and look —
Together they are dancing
In their little garden. The old father
Sits beside the house
With his little grandson,
And teaches him the proper way
To salute a Kozak.

Maryinske, October 16, 1845

Blind Man (Slave), 1843

THE GREAT VAULT

A Mystery

Thou makest us a reproach to our neighbors, a scorn and a derision to them that are round about us. Thou makest us a byword among the heathen, a shaking of the head among the people.

Psalm 44: Verses 13-14

THREE SOULS

Three small birds, like snow,
Flew by the village of Subotiv[201]
And sat upon a tilted cross
Atop an olden church. "God forgives us:
We're now souls, not people,
And from here the view is better,
Of how they'll excavate the vault.
If they'd only dig more quickly,
Then they'd let us into Paradise,
Because that's what God told Peter:
"You'll let them into Paradise,
When the Muscovite takes all,
When he excavates the old great vault."

I

When I was once a human being,
My given name was Prisa;
I was born right here,
And here is where I grew,
Right here, it was, I danced
With children in the graveyard,
And with little Hetman Georgie[202]
We played some blind man's bluff.
And the Hetman's wife,
It was, would come
And call us to the mansion
Where a barn once stood. There she'd
Treat me with some figs and raisins —
She'd give me everything
And hold me in her arms...
And when guests arrived from Chyhyryn,
Accompanying the Hetman,
They would send for me.
They dressed me, gave me shoes,
And the Hetman took me in his arms,
He carried me and kissed me.
In Subotiv I thus grew,
In Subotiv I matured!
Like a blossom; and they always
Greeted me and loved me.
Never did I say a word of malice
To a single person. I was pretty
And dark-browed.
They all courted me,
Began to match me up,
And regarding that,
I prepared embroidered scarves.
On the very verge of giving them,
I confronted trouble!
Early in the morning
During Christmas Lent,
Precisely on a Sunday

---

201 *Subotiv* — Central Ukrainian village where Hetman Bohdan Khmelnytsky's estate was located.

202 *Hetman Georgie* — Reference to Yuri Khmelnytsky, the son of Hetman Bohdan Khmelnytsky. The son was hetman from 1659-63 and 1677-81.

I went running for some water...
And that very well
Had silted up and dried!
Nonethless, I fly!..
I look — there's the hetman
With his officers.
I got my fill of water
And completely crossed his path;[203]
But I did not know
That he headed for Pereyaslav[204]
To swear an oath to Moscow!..
And I just barely carried
All that water home...
Why did I not break the buckets
With the water in them!
All that cursed water poisoned
Father, mother, me,
My brother and the dogs!
This is why I suffer,
And the reason why, my sisters,
I'm not allowed in Paradise.

II

And I was not allowed, my sisters,
For watering the horse
That the czar of Muscovy
Rode in Baturyn[205]
On his way to Moscow from Poltava.[206]
I was still a minor,
When Moscow late at night
Burned the famed Baturyn,
Killing Chechyl,[207]
Drowning youngsters and the old
In the Seyma River.
I rolled among the corpses in
Mazepa's[208] mansions... with me
Were my sister and my mother,
Butchered holding one another,
And lying right beside me;
Forcefully, yes forcefully,
They tore me from my lifeless mother.
Oh, how I pleaded
With the Russian captain
To take my life as well.
No, they did not kill me,
Releasing me instead to be a plaything
For the soldiers!
I barely hid myself
Amid the smoldering ruins.
Just a single house was left
In all the ruins of Baturyn!
And in that house they put the czar

---

203 *Crossed his path* — In Ukrainian folklore, crossing someone's path with pails of water means to bring good luck.

204 *Pereyaslav* — A town in Central Ukraine that Shevchenko considered important for several historic reasons dating to the times of Kyivan Rus. In 1654, it was the place where Hetman Bohdan Khmelnytsky signed the controversial Pereyaslav Treaty with Russia that led to the loss of Ukrainian autonomy.

205 *Baturyn* — A town in northern Ukraine and former capital of the Kozak Hetmanate. It was totally destroyed and thousands of its residents, including women and children, were killed by Russian forces commanded by Alexander Menshikov in 1708.

206 *Poltava* — The site of the 1709 Battle of Poltava, where Peter the Great defeated Sweden's Karl XII. The pivotal battle marked Russia's rise as a great power. Ukrainian Hetman Ivan Mazepa had sided with Sweden.

207 *Dmytro Vasylovych Chechyl (?-1708)* — One of Hetman Ivan Mazepa's officers who defended Baturyn. He was captured by Russian forces and broken on the wheel.

208 *Mazepa's mansions* — Reference to Ivan Mazepa (1639-1709). Ukrainian hetman who sided with Sweden against Russia in the pivotal Battle of Poltava during the Great Northern War. Many Ukrainians consider him a generous patron of the arts and hero who fought for Ukraine's independence. Russia and its Orthodox Church denounce Mazepa at a traitor. His image is on the ten hryvna banknote of independent Ukraine.

To sleep there overnight
As he came back from Poltava.
And I went out with water
To that little house... and he
Waved his hand at me.
Give water to his horse, he said,
And so I gave it!
I did not know how mightily,
How very mightily I sinned!
I barely got back home
And fell dead upon the threshold.
They buried me the next day
As the czar came out,
And my grandma who remained
Amid the ruins,
Had even greeted me in
The roofless house.
And on the morrow she too died,
And decayed right in the house,
For there was no one left to bury her
Amid Baturyn's ruins.
They ripped the house apart
And burned to charcoal
Beams inscribed with writing!..
And I still fly above
The Kozak steppes and valleys!
Why they punish me
I myself know not!
Probably because I pleased
And served most anyone...
And because I gave some water
To the horse of Moscow's czar!..

III

And I was born in Kaniv.
I'd not begun to talk,
I was carried gently swaddled
In my mother's arms
When Catherine sailed the Dnipro
On her way to Kaniv.
In a grove atop a hill beside the river
The two of us sat down.
I cried; I don't know
If it's food I wanted,
Or perhaps because the little thing
Was feeling some discomfort.
My mother entertained me,
And looked out on the Dnipro;
She showed the golden galley
Like a floating mansion. Aboard
The galley were the princes, all the powers,
And some governors... Among them
Was the empress sitting on her throne.
I looked, smiled...
And breathed my last!
Mother also died,
And the both of us were buried
In a single grave.
That's the reason, sisters,
Why I'm punished now,
Why they still won't let me
Even purge my soul.
Did I know, still swaddled,
That this empress —
Was Ukraine's fierce enemy,
And a hungry she-wolf!..
What say you, sisters?

"It grows dark. Let's all fly to Chuta[209]
Where we'll spend the night.
If something's going to happen
We'll hear it all from there."
They darted off, all white,
And flew into the forest,
And together lighted on an oak
Where they spent the night.

[209] *Chuta* — The name of a forest near Subotiv.

THREE RAVENS [210]

I

Caw, caw, cried the rook!
Bohdan is a crook.
He went to thieves in Kyiv
To sell the goods he took.

2

I spent time in Paris, France
And drank away three zlotys
With Potocki and Radziwill [211]

3

The devil walks across a bridge,
And a goat across the water:
Troubles loom. Troubles loom.

Thus the ravens cawed,
Flying in from three directions
And all three lighted on a beacon
On a hill amid a forest.
They puffed out, as if from cold,
All eyeing one another,
Like three old sisters,
Who stayed and stayed as maidens
Till they gathered moss.

I

Here's some for you, and some for you.
I flew far away to steal some gall
From a Decembrist [212] in Siberia.
So, you see, there's a thing
With which to break our fast!
Well, in your Muscovy,
Is something there for nourishment?
Or was there naught and now there's nothing?

3

Eh... there's plenty, sister:
I conjured three decrees
For just a single road... [213]

I

For what kind? With rails?
Well, you've outdone yourself...

3

Yes, six-thousand souls I smothered [214]
Just to build a single verst... [215]

I

Don't lie, 'cause it was five
And that was with von Korf. [216]
She's even bragging, taking credit
For the work of others!
Rotten cabbagehead!..
And you, most gracious Polish lady?
You wine and dine in Paris,
You evil evildoer!

---

210 *Three ravens* — Evil personification of Ukraine, Poland and Russia.

211 *Potocki and Radziwill* — Magnates and participants in an unsuccessful Polish 1830-31 uprising against Russia. Shevchenko has them emigrating to Paris.

212 *Decembrist* — Participant of Russia's Decembrist uprising of military liberals in 1825 against the newly crowned conservative Czar Nicholas I. They promoted representative government and abolition of serfdom. Five Decembrists were executed and others were exiled to Siberia.

213 *For a single road* — Nicholas I issued decrees to construct a rail line from St. Petersburg to Moscow.

214 *Six-thousand souls* — Thousands of serfs died during the railroad construction of disease and hunger.

215 *Verst* — An old Eastern Slavic unit of length equal to approximately 3500 feet or 1.06 kilometers.

216 *von Korf* — In his draft of the poem, Shevchenko first wrote von Grot. There are several von Korfs in Russian history and it is not clear if he had any specific one in mind. The reference, however, is to functionaries who in fact abused serfs in railroad construction.

That spilled a river, maybe more, of blood
And drove your gentry to Siberia,
So that's enough,
You've got your fill of pride.
Behold, such a noble peacock…

2 & 3

And what is it that you've done??

I

What nerve you have to ask me that!
You were not yet born,
When I already ran a tavern here
And also poured some blood!
Just look at you!
Karamzin[217] they've read!
And think they're really something!
Get lost, you upstarts
You have yet to grow your down,
You unfeathered cripples!...

2

There's a touchy one!
It's not the one who got up early,
Who got drunk before the break of dawn…
But the one who overslept!

I

Would you have gotten drunk without me
What with all your priests?
You haven't any talent! I burned down
Poland with its kings;
If it were up to you, you tweeter,
She would still be standing.
And what was it that I did not do
With free and independent Kozaks?
Just whom did I not lease them to,
To whom did I not sell them?
But they're so damned resilient!
I thought that with Bohdan
I almost, almost buried them.
No, they all arose, the rogues,
And joined the Swedish vagrant…[218]
It was quite a happening!
It makes me angry to recall…
I burned Baturyn,
And dammed the river Sula[219]
Just with Kozak officers
In the town of Romney…
And with others,
Just plain Kozaks,
I sowed all of Finland,
In the Orel I piled heaps…[220]
And for the czar
I drove troops to follow troops
To fill the swamps in Lagoda.[221]
And the famed Polubotok[222]
I smothered in a dungeon.
That was quite a celebration!
Even hell was scared.

---

217 *Nikolai Mikhailovich Karamzin (1766-1826)* — Russian writer, poet, critic and author of a 12-volume history of Russia. He was known as a conservative monarchist.

218 *Swedish vagrant* — Swedish King Karl XII (1682-1718), whose army was defeated in Poltava, Ukraine during the Great Northern War against Russia. Ukrainian Hetman Ivan Mazepa sided with Karl.

219 *Dammed the river Sula* — Reference to Peter the Great's vengeance at the Sula River in Northern Ukraine against those who sided with Mazepa.

220 *Finland, Orel* — Ukrainian Kozaks fought for Russia in Finland against Sweden during the Great Northern War. Kozaks and peasants were also used to build fortifications on the Orel River.

221 *Swamps of Lagoda* — Thousands of Ukrainian Kozaks died digging canals around Lake Lagoda in Northwest Russia.

222 *Pavlo Leontiyovych Polubotok (ca. 1660-1723)* — Acting Hetman of Left-Bank Ukraine. He defended Ukrainian autonomy. Accused of treason, he died imprisoned in the Petropavlovsky Fortress in St. Petersburg.

At night in Rzhavytsia
The Blessed Virgin burst out crying.[223]

3

And I too lived it up:
I stirred things up with Tatars,[224]
I hung out with a tyrant,[225]
I drank shots with Peter
And sold out to the Germans.

I

You've done fine:
You've fastened all the Russkies
With German iron shackles —
You may as well lie down and sleep.
In my parts, the devil only knows
Whom the people seek.
I've already sent them into dungeons
And bred horrid hordes of gentry
Dressed in fancy uniforms,
I bred them just like lice;
They're all distinguished bastards!
Their crazy Sich is thick with Jews.
But the Muscovite is no less clever:
He's adept at turning tricks;
He knows just how to warm his hands.
Though I'm fierce,
I'm not able, nonetheless,
To do what Russians do
With Kozaks in Ukraine.
A decree is what they print:
"By the grace of God,
You belong to us, all belongs to us,
Be it pretty or not pretty!"
They now embark upon a search
For *the ancient* in the vaults...
Because there's nothing left to take
In ordinary homes;
They serenely took it all.
The devil knows
Why they rush to
Excavate this lousy vault.
If they'd wait a bit, a bit,
The church would also fall...
Then they'd describe two ruins
In the latest issue of *The Bee.*[226]

2 & 3

Why is it you've summoned us?
To gaze upon the vault?

I

Yes, indeed upon the vault. But there are
Two more wonders yet to rise.
In Ukraine this night
A mother will give birth to twins.
One will, like Gonta,
Be a tyrant against tyrants!
The other will... well, he's one of us!
He will help the tyrants.
Ours already pinches
Before he's left the womb...
And I've read,
That when that Gonta grows,
All that's ours is lost!
He'll plunder all the good,
And won't desert his brother!
And he'll be spreading truth and freedom
All throughout Ukraine!
So you see, my sisters,
What it is that they arrange!
They're preparing shackles
For the tyrants
And all things that are good!

---

223 *Rzhavytsia... Blessed Virgin* — Reference to a 1572 icon of the Blessed Virgin in what is now the village of Irzhavets. Considered a miraculous icon that shed tears for Ukraine.

224 *Tatars* — Moscow was dependent on the Tatars from the 13th through the 15th centuries.

225 *Tyrant* — Reference to Czar Ivan the Terrible (1530-84).

226 *The Bee* — Reference to the *Severnaya pchola* newspaper published in St. Petersburg from 1825-64.

2

I'll fill his eyes
With molten gold!

I

But he's a cursed brute
And will not want the gold.

3

I'll twist his arms
With czarist titles!..

2

And I'll gather
All the evils and the hardships
From across the world!..

I

No, my sisters. Not that way.
While people are still blind,
He needs to be interred,
Otherwise there's trouble!
There, you see, above Kyiv
A sweeping comet's tail,
And the ground that's shaking
Above the Dnipro and the Tiasmyn?
Do you hear? There's moaning
On the hill above the town of Chyhyryn.
O!.. All Ukraine is laughing and lamenting!
The twins are born,
And the crazy mother cackles
That both will have the name, Ivan.
Let's fly!.. — They flew off,
And flying, they sang a little song:

I

Our Ivan will sail
With his crony
To the Lyman on the Dnipr'.

2

Our hunting dog will dash
With me
To eat some vipers
In their nesting grounds.

3

If I want then I'll rush off,
Like an arrow
I will fly to hell.

THREE LYRISTS

One is blind, the second lame,
The third one is a hunchback.
To Subotiv they proceeded
To sing of Bohdan to the laymen.

I

They're ravens, say no more.
They've feathered up the perch,
As if made for them
By Muscovites.

2

For whom else? They surely will not
Place a man to count the stars above...

I

That's what you say.
But maybe on that perch
They'll put a Russian or a German.
Even there a Russian and a German
Will find a piece of bread.

3

What's with all your blathering?
What ravens?
And Muscovites, and perches?
May God forbid!
Perhaps they'll force some breeding
To propagate a Muscovite.

Because as rumor has it,
Conquering the whole wide world
Is what the czar would like to do.

2

Perhaps, it's so! But why the devil
Put them in the mountains?
They're so tall to boot
That you'll reach the clouds
If you climb up to the top...

3

But here's what's what:
There'll be a flood.
The lords will climb
And look to see
How all the bumpkins drown.

I

You're all smart people,
But do not know a thing!
They placed those figures there
For just these reasons:
So that people do not pilfer
Water from the river and so
They secretly don't plow
Abundant sand beyond the Tiasmyn.

2

The devil only knows such blather.
You've no talent, so don't lie.
What say you all, let's sit
Beneath this elm
And get a bit of rest!
In my sack I have perhaps
A couple chunks of bread.
Let's take the opportunity
For breakfast before dawn... —
They sat. — And who, brothers,
Sings about Bohdan today?

3

I sing. And about Iasi [227]
And of Yellow Waters [228]
And the town of Berestechko [229]

2

Today, they'll come in really handy
For the three of us.
'Cause there's a market
Full of people over by the vault,
And among them quite a few elites.
That is where our food will be!
Come on, let's sing!
Rehearsal, please...

I

Oh, bug off!
Better that we all lay down
And get some decent sleep. The day is long.
We'll sing anyway.

3

I too say: let's pray
And sleep.

Beneath the elm the oldsters dozed;
The sun still sleeps, the birds are silent,
But by the vault they're up
And have started digging.

---

227 *Iasi* — City in Romania where the older son of Bohdan Khmelnytsky married Ruxandra, the daughter of Moldavian Prince Vasile Lupu, who was considered the wealthiest man in Eastern Christianity.

228 See glossary or fn. 92

229 *Berestechko* — The site of a 1651 battle in the Volyn Region that involved nearly 250,000 Kozak and Polish forces. Ukraine's Tatar allies pulled out at a critical moment and held Hetman Bohdan Khmelnytsky for ransom. The Ukrainian defeat led to the Bila Tserkva Treaty, which reduced the number of registered Kozaks and allowed Polish magnates to return to their lands in Ukraine.

They dig a day, they dig another,
And on the third they reached a wall
Then took a little break.
They posted *guards.*
The district chief is pleading,
To grant no one entry,
And runs reports to Chyhyryn
To apprise the *higher-ups.*
The mug-faced *higher-ups* arrived,
And looked. "You need, — they say, —
To break the arches,
It's the surest way...".
They broke them down,
And jumped back frightened.
Skeletons lay in that vault
And they seemed to smile,
Because they'd finally seen the sun.
So much for Bohdan's treasure!
A crock, a rotten trough
And skeletons in shackles!
Had they been *in uniform,* then good:
They could have come in handy...
They laughed... And the district chief
Was nearly mad with rage!
Because, you see, he worked so hard
And there's nothing there to take!
All day and night he toiled
And ended up a fool.
Should he get hold of this Bohdan,
He'd dragoon him in the army
To teach the man the meaning
Of fooling higher-ups!!
He shouts, he runs,
As if he was a mad man.
Yaremenko's face he strikes,[230]
He curses all the people
In his native Russian.
And swoops down upon my oldsters.
"What is it, vagrants, that you're doing!!"
"Why, sir, you see,
We're singing songs of Bohdan..."
"I'll give you Bohdan,
You cons, you freeloaders!
And you've composed a song
About a con like you..."
"They taught us, sir."
"Well, I'll teach you!.. Lay into them!"
They took and steamed them
In a bracing Russian sauna —
Thus the songs to Bohdan
Came in handy for the lyrists!!
So it was that Moscow
Dug the small Subotiv vault!
The great vault, though,
They have yet to find.

High upon a hill
In the village of Subotiv
Standing broad and deep,
Is the coffin of Ukraine.
That's the church
Where Bohdan prayed
That the Muscovite share
With the Kozak
Both the good and bad.
Peace unto your soul, Bohdan!
It did not come to pass;
Whatever Muscovites begrudged
Is everything they swindled.
They already dig up mounds
Seeking wealth inside,
They excavate your vaults
And curse you as they dig.
For their effort they find nothing!
Thus it is, Bohdan!
Verily you wrecked Ukraine,
That poor and needy orphan.
For this you get the thanks you get.
There's no one to maintain
The church that is a coffin too!!

---

230 *Yaremenko* — The barn of Kozak Yaremenko is at the place, where Bohdan's mansions stood. (*Footnote by T. Shevchenko.*)

In that Ukraine, the very same,
That quashed the Pole with you!
Now Catherine's bastards
Swarm like locusts.

So it is, Zinoviy,[231]
Friend of Alexei![232]
You gave everything to friends,
But they are all indifferent.
They say, you see, that all of that
Was always really theirs,
That they just leased it
To the Tatars as a grazing ground
And to Poles... Perhaps, indeed!
Just let it be as is!
Foreigners have such a laugh
At Ukraine's expense!
But hold your laughter, foreigners!
The coffin-church will crumble...
And from beneath Ukraine will rise.
It will dispel the gloom of bondage,
It will light the world of truth,
And prayers will be said in freedom
By children once unfree.

Maryinske, October 21, 1845

THE HIRELING

PROLOG

Early Sunday morning
The field was wrapped in mist;
In the mist, upon a mound,
A young maiden leaned
Just like a graceful poplar.
She presses something to her bosom
And converses with the mist:

"O mist, O mist —
My patchy fortune!
Won't you hide me
In the field here?
Won't you smother me,
Force me in the ground?
Will you not relieve me
Of my awful life and fortune?
No, dear mist, don't smother!
Just hide me in the field,
So my hapless fortune is
Seen and known by none!..
I'm not alone, I have
A father, I've a mother...
I have, O mist,
O my mist, my brother!..
A child of my own! O my son,
My unchristened son!
I won't be the one to christen you
In this trying hour.
Strangers are to christen you,
I won't even know
Your name... My child!
I was rich...
Curse me not; I'll pray,
From heaven high above,
I'll requite your fate with tears
And send it down to you."

231 *Zinoviy* — Hetman Bohdan Khmelnytsky's second name.

232 *Alexei* — Czar Alexei (1629-76) who ruled Russia when Khmelnytsky signed the Pereyaslav Treaty that subordinated Ukraine to Russia.

She walked the field, crying,
Hiding in the mist
And through her tears
Sang quietly
Of how a widow drowned her child
In waters of the Danube:

"Oh, in the field is a mound;
There a widow walked,
There she walked and roamed,
Seeking poison herbs.
Poison herbs she did not find,
So she brought two little sons,
Covered them in cloth
And took them to the Danube:
'O quiet, quiet Danube!
Entertain my little children.
You, O golden sand,
Give my children food;
And please bathe them, swaddle them,
And wrap them with yourself!'"

I

There was a grandpa and a grandma.
From way back when,
They lived together in a hamlet
In a grove above a pond.
Like two children,
Both were everywhere.
As little kids they tended lambs,
Later, they got married,
Got some head of cattle,
Got a hamlet, pond and mill,
Grew an orchard in the grove,
And beehives they had plenty —
They acquired everything.
But children they have none,
And closing in behind their backs
Is death with scythe in hand.

Who will greet their golden years,
And stand beside them like a child?
Who will cry and bury?
Who will recollect the soul?
Who will justly use their wealth
To remember and be grateful for good times,
If not a child of one's own?..
It's hard to feed one's children
In a roofless home,
But it's harder still to age
In mansions painted white,
To grow old, to die,
To abandon wealth
To strangers and strange children
For laughter, for misuse!

II

On Sunday, gramps and grandma
Sat beside their house,
Both of them dressed nicely
In their bright white shirts.
The sun beamed, the sky
Was cloudless, it was quiet,
It was pleasant, like in paradise.
Hidden in the heart lay trouble,
Like a beast within a darkened grove.
In such a paradise, why, you see,
Should the old folks worry?
Was it perhaps some bygone trouble
That arose within the home?
Or was it yesterday's forgotten trouble
That stirred up once again,
Or did it just begin to sprout
To set paradise on fire?

I do not know the what or why
Of the old folks' melancholy. Perhaps,
They're set to meet the Lord,
But who will harness up the horses well
For such a long, long journey?

"Nancy, who will bury us upon our deaths?"
"I myself know not!
This I have considered,
And it all became so sad:
We've aged alone...

For whom have we acquired
All this wealth of ours?.."
"Hold on a bit!
Do you hear? There's something crying
Past the gate… like a little child!
Let's just run!... You see?
I guessed there will be something!"

They grabbed each other
And dashed off to the gate…
They come running —
And silently they halted.
Beside their very gate
Was a swaddled child —
But not tightly, it was dressed as well
In simple peasant clothes;
For the mother did the swaddling —
And in the summer used
Her final peasant clothing!..
My oldsters looked and prayed.
And the poor thing seems to plead:
It stretched its tiny hands,
Reaching out to them… and fell silent.
It did not cry, it seems,
But whimpered quietly instead.
"How's that, Nancy?
Just like I said! You see?
There's our fortune, there's our fate,
And we are not alone!
Just take the child and swaddle it…
What a baby, knock on wood!
Carry it inside, while I gallop horseback
To Horodyshche[233]
And cast about for godparents…"

Somehow oddities
Occur among us!
One man damns his son
And drives him from the house,
Another wretch sweats to earn a candle
And to place it, crying,
By some holy icons —
No children!..
Somehow oddities
Occur among us!

III

They gathered three whole sets
Of godparents
To celebrate, and in the evening
Held the christening,
Then named the child Mark.
Mark grows. My oldsters do not know
Where to put, where to sit, where to rest
Nor what to do with him.
A year passes. Mark grows —
And the milk cow bathes in luxury.
And lo, a dark-browed beauty,
Young and fair,
Came by the thriving hamlet
And asked to be a hireling.

"Why not, — he says, —
Let's take her, Nancy."
"Yes, Trokhym, let's take her,
For we're old, we could take ill,
And it's a child after all,
And even though it's bigger,
Nonetheless, he needs good care."
"Yes, indeed, it's needed.
For I have lived my share, thank God, —
I'm worn down a bit. So, what now,
What will you take, my dear?
For a year, or what?"
"Whatever pleases you."
"Ah, no! You need to know,
You must, my daughter, count your pay,
The pay you earn,
Because it's said: one who fails to count
Is one without a thing.

---

233 *Horodyshche* — A town in Cherkasy Oblast of Central Ukraine.

Not so, my dear?
No, you do not know us,
Nor do we know you. You'll live a bit,
You'll look 'round this house,
And we will see you too —
And then we'll talk of pay,
Okay, my daughter?"
"Okay, uncle."
"Welcome to our home."
They connected. The young gal
Is glad and happy,
As if she's married to a lord
And bought herself some villages.
Day and night it's in the house,
Around the yard and cattle;
And around the child she stoops,
As if she were its mother;
On weekdays and on Sundays
She'll wash his little head
And dress him in a clean white shirt
Each and every day.
She plays, she sings,
Makes him little toys, and on holidays —
Won't let him from her arms.
My oldsters are amazed
And pray to God above.
And each night the sleepless hireling,
The wretch, curses her misfortune,
Crying oh so hard;
And no one hears,
Or knows, or sees,
Except the little Mark.
But the child does not know
Why the hireling cleans him
With a stream of tears.
Nor does he know, why she
Showers him with kisses —
She won't eat
Or finish drinking,
She'll instead feed him.
Mark knows not
When late at night
He'll awake at times, stir inside his cradle —
And she's right there,
She'll cover him and cross him,
And rock him gently back to sleep;
She hears the child's breathing
All throughout the house.
Mornings, Mark's tiny hands
Reach out for the hireling
And he exalts the sleepless Hanna
By calling her his mama...
Mark knows not, he grows apace,
Develops and grows more.

IV

As the years flowed on
So too did water toward the sea;
Trouble swerved into the hamlet,
And brought along a lot of tears.
They buried grandma Nancy
And were barely, barely able
To revive grandpa Trokhym.
The accursed trouble made an uproar
And then it went to sleep.
From a shady grove
Bliss came back
And came to rest in grandpa's
Hamlet home.

Mark is now a wandering trader
And in autumn sleeps no longer
In or by the house...
Someone's needed for a match!
"Just who is that to be?" —
Thought the old man
And asked the hireling for advice.
And the hireling would be glad
To send matchmakers to a princess:
"The one to ask is Mark himself."
"Okay, daughter, we'll ask
And then we'll get him married."

They asked around, discussed,
And Mark went seeking go-betweens.
People came with wedding scarves,

Exchanging sacred bread.
They put forth a well-dressed maiden,
A beauty that would not bring
Shame even to a hetman.
That's the wonder they produced!

"Thank you all! — the old man says.
Now, so all may know,
We need to follow through,
Deciding when and where to marry,
And then, of course, to celebrate.
And here's another thing:
Who will be the mother?
My Nancy did not live
To see him off in marriage!.."
His eyes then filled with tears.
The hireling grabbed the doorjamb
And fainted at the threshold.
The house went quiet;
The hireling merely whispered:
"Mother… mother… mother!"

V

At the hamlet in a week
Young wives kneaded wedding bread.
The old father dances with the wives,
Sweeping 'round the yard,
And using all his might;
He summons passers-by and travelers
To come into the yard;
He shares his brew,
And beckons all to join the wedding.
He runs, you know,
Though his feet can barely carry him.
Laughter and commotion reign
Inside the house and all around.
And they rolled out troughs
From the brand new storeroom.
Chores abound: baking, cooking
Sweeping, cleaning…
All are hired hands. But Hanna,
The hireling herself,
Went on a pilgrimage to Kyiv.
The old man pleaded,
Mark had even cried,
That she serve him as his mother.
"No, Mark, it's not proper
That I be your fill-in mother:
They're all rich,
And I'm hireling… they could
Even laugh at you.
May God bless both of you!
I'll go to Kyiv
And I'll pray to all the saints,
Then I'll come back
And join you,
If you'll have me in your house.
I'll toil till I have the strength to do so…"
With her pure heart
She blessed her Mark…
Then cried and went beyond the gate.

The wedding's in full swing.
Music makers work
And so do people's cleats.
Stools and tables slosh with brew.
And the hireling scurries,
Hastening to Kyiv.
To Kyiv she came — she did not rest,
Staying with a bourgeois lady,
For whom she carried water,
Because she had no money left
For prayer services to Barbara.[234]
She carried-carried,
Earning more or less eight kopas[235]
And in the caves from John the Saint
She bought Mark a holy cap,
To free the young man's head of worry;

---

[234] *Barbara* — Reference to an early Christian saint and martyr. Her relics were brought to Kyiv in the 12th century.
[235] See glossary or fn. 137

And from Barbara she got a ring
To give her in-law daughter,
Then having bowed to all the saints,
She began the trip back home.

She returned. Both Mark
And Kateryna met her by the gate,
Led her to their home
And sat her at the table;
They fed her, gave her drink,
Asked about Kyiv,
Then Kateryna sent her
To a room for rest.

"Why their love for me?
Why respect for me?
O my Lord of mercy!
Perhaps, they know...
Perhaps, they've guessed...
No, they haven't guessed;
They're good..."
And the hireling
Broke down and sobbed.

VI

Thrice the river froze,
Thrice it melted in the spring,
Kateryna thrice saw the hireling off to Kyiv,
As if she were a mother;
She saw the poor dear off the fourth year,
Going far into the field to a mound,
Praying to the Lord for a swift return,
Because it's somehow sad without
The hireling at home,
As if a mother left it.
Following the Blessed Virgin's Feast,
After the Dormition, the old Trokhym
Sat on a slab beside the house
In his bright white shirt.
His grandson played
Beside him with his faithful dog,
And the granddaughter
Donned a dress like Kateryna,
Then in a game of make-believe,
She paid a visit to her granddad.
The old man laughed
And welcomed his granddaughter,
As if indeed she were a maiden:
"Where did you hide the flatbread?
Did someone take it in the forest?
Or did you forget to take it?..
Or perhaps you did not bake it?
Tsk, tsk, you pretty mama!"
Then all at once — the hireling
Came into the yard. The old man
And his grandkids ran to meet his Hanna.
"Is Mark yet on the road?"
Hanna asked the granddad.
"Yes, still on the road."
"And I barely made it
To your home,
I did not want to die alone
In a far off place.
If only Mark would come...
It's become so hard for me!"
Then from her sack she gave the kids
Some modest gifts: a few crosses, a few ducats
And a string of beads for Yarynochka,
And a little icon made of crimson foil.
She gave Karpov a pair of horses
And a nightingale,
And for Kateryna, a fourth ring of
Barbara the Saint, and three candles
For the grandpa made of holy wax;
There was nothing for herself and Mark:
She did not buy for lack of money,
And was too sick to earn some more.
"There's still half a breadroll!"
And she gave the children each a half.

VII

She went into the house. Kateryna
Washed her feet and sat her down for lunch.
Old Hanna neither ate nor drank.
"Kateryna!
When is Sunday?"

"Two days hence."
"We'll need
An Akathist to Nicholas,[236]
And to donate to the church;
Because Mark is somewhat late…
Perhaps, he's on the road and ill,
O may God forbid!"
From her old and weary eyes
Dripped despondent tears.
She barely-barely rose
From behind the table.
"Kateryna!
Though I stand
I'm not the same.
I'm unwell, too weak
To even stand up on my legs.
It's hard to die, my Katie,
In a stranger's heated house!"

The poor dear took ill.
They had given her communion,
Anointed her with holy oil —
No, it did not help.
The old Trokhym walks
'Round the yard
As if he had been killed.
Kateryna does not take her eyes
Off the ailing patient;
Kateryna spends her days and nights
Standing right beside her.
Meanwhile, screech owls on the shed
Prophesy misfortune.
The sickly one asks softly
Each day and every hour:
"My daughter Kateryna!
Has Mark not yet returned?
Oh, if I knew I'd live to see him,
I would wait some more!"

VIII

Mark approaches with the chumaks,
Singing as he goes.
He does not hasten home —
He lets the oxen graze.
Mark is bringing Kateryna
Quite expensive cloth,
For his father there's a sash
Made of crimson silk,
And for the hireling, gold brocade
To decorate her cap
And a good red scarf
With a *hem* of white.
For the children there are shoes,
Some figs and also grapes,
And for everyone together —
Red wine from Carihrad[237]
At least three pails all in barrels,
And from the Don[238] there's caviar —
He brings it all, knowing nothing
Of the news back home!

Mark goes along, not worried.
He arrives — thank God!
He opens up the gate,
And says a prayer to the Lord.
"Kateryna, do you hear?
Come running out to greet me!
I'm back! Run quickly!
Bring me quickly in the house!..
Glory unto you, O our Christ the Lord!
I barely held out waiting!"
Then, as if it were a dream,
She softly, softly prayed *Our Father.*

The old man unharnesses the oxen,
Puts away the sculpted clasps,
And Katrusia looks Mark over.

236 *Akathist to Nicholas* — Akathist is a Christian hymn dedicated to Christ, the Blessed Virgin or a saint. Nicholas, a 4th century saint, is the patron of sailors, merchants, children and the poor.

237 See glossary or fn. 43

238 *Don* — Reference to the Don River.

"And where's Hanna, Kateryna?
I've not noticed her!
"She's not passed away?"
"No, she's not died,
Though she's very ill.
Let's go to the small house
While the oxen are unharnessed:
Mark, she waits for you."

Mark walked into the small house,
Stopping at the threshold...
He stood frightened. Hanna whispers:
"Praise, O praise the Lord!
Come here, please do not be frightened...
Katie, leave the house:
There's something I must ask,
And a few things to relate."

Kateryna left the house
And Mark leaned low
Just by the hireling's head.
"Mark! Look,
Have a look at me:
You see how I have whithered?
I'm not Hanna, not a hireling,
I..."
And she fell silent.
Mark cried, and wondered.
Again her eyes were open,
She looked intently, quite intently —
Tears rolled down.
"Forgive me! I suffered
All my years in a stranger's house...
Forgive me, O my son!
I... I'm your mother."
She fell silent...
Mark passed out,
And the ground began to tremble.
He awoke... went to mother —
And mother was by then asleep!

Pereyaslav, November 13, 1845

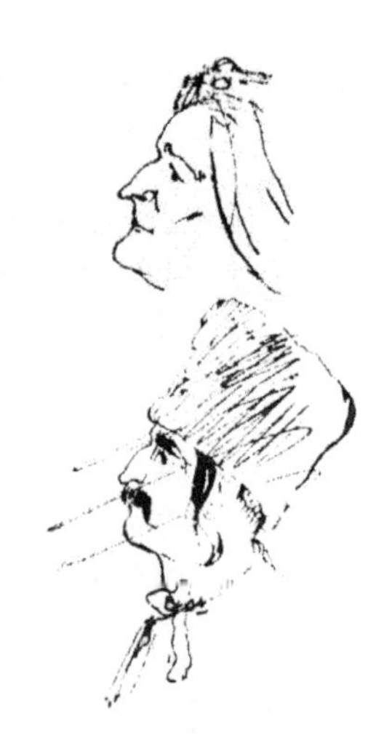

Sketch, 1840

THE CAUCASUS

To my true Yakiv de Balmen[239]

Oh that my head were waters,
and mine eyes a fountain of tears,
that I might weep day and night
for the slain...
Jeremiah 9, Verse 1

Mountains beyond mountains
Shrouded in clouds,
Seeded by grief and showered with blood.
Since time immemorial,
It is there that an eagle
Has punished Prometheus.[240]
Each God-given day
It pecks at his ribs
And pierces the heart that's within.
Pierces, yet it can't drink
Vital blood that is spilled —
The heart pulses again,
And again it knows laughter.
Our soul does not perish,
Nor does freedom expire.
Nor can the greedy plow any field
In the murky abyss of an ocean.
The living soul he will not chain,
The living word he'll not constrain,
He'll not besmirch God's glory,
The glory of the great Creator.

Ours is not to challenge You!
Ours is not to judge Your deeds!
Ours is but to cry, to cry and cry
And to knead our daily bread
With bloody sweat and tears.
Tyrants torment us;
Our truth is in a drunken stupor.
When will it awaken?
When will You lay down to rest,
O weary Lord?
And let us live!
We have faith in all Your power,
And Your living spirit.
The truth will rise!
So too will liberty!
And to You, alone,
All tongues will pray
For all eternity.
But for now,
Rivers, bloody rivers, flow!

Mountains beyond mountains
Shrouded in clouds,
Seeded by grief and showered with blood.

That is where the gracious we
Seized unfed, undressed
And hapless freedom,
Which we harass and hound.
More than a few
Laid down their bones,
All soldiers drilled to die.
And blood? And tears?
There'd be enough to quench

239 *Yakiv de Balmen (1813-45)* — An officer, amateur artist and friend of Shevchenko. He transcribed the poet's *Kobzar* into the Latin alphabet for Slavs who used it. He also helped illustrate the manuscript. De Balmen, a descendant of Scots and Frenchmen, was killed on a Russian military mission to the Caucasus.

240 *Prometheus* — Greek mythological figure punished for stealing fire from the gods and sharing it with people.

All emperors, their children
And their grandchildren,
And to drown them
In the tears of widows. And those
Of maidens shed secretly at night!
And the burning tears of mothers!
And the old and bloody
Tears of fathers —
There's not a river — but a sea,
A fiery sea! Glory! Glory!
To the greyhounds,
To the harriers, to huntsmen
And to our patriarchal czars,
Glory!

And glory be to you,
O azure ice-capped mountains.
And to you, great knights,
Not forgotten by the Lord.
Fight — you'll win the fight,
God is helping you!
Behind you stands the truth,
Behind you stands the glory,
And sacred liberty as well!
The *churek*[241] and the *sakla*[242] — All yours,
They're unbidden, they're not given,
None will take them as their own,
None will lead you bound and shackled.
Ah, but in our land!..
The reason that we're literate
Is to read the word of God!..
And from the deepest dungeon
To the highest altar —
We're all in gold and naked.
Come to us for learning! We'll instruct you
On the cost of bread and price of salt!
We're Christians;
We have the shrines, the schools
And all that's good, God Himself is with us!
It's just the *sakla* that offends our eyes:
Why is it that it stands among you,
We've not given it to you; why should we
Not toss your churek to you, like
We'd chuck it to a dog! Why should
You not pay us for the sun that shines above!
That and nothing more! We're not heathens,
We're true Christians,
Small things are enough!..
At the same time!
If you become our friend,
There's quite a lot you'd learn!
We've got worlds, just consider —
Siberia alone is so vast it can't be passed,
And the dungeons! And the people!..
Why bother even counting!
From the Moldovan to the Finn up north
Every tongue is silent,
Because they all are prospering! In our land
The holy monk reads the Holy Bible
And he teaches that some czar,[243] a swineherd,
Took a neighbor's wife, killed a friend.
And now he sits in heaven! So you see
What kinds we have sitting up in heaven!
You're still dark, you're not enlightened
By the Holy Cross,
Come learn from us!.. Among us, it's steal,
Rip-off, give,
Then it's straight to heaven.
You can even take your family! In our land!
What do we not know?
We count the stars, sow fields of buckwheat,
And we curse the French. We sell people…
They're not negroes,..[244]
Or we lose them in a game of cards…

---

241 *Churek* — An unleavened bread in the Caucasus.

242 *Sakla* — A type of dwelling in the Caucasus.

243 *Some czar* — Reference to the Biblical King David. He took the wife of his neighbor Uriah, whom he sent to battle to be killed.

244 *They're not negroes* — Russia signed the 1841 Quintuple Treaty with four other European powers to suppress the African slave trade, but continued domestic trade in its own serfs.

Indeed they're christened…
But they're simple folk.
We're not Spaniards;[245] God forbid
That, like those Jews, we resell stolen goods.
We're law-abiding!..

Do you love your brother
As per the Apostles' law?
Idle talkers, hypocrites,
Damned by God above.
You love the skin that's on your brother,
Not the soul inside!
You legally extort
To get a fur coat for your daughter,
To settle with your bastard,
To give your wife some slippers,
And to get yourself
That something, of which
The wife and kids know nothing!

For whom, dear Christ, O Son of God,
Were you nailed to the cross?
For us, the meek, or for the word
Of Truth… or so we may scoff at You?
That is how it came to pass.

Shrines, chapels, icons,
Smoke of myrrh and candelabras,
And unflagging bowing
Before Your sacred image.
They implore for theft, for war, for blood,
To spill a brother's blood, and then they
Gift You with an altar-cloth stolen
From a burning ruin!!
We're enlightened! And still we want
To bring enlightenment to others,
To share the light of truth, you see,
With children that are blind.

We'll show you everything! Just let us take
You by the hand.
How to lay the bricks for dungeons,
How to forge some shackles,
And how to wear them too!..
And how to weave a knotted whip —
We'll teach you everything; just give us
All your azure mountains… for
We've now seized the field and sea.

They drove you too, my dear good friend,
My one and only Yakiv! You came to spill
Your good pure blood
Not for Ukraine, but for her executioner.
You had a drink of Moscow's poison from
The cup of Moscow.
O my good, good friend!
My unforgettable dear friend!
May your living spirit soar above Ukraine,
Fly with Kozaks o'er the shores,
Guard the dug up mounds
That stand amid the steppe.
Shed fine tears with Kozaks
And in that steppe please wait for me
As we break our bondage.

But for now I'll sow my thoughts,
My raging anguish — let them grow
And with the wind converse.
The gentle wind
Will mix my thoughts with dew
And they'll reach you from Ukraine!..
You, my friend, will welcome them
You'll read them
With a brother's tear…
And you'll recall
The mounds and steppe,
You'll recall the sea and me.

Pereyaslav, November 18, 1845

---

245 *We're not Spaniards* — Spain was a major slave trader and did not sign the Quintuple Treaty.

TO THE DEAD, THE LIVING, AND TO THE UNBORN
Compatriots of mine in Ukraine and not in Ukraine
My Fraternal
MISSIVE

If a man say, I love God,
and hateth his brother,
he is a liar.

1 John Chapter 4, Verse 20

Dawn, then dusk,
God's livelong day is passing,
Again the people have grown weary,
Everything is resting.
Only I, as if accursed,
Cry by night and day
Standing at a crowded crossroads,
But no one sees,
No one sees, or knows,
Gone deaf, they do not hear;
They swap chains,
They barter truth.
They demean the Lord,
And harness people into
Heavy yokes. They plow evil
Then sow evil. And what sprouts?
You'll see the harvest!
Take pause, unworthy people,
Foolish children!
Behold your quiet paradise,
Behold this land of yours,
Come to love with all your heart
The great Ukrainian ruin,
Throw off your chains, be brothers,
Do not seek and do not ask
In foreign lands
What even heaven does not proffer,
To say nothing of a foreign field.
In your own home there is your truth
Your power and your freedom.
There's but one Ukraine
Upon this world,
There is no second Dnipr',
Yet you rush abroad
Seeking goodly goodness,
Sacred goodness. Freedom! Freedom!
Fraternal brotherhood! Finding it,
You lugged and lugged it
From a foreign field
And what you brought back to Ukraine
Was great words, great power
Not one iota more. You scream
That God has not created you
To bow before untruth!..
And you bend, just as you bent!
And again you strip the skin
Off your sightless brothers,
All those buckwheat farmers.
Then seeking sunlit truth
Again you rush to German lands
That for you aren't foreign!..
If you took along the misery
And all that forebears stole,
It would leave the Dnipro orphaned
With just the sacred mountains!

Oh, would that it transpire,
May you not return,
May you croak where you sprawled out!
Children would not cry,
Nor would mother weep,
And God would not take note

Of all your insolence.
Nor would the sun warm smelly dung
Upon a land that's clean,
That's broad and free.
People would not know your kind of eagle,
And would not shake their heads at you.
Take pause! Be upright,
Or trouble will confound you.
Shackled people soon will
Break their shackles,
Judgment day will come, the Dnipro
And the mountains
Will be called to testify!
Your children's blood will spill
Into a hundred rivers and drain
Into the deep blue sea...[246]
There will not be a soul to help.
Brothers will forsake their brothers
Mothers will disown their children.
And clouds of smoke
Will block the shining sun above you,
Your sons will curse you for eternity!
Clean up! Don't blaspheme God's image
With a pile of muck.
Don't fool your children to believe
They're in this world just to rule...
Because an unschooled eye
Will deeply peer into their very souls.
Deeply! The kids will then find out
Whose skin is on your back,
They'll then condemn, and the clever
Will be fooled by fools.

Had you studied as you should,
Your wisdom would be yours.
Instead you reach for heaven:
"We are not we, and I not I,
I've seen it all, I know it all,
There's neither hell, nor Paradise,
There is no God, just I!
And the short and clumsy German,
Nothing more!" — "Okay, brother,
Who are you?"
"Let the
German say. We don't know."
That is how you study in a foreign land!
The German[247] says, "You're Mongols."
"Mongols! Mongols!"
Naked grandkids
Of the golden Tamerlane.[248]
The German says, "You're Slavs."
"Slavs! Slavs!"
The worthless great-grandchildren
Of glorious great-grandfathers.
You've read with all your might Kollar,[249]
Hanka[250] and Safarik,[251]
And you're keen
To join the Slavophiles...[252]
All languages of Slavic peoples —
All of them you know. And your own,
No way... We too someday will
Speak our language,
If the German shows us how,
On top of which he will relate
Our history as well, —
That's when we'll get into it!..
You've gotten into it
Through German guidance
And spoken in a way
The German, a great teacher,

---

246 *Blood will drain* — Reference to the Book of Revelations, Chapter 16.

247 *The German* — Ironic reference to a theory of some German historians that Slavs were descended from Mongols.

248 *Tamerlane (1336-1405)* — Ruthless Turkic military conqueror feared in Europe, Asia and Africa.

249 *Jan Kollar (1793-1852)* — A Slovak writer and leading proponent of Pan-Slavism.

250 *Vaclav Hanka (1791-1861)* — A Czech philologist and proponent of Pan-Slavism.

251 See glossary or fn. 162

252 *Slavophiles* — Members of a movement that seeks unity of Slavic peoples and admires their cultures.

Does not fathom,
To say nothing of the simple folk.
So much uproar! So much shouting!
"It[253] has harmony, and power,
It's music, say no more.
And history!.. it's the poem
Of a people and their liberty!
What of those needy Romans!
What the hell — not Brutuses!
We have our Brutuses![254] And Cocleses![255]
Glorious, not forgotten!
Freedom grew in our dear land,
It was bathed by Dnipro waters,
Its head rested on the mountains,
And its blanket was the steppe!"
It was bathed in blood,
It slept on piles,
On the corpses of free Kozaks,
Corpses that were robbed!
Just look closer,
Read the glory once again.
Read word for word,
Change not a title,
So much less a comma.
Comprehend it all... then ask yourselves:
What are we?..
Whose sons? Whose parents?
By whom? Why the shackles?..
And then you'll see your glorious Brutuses
For who they really are:
Slaves, footstools, Moscow's mud,
And Warsaw's trash — your lords,
Your most illustrious hetmans.
Why should you be boasting, you!
Sons of poor Ukraine!
That with a yoke you walk so well,
Even better than your parents walked.
Don't boast, they're whipping you,
And from them, at times, they boiled tallow.
Perhaps, you boast, the brotherhood
Preserved the faith.
That it boiled dumplings
In Trapezond and Sinope.[256]
True!.. It's true they ate their fill.
And now you're indisposed.
And on the Sich the canny German[257]
Plants potatoes
That you buy from him.
You eat them in good health
And give praise to Zaporizhia.
But whose blood was used
To water soil that those
Potatoes grow in —
You're indifferent. Just so they're
Good for one's own garden!
And you boast
That we once toppled Poland!..
You're right: Poland fell,
And crushed you too![258]

And thus our parents spilled their blood
For Moscow and for Warsaw,
And to you, their sons, they passed
Their shackles and their glory!

Ukraine has struggled
To the very brink.
Her own children crucify her
Worse than any Pole.
Instead of beer they tap

---

253 *It* — Reference to the Ukrainian language.

254 *Lucius Junius Brutus* — Founder of the Roman Republic in 509 BC.

255 *Horatio Publius Cocles* — An officer and hero in the army of the ancient Roman Republic.

256 *Trapezond and Sinope* — Turkish cities on the Black Sea that Kozaks raided to free brethren taken prisoner.

257 *The canny German* — German Mennonite immigrants founded the Chortitza Colony around the former Sich Kozak stronghold. Russia encouraged such immigration to develop agriculture.

258 *Poland fell...* — Russia took advantage of the Polish partition to seize Ukrainian territory from Poland.

Righteous blood from ribs.
They want, they say, to enlighten
Mother's eyes with contemporary flames.
To lead the dumb and sightless cripple,
Thus following the Germans
Into the modern age.
Good, lead, show,
Let the aging mother learn
How to raise those modern children.
Demonstrate!.. Worry not about tuition,
Mom will recompense.
Your clouded greedy eyes will clear
You'll see the glory,
Living glory of your granddads
And of your evil parents.
Fool not yourselves,
Learn, read,
And study what is foreign,
But don't forsake your own.
For he who won't recall his mother,
Is punished by the Lord,
He's forsaken by his children,
They bar them from their home.
Strangers banish,
And for the evil person
There is no place on earth's expanse
To find a happy home.
I weep when I recall the deeds
Our forebears stamped in memory.
If they could all be disregarded,
I'd give up a half
Of all my happy years.
This then is our glory,
The glory of Ukraine.
Thus, you too should read it,
So that all the falsehoods
Won't be living dreams,
So that lofty mounds will open
Right before your eyes,
So you may ask the martyrs,
Whom, when and why
Each was crucified!
O my brothers, please embrace
Our smallest brother —
May mother smile,
Our weeping mother.
With calloused hands,
She'll bless her children,
With lips set free,
She'll kiss them.
The shameful bygone hour
Soon will be forgotten,
Good glory will revive,
The glory of Ukraine,
And a vivid world, not at twilight,
Will serenely shine...
Embrace, my brothers,
I beseech you, I implore!

Viunishcha, December 14, 1845

Near Kaniv, 1859

THE COLD RAVINE[259]

Each one has his trouble,
I have my disquiet,
Though not my own, it's borrowed,
But it's trouble nonetheless.
Why should there be, you see, any mention
Of what's long since passed,
To awaken bygones —
It's good they went to sleep.
Though that Ravine; the smallest
Trail there exists no more; and it seems
No foot has trodden there, but to recall,
It was the road from Motrona's Monastery[260]
To the terrible Ravine. Haidamaks
Camped in that Ravine, sharpened tips
Of spears and prepared their muzzle-loaders.
They convened in that Ravine,
As if taken from a cross.
A father with his son and a
Brother with his brother
Stood as one to fight
The evil foe, the ferocious Pole.
Where'd you go, O beaten path,
That led into that deep Ravine?
Did you veil yourself
With dark dense woods,
Or were they planted by new tyrants?
So that people would not go to you
To ask for your advice:
How to handle kindly lords,
Evil cannibals,
And newer sets of Poles?
You'll not hide it! Above the Ravine
Drifts Iron Max[261] gazing out toward Uman,
Looking out for Gonta.[262]
Do not hide and do not trample
The righteous sacred law,
Don't refer to Nero[263] as a reverend.
Claim no glory for a war
The czar is willing to deem holy.[264]
For you don't know what petty czars contrive.
But you boast of carrying soul and skin
For the Fatherland!..
By God, the disposition of a sheep;
The fool sticks out his neck,
Knowing not the reason why!
Moreover, he the lazy lazybones[265]
Belittles Gonta.
"The haidamaks aren't warriors —
Bandits, thieves they are.
A stain upon our history..."
You lie, tormentor!
A bandit will not rise
For sacred truth and freedom,
He won't unchain unknowing people
Bound with your own shackles.
He won't kill an evil son,
He won't break a living heart
To defend his country.
You — insatiable bandits,
Hungry ravens.
By what righteous sacred law
Do you trade the land and all its blessings
With the wretches on it?
Be on your guard, or you'll have trouble,

---

259 *The Cold Ravine (Kholodniy yar)* — The 1768 uprising against Polish gentry began in the Cold Ravine, a large forest in Central Ukraine.

260 *Motrona's Monastery* — A monastery in the Cold Ravine founded in the 11th century.

261 See glossary or fn. 83

262 See glossary or fn. 84

263 *Nero (37-68)* — Extravagant and tyrannical Roman emperor.

264 *War ... deem holy* — Reference to Russian war in the Caucasus.

265 *Lazy lazybones* — Reference to Apollo Oleksandrovych Skalkowski (1808-99), Ukrainian and Russian historian who wrote a negative assessment of the haidamak rebels.

Major trouble! Fool the children
And a sightless brother,
Fool yourself and strangers,
But do not fool with God.
For retribution will befall you
On a day of joy.
And a fire will spread anew
From the Cold Ravine.

Viunishcha, December 17, 1845

PSALMS OF DAVID

1

The blessed man won't join
An evil counsel,
He won't go the way of sin,
Nor will he sit beside the scornful.
Instead his heart and will
Draw lessons from the law of God.
He'll bear abundant fruit
Like a greening tree beside the water
Planted in a fertile field.
Thus that man
In his goodness ripens,
But all trace is lost
Of the evil and impious,
Like ashes scattered 'round the earth
By the wind above.
And the evil
Will not rise from coffins
To stand beside the righteous.
Deeds of the good shall flourish,
Deeds of the wicked will expire.

12 [266]

Do You forget me,
My dear God, forever,
Do You turn Your face from me,
Do You abandon me?
How long am I to rack my soul
And have an aching heart?
How long will my fierce foe
Gaze at me and laugh!.. Save me,
Save my soul,
May the clever foe not say:
"I have conquered him."
And the wicked all will laugh,
Should I fall into their hands,
Into hostile hands; save me
From the ruthless torment.
Save me, and with a heart that's pure
I will again sing praises of Your goodness
In a new and quiet psalm.

43

God, we've heard Your glory
With our ears,
And grandfathers tell us
Of those bygone
Bloody years:
How Your strong hand
Freed ours,
And buried hostile corpses.
And Your people praised Your power
Then rested tranquilly in goodness,
Glorifying God!.. And today!..
Again You've wrapped in shame Your people,

[266] *Numbering of the Psalms* — Psalm numbers, beginning with the 9th, differ between faiths. Some use Hebrew numbering; Shevchenko used that of Eastern Orthodoxy.

Again we're plundered by new foes
And devoured just like sheep!..
Without reward
And free of charge You've
Given us to cursed foes.
You've abandoned us
To people's mockery
And to the scorn of neighbors,
You've abandoned us, like a parable
For unwise people.
And they shake their laughing
Heads at us,
And every day ahead
Our shame is there before us.
Robbed, tormented
We now die in chains,
We pray not to foreign gods,
It is You that we beseech:
"Help us, deliver us
From hostile scorn.
The first force you defeated,
Defeat the second one that's graver!..
Awaken, God,
You'll sleep in vain,
Turning from our tears,
Forgetting all our sorrows!
Our soul's resigned,
It's hard to live in shackles!
Rise up, O God, and help us
Rise anew against the tyrant."

52

In his heart the fool won't say
That God does not exist.
In lawlessness he wallows,
He creates no good.
And God looks to see
If someone is still seeking Him.
There's no welldoer, not a single one.
When will they, those unappeased
In sin, find out?
It's not bread they eat, but people,
They neglect to mention God,
They're afraid and startled
Where there is no fear.
Thus the evil fear themselves.
Who will grant salvation to us,
Who is to restore good fortune?
God will renew our freedom someday,
He will break our bondage.
We'll bring glory to You, God,
With abundant praise;
Israel will rejoice
As will the holy Jacob.

53

God, save me, judge me
By Your will,
I pray, O Lord, impart
My words unto their lips.
For mighty foreigners have
Stood upon my soul,
They see no God above themselves,
They know not what they do.
But God helps me,
He protects me
And with His truth
Requites their evil.
I will pray to God
With a lonely heart
And I'll look upon my evil foes
With no malice in my eyes.

81

Among the czars and judges
At the great assembly,
The Ruler of the heavens
Stood to judge the earthly sovereigns.
"How long will you be spilling
The guiltless blood of indigents?

And helping all the rich
In evil courts of law?
Help the needy widow,
Don't condemn the orphan,
And lead the meek
From confinement into freedom,
Protect them from rapacious hands."
They don't want to recognize,
Or to dispel the gloom of bondage,
And the word of God is futile,
The earth's crying too is futile.
Czars, slaves — equal
Sons before the Lord,
You too will die,
Just as your prince
And meager servant.
Arise, O God, judge the earth
And evil judges.
Your truth on earth is everpresent,
So too Your will, and glory.

93

The Lord our God punishes the wicked —
I know this in my soul.
Rise up, God, the prideful man
Offends Your glory.
Ascend high, high
Above the earth
Shut the haughty sightless eye
With the power of Your glory.
How long untruths,
How long, O Lord, will the evil boast
Of them? In gloom and bondage
They have chained Your people...
They've drowned Your good in blood.
The passerby they've butchered,
And they've choked the widow.
Then they said: "The Lord's not watching,
He knows nothing of it."
Wise up, unwise,
He who watches o'er the world
Knows your evil heart
And your thoughts as well.
Observe His deeds,
And His eternal glory.
Blessed is the one among us
Whom the Lord would punish,
Not waiting till a pit
Is scooped out for the evil.
The Lord loves His people,
Loves and won't abandon them,
He waits until the truth
Shall arise before them all.
Who would save me from the wicked
And the evildoers?
If God did not assist me,
The living soul would
Perish in the gloom of hell,
And would be damned on earth.
You, O Lord, help to
Walk on earth.
You make my soul rejoice
And You heal my heart,
Your will shall overcome
Your efforts aren't in vain.
Even if they seize
The soul that's righteous,
And condemn the blood that's good,
The Lord shall be my haven,
My protector He shall be,
He'll avenge their
Bloody and their evil deeds,
He'll destroy them, and their fame
Will turn to infamy.

132

Is there a thing upon this world
Lovelier or better
Than to live together,
Sharing, not dividing, good
With one's good brothers?
Like fragrant myrrh

Dripping from
The honest head
Upon the beard of Aaron[267]
And to brocaded folds
Of a costly vestment;
Or the dew of Hermon[268]
Falling on the lofty sacred
Hills of Zion
And creating good for
All creatures born unto this earth,
And for the earth, and people —
Thus the Lord shall not forget
All his pious brothers.
He'll reign within a peaceful home,
Within a family of the great,
And he'll grant to them good fortune
For all eternity.

136

On the rivers 'round Babylon,
Under willows in the field,
We sat and cried
In distant bondage,
And we hung deaf harps
Upon those willows.
And the evil Edomites[269]
Began to mock us:
"Relate your song to us,
We too perhaps will cry.
Or sing ours,
For you're our captives."
Which are we to sing?..
They sing nothing joyous
In the grip of distant bondage
Upon a foreign field.
And if I, Jerusalem, forget you,
I'll be a slave
Forgotten and abandoned
In a foreign land.
And my evil tongue will wither,
It will be stricken dumb,
Should I forget to recollect
You, our glory.
And you, Edom's children,
Our Lord will recollect,
As you shouted: "Ruin,
Ruin, burn the holy Zion!"
O Babylon's accursed daughter!
Blessed is He, who shall
Requite you for your chains!
Blessed! Blessed! He will in joy
Confront you and smash
Your children against
A cold hard stone.

149

We'll sing new praises to the Lord,
We'll bring Him newfound glory
In an honest congregation,
With an honest heart;
With timbrels and psalteries
We'll exalt the blessing
Of God requiting the unrighteous,
And assisting all the righteous.
The blessed in their glory
And in their quiet chambers,
Rejoice, exalt
And praise the name of God,
Brandishing good swords,
Swords with double edges,

---

267 *Aaron* — Brother of Moses.

268 *Dew of Hermon* — Biblical symbol of reinvigoration and God's blessings. Mount Hermon is a peak in today's Syria standing 9232 feet (2814 meters) above sea level.

269 *Edomites* — Inhabitants of the kingdom of Edom. They were hostile to Israelites in ancient times.

For revenge against the pagans,
And to teach the people.
They'll bind in chains of iron
All the greedy czars,
And hands of their most infamous
Will be bound in shackles.
They will judge the butchers
In their court of justice.
And glory will arise forever,
Glory to the worthy.

Viunishcha, December 19, 1845

TO LITTLE MARYANNE

Grow, grow my little sweetie,
O my poppy blossom,
Prosper while your
Heart's unbroken,
While people have
Not found your
Lovely peaceful valley.
Once they do — they'll play around,
Sap you and discard you.
Neither beauty draping
Years of youth,
Nor hazel eyes
Awash in tears,
Nor your maiden's
Good and quiet heart
Will shield you or protect you
From greedy searching eyes.
The wicked will detect and rob…
And you, poor dear,
They'll throw to hell…
You'll be tormented,
Cursing God.
Don't blossom, my fresh blossom,
My flower yet unfolded,
Wither softly, wither while your
Heart's not broken.

Viunishcha, December 20, 1845

Sketch, 1841

Days go by, nights go by,
Summer passes, yellowed
Leaves are rustling.
Eyes grow dim,
The thoughts, the heart,
And all's asleep, and I don't know
If I'm alive, or marking time,
Or if I merely roam the world,
For I no longer laugh or cry…
Fate, where are you! Fate, where are you?
There's none,
And if You, O God,
Begrudge a fate that's good,
Then grant one that is awful, awful!
Do not let the roamer sleep,
Or the heart to languish
And to lay upon this world
Like a rotten log.
But let live, with the heart to live
And feel love for people,
And if not… then to curse
And set the world afire!
It's dreadful to be held in shackles,
And to die in bondage,
But still worse — to sleep, to sleep
To sleep in freedom,
And to stay asleep forevermore,
And leave no trace
No trace at all, no matter
If one lived, or died!
Fate, where are you!
Fate, where are you?
There is none,
And if You, O God,
Begrudge a fate that's good,
Then grant one that is awful, awful!

Viunishcha, December 21, 1845

THREE YEARS[270]

A day, not one, it ebbs and flows,
And like an arrow years fly by,
Taking all that's good.
They steal good thoughts,
They dash our heart
Against cold rocks
And then they sing amen,
Amen to all the joy
From now until eternity.
They then leave the sightless
Cripple on a lonely crossroads.
Three short years
Flew by in vain…
But in my home
They left much anguish.
They laid to waste
My poor, my placid heart,
Ignited trouble,
And with soot and smoke
They dried good tears
Shed with Katie[271]
On her road to Moscow;
They prayed with Kozaks
Held in Turkish bondage,[272]
And for Oksana,[273] my star
And my good fortune.
Each day God gave they cleansed…
Till awful years crept up
And stole it all once.
There's sorrow when a father or a mother
Or a happy, young and faithful wife
Are placed into a coffin,
What great sorrow, O my brothers;
It's hard to nurture little unwashed
Children in a home not heated,
Weighty anguish, but not the kind
Faced by a fool,
Who loves, gets married,
But she sells herself for three small coins
And even laughs at him.
There is anguish! That is how
The heart is torn.
That's the kind of evil anguish
That had befallen me:
The heart grew fond of people,
It loved people dearly,
And they welcomed it,
They played along and praised it too…
Quietly the years crept up,
Drying tears,
Tears of earnest love;
Then awareness
Slowly dawned on me…
I look closer —
Bite the tongue,
All around me, where'er I look,
I see not people, I see vipers…
My tears dried up,
My youthful tears.
With venom
I now heal the broken heart.
I don't cry, I do not sing,
But like an owl I screech.
So it is, whatever you desire,
Go ahead and do.
Be it loud derision,

---

270 *Three Years (1843-45)* — Shevchenko spent those years in Ukraine. They were prolific and marked a pivotal change in his worldview. Many of his poems from that period included social and political criticism that was suppressed by Russian imperial authorities. He compiled them in a manuscript known as the *Three Years* collection, which was confiscated and kept in secret state archives until 1907.

271 *Katie* — Reference to Kateryna, hero of Shevchenko's eponymous poem.

272 *Kozaks in bondage* — Reference to the heroes of the poem *Hamaliya*.

273 *Oksana Stepanivna Kovalenko (1817–?)* — An orphan, village neighbor and childhood friend of Shevchenko.

Be it quiet praise
Of the thoughts I write; just the same,
My youthful years will not return,
Nor will the joyous word.
It won't return… Nor
With this heart will I return to you.
And where I'll go I do not know,
Where I'll find a haven,
Whom I'll please, with whom I'll talk,
And to whom I may confess my thoughts?
My thoughts! My years,
My three hard years,
Whom are you to lean upon,
All my angry children?
Lean on no one,
Lay yourselves to rest at home…
And I'll ring in
A fourth new year;
Well, good morning, O New Year,
Dressed in last year's peasant coat,
What is that you bring Ukraine
In your patched up sack?
"Prosperity, swaddled in a
New decree."
Go, be well, and don't forget
To bow to poverty.

Viunishcha, December 22, 1845

TESTAMENT[274]

When I die, then bury me
Atop a mound
Amid the steppe's expanse
In my beloved Ukraine,
So I may see
The great broad fields,
The Dnipro and the cliffs,
So I may hear the river roar.
When it carries hostile blood
From Ukraine into the azure sea…
I'll then forsake
The fields and hills —
I'll leave it all,
Taking wing to pray
To God Himself… till
Then I know not God.
Bury me, rise up,
And break your chains
Then sprinkle liberty
With hostile wicked blood.
And in a great new family,
A family of the free,
Forget not to remember me
With a kind and gentle word.

Pereyaslav, December 25, 1845

274 Shevchenko did not name this poem. The title was added to a posthumous *Kobzar* edition in 1867 and is traditionally known as *The Testament*.

Why is it that we love Bohdan[275]?
Because the Muscovites forgot him,
And Germans took the great wise hetman
For a simple fool.

1845-46

THE LILY

"Why, when I was growing,
Was I not liked by people?
Why, when I grew up,
Was I killed so young?
Why is it they now welcome me
Within their mansion walls,
Calling me a princess,
Not diverting eyes
From my lovely blossoms?
They wonder, but where
To put me they know not!
Tell me, my dear brother,
O you, the Royal Flower!"
"I know not, my sister."
And the Royal Flower
Leaned his pink and crimson
Head upon white and gentle face
Of the drooping Lily.
The Lily then shed
Tears of dew…
She cried and said:
"My brother, we've
Loved each other long,
But I've never told you,
Of the torment that I suffered
When I was still a human.

My mother… why did she
Always worry,
And gaze and gaze at me,
Her child, and cry? I know not,
O my only brother!
Who brought harm to her?
I was just a child,
I played, amused myself,
But she always withered,
And our evil master
She condemned and cursed.
Then she died. And the master
Took me in to raise.
I grew up, fostered
In white mansions.
I knew not that I'm a bastard,
That I'm a child of his.
The master then went far away,
Abandoned me,
And the people damned him,
Burning down his mansion…
As for me,
They killed me without killing me,
For what, I do not know,
They just cut my long, long braids,
Then placed a rag on my shorn head.
And they laughed as well.
Even vile Jews would spit.
That's the way I had it, brother,
In my former world.
The people did not let me live

275 *Bohdan* — Reference to Bohdan Khmelnytsky (ca. 1595 — August 6, 1657), hetman of Ukraine who signed the controversial Pereyaslav Treaty with Russia, which led to the loss of Ukrainian independence.

Past my short and youthful years.
I died in winter by a fence,
And come spring
I blossomed by a valley,
With a flower white as snow!
I brought joy into the grove.
In winter, people… O my Lord!
Would not let me in a home.
But in springtime, like a wonder,
People gazed at me.
And girls adorned in flowers
Began to call me snow-white lily;
I would then blossom in a grove,
A greenhouse,
And in a great white mansion.
Tell me, my dear brother,
O you the Royal Flower,
Why is it that God placed me
As a flower on this world?
To bring joy to people,
To the very ones who killed
Me and our dear mother?..
O merciful, dear and sacred God!"
Then the Lily wept again.
And the Royal Flower
Leaned his pink and crimson head
Upon the white and gentle face
Of the drooping Lily.

Kyiv, July 25, 1846

WATER NYMPH

"Mother bore me
In a lofty mansion,
And in the dead of night
She carried me, a babe,
To bathe me in the Dnipro.
Bathing me, she talked:
'Swim, my daughter, swim
With waters of the Dnipro.
Then come ashore
Tomorrow in the thick of night,
Coming as a water nymph.
I'll be out to dance with him,
And you'll tickle him to death.
You'll tickle him, my dear,
So he'll not laugh at me, so young.
Let him drink unto oblivion,
Not my blood and tears —
But blue water of the Dnipro.
Let him frolic with his daughter.
Swim, my only child.
Waves! My waves!
Please welcome a new nymph…' —
Then she sobbed,
And then she ran.
With the current I swam,
Until some sisters met me,
Taking me along.
It's been a week that I've been growing,
Frolicking with sisters
In the dead of night. I am on
The lookout for my father
In his mansion.
Or perhaps they've met already
In the master's mansion.
Perhaps my sinful mother
Indulges once again?" —
And the little nymph fell silent,
Plunging in the Dnipro
Like a little minnow. And quietly
A willow swayed.
Mother came to frolic,
She was sleepless in the mansion.
Master Jan was not at home,
There was no one to converse with.

Walking to the shore,
She recalled her daughter,
Recalling how she bathed her,
And what she said to her.
But it's all the same.
She headed to the mansion
To finally get some sleep.
Not getting there, however,
She overnighted in the Dnipro.
Then the Dnipr' girls
Caught her unawares —
They leapt, they grabbed,
And began to play with her,
Happy with the capture,
They played, they tickled,
Till they stuffed her
In a fishing trap…
Breaking out in laughter.
Just a single nymph
Failed to laugh along.

Kyiv, August 9, 1846

Drink the first, you'll be aroused, [276]
Drink the second, you'll take pause,
Drink the third, the eyes will glow,
A thought will spur a thought.

January 1847

Striuchka's Hut, 1843

[276] There is no known manuscript of this poem. It is attributed to Shevchenko by his Ukrainian friend , writer and critic, Panteleimon Kulish, who recalled in his memoirs that the poet wrote the lines with coal on the wall of a tavern.

THE WITCH[277]

Let death seize upon them, and let them go down quick into hell: for wickedness is in their dwellings, and among them.

Psalm 55: Verse 15

I pray, again I hope,
Again I pour out tears,
And share the burden of my muse
With the silent walls.
Respond, O silent ones,
Lament with me
The falsehoods of humanity
And an awful fate.
Respond!
And perhaps hard luck,
So ever wary, will take your lead,
To respond as well and deign to smile upon us.
It will square us with misfortune,
And will thank us kindly.
It'll cry, pray,
Then lay quietly to sleep.

Such is my advice, O my unknown brother,
Reconcile with God, don't intrude on people,
Seek your brother in a mansion, in a home,
Heed the grave, but heed not glory,
For it can't stop the young from aging,
And won't restore our years of spring!
That, my friend and brother,
Is the way to pray to God,
And as you pray,
Remember me as well.

On a mound amid a field[278]
An enchanted aspen grows.

---

277 *The Witch* — This poem was first entitled *The Aspen.* The title was derived from a Ukrainian superstition. A woman considered to be witch was denied a Christian burial. She was buried instead beside a road and the grave was sealed with an aspen stake.

278 This paragraph does not appear in most *Kobzar* editions. It is taken from the poem *Aspen,* which Shevchenko reworked into two versions of *The Witch.*

That is where a witch is buried.
Cross yourselves, dear girls,
Cross yourselves… and do not wait
For evil lords,
Because you'll meet your end
With ridicule.
You'll garner fame —
Ill fame upon this world,
And on the other!.. God forbid!
For sins so great
God Himself won't help.
Let the lords torment,
Let them trade your brothers
And treat Satan to a
Cup of blood and tears.
They've sold their souls already,
So it's all the same to them.
But you must beware,
Beware — and very much at that!
Beware — love a servant,
If you wish,
Love anyone you please, my dears,
Just not do love the lords.

Near the Feast of Nicholas[279],
Gypsies, tattered, nearly naked,
Walked at night, and walking…
They were free, of course, and sang.
Onward, onward, then they stopped.
They pitched a tent beside the road,
Lit a giant fire,
Gathered 'round it,
Some with shish-kabobs,
Some to merely sit,
Each, however, free as Kozaks
(Used to be). They sit, they doze.
And behind the tent amid the steppe,
A young maiden sings, sounding like
A drunken woman coming from a wedding.

---

[279] *Feast of Nicholas* — St. Nicholas Day, December 19th on the Julian Calendar.

"In a home of newlyweds
The couple went to sleep,
The bride then dreamed
Her mother went berserk,
That her in-law father drowned,
And her own had married.
And… hoo…"
The gypsies listen in and laugh:
"And how'd those people get here?
They're probably from beyond the Dniester.
For all around is steppe… A ghost! A ghost!"
The gypsies shouted, clutching one another.
And that which sang
Appeared before them…
Fear and sorrow!
She shivered in a mended coat,
Blood from bitter frost
Beaded on the hands and feet,
And her lengthy braids
Were tangled all in burrs!..
She stood then sat
Beside the fire and warmed her
Hands upon the very flames.
"Well, okay,
A wretch got married!"
She seemed to whisper to herself.
And she smiled very dreadfully.

GYPSIES
Where ya from, young maiden?

WITCH
Who, me? *(Sings)*
"When I was still a youthful maiden,
They kissed me on the face,
But when I turned into a plain old hag,
If they'd kiss me, I'd be glad."

GYPSIES
A songstress, not half bad!
To get one just like her,
With a bear as well.

WITCH

I sing,
Regardless if I sit or dance,
I always sing, I always sing,
I've forgotten how to talk…
I once spoke quite well.

GYPSIES

Where were you? Did ya go astray?

WITCH

Who, me? Hush… Hush…
With the daughter lies the master,
The fire's out, the moon is rising,
A werewolf grazes in the valley…
At the wedding fete I'd gotten drunk,
And for the girl it did not work.

It's those damned lords
That do such things to maidens…
The son must yet be married off,
I'll go, because without me
The'll know not even how
To place a body in a grave.

GYPSIES

Don't go, poor dear, remain with us,
Life with us, by God, is good.

WITCH

And have you any children?..

GYPSIES

None.

WITCH

Whom then do you feed?
Whom do you lay down to sleep?
Who is it that you rock at night?
When you rest and when you wake,
Who is in your prayers? Oh, children!
Always children! Always children!
And I've no place to hide.
Where'er I go, they're right behind.
They'll someday devour me.

GYPSIES

Don't cry, poor dear, don't worry:
We've neither children nor their crying…

WITCH

I may as well just leap
From a hill into the water…

She then cried and cried.
The gypsies wondered long,
Until they fell asleep,
Each dropping where they were.
But she was sleepless and not troubled,
She sat and stuck her feet
Into the heated ashes;
A waning moon rose o'er a mound
And seemed to peek inside the tent,
Until obscured by clouds.
Why does the rich, the gray
And well-fed man not sleep?
Why does the poor old
Orphan stay awake?
One thinks of ways to pay
For tolling of his funeral bell,
The other contemplates additions
To his estate and mansions.
Only then he'll rest!
Inside a grave…
And the first,
He'll sort of perish anywhere.
And both shall rest
Without a care.
They'll make no mention
Of the poor,
And the second they will curse.
The old one cannot sleep,
Not in a field or a home,
But somehow, nonetheless, must
Live what years remain.
An old gypsy sits a dozing
With a pipe beside the fire,
And looking at the stray,
Perhaps he thinks of something?

GYPSY

Why not lay and why not rest?
Look, the morning star is rising.

WITCH

I'm watching, now you watch.

GYPSY

Come morning we'll move on,
We'll leave you,
If you don't awake…

WITCH

I won't awake!
Now I'll never wake,
I'll just perish anywhere
In a patch of weeds…
(Sings quietly)
"O grove, O shady grove,
O the quiet Danube,
I'll frolic in the grove,
In the Danube I will swim.
I'll unwind amid green algae…
And perhaps I'll bring
An ugly child at least!.."
Whatever, just so long
As it can walk,
And knows enough
To curse its mother.
There… there… do you see?
A cat winks on the mound,

It's winking right at me…
Kitty… Kitty…
The lousy creature isn't coming!
Or else, I'd let you drink,
And next year it would know…
(Sings)
"There's kutia[280] in the corner,
And children in the oven nook.
She begot them, she produced them,
And has no place to put them.
She could drown them,
She could choke them,
She could sell them to a Jew for blood,
Then drink away the cash!"
What, do our people treat you well?
That's just it,
And you don't know!
Just sit closer here.
I'll tell you that I too, you know,
Was in Wallachia![281]
And in Bendery[282] I bore twins,
I rocked their cradle in white Iasi,[283]
Bathed them in the Danube,
Swaddled them in Turkey,
And brought them home —
All the way to Kyiv.
And at home,
Without incense, without an aspergillum,[284]
I had them christened for three coins,
And drank away three others.
I got drunk… I got drunk…
And drunk I still remain!...
And now I'll never rest.
For now I fear not even God
And I feel no public shame.
If I could find those kids somewhere…
Don't you know,
If there's perhaps a war in Turkey?

GYPSY

Once there was, now there's not,
The oldest officer has died.

WITCH

I thought there was, in Turkey,
But now it seems there's none.
So listen up, I'll tell you,
Who it is I'm looking for.
I seek little Natalie,
And my son Ivan,
And worst of all
I seek the cursed lord…
To strangle him! Because
He took me as a youngster,
Cut my hair, just like a boy's
And dragged me everywhere.
We stood with Muscovites beside Bendery —
And Muscovites then fought the Turk.
It was there that I bore twins
Just before the Savior's Feast.[285]
And he, the damned, had left me,
Not even peeking in the house,
And simply left with Muscovites…
And to Ukraine I went again,
Shorn and shoeless,
With my bastards. Whatever.

---

280 *Kutia* — A wheat pudding traditionally served in Ukraine on Christmas Eve. It is made of ground poppy seeds, wheat berries, honey, nuts and sometimes raisins.

281 *Wallachia* — A principality between the Danube and southern Carpathians founded in the 14th century.

282 *Bendery* — A Wallachian city in what today is Moldova. It was captured by Russia from the Ottomans during the Russo-Turkish War.

283 See glossary or fn. 227

284 *Aspergillum* — A brush for sprinkling holy water.

285 *Savior's Feast* — Reference to the Transfiguration of Jesus, a holiday celebrated on August 19 on the Julian Calendar.

I went and asked which way to Kyiv...
Oh, how people laughed at me!!
I nearly drowned myself,
But felt sorry for the twins.
In fits and starts I weaved my way
To my native land... I rested,
Waiting until evening.
Then and only then,
I went into the village,
Because, you see, I did not want
A soul to know.
To my house I crept — there's no fire,
So I thought my dad's asleep —
But dad was really dying.
With no one there to cross his hands!
I was frightened,
The home had reeked of emptiness,
So in the shed I hid the twins,
Then rushed into the house,
And he was barely breathing.
Me to him: "Daddy!
Daddy! Daddy, it is I that's come!" —
I grabbed his arms...
And he took my hand in his
And whispered: "Farewell...
Farewell... And..."
That is all I heard.
I, it seems, collapsed and slept!
If only I had slept forever!
At midnight I awoke —
Something's walking in the house...
And father grips my hand.
I scream, "Daddy! Daddy!"
But he's already cold as ice:
I twisted hard to free my hand.
So, gypsy!
If your daughter was a bitch like that!
Would you forgive?

GYPSY

I'd forgive, by God!

WITCH

Oh, be quiet! Or I'll forget.
I prayed to God...
Maybe not... I fed the children,
Hid them in a crib,
And even made a hood of burlap
So none would know I'm shorn.
I tidied up, I walked around,
While people in the yard
Started working on the coffin.
They finished, laid him in,
Carried, and then buried him...
I alone, abandoned,
Remained upon this world.
"I walked across the valley
Bringing water back,
Alone I baked a wedding loaf,
I gave away my daughter's hand,
And married off my son!..
And... hoo..."

GYPSY
Don't whimper, 'cause you'll wake them all!

WITCH
Do I whimper, crazy man?

GYPSY
Well, okay, okay, what's next?
Tell me more...

WITCH
What's it worth to you?
Will you make some grits tomorrow?
I will bring the corn...
Hold on, I'll remember.
He took to sleeping with his daughter!...
And turned his son into a lackey...
The people drove me from the house...
Oh, yes, oh, yes, I now remember.
I provoked the dogs
Under people's windows,
Joining beggars, twins in tow...
Upon my back, so they would learn...
And then the lord came back,
And that for the community
And everyone involved was
Just too much to handle,
So they drove me from my
Father's house.
Then he took the twins and me
To his mansion chambers.

My twins are growing,
I'm delighted,
And again I love the vicious viper!..
I'm driven to the brink by love!
My son is now a lackey...
Ruined by his father...
And his daughter!
His own, you hear!..
Is this not a sin among your people?
Do they know such ways??

And he gave me a karbovanets[286]
Then sent me to Kyiv.
He sent me there to pray,
So I went, and prayed...
No, gypsy, my prayers were all for naught.
Does any kind of god
Exist among your people?
We, alas, have none!
He's been stolen by the lords
And hidden in a lacquer box.

Returning home —
The rooms are closed,
The lord went somewhere with his daughter,
As he did before with me!
And he took his son, then later... later...
What really happened I know not!..
I dreamed, it seems, I was an owl
Flying by ravines and
Searching for my children...
No, don't listen, it's not the children,
But the lord I searched for.
And now there is no need —
I'll join up with gypsies.
I've married off my son,
And the daughter will remain as is.
She'll crawl beneath the fences
Till she's trampled by the people.
Did you see my son?..
He's so nice!!
He's just like you. Ooo, it's cold!
Lend me money...
I'll buy a fancy necklace,
And with it I will hang you.
I'll then head home...
Look, a mouse, a mouse,
Taking little mice to Kyiv.
You'll not get them there,
You'll drown them
On the way somewhere!
Or the lord will seize them!..

---

286 *Karbovanets* — A Ukrainian monetary unit.

Will I find my children,
Or will I simply perish?! —

She then fell silent, as if sleeping.
The gypsies all began to rise,
Taking down their tent,
Preparing for the road ahead,
And they hit it. They rode the steppe.
The witch got up as well.
And followed after them,
Singing as she went:
"People talk of Judgment Day,
But that day will never come,
For I've been judged already
By people in this world."

They passed village after village,
They walked around the towns,
And, like a marvel,
They brought along the stray.
She danced and sang,
She neither ate nor drank…
Like death she walked
The world with gypsies.
Then coming to her senses,
She began to eat and drink,
And to hide behind the tents
And say prayers unto God.
Old Mariula did this to her,
Giving her some herb to drink.
And so it passed.
She then taught her how to heal,
And what derives from what;
Which herbs,
And where to look for them.
How to brew and how to drink them —
She taught her all and everything,
And the stray learned everything in turn,
And said prayers unto God.
She wandered for a summer then another
Learning from the aging woman.
And in the third
She wandered with her to Ukraine.
She bowed at Mariula's feet
For every lesson taught,
She bid farewell to all the gypsies,
Said prayers unto God,
And then she headed home,
To her native clime —
Glad, so glad and happy,
Like a little child.
Each village that she passed —
She probed the sick,
And gave them herbs to drink,
Helping one and all.
She made it home by fall,
Heated up the empty house,
Whitewashed it, tidied up
And had a little rest,
Like in Paradise. She forgot it all —
The bad and not so bad.
Forgiving all, and loving all
She felt so light,
She seemed to fly above the earth
Just like a blessed angel.
She started living in her home
As if it were a palace,
And the neighbors did not
Turn away,
The entire village loved her,
Because she tended night and day
To all who had an illness.
She helped all,
Accepting nothing in return.
And if she took,
She quickly gave it to the cripples,
Or on Sunday she would light a candle
By the Savior on behalf
Of all the sinners,
But would not keep a coin herself.
"What good is it for me?
(She was wont to say)
Have I any children?!"
She'd then cry, and thus alone upon
This world she lived out
Her few short years…

The girls, it happened,
Spent their days and nights with her,
Even cleaning up the house,
Painting, bringing flowers,
And preparing meals…
They asked not of fortune-telling —
They just loved her as she was!
The little house was quiet, clean,
And bright, like Paradise:
And, know this,
The doors squeaked open,
No one passed her by.
That one comes to say good morning,
That one asks for herbs,
That one brings a braided loaf, a roll, —
They'd bring everything,
Just to have someone to live with,
And to share their goods.
And thus she lived at home,
Feeling warm and fed.
They loved her and respected her,
Meeting every need…
They called her, nonetheless,
Both a witch and unwed mother!

Come spring they brought the lord
Along with gout and pillows,
Plus three or more physicians
From beyond the German lands —
Only he came home. And the children?
He swapped his daughter
For a greyhound
And lost his sons at cards!
(So it goes upon this world!
What are we to do?)
They took him to be treated.
He was treated, treated by three doctors,
And what did they not do?
For naught… he'll no longer sin.
Though he'd like to… She forgave!
She brewed some sacred herbs…
And the merciful left the village
To treat her enemy!
And she asked those doctors
If they'd give the lord the herbs to drink,
And crossed herself so he may live!
But doctors would not let her in,
They chased her off and almost beat her,
So she took her jar and left,
And walking she recalled the children…
She cried… and felt sorry
That she did not help the lord!

Spring disperses winter,
Spreading o'er the earth
A carpet made of green,
Then high above and in formation
Cranes fly back from nesting grounds…
Along the steppes and on the roads
Chumaks head toward the Don.

In heaven and on earth is Paradise,
And I know not
What more can people ask of God?
Meanwhile, slowly dying
Is a sinner not forgiven.
They've administered communion
To this evil man,
Placed him on a bed of straw
And opened up the roof
So his soul might rise.
He's not dying though…
And the doctors
Cannot help!..
It got better somehow,
"Call Lucia…" —
He whispered, and began to shake…
They led my witch into the mansion…
And then doctors even begged for help…
She came, stood at his feet
Then softly read *Our Father*
For the sinner's sake.
The lord seemed to awaken,
Looked around and at her… then shouted:
"No need! No need!
Be off! Or wait…
Have you not forgotten?
Forgive me! Forgive me!.."

And for the first time ever,
Tears glistened in his eyes… "I forgive…
I forgave you long ago…"
And in his hands she placed a candle,
Then crossed herself for him.
The foe before her fell asleep,
Just like a little child,
Leaving her to pray for him
And his eternal soul.

She arranged Sorokousty,[287]
She went off to Kyiv,
Saying prayers to the Lord
For the lord who had departed.
By fall she had returned
To spend winter in the village,
And was greeted like a mother
By all the friendly girls.
And again they went
To her for gatherings,
And again, like mothers, they
Sought to meet Lucia's needs.
And in return she taught them
How to live on earth.
She tells stories how
She too was once a maiden,
And how she loved the lord,
And became an unwed mother.
And how her hair was shorn,
How she brought forth twins,
How she roamed with gypsies
And how Mariula taught her
Every healing art.
All that happened,
She relates it all,
Till the girls begin to cry,
And cross themselves in horror
As if the lord was in the house.
And she relates,
Beseeches and implores
That they not love the lords!..
For God will punish.
You will roam the world
As I roamed it once,
You'll lose your parents
Like I lost my mom and dad.
You'll let loose your children
To a world of human mockery,
As did I… as I… let loose…
My children! Children!
So it was she taught.
Girls crossed themselves
And cried, and at night
Had constant dreams of lords,
Some with horns, some with tails,
Some that cut off braids;
That bite and laugh,
And turn straight-haired girls
Into dogs,
Or give them baths in tar,
Then lead them down the street
And summon people for a look.
Such things were dreamt by girls,
Who still went to her for gatherings.

Verdant spring arrived.
My old one rose,
Went searching in the field for herbs,
And that is where she stayed…
The girls cooked lunch and dinner,
But did not know what happened
To their unrelated mother.
According to the village shepherds,
The old witch was drowned by devils
In a puddle by the mound.
They found her, and all but priests
Then buried her,
And on her mound

---

287 *Sorokousty* — A memorial service held 40 days after a person's death. It is associated with Christ's Ascension 40 days after Easter.

They placed an aspen seedling.
The girls bedecked the mound
With flowers,
And with their tears enriched the aspen.
Upon the mound thus grew
A tall enchanted aspen.

That is where the witch is buried.
Cross yourselves, young girls,
Cross yourselves and
Do not rush toward evil lords,
For you'll die in mockery,
Leaving infamy behind.

Sedniv, March 7, 1847

Witch, 1847

IN SOLITARY CONFINEMENT[288]

Dedicated to my fellow inmates[289]

Recall, my brethren…
May that evil not return.
How you so nicely, and I too,
Peered through prison bars.
And you surely must have thought,
"When will we convene again
For quiet counsel, for a talk
On this impoverished land?"
Never, brethren, never will we
Ever drink together
From waters of the Dnipro!
We'll part, and our misfortune
We'll disperse across
The steppes and forests,
And we'll believe yet more in liberty,
We'll then live
Among the people
Just as people live.
Till that happens,
Love, my brothers, one another,
Love our dear Ukraine,
And pray for her, the hapless,
Say prayers to the Lord.
And forget him, friends,
Do not curse his name.[290]
And remember me
From time to time
In my harsh captivity.

Orenburg, November 1, 1849 — April 23, 1850

I

Oh, alone am I, alone,
Like a single blade of grass.
God has not bestowed me
With fortune or good fate.
The only thing God's given me
Is beauty — hazel eyes,
Which I cried out
In all my lonely maidenhood.
I never knew a brother,
Nor did I know a sister,
I grew among some strangers,
And grew up — not knowing love!
Where's my mate,
Where are you, good people?
There are none, and I'm alone.
Nor will there ever be a mate!

St. Petersburg, April 17 — May 19, 1847

---

288 *In Solitary Confinement* — Shevchenko wrote a cycle of 13 poems while imprisoned in St. Petersburg following his arrest for participation in the banned Cyril and Methodius Brotherhood. The organization, deemed subversive by the czarist regime, advanced popular education, the abolition of serfdom, and the right of every Slavic nation to develop its own language and culture. The Brotherhood also proposed a federation of all Slavs, in which Ukraine would play a leading role.

289 *Fellow inmates* — Other members of the Cyril and Methodius Brotherhood who were in the same prison.

290 *Do not curse his name* — Most likely Oleksiy Mykhailovych Petrov, a Kyiv University student who revealed to the authorities the existence of the secret Cyril and Methodius Brotherhood (See fn. 288). In his denunciation, Petrov mentioned several of Shevchenko's poems, which he characterized as presenting "clearly illegal ideas."

II

There's a glen beyond a glen
And then a mound amid the steppe.
On that mound a Kozak rises,
He is gray and stooped.
He rises all alone at night,
He goes into the steppe,
And as he goes he sings,
He sings a song of sadness:
"They piled up earth
And went back home,
And no one will recall.
Like glass we are three-hundred here!
A company laid dead!
And the earth receives us not!
When the hetman sold out Christians
To put them in a yoke,
He also drove us Kozaks
And sent us on a chase.
On land that's ours,
We spilled our blood
And killed our brother.
We got drunk on brother's blood
And here we lie
Inside this eerie mound."
He fell silent, worried
And leaned against his spear.
He stood atop the mound itself,
Surveyed the Dnipro,
Crying heavily and wailing,
As the azure waves resounded.
An echo bounced across a grove
From a village past the Dnipro,
Third roosters[291] sang their song.
The Kozak slumped,
The glen convulsed,
And the mound let out a moan.

St. Petersburg, April 17 — May 19, 1847

III

It's all the same to me if I shall
Live in my Ukraine or not.
If I'm remembered or forgotten
Amid the foreign snow —
It's truly all the same.
I grew in bondage in the midst of strangers,
And, unwept by kin,
I'll die in bondage, crying.
And I'll take it all with me,
Leaving not a tiny trace
In our glorious Ukraine,
In the land that's ours — but not our own.
The father with his son won't ponder,
He won't tell the son: "Pray,
Pray, my son, they once
Racked him for Ukraine."
It's all the same to me, if that son
Shall pray or not...
But it's not the same to me,
If wicked, evil people
Lull Ukraine to sleep,
And then, ablaze and robbed,
Awaken her...
Oh, it's not the same to me.

St. Petersburg, April 17 — May 19, 1847

---

[291] See glossary or fn. 2

IV

They said, "Don't leave your mother," —
But you left, you ran away,
Mother searched — she did not find,
And now has stopped the search,
Crying as she died.
It's been long that
Sounds were heard
From the place where
You once played,
The dog has wandered off,
A window's broken in the home.
Throughout the day lambs graze alone
In the gloomy garden.
And owls prophesy at night,
Not letting neighbors sleep.
And your patch of cross-shaped periwinkle
Is overgrown with wild chervil
That awaits you with no flowers.
And in the grove the pristine pond,
Where you once swam,
Is all dried out and shallow.
The grove is sad and drooping.
And in the grove the bird sings not.
It too was marked by you.
The valley well has since collapsed,
The willow's dried, bent over,
And thorny bushes overrun
The path you walked upon.
Where did you fly off,
What became of you?
Who is it that you flew off to?
Whom do you delight
In a foreign land and family?
Whom do you embrace?
The heart divines that you're savoring
Life in mansions, and do not miss
The home you left...
I beg God that grief
Shall never waken you,
That it not find you in a mansion...
That you not blame the Lord
Nor condemn your mother.

St. Petersburg, April 17 — May 19, 1847

V

"Why are you going to the mound?"
The mother forced herself to ask. —
"Why the crying as you go,
Why your sleepless nights,
O my darling dove?"
"Yes, mama, yes." And she
Went again, as the mother
Cried and waited.

No pasqueflower[292] blooms
Upon the mound at night.
Instead the girl betrothed
Plants a guelder rose,
Which she waters with her tears,
And asks the Lord,
That He bring rain at night
And also morning dew.
So that the guelder rose may take,
And then begin to branch.
"Perhaps my sweetheart like a bird
Will fly to me from heaven.
I'll weave a nest for him,
And take wing myself,
I'll then chirrup
With my sweetheart
Upon the guelder rose.
We'll cry, we'll chirrup
We'll talk quietly,

292 *Pasqueflower — (Pulsatilla vulgaris)*. A perennial that blooms in early spring.

We'll fly together every morning
To the world beyond."

The guelder rose took root
And then began to branch.
The girl went to the mound
For one year, two years, three.
And on the fourth…
No pasqueflower blooms
Upon the mound at night.
It's a girl crying,
Talking with the guelder rose:
"My guelder rose
So broad and tall,
Sprinkled not with water
Before the break of dawn.
You've been watered by
Broad streams of tears,
Disgraced among the people.
Girls scorn their girlfriend,
They scorn my guelder rose.
Swath my head,
Cleanse it with the morning dew.
And shade me
With broad branches
From the scorching sun.
Come morning,
I'll be found by people,
Who will laugh at me,
And your broad branches
Will be snapped by children."
A bird upon the guelder rose
Sang early in the morn;
Beneath the guelder rose
A girl slept, she did not rise.
The young one had grown weary,
And took a rest forever…
The sun rose above the mound,
Waking people all rejoiced.
But the mother had not gone to bed,
Keeping dinner for her daughter
And weeping heavily as she waited.

St. Petersburg, April 17 — May 19, 1847

VI

Oh, three broad roads
Converged together.
Three brothers left Ukraine,
Bound for foreign lands.
All had left their mother.
One forsook his wife,
Another left his sister.
And the youngest —
His young girl.
The mother planted then
Three ash trees in the field.
And the in-law daughter
Planted a tall poplar.
Three sycamores were
Planted by the sister in the valley…
And the fiancée —
A crimson guelder rose.
The three ashes did not take,
The poplar shriveled up,
Three sycamores dried out,
And the guelder rose had withered.
The three brothers don't return.
The aging mother weeps,
Weeping are the wife and children
In a house bereft of heat.
The sister cries and leaves to
Seek the brothers in a foreign land…
And the fiancée has died,
Being laid to rest inside a coffin.
The three brothers aren't returning,
They're roaming 'round the world,
While the three broad roads
They traveled
Are overrun by thorns.

St. Petersburg, April 17 — May 19, 1847

VII

To N. Kostomarov[293]

The joyous sun was hiding
In the happy clouds of spring.
They served their shackled guests
With cups of wretched tea,
And relieved the sentries,
Sentries dressed in blue.
And I grew a bit accustomed
To doors secured with keys
And to the grated windows.
Nor did I feel sorrow
For all the bygone tears,
My heavy bloody tears,
Long since buried, then forgotten.
And quite a few were shed
Upon a field of futility.
Had it even been a bitter rue,
But nothing grew upon that field!
And I recalled my village.
Who is it that I left behind and when?
My father and my mother
Both lie buried in their graves...
And the heartfelt pangs of sorrow,
That there's no one to recall me!
I look: your mother, O my brother,
Blacker than the dark black earth,
Is walking as if taken from a cross...
I pray! O Lord, I pray!
I'll never cease to praise You!
That I'll never share with anyone
My prison or my shackles!

St. Petersburg, May 19, 1847

VIII

A cherry orchard by the house,
Maybugs[294] hum above the cherries.
Plowmen tread behind their plows,
Girls stroll and sing,
As mothers wait with dinner.

The family dines outside the house,
The evening star is rising.
The daughter serves the dinner,
And the mother wants to teach,
But the nightingale won't let her.

The mother laid her little children
To bed beside the house,
Then, snuggled next to them,
She fell asleep herself.
All grew quiet
Save the girls and nightingale.

St. Petersburg, May 19-30, 1847

---

[293] *Mykola Ivanovych Kostomarov (1817-85)* — Ukrainian historian, friend of Shevchenko and founder of the banned Cyril and Methodius Brotherhood, of which the poet was a member.

[294] *Maybug* — A European beetle *(Melolontha melolontha)* that makes a low buzzing sound in flight.

IX

Early morn the newlyweds
Departed from the village,
Following the couple
Was a single lass.
Her aging mother noticed
And went chasing 'cross the field...
She chased her, brought her in;
She complained and talked.
Till she laid her in the ground,
And herself became a beggar.

Years went by, but the village
Did not change.
Just an empty house has leaned
At the village edge.
On a crutch a soldier
Limps past the empty house.
He looks about the orchard,
Peers inside the house.
In vain, O brother,
For no dark-browed beauty
Will be looking from the house.
You'll not be asked for dinner
By any aging mother.
Ah, but once... 'Twas long ago!
Wedding scarves were weaved,
And silken thread was used
To adorn a kerchief.
He hoped to live, to love
And to honor God!
Instead... there's no one
In the world to lean on.
He sits beside the empty house,
It's getting dark outside.
And through the window,
Like a grandma, peers
A single owl.

St. Petersburg, May 19-30, 1847

X

Captivity is hard, but
If the truth be told,
There was no prior freedom.
But even so, I somehow lived.
And though foreign, it
Was a field nonetheless...
Like awaiting God,
All's come to waiting
For my evil destiny.
I await it, I expect it,
And curse my foolish mind,
For being fooled by fools,
And drowning freedom in a puddle.
When I think, the heart turns cold,
That I'll not be buried in Ukraine,
Nor will I live in my Ukraine,
To love people and the Lord.

St. Petersburg, May 19-30, 1847

XI
THE REAPER

Across the field he goes
Not mowing swaths,
Not mowing swaths — but mountains.
The earth moans,
The sea too moans,
It moans and murmurs endlessly.

The reaper late at night is
Greeted by the owls.
The reaper mows, he does not rest,
Taking heed of no one,
Don't even try to plead.

Do not ask and do not plead,
He does not hone his scythe.
Be it suburb, be it city,
The old man cuts through like a razor.
Everything he's given.

A peasant and a barman,
And an orphan-kobzar.
Singing as he goes along,
The old man mows,
And piles high his harvest,
And does not pass the czar.

Nor will he pass me by,
He'll cut me down in foreign lands,
He'll choke me in a prison cell,
And none will place a cross for me,
Nor remember that I was.

St. Petersburg, May 30, 1847

XII

Will we ever meet again?
Or have we parted now forever?
And dispersed the word
Of truth and love
Throughout the steppes and thickets!
So be it! It was not our mother,
But we had to have respect.
That's the will of God. Obey!
Submit, pray to God
And remember one another.
Love your Ukraine,
Love her… in trying times,
And in your hard and final minute
Pray for her unto the Lord.

St. Petersburg, May 19-30, 1847

I was sleepless, and the night
Was like an endless sea.
(Though this happened not in autumn
But in captivity.)
With a wall you'll not discuss
Your sorrow or your *youthful dreams.*
I toss about, await the light,
And outside the door
Two sentries speak about
The lousy life of soldiering.

I

She was loose and buxom,
And a C-note was the least she gave,
But the baron was a sorry sort.
And me, you know, they eyed me,
Took me to Kaluga,[295] and recruited me.
So there's a story for you!

2

And I... when I recall, it's even dreadful.
I myself enlisted as a soldier;
I'd met a girl in my village... We went out,
Her widowed mother gave her blessing.
But the cursed master would not give her.
"Too young, — he said, — You gotta wait."
And I, you know, kept seeing Hanna.
In a year I tried again to get what I was due;
I went to ask and took the mother with me.
"Sorry, do not ask, he says, —
Five hundred, if you give it,
You can take her right this minute..."
What to do! The woe! Borrow?
But who would lend a wad like that?
Then, my brother, I went off to earn it.
Where did the feet not carry me,
Before I earned that cash.
I spent two years traversing
The Don and Black Sea shores,
And bought a lot of lavish gifts...
Then to the village I returned
To see my girl at night —
But the mother by the oven
Is the lone one there,
And she, the wretch, is dying
And the house now reeks of emptiness.
I stoke a fire, turn to her...
But she already smells of earth,
And me she does not recognize!
I went to see the priest and neighbor,
I brought the priest, but came too late —
She'd already died. And there's

295 *Kaluga* — A Russian city about 100 miles (160 kilometers) southwest of Moscow.

No trace of my dear Hanna.
Still, I asked the neighbor about Hanna.
"Why, don't you know?
Hanna's in Siberia.
She went, you see, to dally with
The master's son until she bore
A child and drowned it in a well."
It's like my heart was burned.
I barely, barely left the house
Before first light of dawn.
Knife in hand, I dashed off to the mansion,
Not feeling ground beneath my feet...
But the master's son had left,
He'd been sent to school in Kyiv.
So it was, my brother!
Remaining were my mom and dad,
And I enlisted as a soldier.
When I recall, it's all still dreadful.
What I wanted
Was to either burn the mansion,
Or to take my life.
But God had mercy... Say, do you know
That he got a transfer to our unit
From the army or wherever?

I

So then,
Well, now the fun begins.

2

Let him be. God will help,
And all will be forgotten.

They kept talking for some time,
And I dozed off before first light,
Then I dreamed of masters' sons,
And they, the wicked, would not let me sleep.

St. Petersburg, May 19-30, 1847

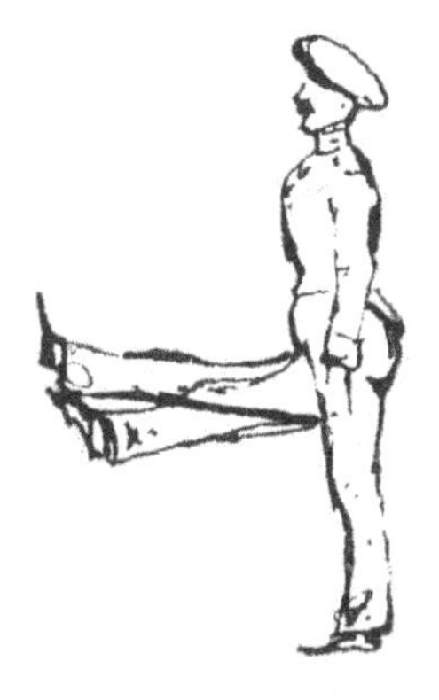

Sketches, 1841-42

THE PRINCESS

A Poem

Rise, my evening star,
Rise above the hill,
We'll talk quietly
In bondage.
Tell me how the sun is setting
Far beyond the hill,
And how the rainbow
Borrows water from the Dnipro River.
How the tall black poplar
Spread its branches out…
And how the willow tree has leaned
Beside the water's edge;
It's even sent green branches
Just above the water,
And unchristened children
Swing upon those branches.
How a werewolf spends the night
On a mound amid the field,
And how the screech owl
Heralds trouble from the woods
And rooftops.
How the pasqueflower by the valley
Starts to bloom at night…
As for people… Let them be.
I know all the good ones.
I know them very well. O my star,
My only friend!
Who knows what happens back in
Our Ukraine? I know. I'll tell you;
And I won't lay down to sleep.
You'll share it quietly
With God tomorrow.

The village! And the heart can rest.
A village in our dear Ukraine —
As pretty as an Easter egg.
Ringed by woods of green.
Blooming orchards, whitened homes,
And on the hill's a palace.
It all seems like a wonder.
All around are broad-leafed poplars,
Over there are woods, and woods, a field
And azure hills beyond the Dnipro.
God soars Himself above the village.

The village! Oh, the village!
Happy homes!
Palaces, happy from a distance,
May you be overgrown with thorns!
So people may not find a trace,
May they not know where to even look.
I know not where they came from
In our blessed village,
In our glorious Ukraine, —
A wayward prince.
There was a princess too.
They were still young,
And lived alone. They were rich,
Had a palace on a hill,
An ample pond down in the valley
A green orchard on the slope,
With willows, poplars,
And in the field, windmills.
And below — a village stretching
By the water.

It was once a happy place.
It used to be that music played
In summertime and winter,
Rivers of wine were poured
To quench voracious guests…
And the strolling prince, all flush,
Himself poured drinks for all the timid,
Even shouting, "Vivat!"
The prince is dancing, guests are dancing;
They all rolled over on the floor…
He revives again tomorrow,
To drink again, to dance again,
And thus the days go by,
As peasant souls begin to squeal.

Judges beg the Lord above…
The drunkards, know this, shout:
"A patriot! And a paupers' friend!
Our famous prince! Vivat! Vivat!"
And the patriotic paupers' brother…
Takes a peasant's calf and daughter…
And God knows not, perhaps He does,
But stands aside in silence.

The princess sits confined,
The paupers' brother
Won't allow her even on the porch.
What to do?
She eloped and married.
Both the mother and the father
Did not give permission,
Saying: "Do not climb so high."
But no, a prince's hand. Indeed, a prince!
Now, O princess, pride yourself!
You'll perish, dear, you'll perish
Just like primrose on a night in spring.
You'll wither, knowing nothing,
You'll not know how God is praised,
How people live and love.
And, O Lord, she longed to live!
And longed to love,
And see the world
If only for a year, for just an hour.
It did not come to pass,
Though she had it all,
And it was all acquired
By her aging mother.
Your beauty was her painting,
Nearly worthy of a prayer
Said before a saint…
O my youthful beauty,
You're beset with grief!
It would be best to live,
To live and render praise to God,
To create good deeds
And use God's gift of beauty
To bring delight to people.
But for young and hazel eyes
To waste away alone…
Perhaps, God wants it so?
O God! O God! You grant on earth
Free will and wisdom,
You grant beauty
And a heart that's pure…
But You don't let live.
You don't allow an eyeful
Of Your joyous paradise
Or of Your great wide world,
Nor time to pray enough
Before eternal sleep.

There's no happiness on earth
If there's no one here to love.
So it is with her,
My lost and lonely,
And still youthful princess,
Whose heart will wilt
As will her beauty,
And she'll die alone in vain.
It's dreadful!.. And she prayed,
And asked the Lord to live,
For there will be someone to love.
She'd already thought herself a mother,
Took pride and loved her child.
The Lord let her live to feel
Joy upon this earth.
To see and kiss her only child,
And to hear it first let out a cry…
O children! Children! Children!
God's great blessing!
The tears dried up and vanished,
The sun shined once again.
The princess with her child
Became another person.
As if born anew upon this world —
Playful, joyful…
And she sewed
Her little princess shirts,
Then embroidered
Little sleeves with silk.
She bathed, rocked

And nursed the child herself.
Because princesses know only
How to bear a child,
But princesses know not
How to care and nourish.
They're then surprised:
"I'm forgotten by my Paul or Filat!"
Why should the child recollect you?
Just because you gave it birth?
My princess raised her child
On her own,
Not granting access
To her drunken prince.
The child was raised with love
Like an apple in an orchard.
It began to talk,
And the princess
Only taught it "mama,"
To utter "papa" was not taught…
She bought the child
Many picture books in Romny.[296]
She entertained, she talked
And with those books
Began to teach the child
Her ABCs and prayers.
Each blessed day she bathed the child,
Observed an early bedtime,
And would not let a speck of dust
Fall upon the little girl.
She spent the night not sleeping,
But hovering beside her.
It gave her pleasure to behold
And to love her princess…
She thought of matches
And rejoiced and cried along with her;
Already she undid
The girl's long, long braids.
And the wretched dear recalled
Her drunken prince — in uniform.
And closed her teary eyes.
And the child seems to have an inkling,
And appears it sought to say:
"Don't cry, mama, don't undo
My long, long braids —
The ends will split…"
Each blessed day
The pretty girl brings her mother joy.

To the world's amazement,
She grows just like a poplar…
But not for long will
She bring joy to mama. God
Is punishing the princess in this world…
And for what? It's a mystery to people,
For they know not
Why goodness dies
And evil thrives.
As the princess ailed,
The prince came to his senses.
He swept across the village
In search of hags and healers.
They came… Observed.
They healed and healed…
Until she, the luckless,
Was laid out in a coffin.

The village princess was no more,
Again the husli[297] mourned.
And in that village is her orphan,
Her one and only child!
Like a fallen fruit,
Unnourished and unshod,
She wears her shirt until it's tattered.
The dear got sunburned in the heat.
She eats stalks, makes ponds from
Dammed up valley puddles, where
She plays with other children.
Clean up, my dear! For mother looks

296 *Romny* — A town in Ukraine's northern Sumy region. Until the mid-19th century, it was known as Ukraine's commercial capital.

297 *Husli* — Ancient string instrument of Kyivan Rus.

But does not recognize her child from
Any other. And thinks: you are no more…
Clean up, my dear, so she may spot you,
You, her one and only…
So she may praise the Lord
For your happy destiny.
She washed. And decent people
Spruced her up and took her
To Kyiv to study. And what will be there,
We shall see. Husli played another tune,
The prince and guests all frolic,
The palace floor resounds,
As hunger moans throughout the village.
It moans, it moans throughout Ukraine.
God's punishment. Hungry people
Die by thousands.
And stacks of grain decay.
And the lords sell even chaff to Jews.
The famine makes them glad,
And they pray to God
For yet another year of failed crops.
Then our brother from the manor may
Strut his stuff in Paris or another land.
Meanwhile, God dozes.
It would otherwise be strange,
To hear and see —
And to hold back retribution.
Or perhaps He's just too patient…

Years go by; people die,
Famine rages in Ukraine,
It rages in the princely village.
The prince's sheaves have rotted.
It's all the same to him —
He drinks, he dances
And awaits the Jew with money.
No petty Jew arrives…
Grain has flourished,
People revel, ask of God…
And behold, they bring the princess
From Kyiv. She's like a sunrise
In the looted village.

Dark-browed and hazel-eyed,
A perfect copy of her mother.
Except she's mournful and unhappy…
Why mournful?
Or perhaps she was born that way?
Or perhaps she's young and
Has not loved another? No. No one.
She nonetheless danced happily,
She viewed the world from Kyiv
Like a weasel[298] from its nest. Until
She saw the shattered villages. She has
Since become unhappy.

She flew around the village
Like a gray-winged dove.
She called on all, saw everyone,
And they all cheered up.
She greeted some with words,
And some she had to feed…
She walked around the village
Every blessed day. She helped
Anyone. And orphans came
To visit in her palace. They
Referred to her as their holy mother.
And the villagers all prayed for her…
Meanwhile, Jews with cash in hand
Showed up in the village.
The prince rejoices,
Selling rye with chaff.
And sends out half-dead people
To thrash the grain for him.
They thrashed, not bad of them,
Then winnowed his entire barn
In just a single hour…
The prince would not stop for rest,
And called to toast the bargain,
He drinks, he dances,

---

[298] *Weasel* — This is a neutral reference. A weasel does not have the negative connotation in Ukrainian that it does in English.

Though far off in the grove... Because
His daughter's resting
In the palace chambers.

Throughout the grove
There's hubbub, noise and din,
And sounds of shameless songs.
The air resounds
With piercing women's laughter.
The host roars out
And bellows: "We'll drink,
As long as our dear daughter sleeps."

But the daughter sits
Locked inside her somber chambers,
And beholds the crimson moon
Quietly emerging from behind a cloud,
Ablaze above the hill.
And the hills appear alive.
From the grove, the oaks, as if by wonder,
Cast their quiet shadows on the field.
The eagle owl lets out a scream,
The screech owl flies
From thatch to field,
As frogs all croak and drone.
Behold, young eyes,
The rising of God's stars,
Behold the rising moon and
How it reddens up above...
Behold, while you feel warmth,
And stars won't let you sleep.
She leaned her youthful
Head upon her hands,
And my princess sadly watched
Till midnight the shining stars above.
She watched...
And began to cry.
Perhaps the heart had softly whispered
Of some anguish to her?
No matter. She cried a bit,
She smiled, prayed and went to bed.
And fell quietly asleep.

All that lay inside the grove
Was strewn about at random —
Guests and bottles; where they fell
Is where they stayed. Himself
He did not fall, he was downing
His last drop. And drank it. He rises,
Does not fall,
And goes into the chambers...
Take pause!
Where to, filthy viper?
What's your purpose?
He takes no pause, but grabs a key,
He comes, unlocks the door,
And crawls in with his daughter. Awake!
Awake, O purest one. Take hold,
Kill the viper, or he'll bite!
Kill, and God will not condemn!
Like Cenci[299] who had killed the cardinal,
Her father,
And had no fear of Sabaoth.[300]
No, she did not awake, but sleeps,
And though God sees, He's silent,
And tolerates great sin.
All is silent. Time elapses.
Then a scream, then shouts for help
And from the palace cries are heard —
Heard by owls. Once again it's silent.
At that time, the sheaves and barn
Caught fire, and stars
All vanished from the sky.
Had there been a word,
If but a single voice was heard.
The gentry in the grove

299 *Beatrice Cenci (1577-99)* — Daughter of an abusive Italian aristocrat who committed incest against her. She and three other family members were beheaded for the father's murder. Despite the mitigating circumstances, Pope Clement VIII showed no mercy.

300 *Sabaoth* — An army, great number or multitude.

Did not so much as stir,
But people met and watched,
As smoke rose in the sky.

Early morn, the guests got up.
They see there's trouble,
Then earnestly and quietly
Left their friend, the prince.
We too will forsake him,
As will God forsake.
But, O my luckless princess, my
Defiled blossom, you'll not be
Forsaken by your adverse hour.
You will still atone for sins,
For father's sins on earth. O fate!
O ruthless fate!
Leave her be at least in her old age,
At least in sparse and foreign fields.
But you'll not leave her,
You'll drive her to the edge,
To her very coffin,
And you alone will bury her.

In the village no one heard or saw
Where she disappeared.
They thought the wretched dear
Had perished in the blaze.

The village stands.
The palace on the hill
Is mournfully discolored.
The prince is sick,
Too weak to rise.
There's no one to assist,
Nor will anyone so much as see
The sinful patient
In his wicked palace.
Recovering a bit, people
Beg the Lord that the princess
May return to them.
But she's gone
And the saint will never come…
Where did she go?
She joined the nuns in sacred Kyiv.

She was born on earth to live and love,
To radiate God's beauty,
To be a saint and stand by sinners
And do good works for all.
But here's what happened.
The good was wasted with the nuns…

Roaming 'round Ukraine,
I somehow lurched to Chyhyryn,
And to the nunnery
That stands alone beside a swamp
Beyond the sands amid some willows.
It's there an aging nun
Shared with me the news.
That some princess came
Two years before
From a place beyond the Dnipro.
She rested and gave her soul to God…
"She was yet young and oh so pretty.
She'd been badly sunburned
And had taken ill.
She did not lie for long,
Perhaps three weeks,
And confided every detail…
To me and Sister Ksenia.
And she died with us.
Where she went,
To which righteous cities.
And here with us,
The poor dear rested.
Here's her sacred grave…
We've not yet placed a cross."

Orsk Fortress, End of June — December 1847

N. N.

The sun sets, hills grow dark,
The bird falls silent, the field is hushed.
All rejoice, for they will rest,
And I gaze… my heart floats gently
To a twilit orchard in Ukraine.
I float, I float and ponder,
And it seems the heart's at rest.
The field grows dark,
So too the grove and hills,
A star ascends the dark blue sky.
Star! O star! — and tears roll down.
Have you now risen in Ukraine?
Do hazel eyes now seek you
In the dark blue sky? Have they forgotten?
If they've forgotten, may they sleep,
And hear nothing of my fate.

Orsk Fortress, End of June — December 1847

N. N.

My thirteenth year was passing.
I herded lambs beyond the village.
Was it the shining sun
Or was it something deep within?
I was filled with lovely, lovely feeling
As if I were with God . . . .
They had called us in
To get our helpings,
But there I sat amid the weeds,
Praying to the Lord… And I know not
Why praying was so pleasant
When I was but a little boy,
Or why I felt such sense of joy.
God's sky above, the village,
The lamb, it seems, felt joyous!
The sun warmed, but did not burn!
But sunlit warmth did not last long,
The prayer did not last…
The sun scorched, turned red
Setting paradise on fire.
I gaze as if awakened:
The village has turned black
God's azure sky has faded.
I beheld the lambs —
They are not my lambs!
I turned to see the homes —
I do not have a home!
There's nothing God has given me!..
And tears gushed out,
Heavy, oh so heavy tears!..
And a girl not far,
Sorting hemp beside the road,
Heard that I was crying.
She came, greeted,
Wiped my tears
And kissed me…

It seems the sun beamed once again,
It seems all on earth
Became my own... fields,
Forests and the orchards!..
And we, both joking, drove
A stranger's lambs to water.
  Nonsense!..
  And even now, when I recall,
The heart cries and aches
Over why the Lord did not let me
Live my years out as a youngster
In that lovely paradise.
I'd have died behind a field plow,
Knowing nothing of this world.
I'd not be an outcast in that world
Cursing man and God!

Orsk Fortress, End of June — December 1847

The sun is cold on foreign land,
But it scorched back home.
I was not happy,
Even in our famed Ukraine.
No one loved or greeted me,
And I leaned on none,
I just wandered, prayed to God
And cursed the cruel gentry.
I recalled the dreadful years,
The awful bygone years,
When Christ was hung,
And even now the Son of Mary
Would not flee His fate!
Nowhere am I happy,
Nor will I likely be,
Not in Ukraine, good people,
And thus not in a foreign land.
I'd like... But for that,
I wish the Muscovites would not
Craft coffins out of foreign lumber,
Or for the sacred winds, at least, to
Bring a speck of earth from beyond
My holy Dnipro,
Nothing more. That, people,
Is my wish. But why bother...
Why even trouble God,
If it will not be our way.

Orsk Fortress, End of June — December 1847

A DREAM

O my lofty hills,
Not so much tall
As pretty, pretty,
And from a distance, blue.
From ancient Pereyaslav,[301]
From *Vybla Mound*,[302]
That's even older... like clouds
Resting past the Dnipro.
I take an easy pace,
I look — and suddenly ahead
There seem emerging wonders.
Gently from a cloud
Appear a lofty cliff, a grove, ravine;
Small white houses peek,
Like children in white shirts,
Playing blind man's bluff.
And beneath them all the Dnipro,
Our gray Kozak,
Frolics with the meadows.
And yonder, over yonder
On a hillock past the Dnipro,
There seems to be a chapel,
A smallish Kozak church
With a leaning cross.
It's stood there long
To await a Zaporizhian
Coming from the Meadow...[303]
It converses with the Dnipro,
And diverts its longing.
It has aging window panes,
Like a green-eyed corpse,
Peering at the world
From the confines of a coffin.
Perhaps, you seek revival?
Don't await that glory!
Your people have been robbed,
And evil lords...
What use have they for
Kozak fame and glory?!..
And Trakhtemyriv[304] has strewn
With hapless fate
Its shabby houses on the hills,
Like a drunken beggar
Tossing sacks at random.
And there's old Monastyryshche,[305]
Once a Kozak village.
Was it ever really that?..
It all went to the czars for play:
Both Zaporizhia and the village...
And the holy monastery, the treasury, —
All, all was taken by the greedy!..
And you? You gave the hills away!!..
May one never look at you, the damned!!
No, no... You're not the damned...
But rather hetmans,
Instigators, evil Poles!!..
Forgive me, lofty ones!
Tall and azure ones!
The best on earth! Most sacred!
Forgive!.. I'll pray to God...
I love her so, I love her oh so dearly,
My impoverished Ukraine,
That I'll curse our sacred God,
I'll lose my soul for her!

Above Trakhtemyriv high upon a cliff,
Like an orphan come to drown herself...
In the deep, expansive Dnipro...
There stands alone a single house...
From that house Ukraine appears

301 See glossary or fn. 204
302 *Vybla Mound* — An ancient burial mound near Pereyaslav that offers panoramic views of the area.
303 See glossary or fn. 122
304 *Trakhtemyriv* — An ancient town on the right bank of the Dnipro. It once had a monastery and hospital for Kozaks.
305 *Monastyryshche* — A village near Trakhtemyriv with ruins of an ancient monastery.

With a view as well
Of the entire Hetmanate.[306]
Sitting by the house is a gray old grandpa,
As the sun sets low above the Dnipro.
He sits, he looks, he thinks,
And tears drip down… "Hey-hey!.. —
The old man said. — Morons!
They destroyed God's paradise!..[307]
The Hetmanate!!.." And his pensive
Brow turned gloomy…
He probably wished to say
Some heavy heart-felt words.
But said nothing…
. . . .

"I wandered 'round the world a lot,
I wore both peasant garb and overcoats…
Why speak of trouble
For the Kyrgyz past the Urals,
For they, by God, live better
Than we here in Ukraine.
Or perhaps it's that the Kyrgyz
Are not Christians yet?
You've created trouble, Christ!
And converted?!
God's people?! Our stupid
Kozak heads rolled for truth,
And for the faith of Christ,
They got drunk on foreign blood
And our own as well!..
Did we improve?.. No way!
We're now worse off,
They've chained the people
Without knives, with no auto-da-fe
And now they murder… O, O lords,
O you Christian lords!.."
My gray-haired one grew silent,
Beaten down with longing,
He drooped his brawny head.
The evening sun gilds the edges of a grove,
It pours gold upon the field and Dnipro.
Shining all in white
Is the cathedral of Mazepa,[308]
In the distance glimmers
Father Bohdan's Mound,[309]
Weeping willows on the Kyiv road cover
Triple Mounds of Brothers.[310]
The Trubailo and the Alta[311] have
Converged beside an ash,
United like a brother with his sister.
All, it's all so pleasing to the eye,
But the heart sheds tears,
And does not want to look!

The shining sun has bid farewell
To the rich black earth below,
The round-faced moon appears above
With a star, his sister.
They both appear amid a cloud,
And all the clouds rejoice…
And my old one looked,
As tears rolled down…
"To You I pray, dear God,
To our true great Lord!
That You, who rules the heavens,
Did not let me perish.

306 See glossary or fn. 11

307 *Destroyed God's paradise* — Reference to squabbling Kozak leadership that sometimes even solicited the help of marauding Turkish, Tatar and Russian armies.

308 *Cathedral of Mazepa* — Cathedral of the Ascension in Pereyaslav built between 1695 and 1700 with funds provided by Hetman Ivan Mazepa.

309 *Father Bohdan's Mound* — An ancient burial mound that according to legend dates from the time of the Scythians in the 2nd century. Shevchenko mentioned it in his archaeological notes.

310 *Triple mounds of brothers* — The Trybratni, or Three Brother Mounds, about three miles (five kilometers) from Pereyaslav. They are believed to date from Scythian times.

311 See glossary or fn. 21

That you gave me decent strength
To conquer all the anguish,
And brought me, an aging man,
To these sacred hills
To live my years alone,
To praise You,
And delight the heart
With all the beauty that is Yours…
And to bury in these lofty hills
All that's beaten
By the sins of man,
And then to soar above them…"
The tears he wiped were hardly cool,
And weren't the ones of youth…
He recalled his blessed bygone years…
What occurred? When, where and how?
Some was lived, and some was dreamed.
The seas that he traversed!..
And the shady verdant grove,
And the dark-browed youthful beauty,
And the shining moon amid the stars,
And the nightingale on the guelder rose,
That in turns would hush and chirp,
Singing praises to the sacred Lord;
And all, all of it was in Ukraine!..
The gray-haired grandpa smiled…
Because, perhaps, the truth be told
It transpired that they courted,
But parted, never married.
She left him to a life alone,
To live his years within that house!..
Again my old man was concerned,
He walked outside for quite some time,
Then said a prayer to God,
And went inside to sleep.
And the moon was shrouded by a cloud.

Such was the dream I dreamt
In a foreign land!
As if born again to freedom
In this world of ours.
Permit me, God, whenever,
Even in old age, to stand
Upon those looted hills
Inside the little house.
Let me bring a heart
That's ground by grief
And tortured,
So it may rest
Upon the Dnipro hills.

Orsk Fortress, End of June—December 1847

In Kyiv, 1843

Pencil, August 1845

Sepia, December 29, 1849

Italian & White Pencil, 1857

Etching, December 1860

Self-Portraits

By A. I. Denier
St. Petersburg, March 30, 1858

By I. V. Hudovsky
Kyiv, Summer 1859

By Unknown Photographer, 1859

By A. I. Denier, St. Petersburg, 1859

Photo Portraits

ДЛЯ ПИСЬМА КРѢПОСТЕЙ
ДО 1000 РУБЛЕЙ

ЦѢНА ТРИ РУБЛИ.

Тысяча восемьсотъ тридцать восьмаго года Апрѣля двадцать втораго дня, я нижеподписавшійся уволенный отъ службы гвардіи Полковникъ Павелъ Васильевъ сынъ Энгельгардтъ отпустилъ вѣчно на волю крѣпостнаго моего человѣка Тараса Григорьева сына Шевченка, доставшагося мнѣ по наслѣдству послѣ покойнаго родителя моего Дѣйствительнаго Тайнаго Совѣтника Василія Васильевича Энгельгардта, записаннаго по ревизіи Кіевской губерніи, Звенигородскаго уѣзда въ Селѣ Кириловкѣ; до котораго человѣка мнѣ Энгельгардту и наслѣдникамъ моимъ впредь дѣла нѣтъ и ни во что не вступаться, а воленъ онъ Шевченко избрать себѣ родъ жизни какой пожелаетъ.

Shevchenko's Emancipation Certificate, April 22, 1838

7.

Мени тринадцятый минало
Я пасъ ягнята за селомъ,
Чи то такъ сонечко сіяло
Чи такъ мени чого було?
Мени такъ любо, любо стало
Неначе въ бога...
Уже прокликали до паю
А я соби у бурьяни
Молюся богу... и незнаю
Чого маленькому мени
Тойди такъ приязно молилось
Чого такъ весело було?
Господнє небо, и село
Ягня здаеться веселилось!
И сонце грило, не пекло!
Та недовго сонце грило
Недовго молилось....
Запекло, почервонило
И рай запалило.

My Thirteenth Year

1.

Ануте знову віршовать,
(Звичайне нишкомъ) нуте знову
[illegible] на основи
Старинну [illegible] лицьовать.
А сирічъ... якъ вамъ сказать —
[illegible]... нуте знову
Людей и долю проклинать
Долю знати що не стане
Та насъ доки дали
Людей знати що витали
Та насъ поховали.
[illegible] не [illegible]
И [illegible] небуде
И небуде [illegible]
[illegible] спуть [illegible]
И [illegible]
[illegible]
[illegible]
[illegible]
[illegible]
[illegible]
[illegible]

Let's Write Some Poems Again

Manuscripts from *Mala Knyzhka (Little Book)*
Shevchenko's Clandestine Original, 1848
(Shown Actual Size)

Pochayiv Monastery. Watercolor, 1846

Bohdan's Church – Subotiv. Watercolor, 1845

Ukraine

Kateryna. Oil, 1842

Tribunal. Etching, 1844

Village Family. Oil, 1843

Friends. Etching & Aquatint, 1859

Fort Kara-Butak. Watercolor, 1848-50

Fire in the Steppe. Watercolor, 1848

Prayer for the Deceased
Sepia, 1856-57

Impoverished Kyrgyz Boys
Sepia, 1853

Content Angler
Sepia, 1856-57

Kazakh Boy Lights Stove
Sepia, 1848-49

Panteleimon O. Kulish, Writer
Oil, 1843

Ira F. Aldridge, Actor
Italian and White Pencil, 1858

Yelizaveta V. Keykuatova, Wife of Landowner.
Oil, 1847

Fyodor P. Tolstoy, Artist.
Engraving, 1860

Portraits

Sketch of Crucifixion. Sepia, 1850

St. Sebastian. Sepia and Ceruse, 1856

Losing at Cards

In the Animal Shed

Punishment with Dowel

Running the Gauntlet

Parable of the Prodigal Son
India Ink and Bister, 1856-57

Oak. Etching and Aquatint, 1860

Dzangiz-Agach (Lone Tree). Watercolor, 1848

Trees

IRZHAVETS[312]

The Swedes once stirred up
Great renown,
Fleeing with Mazepa[313]
From Poltava[314]
Toward the city of Bendery.[315]
Hordienko[316] followed...
Mother gave advice
On how to reap the wheat
And how to seize Poltava.
Oh, they would have reaped
Had they stood as one,
And if the Fastiv colonel[317]
Had united with the hetman,
Spears would not be stuck as trophies
In the rooftops
Of our sidekick, Peter.[318]
Nor would gloried wretches flee
From Khortytsia[319]
And they'd not be blocked
By the evil colonel of Pryluky...[320]
Nor would the Blessed Virgin
Shed tears in the Crimea
For what befell Ukraine.
As they wandered day and night,
As the Zaporizhians left the Sich,
They took with them the Blessed Virgin,
They took nothing else,
And brought Her to the khan,
The master of Crimea,
For still more Zaporizhian grief.

The black cloud blocked the white one.
The wicked Tatar
Came to rule the Zaporizhian.
Though the khan allowed
New units to be formed on sandy tracts,
He forbade the Zaporizhians
From building any church.
So they put the Blessed's image
In a Kozak tent,
And furtively they prayed to Her...

Oh, may God have pity on you!
O my beautiful, my lush and wealthy land!
Who has not tormented you?
Told truthfully, the tale of any magnate
Would frighten hell itself.
Dante too would be surprised

---

312 *Irzhavets* — A village in the Poltava region where a miraculous icon of the Virgin Mary was located.

313 See glossary or fn. 208

314 *Poltava* — The site of the 1709 Battle of Poltava, where Peter the Great defeated Sweden's Karl XII. The pivotal battle marked Russia's rise as a great power. Ukrainian Hetman Ivan Mazepa had sided with Sweden.

315 See glossary or fn. 282

316 *Kost Hordienko (?-1733)* — An officer of the Zaporizhian Sich. Brought 8,000 troops to Poltava on the side of Mazepa and Karl XII.

317 *Fastiv Colonel* — Reference to Semen Paliy (ca. 1645-1710), historic name of Semen Pylypovych Hurko, a colonel and hero of an uprising against Polish nobility in Right-Bank Ukraine. Also a veteran of wars against Crimean Tatars and Ottoman Turks. Hetman Ivan Mazepa considered Paliy to be a social radical, feared his popularity and arrested him. Czar Peter exiled Paliy to Siberia, but released him after Mazepa sided with Sweden. Paliy fought on Russia's side at Poltava.

318 *Our sidekick, Peter* — Sarcastic reference to Peter the Great. Spears stuck in thatched rooftops is an image derived from the folksong, *Oy, polety halko.*

319 See glossary or fn. 55

320 *Pryluky's evil colonel* — Hnat Ivanovych Halahan (?-1748), a Kozak commander who helped Russian czarist troops destroy the Zaporizhian Sich. Pryluky is an ancient town in north-central Ukraine.

By a semi-lord of ours.
And all that grief, all, they say,
Is straight from God!
Could it be that He takes pleasure
In tormenting people?
Especially my poor Ukraine.
What has she done? Why does she perish?
What is it that has put her children
In such silent bondage?

The kobzars told us of our
Wars and feuds,
About the years of anguish...
About the vicious torment
Done to us by Poles —
They told us all.
But the Swedish aftermath!
They too were scared!
The blind wretches were
Struck dumb by fear.[321]
And thus the faithful dogs of Peter,
The army voivodes,[322]
Tore apart and gnawed Ukraine...
From afar the Zaporizhians heard
How bells rang out in Hlukhiv[323]
And how the cannons roared.
How they drove their brothers to
Build a city in the mud.[324]
How the aging mother
Wept for all her children.
How the children dug a line[325]
By the Orel River.
How they perished
In the snows of Finland.
The Zaporizhians heard,
They heard in faraway Crimea,
Of the Hetmanate's mortal danger,
Of its guiltless passing.
They heard, the poor guys heard,
They heard but all kept silent.
Because they got it good and hard
From mirzas[326] in the foreign land.
The grunts were tortured;
How they cried, and with them
Cried God's Mother,
Who shed holy tears,
The kindhearted Virgin wept
As if weeping for her Son.
And God looked down upon those tears,
Those tears of purity!
He beat Peter, He beat the tyrant
On a sudden road.
The Zaporizhians returned
And brought with them to the Hetmanate
That wondrous image
Of the Blessed Virgin.
In Irzhavets they placed it
In a church made out of stone.
And there she cries until this day
For the sake of all the Kozaks.

Orsk Fortress, End of June — December 1847

321 *Struck dumb by fear* — The kobzars left a rich oral history of Ukraine, but no record of the defeat in Poltava. Its aftermath was a reign of terror and pronouncement of an anathema by the Russian Orthodox Church against Mazepa and his followers. The ROC has never rescinded the anathema.

322 *Voivoda* — Army commander.

323 See glossary or fn. 156

324 *City in the mud* — St. Petersburg was built on swampland.

325 *Dug a line* — Kozaks were ordered to dig defensive fortifications on the Orel River, a left bank tributary of the Dnipro.

326 *Mirza* — Tatar military commander.

O my thoughts! O wicked fame!
For you I'm punished to no purpose
In a foreign land.
I suffer... but I don't repent!..
I love you like an earnest, faithful wife,
Like my luckless dear Ukraine!
Do with me, the cheerless,
Whatever deeds you wish,
Just don't leave me,
I'll hobble off to hell with you. . . .
. . . .
You greeted
Vicious Nero, Sardanapalus,[327]
Herod, Cain, Christ and Socrates.
How obscene of you! You loved equally
The tyrant Caesar and the noble Greek!..
Because they paid. And what can I,
A poor man, bring?
What would make you kiss a wretch?
A song and muse?.. O my grove, my grove,[328]
I can't compare with those
Who also sing that song in vain.
It's strange and boring when I ponder
How often brawny heads have rolled
For that wonder's sake! Like dogs, brothers
Gnaw at brothers, never taking pause.
And that wonder's loved by all:
An unwed mother in a tavern,
And everyone is drunk.

Orsk Fortress, End of June — December 1847

327 *Sardanapalus (668-627 BC)* — Said to be the last Assyrian king. According to legend, a self-indulgent ruler who burned himself, his concubines and treasures when his besieged capital was flooded amid a rebel uprising.

328 *O my grove, my grove* — Words to a popular folk song.

TO THE POLES

Back when we were Kozaks
And the Union[329] was unheard of,
Oh, that's when life was happy!
We met as brothers with free Poles,
Took pride in our free steppes,
Girls loved the boys in orchards,
And blossomed like a lily garden.
Mothers all had pride in sons,
Sons who grew up free... The sons
All grew, and grew,
Bringing joy to sorrows
Of advancing years...
Until the Latin priests arrived,
To set ablaze our quiet paradise
In the name of Christ.
They spilled a sea of blood and tears,
They took orphans,
Whom they tortured
And then crucified,
Also in the name of Christ...
Kozaks heads began to droop
Like a field of trodden grass.
Ukraine is crying, moaning-crying!
One head hits the ground,
Yet another follows. The tyrant rages,
And the Latin priest with a rabid tongue
Screams: "Te Deum! Hallelujah!"

That my friend, my brother, Pole,
Is how the greedy Latin priests
And magnates
Made us different, split us up,
Otherwise, we'd still be living
Like we lived before.
Extend your hand to Kozaks
Extend an honest heart!
And in the name of Christ,
We'll renew our quiet paradise.

Orsk Fortress, End of June — December 1847

THE MONK

It once happened
On Kyiv's Podil...[330]
What happened won't return,
What's awaited won't return,
It won't...
I will wait, my brother,
I'll, nonetheless, keep watch,
Inflicting pain upon my heart.

In Kyiv on the Podil
Our fraternal freedom reigns
With no plebian, with no lord.
In its own fine overcoat
It happily turned out.
It decks the roads with satin,
Covers them with silk
And veers away from no one.

---

329 *Union* — The Union of Brest in 1596 by which part of the Ukrainian Orthodox Church accepted jurisdiction of the Catholic Pope. Poland sought to expand the Union in all of Ukraine. This prompted armed resistance by Ukrainian Orthodox forces.

330 *Podil* — An old part of Kyiv's city center along the right bank of the Dnipro where important religious and educational institutions were located. The Mohyla Academy, a university established in 1632, was reopened there in 1991 after a period of persecution of Ukrainian learning by Russian and Soviet imperial authorities.

In Kyiv on the Podil
Kozaks sing and dance.
They pour pail after pail of wine,
As if it were just water.
The Zaporizhians bought up
Cellars, taverns, barmaids,
All the wines and meads,
And they down it by the ladle.
Music plays and roars,
Making people happy.
And students at the Brotherhood
View it all in silence.
The barebones school has no free reign,
For it would otherwise oblige...
Who's the one with music
That's surrounded by the people?

Dressed in crimson satin pants,
His bloomer bottoms sweep the street.
It's a Kozak walking. — O years!
O years! What do you mete out? —
Suddenly the old man
Struck his heels,
And raised a cloud of dust! Like this!
And the Kozak sings along as well:

"On the road's a crab, crab,
Let it be like that, that.
If indeed a maiden plants a poppy, poppy.
I'll give my heels hell,
And if there's strength remaining,
I'll share it with another.
And how those heels
Took a beating.
I'll dance away,
I'll give my heels hell
And if there's strength remaining,
I'll share it with another!"

The gray old man
Danced his way to the Mezhyhirsky Savior.[331]
He was followed by the brotherhood
And all of sacred Kyiv.
He danced his way up to the gate,
Shouted, "Hello! Hello!
Greet, O holy monks,
A comrade from the Meadow!"
The sacred gate then opened,
And the Kozak entered,
And the gate then closed,
It shut the Kozak in forever.
Who's this gray-hair
That bids the world farewell?
Semen Paliy,[332] a Zaporizhian,
Not done in by all his troubles.

Oh, the sun ascends up high
And sets down low at dusk.
The old monk paces in his cassock
Up and down his cell.
He goes to Vyshhorod[333]
To take a look at Kyiv,
And there upon a hill he'll sit,
And feel a bit of sorrow.
The monk descends into the valley
To drink water from the Dzvonkova[334]
And remembers just how hard it was
To live his life on earth.
To his cell the monk returns
To stand between the silent walls
Where he recalls his years,
All his years of youth.
He takes in hand the Holy Scripture
And begins to read aloud...
And in his thoughts
The old monk soars
To someplace far away.

---

331 See glossary or fn. 186
332 See glossary or fn. 317
333 *Vyshhorod* — A village near Kyiv.
334 *Dzvonkova* — A natural spring at the Mezhyhirsky Monastery.

The words of God grow silent,
And in the cell, like at the Sich,
The famous brotherhood revives.
And the gray-haired hetman,[335] like an owl,
Looks the monk straight in the eye.
Music, dances and Berdychiv.
Shackles rattle... Moscow,
Pinewood forests, snows, the Yenisei [336]...
And tears rolled from his eyes
Down onto his cassock... Bow low!
And subdue your aging flesh.
Read the Holy Scripture,
Read and read and hearken to the bell,
But don't indulge your heart.
It led you to Siberia,
And deceived you all your life.
Lull your heart to sleep
And forget your Borzna
And all the deeds at Fastiv. [337]
All will die, and you will die yourself.
None will recall, just so you know...
And the old man burst out crying.
He paced his cell. He paced,
Then sat and worried:
"Why was I born into this world,
Why did I love my dear Ukraine?"
The large bell in the tower tolled
For morning prayers. My monk got up,
Donned his hood, took his staff,
Crossed himself, took his prayer beads...
The old monk hobbled off
To say his prayers for Ukraine.

Orsk Fortress, End of June — December 1847

We ask each other,
Why did mother give us birth?
For good? For evil?
Why is it that we live?
What is it we desire?
We die, never learning,
And leave our deeds behind...
What earthly deeds,
O my dear God, shall judge me?
Would that those children
Born in bondage
Did not grow to scorn
Your Holiness,
And to bring You shame.

Orsk Fortress, End of June — December 1847

Alone it's strange. But where to go?
What to do and what to start?
To curse fate and people is, by God,
Not worth it. But how to live abroad?
What to do in custody?
If shackles could be gnawed,
I'd gnaw them bit by bit. But they're
Not the kind.
They're not the kind
That blacksmiths forged,
They did not temper iron that could
Be gnawed right through. Such anguish!
For the slaves and orphans
In the boundless steppe beyond the Urals.

Orsk Fortress, End of June — December 1847

335 *Gray-haired hetman* — Ivan Mazepa.

336 *Yenisei* — Siberian River that empties into the Arctic Ocean.

337 *Borzna and Fastiv* — Areas of Semen Paliy's exploits. He was born in Borzna.

Row by row
Three nights I stitch,
I stitch, embroider,
And I'll dance on Sunday.

O my bright-red scarf of silk,
Marvel, girls,
Marvel, guys,
Marvel at it, Zaporizhian Kozaks.

Marvel, woo,
And marry someone else.
Scarves as gifts...
But Kozaks will be Kozaks!

Orsk Fortress, End of June — December 1847

THE KERCHIEF

Was it the will of God?
Was it her destiny?
Bred in servitude, she grew
To love an orphan.
Like a dove, the poor young lad
Was with his luckless girl
From the morning till the evening star,
Sitting by a widow's home.
They just sat, they talked,
And awaited the Immaculate.[338]
Their wait was over... From Chyhyryn
And throughout glorious Ukraine,
Great bells began to toll,
Calling boys to saddle up.
To sharpen swords and sabers,
To gather for a fest,
For a merry romp,
For a bloody courtship.
Early on a Sunday,
Horns and bugles sounded.
The famed companions[339]
Started marching,
And hit the road before the sunrise.
The widow bid her son farewell,
The only child she had.
The sister saw her brother off.
So too the orphan girl
Saw her poor young Kozak off:
His horse she watered at the well
Beneath the morning star,
She brought his arms —
A golden sword
And arquebus[340] rifle.
For three fields, three miles,

338 *Awaited the Immaculate* — Reference to two religious holidays, the death of the Blessed Virgin on August 15 and Her birth on September 8. Weddings in Ukraine were traditionally held after the second holiday.

339 *Famed companions* — A light cavalry Kozak unit subordinate to the hetman that often served as police.

340 *Arquebus* — A muzzle-loading rifle used in the 15th to 17th centuries.

She saw him off
And in the valley said farewell.
A silk embroidered kerchief
Was her gift to him
So he'd recall her in a foreign land.
O kerchief, O precious kerchief!
Laced, embroidered, sewn.
To have his saddle trimmed with you
Gives a Kozak joy.

She returned, she worried,
And watched the beaten path.
Adorned with flowers,
Always tidy,
She expected his return
Every blessed day.
And she climbed the mound on Sundays
To watch for him all day.

Summer passed, another passed
And on the third the famed companions
Streamed back to their Ukraine.
One army comes, a second comes,
And the third is wrapped in silence —
Don't look, O luckless one, —
They bring you only grief.
They bring a painted coffin,
Draped with nankeen cloth,[341]
And behind it is an officer
In an overcoat of black.
It's the very colonel of the famed,
The wizard[342] of the Sich.
Close behind are chieftains,
Weeping as they go.
The chieftain gentlemen
Bear Kozak weapons:
Cast armor that's been hacked,
A golden sword,
Three arquebus rifles,
And three matchlocks too...
And on the weapons...
Crusted Kozak blood.
The jet black horse they lead
Limps with shattered hooves...
And the saddle on his back
Is covered with a kerchief.

Orsk Fortress, End of June — December 1847

Girl with Scarf, 1842

341 See glossary or fn. 5

342 *Wizard of the Sich* — Possible reference to Ivan Sirko (1610-80), a Kozak officer whom legend renowns as a wizard impervious to bullets and swords.

TO A. O. KOZACHKOVSKY[343]

This happened long ago.
It was still in school
That I'd lift a five-spot from the
Cantor-teacher.[344]
For I was nearly naked, oh so poor —
So I'll buy a sheet of paper. And I'll
Make a little book.
I'll decorate the border
With flowery patterns and with crosses.
I then copy Skovoroda[345]
Or *Three Kings with Gifts.*
Then alone amid the weeds,
So no one hears or sees,
I sing a song and cry.
In my old age it's come to pass
That I again must hide with poems,
To adorn my books and
Weep alone amid some weeds.
And weep heavily. And I don't know,
Why does God so chasten me?
In school the youngster grew
And suffered,
In school the hair turned to gray,
The fool they'll bury still in school.
It all stems from the five-spot,
Which I, the little boy,
Had purloined from the cantor,
And thus the Lord so chastens me.

So listen up, my dear old friend,
O my raptor-Kozak.
Of how I agonize in bondage,
Of how I roam the world.
Listen up, my brother, and teach
Your little children,
Teach them not to learn in youth
How to write a poem.
If despite it all
One of them should hasten,
Then quietly, my brother,
Let it go off to a corner
To pen a verse and softly cry,
So God won't hear,
And you won't see.
So it does not come to pass,
My brother,
That he too will be chastened.
As I now, my brother,
Sit in bondage punished.

On Sundays like a thief,
I steal beyond the ramparts to a field.
Passing willow beds, as if to freedom,
I'll rise above the Ural
On the broad, broad steppe.
And the aching beaten heart
Twitches like a leaping fish.
It softly smiles
And like a dove it soars
Above the foreign field,
And I, it seems, revive
Upon that field and in liberty.
And I climb a lofty hill,
I look and then recall Ukraine.
And fear the recollection.
Steppes are there and steppes are here,
But here they're not the same,
Reddish-reddish nearly crimson,
But there the steppes are azure, green
And laced with fields, with grain,

343 *Andriy Osypovych Kozachkovsky (1812-89)* — A physician and friend of Shevchenko. He treated the poet for an illness in Pereyaslav in 1845.

344 *Cantor-teacher* — After his parent's death, Shevchenko studied with his village church cantor, Pavlo Ruban.

345 *Hryhoriy Savych Skovoroda (1722-94)* — Ukraine's itinerant and pre-eminent philosopher. He was a Neo-Platonist.

Tall mounds and shady groves.
And here are weeds, and sand,
And willow beds...
If there only was a mound
To even speak in jest of ages long ago.
It seems that people never lived.
From ancient times until today
The desert hid from people,
But nonetheless, we found it.
We've built fortresses already,
And soon there will be mounds,
Because we'll do it all someday!
O my fate! O my country!
When will I escape these desert wastes?
Or maybe, God forbid,
I'll simply perish here.

And the crimson field will blacken...
"Move it, to the barracks!
Move it, back to bondage!"
Someone seems to shout above.
And I awaken. I return beyond the hill,
Steal past the Ural, and like a thief
I slip back through the ramparts.

And this, my friend, is how I celebrate
My holy Sunday.
And Monday?..
My friend, my brother!
Night will come
Into the stinking house,
So too will the thoughts.
One hundred times
They'll break the heart and hope,
And things I can't express...
All things on earth they'll chase away.
And they'll stop the night.
Time will deafly flow
In years, in ages.
And more than once I'll soak my bed
With my bloody tears.[346]

I'll count the days and years.
Whom did I love and where?
What good did I do for whom?
No one on earth, for none on earth.
As if I roamed a forest!
And there was freedom,
There was power,
But power got worn down by loans,
Then freedom as a guest got drunk,
And blundered into Nicholas...[347]
And renounced intoxication.

Dear God won't help,
As people say.
On earth there will be penance,
But not a chance of going back.

I beg God for dawn;
Like freedom, I await the sunlight.
The cricket ceases chirping;
They sound reveille.
I beg God for dusk,
Because they stage a spectacle
In which they drill an aging fool.
So he may know respect for freedom,
So he may know that fools are beaten.
The years of youth pass by,
Destiny has passed, and hope
In bondage does its thing again,
Again it gives me trouble,
Bringing sorrow to the heart.
But perhaps, I'll yet again see goodness?
But perhaps, I'll cry
Through all the grief?
I'll drink water from the Dnipro,

---

346 *With my bloody tears* — Reference to Psalms Chapter 6, Verse 6: "I am weary with my groaning; all the night make I my bed to swim; I water my couch with my tears."

347 *Nicholas* — Reference to Czar Nicholas I, Russian autocrat who personally forbade Shevchenko to write or draw during his decade-long internal exile.

And you, my friend, I'll see again.
And perhaps, my friend, we'll talk again
In your quiet home. I'm afraid!
Afraid to ask myself, —
Will this ever come to pass?
Or perhaps, only from
The realm of heaven
Will I see Ukraine and you.

And it sometimes happens
That not a tear remains;
And I'd plead for death...
But you, Ukraine,
The Dnipro's plunging banks,
And hope, my brother,
Don't allow me to beseech
The Lord above for death.

Orsk Fortress, End of June — December 1847

SOLDIER'S WELL

To Y. Kukharenko[348]

"Life on earth, by God,
Ain't worth it!.."
"Then go drown yourself!"
"And the wife! The kids?"
"So there, you see, don't lie!
Just sit and write this tale... Perhaps,
Poor chap, you'll say things
In a different way."

Write like this: there was
A village —
And not to crawl to foreign lands,
Write — in our Ukraine.
And in that village lived a widow,
And the widow had a daughter
And a son of seven years.
Good is having kids in comfort,
So you praise the Lord...
But perhaps the needy widow
Is not much in the mood for Him,
Because she almost perished
From the troubles heaped upon her.
She thought — a nunnery,
Or to drown herself,
But felt sorry for the kids!
Of course, a mother, say no more.
Or perhaps she had a dream
Of an in-law son,
Because Katrusia was now growing.
Or will she waste her maiden years
Making eyes for naught?..
No, she's not that kind of maiden!

Indeed in that same village,
A hardworking orphan
(For orphans everywhere are lazy)
Grew up as a hireling,
As if he were a father's child!
One way or another
The pauper earned some cash,
Bought some clothes, an overcoat,
And out of nowhere on that orphan's kopeck,
Bought a little house and orchard.
He thanked good people
For their bread and salt,
For an education, then whoosh,
He made a beeline to the widow
To get some wedding scarves!

[348] *Yakiv Herasymovych Kukharenko (1800-62)* — Ukrainian writer, ethnographer and general of the Black Sea Kozak Host. Shevchenko met him in 1840 and supported his literary efforts.

They did not haggle with matchmakers
(As gentry often do),
The priest too did not negotiate,
And to everyone's amazement
Wed them on a weekday
For a mere three kopas...[349]

The widow's tears dried up.
That, my friend, is how to live,
Life on earth will then be happy.
Life on earth will be worth living,
When you have someone to love.
Though this they say as well, poor chap:
Love yourself, and God will help.
But when it's time to die?
Do you croak on all your cash?
No, poor chap!
Love — the blessing of the Lord!
Love, my friend, your wife, your kids;
Share your income with the poor,
It will be easier to earn.

The poor kids married.
People wondered
How will they, the orphans,
Live upon this world?
One year passes, then a second,
And again they wonder,
Where did both those luckless orphans
Acquire all their goods?
Outdoors and in their barn,
On the field and in the stackyard.
And children just like blossoms,
And both the handsome dark-brows
Dress in overcoats,
They ask beggars in for lunch,
And the rich — don't pass them by.
They did not pass, the self-absorbed,
But, nonetheless, they felt regret
That orphans shared
Such goods with beggars![350]
"If it's rotting, they should sell it,
They have children, after all!.."
Hear this about what envy
Does on earth,
And also naked greed.
They went, they went
Until at night, regretfully,
They set the house on fire!
Let it be uncertain
How enlightened nobles are:
Then there'd be no sorrow; not so?
This way it's the lowliest of bumpkins,
Who engages in such cruelty.
It's tough, my brother,
To comprehend the ways of people,
But to love a viper in one's youth
Is altogether worse.
It entrances with a serpent's hazel eyes...
But confound it, you forgot, you fool,
That death is just behind your back.

All had burned right to the ground,
The children burned as well.
And the neighbors, rich and poor,
Rejoiced. The rich, you see, rejoiced,
For they were now yet richer,
And the poor felt joy,
For they were now the couple's equal.
They assembled to express regret,
Thus provoking more regret.
"What a pity! Such a pity!
If only there was knowledge
Of how to mind a kopeck,
Then, even so, this would not be so...
Ain't it so, Maksym!
(Because Maksym is what they called him.)
Sell your cattle,

349 See glossary or fn. 137

350 *Shared such goods with beggars* — There was a custom in Ukraine to feed the homeless and hungry on holidays.

Come work for me and be my hireling,
What will be will be.
We'll again be chumaks,
Till we make something of ourselves,
And then we'll see..."
Maksym said thanks for the advice.
"I'll see what's up ahead;
If I can't handle it,
Then again I'll likely be a hireling...
Where's my dark-brow, Kateryna?!
She always had advice that's good,
And she'll advise me now!.."
The last advice will hurt forever.
Your cows and oxen all dropped dead
And Katrusia[351] wandered off
With soldiers!

Now, write this, poor chap.
Maksym thought and worried;
Then he prayed to God.
Twice he said: "God! O God!"
And nothing more.
From the empress came an order
That all heads be shorn.[352]
"I did not let the widow drown,
I'll not let her wander with a sack." —
Said Maksym and left his land.
Because the community, you see,
Took the widow's son to
Be drafted in the army.[353]
Such dark and shifty deeds
Occur upon this world!
And you, the literate,
Should be beaten,
So you don't shout, "Ah! Allah!
Life on earth ain't worth it!"
Why, confound it,
Don't the simple shout?

2

But do they really live? And do they know,
As you once said, of love and blessings?

I

What, what? I can't quite hear...

2

They, I tell you, all will sprout.
Or, as you put it, grow,
Like cabbage in a garden.

I

In your words! But okay,
Suppose indeed they do not live...
I'll put it any way you wish.
But you don't let them live,

---

351 *Katrusia* — Diminutive for Kateryna.

352 *Heads be shorn* — A reference to a decree by Catherine II in the early 1780s instituting the military draft in Ukraine. A shorn head meant a military crew-cut.

353 *Drafted in the army* — Wealthy villagers frequently sent poor men to serve in place of their sons, despite a law that prohibited sending an only breadwinner to the army.

Because you all live for yourselves,
Having shut your well-read eyes.

2

So, if we write like this,
We'll not finish until evening.
Okay, where's that luckless son-in-law?

The widow's son came home,
The son-in-law became a soldier.
None felt sorrow for him,
They even mocked him in the village!

So, really, I don't know,
If she returned,
Kateryna, to her mother,
Or did she truly perish?
Rumor had it, that they led
A woman shorn of hair
Through the streets of Uman —
She stole something...
Then she drowned herself.
But that is neither here nor there,
People drown and strangle others!
Or perhaps it's true
Just like pears upon a willow.
I just know they wrote
Some song about her.
I heard it once when girls
Sang it at a party:
"Rustle, rustle through the oaks,
The boys lost all their hats,
Just the hireling did not lose his,
He came to love the widow's daughter..."
A shameless song, it's bad but good.
The years passed softly by, —
Write this, — and for their sins
The Poles were punished by the Lord[354]
And the shriek owl
Shrieked above the Urals,[355]
Bards wrote words of praise
For combat and the empress. Just we,
Thank God, sat tight and quiet.

After that great winter,[356]
The legless Maksym came home too.
He says he lost it in a battle
And earned a little cross of silver!

"Why'd he hobble back? He's got no home,
He's got no one, not a sister, nor a brother.
Why'd he wander in?"
"He can't be figured out!
Did you hear they say: it's easier
To die in native rubble
Than in foreign castles,
Did you hear?" — "Why no.
Eh, good man, let's write this faster,
'Cause you and I both want to sleep."

---

354 *Punished by the Lord* — Reference to Koliivshchyna, a bloody Kozak-peasant uprising against Polish landowners in 1768.

355 *Owl shrieked above the Urals* — Reference to Russia's largest peasant revolt against landowners (1773-74). It was led Emelyan Pugachev. Shevchenko's reference to him is a play on words in Ukrainian, which typically uses the letter "h" where Russian uses a "g." *Puhach* is a shriek owl. *Puhaty* means to shriek.

356 *Great winter* — The unusually cold and long winter of 1788.

The crippled soldier worried,
Where was he to go? The widow's
Son is with the pikemen[357]
And the widow's in the great beyond.
To whom is he to turn?
Where is he to spend the winter?
It's fall already,
Winter soon will rage.
There is no fortune in his world,
It fled into a field!..
He appealed to the cantor
To spend winter in the school.
Because the Muscovites,
Thank you kindly,
Taught him how to read and write.
He then wove a braid,
Because soldiers,
One and all, you see,
Wore gray braids with curls
And dusted them with flour,
Only God knows why!
Maksym, indeed, was literate,
And at times, he helped the cantor
In the choir loft,
And read the Psalms at funerals.
He carried contributions
With school kids to the priest.
And at Advent, the poor guy
Petitions in the name of Christ!
But you may write just what you will,
But do not lie to people.
From him you would not hear
A single unkind word.
"Fortune and misfortune —
All of it, — he says, — comes
From God above."
He won't sigh, nor will he cry,
As if he were a child.
And dogs would never bite
Maksym the soldier.
And on a Sunday or a feast day
He'll tidy up a bit,
And hobble over to the widow's house
To see the burned out ruin.
He'll sit down in the orchard...
He'll recall the widow,
And he'll read the Psalms
For her sinful soul.
Softly he'll appeal
For the health of Kateryna.
He'll wipe his tears — all's from God —
Then he feels happy.
And on the Feasts of Peter and the Savior[358]
He won't rest in school,
But he takes a spade and shovel,
Then hobbles to the field...
Along the road beside a valley —
So, you'll not guess
What the cripple's up to, —
He's digging out a well!
And dug it out. They blessed the well
That summer on the Feast of Makoviy,
And for passers-by they marked the spot
With a planted oak tree.
But the summer after, children
Found the lifeless soldier
By the well down in a valley —
The poor soul went one last time
To see the well he dug.
He was buried in the valley
By all in the community,
And to honor him
They named the well and valley
As the Soldier's. They still
Bless water there on the Savior's Feast
Or on that of Makoviy.
And the oak tree turns a vibrant green.
Whoever walks or rides —

---

357 *Pikemen* — Ukrainian Kozak or Russian units armed with pikes and rifles.

358 *Feasts of Peter and the Savior* — The Feast of Sts. Peter and Paul is marked on July 12 according to the Julian calendar. The Savior's Feast is on August 19.

Does not pass
The verdant oak.
In its shade they sit,
Drinking cool fresh water,
Thinking of Maksym...

Live that way, you halfwits,
And life will not be boring.

Orsk Fortress, End of June — December 1847

They say, once a dog is accustomed to chasing a wagon, it will chase a sled.

That's the vein I write in now,
Only wasting ink and paper...
But once! By God, I do not lie!
If I recall or witness something,
I dash off words that make me cry.
And it seems I fly
If for an hour to my dear Ukraine.
I glance at her, I look,
And it seems I've done somebody good,
So my heart then sweetly rests.
Were it said I do not love,
That I forget Ukraine,
Or that I now curse evil people
For what I must endure,
By God, my brothers, I forgive
And beseech the Merciful
That what you may recall about me
Is not a thing of evil.
Though I've done no harm to you,
Nonetheless, I've lived among you,
And perhaps some good remains.

Orsk Fortress, End of June — December 1847

Come on, let's write some poems again.
Secretly, of course. Come on,
While something novel forms a basis,
Let's refurbish God's old tale.
Or... how to tell you,
Without lying. Let's again
Curse fate and people.
People, so they'll show respect
And know us.
Fate, so she won't slumber,
So she may take good care of us.
But you see the fix she's put us in:
Indifferently, she left a child
At a crossroads,
And he's poor, young
But with whitened whiskers, —
Just a kid, of course, —
And he softly hobbled off
To live beneath a foreign fence
Far beyond the Urals.
He found himself amid a desert,
He found himself in bondage...
How, cruel fate, can one not curse you?
I won't curse you, fate,
Instead I'll hide behind the ramparts.
And I'll secretly write poems,
I'll roam the world,
And I'll expect you, my fate,
As a guest in bondage
From beyond the mighty Dnipro!

Orsk Fortress, January — Early May 1848

THE BRANDED CONVICT[359]

I once met an old, old grandpa
Rambling in a foreign land
Above the Ilek River.[360]
The old countryman of ours,
A branded con,
Survived a lot of torture.
In a field on a Sunday
We somehow met and got to talking.
The old man mentioned his revered Volyn,[361]
His youthful fate and freedom,
And the humdrum of his life.
We sat down amid the grass
Beyond the ramparts.
And talking, we confessed our sins
To one another.
"A long life! — The old man said.
All's from God!
From God is all!
Foolish man does naught alone.
My efforts, as you see, were futile, all in vain,
I ruined my life all by myself.
I blame none for that,
Nor do I ask a thing of others. Thus,
My son, my only friend,
I'll die in bondage in a foreign land."
Then the old and branded con
Quietly shed tears. My gray old brother!
Until hope lives in a home,
Let it live, don't drive it out.
Let it sometimes warm
That cold and empty home.
From aging eyes flow youthful tears,
And the heart
Washed in those tears will rest,
To soar from foreign places
To its native land.

"A lot has passed, —
Remarked the aging man. —
Much water's drained
From the Ikva[362] to the sea…
Above the Ikva was a village,
And that village is the place I grew
For misfortune and perdition.
O my destiny so cruel!..
The old lady of our manor
Had some lordling sons;
They were all my age.
She took me to the mansion
As a plaything for her sons.
Like so many pups,
The lordlings grew and grew.
I'm not the only one they bit.
And then they taught them
To be literate. And to my misfortune
I was taught as well.
With tears! With blood!
Thus the learning flowed… Us!
Those cheaper than a lordly dog,
To be granted literacy?!
To pray to God
And behind a plow to stumble,
Nothing more,
Is what the slave should know.
That's his destiny.
And thus I learned, I grew,
And asked for freedom —
She won't give it. Nor will the cursed
Woman let me join the army.
What to do upon this earth?
To the plow I went…
But she got the lordlings
Positions in the guard…

---

359 *Branded convict* – Some convicts in the Russian Empire were branded on the forehead.
360 *Ilek River* — A tributary of the Ural River in Orenburg Oblast of Russia and Kazakhstan.
361 See glossary or fn. 69
362 *Ikva* — A tributary of the Styr River in Volyn.

A dark and dire hour came!
Tough years were yet to follow!
And thus I worked behind a plow.
I was but a meager orphan.
And at the neighbor's was a girl
Working as a hireling. And I…
O my destiny! My meager destiny!
O my Lord! O my only!
She was but a child,
She... We are not to judge Your deeds,
O great God of ours!
She thus grew to my grief and ruin.
I hardly had a chance to look
And thought of getting married,
To live, be happy,
To praise the Lord and people…
But as it happened…
We bought a lot of goods,
Brewed a batch of beer,
But did not get to drink it.
The aging lady's gray-haired punk went
And stole the goods. He spilled
The beer, and made the
Bride an unwed mother…
It was all in vain.
It's passed. 'Nuff said…
It's awkward now to mention it.
What's done, is done. It's past and gone…
I left the field and the plow,
I left the home and town,
I left everything. The devil gave advice.
I became a civic clerk.
The year somehow elapses,
I write, meet people,
And choose good guys as friends.
A second year goes by.
In the summer of the third,
The lordlings all converged,
All of them engaged.
Living in the court,
They danced, played cards,
And waited for their wedding,
Chasing village girls
Like a herd of studs.
Of course, they're lordlings.
We await, and we await
That wedding.
And on the Pentacost,
Both of them were married
In the local Latin church.
They were Poles.
God Himself in this great world
Had never, never seen
Anything more pretty
Than that youthful couple…
Merry music played…
And from the church
They led them to refurbished chambers.
We met them all,
Little princes, lordlings and the couple,
And all of them we butchered.
The wedding was awash in red.
Not a single Catholic got away,
All were killed, like piglets
In a smelly bog. And we,
Having finished,
Went to find another house, and
We found ourselves a room
In a house of green
And in a shady grove.
In meadows, in expansive steppes,
In deep and steep ravines.
Everywhere a house.
With room to romp
And room to rest.
They chose me as the master,
Everyday my household grew,
And then it reached a hundred.
Blood flowed like it would from piglets.
I butchered anything named lord,
Without mercy, without malice,
I butchered just because.
I myself don't know,
What was it that I wanted?
Three years I walked with knives,
Just like a drunken butcher.
To tears, to blood, to flames,
To everything I grew accustomed.

At times, you'll spear a child
And roast it like you would a frog,
Or you'll strap a fair young naked lady
To a horse and in the steppe you let it run.
Everything transpired, everything,
And it all began to trouble me…
I went mad, and it was hard
To live in dens.
I thought of slicing up myself,
To roam the world no longer.
I would have done it,
But to me, a semi-human,
A wonder,
A wondrous wonder happened…
The day was dawning,
And with a knife stashed in my boot
I left the forest in Brovary[363]
To cut myself to death. I look,
And our great sacred Kyiv
Seems to hover in the sky.
God's shrines shine with holy wonder,
As if talking to the Lord himself.
I look, but feel faint.
Bells tolled quietly in Kyiv,
As if they were in heaven…
O my dear Lord!
You are such a wonder. I cried,
Till noon I cried.
I felt so much delight.
No weariness was left,
It seems I was reborn…
I looked around,
Then having crossed myself,
I went quietly to Kyiv
To pray to all the saints,
And to ask the people
For their judgment,
For their human judgment."

Orsk Fortress, January — Early May 1848

Oh I'll glance, I'll look
Upon that steppe, upon the field;
Will God the merciful not grant freedom
If only in my waning years?
I'd go back to my Ukraine,
I'd go back to my old home,
They'd greet me there,
They'd be glad to see the old man;
There I'd rest, though not enough,
As I prayed unto the Lord,
There I'd… It's not even worth a thought,
Nothing will result.
How does one live in bondage
Not having any hope?
Teach me, gentle people,
Or I'll be driven mad…

Orsk Fortress, January — Early May 1848

363 See glossary or fn. 32

O Lord, allow none,
Like me, an old man now,
To perish in captivity,
To pass the years in vain.

I'll go along the steppe and meadow,
I'll divert my longing.
Don't leave, they say,
They'll not allow a stroll
From the confines of this house.

Orsk Fortress, January — Early May 1848

An axe once lay behind God's door.[364]
(God walked the world back then
Creating wonders with Saint Peter.)
But a Kazakh raising trouble,
Causing great calamity,
Lovingly and quietly
Went and stole that axe.
He headed off for kindling
To the verdant oak-wood forest.
He picked a tree, and whack!
Then the axe escaped his grasp —
Mowing down the forest.
It was scary and quite sorry to behold.
Ancient oaks and sundry trees,
All laid down in rows, and from
The valley comes a fire,
A cloud of smoke obscures the sun,
And from the Urals
To the *Tengiz*, to the *Aral*[365]
Water boiled in the lakes,
Villages and towns ablaze,
People crying, creatures moaning,
Hiding past the Tobol[366]
In snows of cold Siberia.
For seven years God's axe
Cut down the verdant forest,
The inferno did not cease.
God's world grew dim
Amid the smoke.
. . . .
On the eighth year
On a summer Sunday,
The sacred sun came out
Like a doll in bright white lace.
Where once there was a town or village —
A desert stood,
Tinted like a swarthy gypsy.
The charred remains
No longer glowed,
Winds swept away the ashes,
Not a blade of grass was left.
Tottering alone amid the steppe
Stood a green and single tree.
Scattered in a reddened desert
Lay baked shards and ruddy clay,
Thorny weeds and thistle,

364 *Behind God's door* — A Ukrainian idiom that means something is safe or secure.
365 *Tengiz and Aral* — Two seas in Kazakhstan.
366 *Tobol* — A river in Kazakhstan and Russia.

With random sedge and feather grass
Casting shades of black upon a
Valley near a hill
That at times a wild Kazakh
Softly climbs upon a tired camel.
Then something vague ensues.
It's as if the steppe
Speaks to the Lord.
The camel cries, the Kazakh
Drops his head,
Gazing at the steppe
And on the *Karabutak.*[367]
He then recalls the *Synhychabach,*[368]
Rides quietly down the hill,
And vanishes amid the desert clay...

All alone beside a valley on a roadside
In the steppe stands a tall and single tree
Abandoned there by God.
Abandoned by the axe.
Not burned by any flames,
It whispers to the valley
About that bygone hour.
And Kazakhs don't go past
That sacred desert tree.
They ride into the valley,
Gaze at it and pray,
And with offerings
Beseech the tree
To spread its shoots
In their impoverished land.

Raim, June 19-25, 1848

Chirkala-Tau, 1851

367 *Karabutak* — A small river in Kazakhstan.
368 *Synhychabach* — A single tree.

CZARS (KINGS)

O aging sister of Apollo,
If perchance for just an hour
You could saunter over for a visit
And relate to us the days of yore,
And if you could lend your
Godly voice to an elegant and tidy ode,
Then the two of us can sing some praises
To kings or something else.
For if the truth be told,
I've grown tired of
Those peasants, lordlings,
And the unwed mothers.[369]
I'd like instead to vent my spleen
On crowned heads,
On those anointed by the Lord...
And yet, I'll not cut it, but if you help
And if you demonstrate how those
Birds are plucked and gutted,
Then we'll perhaps lay hands
On anointed locks of hair.
Leave your holy Mount Parnassus, Auntie,
And mosey over, if even for an hour,
And lend, at least, your old
And godly voice.
And in good rhythm and good measure
For just a little hour,
We'll show that laureled company
From the front and back
To all unseeing people.
In good time, we'll do it, mentor.

I

There's no one to be seen
In the city of Jerusalem.
Its gates are shut, as if the plague
Had spread along the boulevards
In the town of David,
In a town secured by God.
No, there is no plague;
But Israel has been visited
By more terrible distress
And a fiercer hour still —
A monarch's war!

The king's princes, all his forces,
All his squires, his entire people,
Having locked the sacred ark
Within the city walls,
Went out, weak,
To fight upon a field, making
Orphans of their children.
And in the city,
Young and dark-browed widows,
Having locked themselves in parlors,
Cry and gaze upon their children.
They curse their prophet
And their master,
The insatiable King David.
And he, with hands on hips
And in a crimson robe,
Just strolls along the rooftop
Of his cedar palace,
And like a tomcat spies
A piece of lard,
He eyes the verdant garden
Of his neighbor named Uriah.
And in that garden,
In her happy terrace,
Like Eve in Paradise,
Bathed Bathsheba,
Uriah's wife and
Subject of the king.

[369] *I've grown tired... unwed mothers* — Shevchenko's facetious reference to his earlier poetry.

At one with God,
She washed her fair white bosom,
And turned the holy king
Into a senseless fool.

Dusk descends outside, as Jerusalem,
Cloaked in darkness, dozes off in sorrow.
And in the cedar palace, David walks
As if demented, and the king-insatiate
Converses with himself: "I... We will rule!
I'm the king above God's people!
I myself am God on earth!
I'm everything!.." — A while later
Slaves brought dinner
And a pail of decent brew...
And the king said slaves
Should bring his subject in for dinner,
That very same Bathsheba.
Not a shabby looker,
Bathsheba came to see
The prophet-king. She dined with him,
Drank some brew, and after dinner
Went to rest a bit with her king, the ruler.
And Uriah slept.
In his dreams
The wretch could not imagine
What transpired in his home,
That what the king had stolen
From that home
Was not gold or silver,
But his greatest treasure —
He had stolen his Bathsheba.
Lest he know about his loss,
The king then simply killed him.
And the king cried a bit before the people,
He fooled old Nathan with a psalm...
Again he's happy, he is drunk again,
He's tending to his subject.

II

David, the old prophet and a king,
Was not so very pious.
He had a daughter Tamar
And a son named Amnon.
Nothing strange.
Even saints have children,
Though they're not the same
As common ones. But like this.
Amnon is his happy, handsome first-born!
He's taken ill and lies in bed?
David moans and cries,
He rips his scarlet cloak,
Pouring ashes on his head.
"Without you I won't live a day,
My son, the best of all my children!
Without you I won't see the sun,
Without you I will die! I'll die!"
And he goes crying to his son.
He tiptoes quickly, nearly running.
And the son, a healthy strapping bull,
Moans from prolonged malingering
Within his cedar mansion;
He lies around, sneering at the fool.
Now the poor guy wails, now he cries,
Asking father to have
His sister Tamar come.
"My dear father and my king!
Bid my sister Tamar
Bake a shortcake for me,
And have her bring it here herself,
Then I, biting into it, will rise again
From the grip of illness."
Early morn, Tamar baked and brought
The shortcake to her brother.
Amnon takes her by the hand, leads her
To the darkened mansion, and lays his
Sister in his bed. Wringing hands,
The sister cries. And, struggling,
She screams out at her brother:
"Have sense, Amnon, my evil brother!

O my only brother! I, I'm your
Only sister. Where will I now turn,
Where will I hide the sin, the shame
And infamy? You will yourself
Be cursed by God and people!.."
Nothing helped. That's how princes live,
Debauching here on earth.
Take note, children of humanity.

III

And here on earth
David has yet long to live.
He grew decrepit, so they
Covered him with cloaks aplenty,
But failed, nonetheless, to
Warm their prodigal old tomcat.
Then his squires pondered
(How well they knew his wolfish nature),
And to warm him up, they took girls
Better looking than the princess,
And brought them to the aging codger.
Thus they heat their king
With their youthful blood.
And they dispersed, having closed
The door behind them.
The old tomcat licked his chops,
And stretched his claws toward
The Shunammite.[370]
Because she, to her misfortune,
Was the prettiest of all,
Of all the girls; like a pure white
Lily growing in a valley —
Alongside other flowers. Thus she
Warmed her king, using her own body,
And the girls played
Among themselves undressed.
I know not
How she warmed him,
I only know the king was warmed,
And... and did not even know her.

IV

Strolling quietly across his courtyard
Is old and happy Rohvolod.[371]
The guard, the squires and the people
Shine around him all in gold.
The Prince is set to celebrate;
From Lithuania a prince and suitor
Seeks wedding scarves
From his Rohnida.[372]
Rohnida lit a fire
Before the gods of Lel and Lado;[373]

---

370 *Shunammite* — Biblical reference to Abishag the Shunammite, who served as King David's bed companion. (1 Kings Chapter 1, Verses 1-4)

371 *Rohvolod (Also Rogvolod & Ragnvald, c. 920-978)* — Prince of Polotsk, an autonomous principality of Kyivan Rus. It was located in what today is north and central Belarus. Volodymyr the Great, Prince of Novgorod before ascending to power in Kyiv, sought an alliance with Rohvolod through marriage with his daughter, Rohnida. She refused. This led Volodymyr to attack and kill Rohvolod and to seize her as his wife.

372 *Rohnida (Also Rogneda & Ragnhild, 962-1002)* — Daughter of Rohvolod. She was betrothed to Kyivan Prince Yaropolk. According to an ancient chronicle, Yaropolk's half-brother, Volodymyr the Great, killed her parents, raped, abducted and made her his wife. One of her four sons was Kyivan Prince Yaroslav the Wise. In this poem, Shevchenko depicts her suitor as the Prince of Lithuania.

373 *Lel and Lado* — Lel, the ancient Slavic god of spring, youth and marriage. Lado, goddess of love and beauty.

She drizzled it with costly oil
And sprinkled it with incense.
Like Valkyries around her, girls dance,
Play and sing along:

"Hoy, hoya, hoya!
Let's adorn the room with flowers,
And expect some guests."

Dark plumes of dust rise like
Clouds on roads beyond Polotsk.
Squires and old boyars
Go out to meet the Prince of Lithuania.
Rohnida with Rohvolod went in person
With the girls, with the people.

But the one who comes
Is not a prince from Lithuania,
The one unknown and long awaited.
Instead it's Volodymyr,
Prince of Kyiv, like an auroch[374] bull
Or wild boar coming for Rohnida
With members of his Kyivan court.

They came, besieged the town,
And set the town on fire.
And Volodymyr, Prince of Kyiv,
Killed old Rohvolod before his people,
Slaughtered them,
And forced a marriage on the princess,
Going back to his domain,
Going back with furor.
He would then defile her,
The young Rohnida,
And would cast her out.
And the princess roams
The world alone,
She'll do nothing to the enemy.
Such are those saints, the kings.

V

Would that headsmen cut them down,
Those kings, the human executioners.
They're a bother, may you know,
Like a fool you mind them,
Not sure of your own footing.
So what am I to do
With all these royal rascals?
Tell me, elder sister of Apollo,
Teach me, dear, help me crawl a bit
Around the throne;
A necklace, if I earn enough,
I'll buy for you at Eastertime.
We'll be shorn as lackeys,
And newly dressed in livery,
We'll zealously adore the kings.
It's a shame to blunt the pencil.
For good will never be
Where there is no sacred freedom.
Why then even fool ourselves?
Let's proceed to villages, to people.
And there, where people live,
Is where it will be good.
That is where we'll live and love,
And praise the blessed Lord.

Kos-Aral, End of September — December 1848

[374] *Auroch* — An extinct ancestor *(Bos primigenius)* of domestic cattle known for its large size and strength.

Blessed is he who has a home,
And in that home a sister,
Or a kindly mother. A blessing,
Such a blessing I,
Quite frankly, never had,
But somehow I just lived.
. . . .
I once was driven in a
Far-off foreign land
To lament not having family,
Not having any haven, Lord!
. . . .
We suffered long at sea,
Then sailed to the *Darya,*[375]
Dropping anchor in the river.
From the *vataha* they brought letters,[376]
Everyone read quietly,
And my friend and I lay down,
Talking this or that.
Then I thought
Of where to find on earth
The blessing of a letter or a mother.
"Do you have one?" — "A wife and children,
A home, a mother, and a sister!
But no letter…"
. . . .

Kos-Aral, End of September — December 1848

THE SEXTON'S DAUGHTER

This happened long ago,
When hoodlum fighters roamed
Our villages, duping girls
Beating boys, scoffing
At society and bullying
A village like a band
Of *quartered* Hussars.
This happened long ago
During the sacred Hetmanate.[377]

On a Sunday in a village
In a tavern on a table
Sat a group of minstrels
Playing dances for a coin.
All around the dust kicked up.
Girls danced
And so did boys… "It's over!
Play another!" — "That's a good one!"
And again the zithers roared,
And again the girls hop like magpies,
And the boys with arms akimbo,
Squat and kick their feet.
. . . .
The best young man, Mykyta,
Stands upon a bench in pauper's gray attire,
The best young man, a bastard though,
A bastard, and a poor one too,
Drawing no one's interest,
And he stands there, just like that…
He props the ceiling with his shoulders.
His heart melts when
He sees the sexton's daughter…
And she, adorned in flowers,
Is as pretty as a picture,
And she stands alone and seems to
Look Mykyta's way!.. He's on fire!

---

375 *Syr Darya* — River in Central Asia. It once emptied into the Aral Sea, but dried up because of Soviet irrigation projects.

376 *Vataha* — Fishermen's winter quarters.

377 See glossary or fn. 11

Mykyta blazes
Dressed in peasant gray attire!
He draws a coin, his last,
And with it calls a tune,
And though unequal to her, he
Asks the sexton's daughter for a dance!!
"Hands off, you drifter!"
And the sexton's daughter laughed,
"Are you out of servant girls!"
The sexton's daughter mocked
The poor Mykyta.
Publicly she mocked him
For his pauper's gray attire!
You'll get yours, sexton's daughter!
You'll cry, my dearie, for that laughter!..
Where's Mykyta?
He took off on a distant trip...
He's not been heard from since...
After that, something's happened
To the sexton's daughter!

She came home in tears,
And went to bed in tears,
Having had no dinner!.. Sleepless,
Just as she lay, so she rose from bed,
Seemingly gone mad. What to do?
She herself knows not!
And Mykyta, like a screech owl,
Always stays before her eyes
In his pauper's gray attire!
An apparition, nothing more!
O sexton's daughter!
Untimely was your laughter
At the one unequal to you...
You began to pity him...
Your soul was gripped by shame,
By aches and melancholy,
Then you wept, you cried! Why?
Because you've fallen deep in love
With that poor Mykyta!
Wondrous earthly wonders
Vex the human heart!
In the evening it rejects,
Come morning it desires!
And how deeply it desires,
It will go on searches
To the far ends of the world...
Thus the sexton's daughter
Knows not where to go...
Just as well to drown.
Just to see Mykyta...
Beware, young girls,
Of laughter at unequals,
So what befell the sexton's daughter
Does not befall you too!

She withered like a blade of grass.
Mother, father worried and took her
On a pilgrimage to Kyiv.
They gave her sacred herbs to drink,
Nonetheless, it did not help!
She beat a path atop the mound
And always went to look for him.
But the path grew over
As she became too weak to rise.
That's what laughter did!
He vanished,
Half-forgotten,
Indeed he's been forgotten,
Or did he ever live? Year by year
Three years went by.

On the fourth year on a Sunday
In a tavern in a village,
Sitting at a spacious table,
Blind minstrels
For a coin,
Played the tunes
They did a year before the last.
Girls danced the same fine steps
They did a year before the last.
An earnest
Kozak in a dark blue hat,
A fancy overcoat, and pants as
Red as berries on a guelder rose,
Flies in kicking, squatting and

Belting out a song:
"Say thanks to father,
Thanks to mother
That they gave us life!
When they gave us life,
They scattered rye
Upon the stove at night…"
"Vodka! Mead! Where's the otaman?
The community? The policeman?
Come and fight,
You lousy, quivering young dudes!
Or box, 'cause I'm a fighter!.."
Not one Sunday,
Nor two, or three or even four!
The village humored
That big pain, the fighter,
Like it would a boil… He's capricious
Like a lordling… Where'd he come from?
Such a ne'er-do-well? The entire
Village cannot feed this damned intruder.
And he just dances, drinks
And gives guys grief about the gals.
And all the girls swoon for him.
He's so handsome and well-off!
He no longer fights with people,
He merely strolls and in the evenings
Wanders to the sexton's garden.
And the sexton's daughter meets him,
Sings and says:
"Is this not Mykyta
In an overcoat with fancy sleeves?"
It is he, the one you mocked
Once in the village.
And now, you, yourself
Go see him in the garden,
You go yourself to see the bastard
As you would a lord!
It was not a day, nor two
That the sexton's daughter
Went into the garden,
It was not a day, nor two
That she sought to please
The lord, Mykyta!

Her indulgence of him
Took her to the very limit.
She lost control!
Days went by,
Months go by,
Summer passes, autumn passes,
As did the seventh month, the eighth
And now the ninth approaches.
Your anguish too approaches!
. . . .
In the sexton's garden is a well,
Beneath a willow in the valley…
Barely walking to the well,
Is the sexton's daughter,
But not to get a drink of water,
But to worry some,
To cry and think,
How is she to be a maiden?
How can she escape her shame,
Where is she to hide?
. . . .
One evening in the winter,
Dressed only in a peasant coat,
The sexton's daughter went
Out barefoot, carrying her child.
She walks toward the well
And again retreats.
And like a viper from the guelder rose
The bastard watches her!
The sexton's daughter placed her son
Upon the parapet, then ran…
And from behind the guelder rose,
Mykyta crept
And threw the child down the well,
As if it were a puppy!
Himself he went a singing
To tell police to find the child
With help from the community!!
Early Sunday morning
People gathered, drained the well,
And looked there for the child.
They found, they found your son,
O sexton's daughter, in a pile of mud.

And they took the hapless one,
Fettered her in shackles,
Took confession, gave communion,
Reproached the father and her mother,
Publicly condemned her
And placed her living in a coffin!..
Along with her own son!
Then they covered both with earth!
They raised a tall stone pillar,
So that people know of her,
And may teach their children,
And for girls to learn,
When their parents fail to teach.

The fighter vanished from the village;
And in Poland people met
Some dandy; he would ask,
"Is she alive, he says,
The sexton's daughter?
Does she mock unequals?"
It's the selfsame he.
God punished him for his great sin
Not by death — he'll live,
He'll walk the world
As a human devil
And you, young girls, he'll fool
Forever.

Kos-Aral, End of September — December 1848

Well, mere words, it seems...
Words, the voice — and nothing more.
The heart, however, races — it revives
With hearing!.. To know, the
Voice derives from God, and words
Disperse among the people! . . . . .
Having bowed,
Not that I was full of sorrow,
I just stood upon the deck
And looked out at the sea,
Like I would at Judas...
The crimson-faced Diana
Began to peer out through the mist...
And I had thoughts of sleep, but rose
To watch the round-faced maiden,
Or girl, rather!.. A sailor,
A countryman of ours from Ostrivna,[378]
Stood watch,
And worried over something,
Then sang, — quietly, of course,
So the captain would not hear,
Because the hothead was an angry sort,
Though a countryman of ours.
The sailor sang, like the Kozak
Who grew up orphaned as a servant,
And serves now as a soldier!..
Long, long ago,
I heard a girl standing by a willow
Sing a quiet song.
And I, a little boy, felt pity
For that wretched orphan,
That he was weary,
That he leaned upon a fence,
As people talk and say:
"He's most likely drunk."
And I cried, I felt pity
As a little boy
For the wretched orphan.
. . . .
Why have you now cried as well?
For what do you, an old man now,
Feel pity in this bondage —
That the world is bound and closed!
That I myself am now a soldier,

378 *Ostrivna* — An early 19th century Ukrainian settlement near the Russian city of Orenburg.

That the heart is torn and beaten,
And what was kind
And precious in it
Has been spilled and lost,
That this is how my life turned out, —
Not so, dear fellow?! — "Ah, yes..."

Kos-Aral, End of September — December 1848

Like a soul tax,[379]
I'm surrounded in a foreign land
By tedium and autumn.
Where, O my good God, where am I to hide?
What is there to do?

'Round this *Aral*[380] I roam and write.
Furtively I versify, I sin.
God knows what prior episodes
I sort within my soul and list;
So that sorrow, like a Muscovite,
Won't intrude into a lonely soul.
Even so, the vicious thief intrudes,
And that's that.

Kos-Aral, End of September — December 1848

P. S.[381]

There's no ire for the evil person,
Ill repute stands guard beside him.
There's ire for the type of good guy
Who knows the ways of tricking fame.

It's still disgusting when I recall
The gothic manor with a clock;
A village tattered all around;
And the peasant doffs his cap
When he sees a flag. It means
The lord carouses with his entourage.
This well-fed boar!
This lazy idler. An earnest lord,
Descendant of a stupid hetman,[382]
And a super fervent patriot;
And on top of that a Christian.

379 See glossary or fn. 134

380 *Aral* — A former island in the Aral Sea. Since Shevchenko's time, it became connected to the mainland.

381 *Petro Petrovych Skoropadsky (1805-48)* — A landholder and serf owner in Central Ukraine. In this poem, Shevchenko satirizes Ukrainian pseudo-patriots. The Ukrainian name Petro is Peter in English.

382 *Stupid hetman* — Reference to Hetman Ivan Illych Skoropadsky (1646-1722), successor to Ivan Mazepa. Shevchenko considered Skoropadksy weak and superficial.

Each year he goes to Kyiv,
Among the lords he wears a peasant coat,
Drinks horilka[383] with the peasants,
And in a bar engages in freethinking.
That's his story, it's all fit to print.
And in his village, he's even got
His pick of girls. And easily each year
He holds his bastards, roughly ten,
To be christened in the faith.
There's so much of that.
A scoundrel all around!

Why don't they call him that?
Why don't they spit on him?
Why don't they trample!!
People, people!
Just ask you for your mother,
And you'll give her up
For a chunk of rotten sausage.
For him there is no sorrow,
For the shady drunken Petro.
But there's great sorrow for the people,
For those foolish children!

Kos-Aral, End of September — December 1848

H. Z.[384]

There's nothing worse in bondage
Than recalling freedom. And you,
My darling freedom, is just what
I recall. Never have you seemed
So young and pretty,
So very wonderful
As in this foreign land right now,
And in bondage too. Fate! O fate!
O my hailed freedom!
Glance my way, at least,
From beyond the Dnipro,
Smile, at least, from far beyond . . . . . .

And you, my one and only,
From beyond the sea you rise,
From beyond the mist,
O my devoted rosy star!
My one and only,
You bring along my years of youth.
It seems the sea ahead of me
Is blocked by happy people
And broad villages
With cherry orchards.
And those people and that village,
Where once they greeted me
As they would a brother. Mother!
Dear old mother![385] Do happy guests
Still gather in the old one's home to dance,
To simply dance, as in days gone by,
The old-fashioned way from
Early morn till late at night?
And you, my dark-haired children,
Happy girls,
Do you still dance at grandma's house?
And you, O fate! And you, my serenity!
My dark-browed joy,
Do you still softly, grandly
Stroll among them?

383 *Horilka* —The Ukrainian word for vodka and some hard liquors like whiskey. It is derived from the verb *hority*, which means "to burn."

384 *Hanna Ivanivna Zakrevska (1822-57)* —Wife of estate owner Platon Zakrevsky, a descendant of Kozak officers. Shevchenko had high regard for Zakrevska and painted her portrait.

385 *Tatiyana Hustavivna Volkhovska (1763-1853)* — Owner of Moysivka village in Central Ukraine. Shevchenko met her in 1843 and was warmly welcomed in the village.

Do you still charm
The souls of people
With eyes so blue they're dark?
Do people still remark in vain
About your graceful stature?
My joy! My only joy!
When they gather round you, fate,
Girls will chirp out of decent custom,
And perhaps the kids, by chance,
Will all remember me.
Perhaps some girl may even say
Some nasty thing about me.
Smile, my heart,
So quietly, so gently,
So none may even see…
And nothing more.
And I, my fate, will pray
To God in bondage.

Kos-Aral, End of September — December 1848

Were we to meet again,
Would you be frightened, yes or no?
What gentle word would
You then speak to me?
None. You'd not recognize.
Or you'd recall me later,
Saying: " 'Twas a dream dreamt by a fool."
But I'd rejoice, my wonder!
You're my dark-browed destiny!
If I'd see you, I'd recall
That happy, youthful
Woeful grief of yore.
I'd then cry, I'd cry!
And I'd pray, because
The sacred former wonder
Parted not in righteous,
But in wicked dreams,
Washed away by tears.

Kos-Aral, End of September — December 1848

MARYNA

Like a nail driven in the heart,
I carry this Maryna with me.
Long ago I should have written
Of this raving woman.
But what of it? They'd say I'm lying,
That I'm, you see, just mad at lords
And always write such things
About their shocking customs…
They'd put it simply —
The fool badmouths
For he is but a serf,
An unschooled commoner.
Not true! I, by God, don't badmouth!
That I'm no lord provokes no sorrow,
But I'm sorry, very sorry
For those enlightened Christians.
. . . .
Though you bow before the Lord,
A wild beast won't do
What you do to your brothers…
Tyrants tailor laws for you,
Making you indifferent, and
When the time is right,
You make a yearly trip to Kyiv,

To confess before a monk, how swell!..
There's also this to mention:
Why am I concerned?
I'll now hear neither bad, nor good.
And he who does not hear, say I,
Is indifferent anyway.
Come soaring from Ukraine,
O you, my only friend,
My pure unsullied muse,
O my faithful partner,
And tell me, O my guiding star,
About Maryna,
How and why she suffered
With the evil lord.
But quietly, so they won't
Hear or learn of this.
Or they'll say we're
Highway robbers,
And dispatch us even farther.
Both of us would perish...
. . . .
. . . .
. . . This happened not so long ago.
A wedding rollicked in a village
And a lord rode
From a Catholic church,
Or perhaps a steward, not a lord.
Amid whirling of the guests,
Amid the clamor and the laughter,
No one saw that steward,
That lazy Pole ride by.
He, however, saw things well,
Especially the bride.
Why, pray tell, does God
Have mercy on a beast,
The likes of such a steward?..
Two years have passed
Since he arrived with
German plows, impoverished,
In this corner of our land.
But nothing's said of how
He cast those poor unmarried mothers
With their bastards out into the world!
And he's married, has two kids,
Both like little angels.
Look, the young lady
Like a dame, went out to
Stroll with her two children.
And my lord crawls from his coach,
Summoning the bridegroom.
And then he greets the kids,
His wife, the poor young dame,
Giving her three kisses.
And they strolled off,
Chatting, to their mansion...
Soon they brought the bridegroom.
The next day, they took him into town
And dragooned him in the army!
And that, as is our custom,
Is how people mindlessly end up!
And the bride? Most likely
She's been fated by the Lord
To waste her youth and beauty
Without a mate to love...
Like a spell dispelled,
All had crumbled, washed away,
And was she to ask again
To serve as someone's hireling?
No, not again:
Already she's a chambermaid,
Whom they call Marysia,[386]
Not Maryna! Above all,
They don't let the poor dear cry,
So she hides and cries herself.
The fool, she feels pity for the peasant
And sorrow for the holy bumpkin,
But just nicely look around —
No need to seek a finer paradise,
All you want, just ask,
They'll give you all, and then some more!
No need, you say, provide a home instead!
This you'd best not ask for,

[386] *Marysia* — Polish for Maryna.

'Cause this... you're fit
And know yourself...
Look, the lord himself, just like a stallion,
Is prancing 'round and 'round you,
For good or ill, but you'll
Be kinfolk of a lord,
Unless you hang yourself!..
   On her behalf, the mother
   Pleaded with the lord.
   He gave orders to bar entry,
   And if she comes, to beat her —
   What is she to do?
She went weeping to the village,
She had that one and only child,
And now it was no more . . . .
. . . .
Like the cawing of a flying raven,
I thus recount the tears, the pain,
And those little idle bastards,
Though no one pities them.
   I recount and cry.
I pity them!.. O my dear God.
Grant sacred power to my words —
To penetrate the human heart,
To elicit human tears,
So the soul is blessed with grace,
So quiet sorrow may descend
Upon their eyes, so there is pity
For my little girls, so they may
Learn to walk the righteous paths,
To love the Lord
And grace their brother...
                    She trudged
Back home and looked:
Flowers behind holy icons,
Flowers on the windowsill,
Crosses decorate the walls,
Like a lovely painted picture...
Maryna! It's all Maryna's,
Her own work!
Except there's no Maryna.
She barely-barely left the house,
Climbed the hill to watch
The cursed mansion,
And went up to that mansion,
Sat beneath a fence
And cried the whole night through.
The mother was still weeping
As shepherds drove their flocks
From the village to the field.
The sun already rose,
The sun already set,
Even twilight ended,
But the wretched dear
Won't go back into the village,
But sits instead beneath a fence;
They tried to drive her off,
Even sicced the dogs on her —
She won't budge, that's that...
   And Maryna's dress is white,
   Just like a novice nun's,
   She prays to God and cries,
   Sequestered in the parlor.
   Beside the lord, no one
   Steps into that parlor,
   He brings her food himself,
   He pleads, he begs
   That she lift her eyes for him,
   That she wipe her tears...
   She does not care to look,
   Nor does she care to eat.
   The evil Pole is agonized,
   Not knowing what to do.
   And Maryna wilts and withers
   In the great white mansion.
   Summer's gone,
   Winter's at the doorstep,
   And Maryna sits around,
   Saying not a word,
   And shedding not a tear...
   Thus the wretch was driven
   By that Polish steward...
   She'll, nonetheless, do nothing,
   Even if you slice her up,
   'Cause that's how she was born.
   One evening in the winter,

Maryna gazed out
At a shady grove,
And from behind that grove
Rose a plump and crimson moon…
"I too was young…"
She whispered and she pondered,
And afterwards she sang:
"Guests converged upon a house,
A house upon a hill,
They loosened braids,
Took off ribbons,
While the lord requests
Some salted pork,
And the devil asks to eat.
Geese, white, white geese
Flew off to nesting grounds,
The gray ones chose the sea!.."[387]
. . . .
Dogs outside began to howl,
Their handlers roared with laughter,
And the lord, his face so flushed it burns,
Goes to see Maryna in the parlor,
Like a drunken *Kiryk*[388]
As if at home,
The wretched mother, know this,
Sits outside and shivers by a fence.
The old one's lost her mind, it seems.
A bitter frost is crackling,
The crimson moon turns pale,
And the watchman cautions timidly
Not to wake the wicked lord.
Now look — the mansion is ablaze.
Fire! Fire! And just where in heavens
Have all those people come from?
As if they sprouted
From the ground,
Grew in place,
Then flowed in waves to marvel
At the blazing fire.
And there was some marvel to behold!
Stark naked by the mansion danced Maryna
With her mother! — And dread —
With a bloody knife in hand
She sang a little song . . . .
"Is this not the kin
Who gathered up her dress!..
When I was still a lady
With a fancy overcoat,
Lordlings courted me,
And kissed me on the hand!.."

(To the mother)

Did you come to see my wedding
From the world beyond?
They'd undone my braid
But the lord arrived… Shoo! Shoo!
Those aren't geese, they're lords,
Look, they've flown to nesting grounds,
Shoo! Be off! Off to Satan.
Be the devil's guest! Hear ye! Hear ye!
All the bells of Kyiv ring.
You see the fire burning,
And the lord just lies there reading,
Asking for a drink… And do you know,
I butchered him?..
Look, he's the charred log on the chimney.
Why, why do you so gaze at her?
It's my mother! Mother! Do not look!
Or you'll devour her.
Here, choke on this!

---

387 *Gray ones chose the sea* — Reference to the song, *Shoo, Shoo, Gray Geese* (*Гиля, гиля, сірії гуси*) Contemporaries said it was one of Shevchenko's favorites.

388 *Drunken Kiryk* — Unexplained reference. Some suggest Shevchenko picked it up in a village where it was locally understood. Others say it comes from a song about a sober man whom a priest makes out to be a drunk.

(Gestures obscenely[389] and sings)

"She was smitten by a Muscovite,
Even grinning with her teeth!
Muscovites! O Muscovites!
They brought a load of aprons,
Lordlings came
With ducats,
And sons of urban priests
Carted in the necklaces!..
Ring, bell, ring,
Disperse the cloud above,
Leave the cloud for Tatars,
Let sun shine on the Christian,
Ring, bell, ring!"

MOTHER

Maryna, darling, let's go sleep!

MARYNA

Let's go sleep,
Because come early morn
We'll go to church;
Look, the ugly man
Is crawling up to kiss me.
Here, take this!..

MOTHER

Let's go sleep.

(To the people)

Christened people, help!

MARYNA

Take me! Take and tie me,
Lead me to the lord and parlor!
And will you go to see
The ladylike Maryna
Sitting locked up at the lord's?
And your only child,
Your little dear Maryna,
Wilts and withers, dying, dying…

(Sings)

"Shoo, shoo, O geese of gray,
Shoo on past the Danube.
I tied the knot,
Now sit and ponder."
Birds are free and happy
Flying in an open field.
But I have waned in bondage.

---

389 *Gestures obscenely* — Reference to the mano fica (*дуля*), a closed fist with thumb protruding between the index and middle fingers.

(She cries)

I should have grabbed a necklace,
So I could hang myself…
That, you see, I now regret…
Drowning is my recourse!
Why, dear mother, do you weep?
Don't cry, my dear, but look,
It's I, your little sweet Maryna.!
Look, a black serpent
Slithers on the snow… I'll flee,
I'll fly again to nesting grounds,
'Cause I am now a cuckoo.
Did he not come to visit?
Perhaps they killed him in a war?
You know, I had a dream:
It seems the moon rose in broad daylight,
And by the sea we both are strolling;
I look, it seems the stars have
Dropped into the water,
Only one remained,
All alone up in the sky;
And like someone crazed, I seek
To ford the Danube,
And I wade disheveled 'cross the river,
With a bastard in my arms.
People laugh at me,
Calling me a fool and an unwed mother,
And while you laugh, I cry,
Or rather, I don't cry,
But roar with laughter…
Watch me fly, 'cause I'm an owl…
— And she flapped her arms like wings,
Jumping 'cross the yard,
Running toward the field,
Howling like a beast.
The old mother hobbled after,
To catch up with Maryna.
Every lord had roasted,
Like little suckling piglets,
The once white mansion burned,
And people quietly dispersed.
Maryna and her mother vanished.
Come springtime when they plowed,
They found two corpses in the field,
And interred them on a mound.

Kos-Aral, End of September — December 1848

THE PROPHET

To My Dear Friend N. V. Tarnovska[390]
In Remembrance of December 17, 1859

Like righteous children
Is how the Lord loved people,
Sending them an earthly prophet —
To proclaim His love!
To assert the sacred truth!
Like our mighty Dnipro,
His words poured out and flowed,
Falling deep into the heart!
They heated frozen souls
With an unseen fire.
They came to love the prophet,
Everywhere they followed Him,
And learned people cried for Him.
And the evil!
They defiled God's sacred glory…
They devoured a sacrifice to

[390] *Nadia Vasylivna Tarnovska (?-1891)* — A close friend of Shevchenko. Both were godparents to a child of a deacon in the Ukrainian village of Kachanivka.

Foreign gods. Blasphemy!
And the holy man… woe to you!
They stoned him in the city square.
And rightly did the Lord so great
Deem that shackles should be forged,
That sunken dungeons should be dug
As if to bridle raging wild beasts.
O you cruel and vicious race!
Instead of giving you a gentle prophet…
He granted you a czar!

Kos-Aral, End of September — December 1848

THE OWLS

On a field of rye at night
On a broad expansive meadow,
Gathering slowly was a parliament of
Owls —
To joke,
To ponder,
To protect impoverished birds,
To consume the eagle's kingdom
And burn it down completely,
To hang the eagle on a spike,
And then at the appointed hour
To institute a new republic!
That would be all, it seems? But no,
Lest they trample down the grain…
It would come as no surprise,
If upon that field
Someone else would set a snare, and lo!
Indeed a ragged peasant did exactly that.
Then he slept among the haystacks,
And come morning,
Without washing,
He went to see his guests…
"They're ugly!
And each of them an owl —
Boil or broil, either way a hassle!"
Not to carry home such meager goods,
He killed off some,
Subdued the others,
And gave them to the ravens for amusement,
And told no one about it.

Kos-Aral, End of September — December 1848

A Kozak steals
Like a thief at night
Among the craggy rocks
Above the darkened Dniester.
As he goes he gazes
At the murky water,
As if to look into a rival's eye,
As if he sought to say:
"O Dniester and your murky water,
Carry me to freedom!
Or drown me at the least
If such should be my fate." —
He stripped down on a rock,
Jumped into the water,
Swimming so the blue wave roars.
And in a roar it casts him
On the other shore.
The poor lad shuddered,
Naked, shoeless
But in freedom, and he asks
The Lord for nothing more.
But wait: perhaps

Upon that foreign field, good brother,
You might ask Him for good fortune
And a better fate.
He walked along a darkened gully
Singing as a went:
"Beneath a hill at the foot of a cliff
Rolled squeaky chumak carts.
And behind them walked
A dark-haired beauty
Crying, wailing as she went." —

Do as you see fit, curse me,
Or don't curse me,
And do not even read me, —
Myself… I ask of nothing,
I'll just write it for myself,
And again I'll waste some lead,
And perhaps, God willing,
I will shed some tears
And they will do me fine . . . . .
Let's pick it up again.
He left his mother and his home,
He left his wife, a pity, nothing more.
To Bessarabia went this Kozak;
Grief drove him to the sea to drink;
Though they say:
"Had there been a whip in hand,
The lowly peasant, like an ox,
Could be harnessed hungry to a plow."
. . . .
It nearly came to pass, not so?
From childhood, this Kozak
And his aging mother
Roamed around with sacks,
Thus he grew up as an orphan
And a hireling: a tramp, they said
And accordingly he married,
Taking as his wife a pretty but a
Needy girl, a hireling, of course.
And the lord!..
(Our fortune and misfortune,
As the people say, are granted both by God)
The damned one spied her! Noble eyes!
Now he showers her with gifts,
Gifts she does not want,
Nor does she wish to love this lord.
What to do? Assail the husband,
Cutting short his years…
And the wife may then be bidden.
Thus it almost happened.
Serfdom's cruel damnations
Drove to ruin my Kozak,
Despite his savvy on the land . . . . .
. . . .
But he loved his little wife
And — O my one and only Lord! —
Like a lady, like a child,
He kept her graced in necklaces!
But the poor guy was worn out,
Forced to sell his home
And become a hireling.
That's how the cursed lord
Burned the man but good.
And the little wife feigned ignorance,
And danced around the garden
Decked out in lovely necklaces —
Just like a beauty queen! —
What to do here? —
And the poor man ponders.
"I'll leave them and I'll flee.
But who will feed them,
Who is to provide for them? One is old,
And cannot rise,
The other's young and thinks of fun!
How to solve this? What to do?
O my grief! Such grief!"
He then left and took a sack
And headed for the deep blue sea!
In search of destiny. He thought
To bring his wife at least…
The aging mother will remain
To live out life at home!..
So it goes upon this world.
He thought he'd live, he'd be alive
To praise the Lord,
But he came to live in foreign lands,

And to only shed a stream of tears!
Nothing more. He's weary
On a foreign field.
The drudge acquired everything,
But he had no fortune!
That blessing known as luck...
He has no pleasure on God's earth,
He's weary in a foreign land,
And belongings make him sick!
He wants at least to see
His dear and native land!
The soaring mounds!
The steppes so broad!
His garden! His little wife,
That hazel-eyed young beauty!
So he swam the Dniester to this shore,
A vagrant who abandoned freedom...
O my God!
What a wonder is the field,
A field of one's own!
How broad you are...
How broad!.. Like liberty itself . . . .
. . . .
He came back home at night.
The mother moaned beside the stove,
And the wife slept in the storeroom
(Because the lord took ill).
The wife awoke, and like a leech
She clung to him, crying in a
Shower of tears.
But among us it so happens
That one can aim a dagger
At a lover's heart
Even as he's kissing!.. My poor
Young girl's come alive!
And where in heavens did
All this wondrous food appear?
Yet she somehow seems
Not quite alive,
Leaning on his shoulders...
She gave him drink, gave him food,
Then led the blissful one to rest.
The poor guy lays there
Thinking, musing,
Of how they'll both go wandering,
And then he gently slept...
But the youthful little wife
Leapt up to the lord,
And told of this and that.
. . . .

Lovingly and dearly
They came, grabbed the wretch,
Then took the vagabond
And vagrant... From home
Directly to a draft board

But fate did not abandon him.
He won promotions,
Then went back to his village,
Leaving service altogether.
By then his mother had been buried,
And the lord had also died,
And the little wife just roams
All over, like a soldier's spouse...
Among the Jews, among the lords,
And barefoot...
He found her, took a look...
And gray-haired as he was,
He raised his worn out arms
Up to God above,
And then he cried just like a child...
And forgave the wretched woman!
Thus, good people, you must learn
To forgive your foes,
Just like this unschooled man! . . . .
But where shall we, all sinners,
Find that kind of grace?
. . . .
. . . .

Kos-Aral, End of September — December 1848

Beside the setting sun
Drifts a little cloud,
Making crimson beds
And beckoning the sun to sleep
Upon the deep blue sea:
It draws a rosy blanket
Like a mother for her child.
It delights the eye.
An hour, just a fleeting hour,
And it seems the heart's at rest,
Conversing with the Lord...
But a mist, like an avenger,
Cloaks the sea
And crimson cloud,
Spreading darkness in its wake,
Then the silent gloom
Shrouds your very soul.
Not knowing where to go,
You wait for dawn
Like children for their mother.

Kos-Aral, End of September — December 1848

The sky's unwashed, the waves are spent.
And reeds, devoid of wind,
Still sway much like a drunkard
All along the shore. O my dear Lord!
How much more am I to roam the world
Along this useless sea and in this open jail?
Silent is the yellowed grass,
Which sways amid the steppe as
If it were alive;
It does not wish to speak the truth,
And there's no one else to ask.

Kos-Aral, End of September — December 1848

My thoughts, my thoughts,
You're all I have,
Don't you too abandon me
In a trying hour.
Fly to me, my gray-winged doves,
From beyond the sweeping Dnipro
To frolic in the steppe
Along with Kyrgyz paupers.
They are bare... yet
Still pray to God in freedom.
Fly to me, my darlings,
I'll welcome you with
Gentle words, like children,
And I'll cry with you.

Kos-Aral, End of September — December 1848

On foreign soil I grew up[391],
On alien land I now turn gray:
It strikes me in my loneliness —
That God created nothing better
Than the Dnipro and
Our famous land...
But then I see it's only better
Wherever we are not.
In a troubled time not long ago,
I chanced upon a visit
To Ukraine and to its finest village...
To the one where mother
Swaddled me and toiled late at night
For a candle to be lit for God;
Bowing deeply, she placed one
For the Virgin, praying that
Good fortune would truly love her child...
It was good, dear mother, that you
Died so early, or else you would have
Cursed the Lord for the destiny I met.

It's frightening how bad
That lovely village has become.
People blacker than the blackest earth
Wander aimlessly about,
Verdant groves have shriveled,
Homes once white
Are stained and rotten,
Ponds are filled with weeds.
It seems the place has burned,
The people have gone mad,
As serfs they trudge without a word
And bring along their little children!..
. . . .
And I, having shed some tears,
Left again for foreign lands.

And it's not just in that single village,
But all throughout our famed Ukraine
That evil lords have harnessed people
With their heavy yokes...

[391] *I grew up* — Shevchenko left Ukraine with his owner in 1829 at the age of 15. He did not return until 1843.

They're dying!
Sons of knights are dying
Burdened with those heavy yokes,
And lords most evil
Sell whatever pants they have
To Jews and their fine brothers...
. . . .
Bad, it is, extremely bad!
To perish in this desert.
But in Ukraine it's even worse
To see, to cry — to say no word!

And if you see that evil not,
Then all seems lovely, oh so peaceful,
And Ukraine seems
Filled with good.
Between the mountains
Runs the Dnipro,
Like a child awash in milk,
The river preens, indulges
For the sake of all Ukraine.
Broad villages above him flourish
All in green,
And in those happy villages
Are happy people too.
It would perhaps so come to pass,
If not a trace of gentry
Remained in our Ukraine.

Kos-Aral, End of September — December 1848

Widow's House in Ukraine, 1843

It's not for people,
Not for fame that I pen
These laced and florid verses.
They're for me, my brothers!

Composing them relieves my bondage,
It seems that words come flying
From beyond the Dnipro.
They spread across the paper,
Laughing, crying,
Like a group of children.
They delight a lonely, needy soul.
They please me.
It's a pleasure to be with them,
Like a wealthy father
With his little children.
I'm joyous and I'm happy
And plead with God
That He not put my kids to sleep
In this distant land.
May the gentle children fly toward home
To convey how hard on earth
It was for them.
And in a happy family
They'll welcome all the children,
And a gray-haired father will approve.
The mom will say: "Would that
All those children were never ever born."
And the girl will think:
"I fell in love with them."

Kos-Aral, End of September — December 1848

Two lofty poplars grow
Beside a grove
Amid an open field
On the apex of a mound,
Each leaning on the other.
They sway without a breeze
As if wrestling on that field.
Those poplars are two sisters —
Each of them a sorceress.

Both were smitten
By Ivan; and Ivan, a normal Kozak,
Would disparage neither,
Courting one dear then the other...
Until one evening in a valley
All three of them convened.
"So that's the way you are, you bully!
You're heartless to us sisters..."
And they went to find some
Toxic herbs
To poison Ivan in the morning.
They found the herbs, dug them up
And then began to cook.
They cried, they wept...
But there's no denying,
The cooking is a must.
They made a brew,
They poisoned Ivan
Then on a mound they buried him
Amid a field beside a grove.
Indifferent? No, not really.
For early morn each blessed day,
The sisters went to
Cry for Ivan at his lonely grave,
Till they themselves were poisoned
By those awful herbs.
And God placed them both as poplars
Amid the field on the mound
As a lesson for the people.
And those poplars
On the mound above Ivan
Beside a grove;
They always sway,
Be it windy, be it still.

Kos-Aral, End of September — December 1848

If I had shoes,
I'd go a dancing…
Oh such grief!
I have no shoes,
But music plays and plays!
It delivers sorrow!
I'll go barefoot through the field,
I'll go find my fortune…
O my fortune!

Look at me, a dark-browed beauty,
Look this way, my faithless fortune…
I've no luck!
Girls dressed in crimson shoes
All frolic with the music…
But I roam the earth.
Without splendor, without love,
My pretty brows are wasted,
I waste them as a serf.

Kos-Aral, End of September — December 1848

I am wealthy,
I am pretty,
But I have no mate,
Just a hapless life.
It's oh so hard to live on earth
And to have no one to love,
To wear fancy satin coats
For no one but myself.
I'd fall in love,
I'd wed a handsome
Dark-browed orphan,
But I have no freedom!
Mom and dad they do not sleep,
They stand on guard
And will not let me go alone
To frolic in the garden.
And when they do,
It's with the ultra-ugly old guy,
With the loathsome rich man,
With my evil foe!

Kos-Aral, End of September — December 1848

I fell in love, I got married…
I got married
To a hapless orphan boy —
That's my destiny!

People proud and evil,
Split us up, then took him
To an army station —
And gave him to the Muscovites!

And I, a soldier's wife,
Grow old and lonely
In a stranger's house —
That's my destiny!

Kos-Aral, End of September — December 1848

My mother bore me
In a lofty mansion,
Swathing me in silk.

In gold, in satin,
Like a gilded flower,
I thus grew, I grew.

And wondrously I grew:
Dark-browed, hazel-eyed,
And fair.

I was smitten by a poor man,
Mother did not let me marry,
So in a lofty mansion

I remained a maiden
All my life.
Such was my misfortune.

Like a single blade of grass
In the valley down below
I now grow old alone and lonely.

I do not see God's lovely world,
I cuddle up with no one…
And my aging mother…

Forgive me, mother dear!
I'll curse you
Till the day I die.

Kos-Aral, End of September — December 1848

Oh, I sent my husband
On a trip,
While I beat a path myself
From one bar to another.
I would see my friend
To borrow millet,
So I could feed my children
In a house unheated.
And I fed them,
Then I laid them all to sleep.
Myself I saw the cantor
So I could get a five-spot,
And spent the night with him.
My husband came back
From Crimea and could barely
Drag his feet.
The oxen died,
The carts broke down,
The chumaks came
With just their whips.
He came back home
And hit the sack:

His children, bare and hungry,
Crawl about the oven nook.
"And where's your mother, children?"
Asks the wretched father.
"Daddy! Daddy! Mommy's
Dancing in a tavern."

Kos-Aral, End of September — December 1848

Sketch, 1841

I'll hone my friend,
And in my bootleg I will hide him,
Then I'm off in search of truth
And for a stab at glory.
I'll not cross the meadows,
Nor traverse the shores,
I'll not take the highways,
It's the byways I will follow.
I'll ask a Jew,
A wealthy lord,
A lousy noble
In his lousy coat,
And a monk if I should meet one,
Though he should not be frolicking,
But rather teaching people
From the Holy Book,
That neither should a brother kill
Or rob a brother,
Nor send a widow's only son
For service in the army.

Kos-Aral, End of September — December 1848

The snow is driven by the wind…
Along a lonely street.
A wretched widow hobbles down it
Past a fence and belfry,
Her hands stretched out to
Wealthy folks
Who forced a crew cut on her son
Two long years ago.
A life is what she hoped for…
At least to rest in her old age
With her in-law daughter.
For naught. She begged for alms
And got a kopeck…
With that coin she lit a candle,
That flickers by the Virgin's icon
As a prayer for her son.

Kos-Aral, End of September — December 1848

Beside the house I'll sit,
Upon the street I'll gaze,
To watch the girls
Play a game of khreshchyk.[392]
Without their Hanna,
Without my little Hanna.
They play not very happily,
Nor do the girls sing quite the same.
And my dear's not here.
She cooing somewhere
At my in-law mother's,
Awaiting my return.

Kos-Aral, End of September — December 1848

---

392 *Khreshchyk* — A game similar to Red Rover in which a one pair of players holds hands, trying to capture another.

In a verdant grove
A cuckoo sang its song,
Nearby a girl cried —
Because she's got no mate.
Her young and happy
Maiden years
Drift from this world
Like blossoms
Floating down a stream.
If I had a mother, father
And if they had some riches,
There would be someone to love,
There would be someone to take me.
But there's no one, so I'll die an orphan,
And spend my lonely maidenhood
Beneath a fence somewhere.

Kos-Aral, End of September — December 1848

SHVACHKA[393]

"No vodka's downed,
No mead is drunk.
You, cursed Jews,
Won't run your taverns.
No beer is drunk,
But I will drink.
I'll not let the hostile Poles
Live in our Ukraine.
Let's go this Sunday,
Fathers-otamans, to Fastiv,[394]
And on our foes, the Poles,
We'll slip a bright white shirt.
No, not white, but red...
Let's go frolic and
In the midst of our adventure,
We'll recall our elder father,
The Fastiv colonel,
Our glorious Semen.[395]
Let's go brothers: beside me
You'll not perish, boys."

Haidamaks in secret
Spent the night in Perepyat.[396]
The boys in Fastiv
Romped all night
Until the break of dawn.

---

393 *Mykyta Shvachka (ca. 1728–?)* — A Haidamak leader of the 1768 Koliyivshchyna uprising. He was known for exceptional brutality. Shvachka was sentenced to life at hard labor in Siberia, where he presumably died.

394 *Fastiv* — A town near Kyiv that was a center of the anti-Polish uprising of the early 18th century.

395 See glossary or fn. 317

396 *Perepyat* — A village near Fastiv.

Oh, our glorious Paliy,
Rides in from Mezhyhirya
To see the deeds of Shvachka
In the famous town of Fastiv!
Good deeds! Jews and Poles
In Fastiv tumbled not by hundreds,
But by thousands. Squares
Were reddened by the blood.
Taverns burned like candles,
As did Catholic churches.
A sacred chapel in the fortress
Was not set ablaze. It is
In that chapel that Shvachka sings
His *Hallelujah.*
He praises God, he's happy,
And he orders
That his jet-black horse be saddled;
He'll ride the steed to Bykhiv,[397]
And in that famous town,
Both he and Levchenko[398] will frolic,
And they'll trample on the corpses
Of noblemen and Jews.[399]

Kos-Aral, End of September — December 1848

Beer and mead will not be quaffed,
Water won't go down,
Trouble's hitched a ride
With a chumak in the steppe.
With an aching head,
An aching belly,
The chumak fell beside his cart,
He fell and there he lies.
From the famed Odesa[400]
They brought along the plague.
Abandoned by his comrades,
He's all alone with grief.
Standing glumly by the cart
Is his team of oxen.
A flock of rooks[401] flies in from the steppe
Toward the stricken fellow.
"Don't peck this chumak's corpse, my rooks,
For if you do you'll die with me.
Fly instead to my dear father,
Ask of him to serve a service
And to read the Book of Psalms
For my sinful soul,
And tell my girl, so young and pretty,
Not to wait for my return."

Kos-Aral, End of September — December 1848

397 *Bykhiv* — Town near Fastiv. Its actual name is Byshiv.

398 *Fedir Levchenko (dates unknown)* — Participated in the Koliyivshchyna uprising and capture of the town of Hostomel near Kyiv.

399 Please refer to introduction on Shevchenko's real life attitude toward Poles and Jews.

400 *Odesa* — The Ukrainian spelling of Odesa uses only one "s."

401 *Rook* — A European bird (*Corvus frugilegus*) that is similar to the carrion crow.

On the street there is no joy,
In the house my father scolds,
And mother will not let me go
To parties at the widow's house.
What then can I do,
And where am I to go?
Am I to love another,
Or should I drown myself?
I'll put on earrings
And a pretty necklace,
Then I'll go on Sunday
To the village fair.
I'll tell him: marry me
Or leave me be…!
Because the way I have
It now with mom,
It's much better
That I drown.

Kos-Aral, End of September — December 1848

That Kateryna has a fancy house,
Guests converge upon it
From the famous Zaporizhia.
One is Semen Barefoot,
The second, Ivan Nude.
The third's a famous widower,
Ivan Yaroshenko.
"We crossed Poland
And traversed Ukraine,
But did not see a girl
The likes of Kateryna."
One says, "If I were rich,
My brother, I'd give
All my gold
To spend an hour with Kateryna."
The second says, "If I were strong,
My friend, I'd give
All my strength
To spend an hour with Kateryna."
The third one says, "Children,
There's nothing in the world
I would not do
To spend an hour with Kateryna."

Kateryna pondered,
And told the third:
"I have an only brother,
Who's held captive by our foes!
Somewhere in Crimea,
Is the place he suffers.
He who frees him, Zaporizhians,
Will become my mate."
They rose together,
Saddled up, and went
To free the girl's brother.
The first one drowned
In the Dnipro delta.
They placed the second on a spike
In the town of Kozlov.[402]
The third one, [Ivan] Yaroshenko,
Widower of glory,
Frees the brother
From his vicious bondage
In Bakhchysaray.[403]
In the morn, the door squeaked open
To the spacious house.
Get up, get up, Kateryna,
Come to meet your brother.
Kateryna looked and stated:
"He is not my brother,
He's my sweetheart,
I was only fooling you…"

[402] *Kozlov* — Ukrainian name for the Tatar city of Hezlev, today's Yevpatoria on the Crimean Peninsula.
[403] *Bakhchysaray* — Capital of the Crimean Khanate.

"Fooled me!.." Kateryna's head
Then rolled across the floor.
"Let's go, brother,
Let's leave this evil house."
The Zaporizhians rode off
To chase the wind ahead.
Dark-browed Kateryna
Was buried in a field,
And the glorious Zaporizhians
Became good buddies in the steppe.

Kos-Aral, End of September — December 1848

The sun rises, the sun sets,
Above the grove each day.
Along a valley in the evening
Walks a gloomy Kozak.
He roams an hour, then another.
His dark-browed girl does not come.
His fickle lover does not come
From the darkened meadow...
But riding from the woods and valley
Comes a rakish lord
With dogs and huntsmen by his side.
They sic the dogs upon the lad,
Twist his arms behind his back
And mete out mortal torture;
The lord locks the youngster
In a dungeon...
And lets the girl roam the world
As an unwed mother.

Kos-Aral, End of September — December 1848

I went for water in the valley,
And saw my sweetheart with another.
And the other
Is an evil temptress,
A wealthy neighbor
And a youthful widow.
With this viper yesterday,
I sorted hemp stalks in the field,
And told her all,
Of how he'll marry,
If he dearly loves me.
And this nasty bitch
I invited to my shower.
Ivan, O my Ivan,
My dear and loving sweetheart,
May God's power
Strike you down
On a road to doom.

Kos-Aral, End of September — December 1848

It's not so much the enemies,
As people who are good —
Remorsefully they rob
And tearfully condemn,
They'll invite you in their home,
They'll greet you,
Ask about you,
To later laugh,
To laugh at you,
And then to do you in...
One can somehow live on earth
Without an enemy,
But these good people
Will unearth you
Wherever you may be,
And such good souls
Will not forget you
Even in the great beyond.

Kos-Aral, End of September — December 1848

Hush-a-by, hush-a-by baby,
I lull you by day and by night.
Someday you will curse us
As you wander Ukraine.
Curse not your father, my son, O my son,
Do not recall him.
It is me, your dear mother, the damned,
That you should be cursing instead.
When I am gone don't mix with the people,
But go to a forest,
It will not ask, nor will it see;
That is the place you should frolic.
Should you find there a red guelder rose,
Embrace it,
For I, my dear baby,
Once loved it.
When you go to the villages and enter the homes,
Do not be sad,
But if should you see any mother with children,
Then, my dear son, it is best you not look.

Kos-Aral, End of September — December 1848

Oh why, green field,
Have you blackened?
"I've blackened from the blood
Shed for liberty and freedom.
Four miles 'round
The town of Berestechko[404]
Zaporizhians of renown
Shroud me with their fallen corpses.
I'm covered too by rooks
That have flown
In from the north...
They peck the eyes of Kozaks,
But do not want the corpses.
Though I'm green, I've blackened
For your liberty...
I will green again,
But you'll not return to liberty.
In silence you will
Plow me, and as you plow
You'll curse your fate."

Kos-Aral, End of September — December 1848

A mist, a mist rolls through a valley,
In a family, life is good.
With a youthful spouse,
It's even better
On the far side of a hill.
I'll go along a shady grove,
To find myself a mate.
"Where are you? Where? Reply!
Come my sweetheart,
Squeeze me tight.
Come my sweetheart, let's go out,
We'll then ride off and marry
So that ma and pa won't know
Where we spend the night."
We got married, hid ourselves,
But I should not have loved you.
Life alone would be much better
Than strife on earth with you.

Kos-Aral, End of September — December 1848

At a predawn hour,[405]
On a holy Sunday,
In the famous, oh so famous
Town of Chyhyryn,
All the bells began to ring,
Cannons opened fire,
Calling all distinguished citizens
To meet upon the square.
Bearing holy banners
And icons of the Blessed Virgin,
Priests and people from all churches
Ascend upon a hill,
Buzzing like God's honey bee.
From the sacred monastery,

---

404 *Berestechko* — The site of a 1651 battle in the Volyn Region that involved nearly 250,000 Kozak and Polish forces. Ukraine's Tatar allies pulled out at a critical moment and held Hetman Bohdan Khmelnytsky for ransom. The Ukrainian defeat led to the Bila Tserkva Treaty, which reduced the number of registered Kozaks and allowed Polish magnates to return to their lands in Ukraine.

405 This poem idealizes Kozak pageantry, but misrepresents its two characters. In reality, one of them was assassinated by supporters of the other.

Comes the archimandrite,
All radiant in gold.
He reads the Akathist[406]
And prostrates to the ground.
At this early hour,
Colonels gathered
Quietly and solemnly
To ascend the lofty hill.
And the army, like a sea,
With their banners and bunchuks,[407]
Marched up from the Meadow,
Playing bugles as they went.
Atop the hill they stopped.
Citizens bowed deeply
As cannons all fell silent,
And bells no longer rang.
On the hill the archimandrite
Leads a public prayer,
Asking God and praising Him
So He may grant the wisdom
To elect a worthy hetman.
All as one and all together
People picked their hetman —
The preeminent Loboda, Ivan,[408]
The aged knight
And soldier's brother.
Cannons pounded,
Bugles blared,
All the bells rang out,
And they covered the new hetman
With their banners and bunchuks.
The old hetman weeps,
He lifts his arms to God,
Bows three times
To the splendid gathering,
And speaks as if
He were a pealing bell:
"Thank you, youthful gentlemen,
Zaporizhians of renown,
For the honor, for the fame,
For respect that you have shown me,
But you'd do even better
If you chose a young
And eager fellow,
The preeminent Zaporizhian,
Pavlo Kravchenko-Nalyvaiko.[409]
I am old, and to rise I'm indisposed.
I'll counsel him,
I'll teach him like a father
How to rise against the Pole.
It's now a dire hour
In our glorious Ukraine.
I'm not the one to lead you
In a fight against the Poles.
It's not for me, an aging man,
To bear the mace of power.
It's Nalyvaiko who should
Hold it for the glory of all Kozaks,
To strike fear in Warsaw
Among the hostile Poles."
The public buzzed like bees,
Bells rang out,
A cannon roared,
And they covered with bunchuks
The famous Zaporizhian,
Pavlo Kravchenko-Nalyvaiko.

Kos-Aral, End of September — December 1848

---

406 *Akathist* — A Christian hymn dedicated to Christ, the Blessed Virgin or a saint.

407 *Bunchuk* — Military regalia used by Kozaks. It is a pole topped by a ball or point with horsehair streaming down. Pronounced with the accent on the second syllable.

408 *Loboda (?-1596)* — Reference to Hetman Hryhoriy Loboda. He was assassinated by supporters of Severyn (Pavlo) Nalyvaiko for seeking accommodation with Poland.

409 See glossary or fn. 15

I roamed the thicket
Gathering nuts,
And just for fun
I fell in love
And for the miller I went nuts.
The miller mills and winnows,
He turns around and
Just for fun he lays a kiss on me.

I roamed the thicket
For a mushroom
And in my bloom
I fell in love with a handsome saddler.
The saddler sews a collar pad,
He cuddles and embraces me
In my maiden's bloom.

I roamed the thicket
For some tinder
And I, a maiden oh so tender,
Was smitten with a cooper.
The cooper hammers buckets,
He cuddles me and hugs me,
A maiden oh so tender.

If you really want to know,
My mother, whom you'll call
Your son-in-law —
Each and every one, my mother,
Each of them come Sunday
You will call your son.

Kos-Aral, End of September — December 1848

Early Sunday mornings,
The sun had yet to rise,
But I, a youthful maiden
Went sadly to the road.
I went past the grove and valley,
So my mother would not see me.
I waited for my youthful chumak
To return from his long road.
Out beyond the willows
I finally met the chumak carts.
His oxen trod,
His light-red oxen,
They trod, chewed cud,
But my youthful chumak
Was not beside his oxen.
Near the road amid the steppe
They had dug his grave with yoke pins.
They wrapped his body
In some matting,
And lowered Ivan in his grave
High upon a mound.
O my dear God!
My dear and merciful,
I so truly loved him.

Kos-Aral, End of September — December 1848

Bending in the wind
Is not a poplar,
But a youthful maiden
Tempting her own fate.
"In the sea
I hope you drown, O fate,
For even now you
Grant me not a soul to love.
I know not
How girls are kissed,
How they are embraced
And what happens after that.
Nor will I ever. O mama,
It's so hard to be a lonely maiden,
A spinster your whole life,
And to have no one to love."

Kos-Aral, End of September — December 1848

I beat a path, my dear,
Across the valley
O'er the hill,
And to the marketplace.
I sold bagels
To the Kozaks,
And, my dear,
I cleared a five-spot.
Two shahs,[410] two whole shahs
I drank away,
And hired a piper
For a kopeck.
Play your pipe for me,
My piper,
So I'll forget
My grief.
That's the kind of girl I am,
I am!
Propose to me, my dear,
I'll wed.

Kos-Aral, End of September — December 1848

The broad valley,
And tall mound,
The evening hour,
And our dreams,
Our heart-to-heart
I'll not forget.

But what of it?
We never wedded,
And we parted
Like two strangers.
Precious years of youth,
Meanwhile,
All rushed by for naught.

We both withered —
I'm a captive, you're a widow,
We don't live, but stagger,
And recall those years
Of how we once had lived.

Kos-Aral, End of September — December 1848

410 *Shah* — Ukrainian name for a coin used in the Russian Empire. The *h* is not silent.

In the garden by the ford,
Periwinkle fails to sprout.
A girl for unknown reasons
Draws no water from that ford.
On the stakes along a fence
Wither hopvines in the garden,
Yet the girl won't leave her house.
A willow tree is leaning
In the garden by the ford.
Saddened is the dark-browed beauty,
She's troubled very much.
She cries, she cries and weeps,
And struggles like a little fish…
Laughing at the youthful girl
Is a nasty man.

Kos-Aral, End of September — December 1848

If I had a necklace, mama,
I'd hit the city right tomorrow,
And in the city, mama,
Playing in the city, mom,
Is music by folk trios.
And girls make eyes at boys.
Mama! Mama!
I've no fortune.

I'll go pray to God,
I'll go and be a hireling,
I'll buy some shoes, O mama,
And hire some folk musicians.
May people be not startled
If I go out and dance.
Oh, such fate!

May my years be spent not as a maiden,
Braiding and rebraiding tresses,
Letting eyebrows waste at home,
Living out my years alone.
And as I make a living,
My dark brows are fading,
I have no fortune of my own.

Kos-Aral, End of September — December 1848

"I've no desire to marry,
I do not wish to wed,
Nor do I want to feed
Some children by the oven nook.
I do not want, O mama,
To trod behind a plow,
With velvet garments on a field.
I'll get married to my faithful comrade,
To my famous Zaporizhian father
And to the broad Great Meadow.
I'll live well on Khortytsia, O mama,
I'll walk around in velvet,
Drinking wine and mead."
The foolish Kozak wandered off
In search of fame and glory.
He left his aging mother
As an orphan in her home.
On a Sunday she recalled
Sitting down to eat a meal:
"My son Ivan is gone,
Not a word from him."
It wasn't two, it wasn't three
Nor four entire years
That our Zaporizhian
Came back home,
All broken and diseased,
Patched and ragged
As a cripple.
That is Zaporizhia for you,
And the wretched mother!
Not a soul to greet you,
Not a soul to share your grief with.
Better to have married young.
The happy years of youth are gone,
There's not a soul with whom
To warm a heart gone cold.
There's not a soul to welcome,
Or to heat a home with,
There's not a soul to
Give the cripple just a sip of water.

Kos-Aral, End of September — December 1848

THE PLAGUE

The plague meandered with a spade,
Digging, digging graves,
Stuffing them with corpses, corpses,
And not singing *of the saints.*[411]
Be it city, be it village,
It sweeps up like a broom.
It's spring, the orchards bloom;
They're like a tapestry,
Awash and sparkling
With God's dew. The earth
Is happy, it prides itself with blossoms,
Shaded groves and orchards.
But poor people in the village,
Like a flock of frightened sheep,
Are locked inside of houses,
Dying. Moaning oxen roam
The streets with hunger, and
Horses graze in gardens, but no one
Comes to chase or feed them,
As if the people were asleep.
Indeed, they're sleeping,
You should know they're sleeping,
They've forgotten sacred Sundays,
For it's been long since
Bells have rung.
Absent smoke, the chimneys mourn,

411 *Singing of the saints* — Reference to the memorial hymn, *With the Saints Give Rest (So sviatymy upokoi).*

Beyond the orchard, past the fence,
Burgeon somber graves.
Between the houses by the orchards,
Cloaked in tar and leather,
Sextons chain the corpses
To drag them past the village gate —
They then cover them without a coffin.
Days go by, months go by, —
Evermore, the village will be silent.
It's now still;
All is overgrown with nettle.
The sextons laid beside the houses.
From those houses no one came
To bury their poor souls as well,
And so they rotted by the houses.

The village in an open field
Turns green like an oasis.
No one enters,
Just the blowing wind
That scatters yellowed leaves
Across the golden field.
Greenery lingered in the village
Till people from the field
Sparked a blaze,
Burning down the verdant village.
It burned and smoldered,
Then wind dispersed the ashes,
Not a trace remained.
Such was the grief
Created by the plague.

Kos-Aral, End of September — December 1848

The mail has yet again delivered
Nothing from Ukraine to me…
For sinful deeds, perhaps,
I'm punished in this desert
By an angry God.
Mine is not to know the reason,
Nor do I want to know.
The heart weeps, nonetheless,
Even to recall unhappy episodes
And those unhappy days
That once befell me in Ukraine…
They once avowed and pledged to me
Their brotherhood and sisterhood,
Until all dissipated like a cloud,
Without a tear, that sacred dewdrop.
In old age it's come to pass,
That people I… No, no,
They're dead of cholera,
For otherwise they'd have sent
That little scrap of paper . . . .
. . . .
Out of grief and sadness,
Lest I see others reading letters,
I'll take a walk along the seashore.
To divert my woe,
I'll recall Ukraine,
And sing a little song.
People promise and betray,
But the song will give me counsel,
Advise and entertain,
And speak the truth to me.

Kos-Aral, End of September — December 1848

In captivity and loneliness,
The heart is shared with no one.
I search for someone nonetheless,
To have a conversation.
I seek God, but what I find
Is best not mentioned.
Lo, what fate and time
Have done to me;
And my blessed years of summer
All passed beneath a cloud,
So there's not a single memory
That may be well remembered.
But the soul must be diverted,
Because it yearns and pleads
For a gentle word at least; there's none,
Instead it seems that snow amid a field
Drifts upon a corpse yet warm.

Kos-Aral, End of September — December 1848

"Oh my aging father breathed his last,
My kindly mother also died,
There's no one left to
Share a word of heartfelt loving counsel.
What am I, an orphan,
To do upon this world?
Go live among the people,
Or stay at home and grieve?
I'll go into the verdant grove,
And there I'll plant some rue.
If my rue will flourish,
That is where I'll stay,
I'll have a sweetheart in my home,
He will be its husband.
If not, I'll go
In search of destiny."
The grove is green
The rue has flourished,
But the orphan girl
Wilts and wastes in servant quarters.

Kos-Aral, End of September — December 1848

Not returning from his mission
Is my hussar Muscovite.
Why my feelings of regret,
Why the tinge of sorrow?
That he wore a soldier's tunic,
That he grew a hussar's mustache,
That he called me Masha?[412]
No, those aren't the reasons for regret;
But my looks are fading,
No one comes my way.
And on the streets
The girls, damn them, laugh,
And denounce me
As a hussar girl.

Kos-Aral, End of September — December 1848

This came to pass not long ago,[413]
In the famous town of Vilna,[414]
There was then... For this poem
I can't quite find the word for it...[415]
It was a hefty, very hefty,
But they made a clinic out of it,
And chased off all the baccalaureates
Because they didn't tip their hats
As they passed the Ostriy Gate.[416]
A fool, they say, betrays himself
By the way he walks. Thus, I swear,
I cannot name the student,
What are we to do?
He was an only son,
His mother was a countess,
Proud and Lithuanian.
He was good and wealthy,
He studied well, not like a lord,
And tipped his hat when
Passing by the city gate.
Things were good, but
Trouble struck!
He fell in love, for he was young,
With a Jewish maiden,
And thought, of course,
To marry her, so long as
Mother did not know,
Because it could not be denied,
That this was quite a curse!
Like a pretty picture, she sat
Till late beside the window,
And dabbed her tearful eyes,

412 *Masha* — The Russian diminutive for Maria. It in not used in Ukrainian.

413 *Not long ago* — Reference to what may have been a real event in Vilnius. Polish writer Jozef Ignacy Kraszewski developed a similar theme in *Novel Without a Name.*

414 *Vilna* — Today's Vilnius, the capital of Lithuania.

415 *The word for it* — Probably the university. Participation by its students in the Polish liberation struggle prompted the czarist regime to close the institution. It was turned into a hospital.

416 *Ostriy Gate* — The former city gate of Vilnius. Residents tipped their hats as they passed an icon of the Blessed Virgin at the gate.

Because she truly loved —
It was frightful how she loved!
She went to school
And strolled along the boulevard,
But always with her father,
For which there was no choice.
And some banker
From the town of Lubsk
Sought to wed the Jewish maiden.
What on earth to do?
It's all the same to drown
In the Zakret.[417]
The student has no will to live
Without his Jewish girl.
And this the old Jew seems to know —
When he goes to work each morning,
He locks his only daughter
In the confines of the house,
And hires old Rukhla as a sentry.
No, dear fellow, Rukhla
Will not help.
Perhaps the girl had somewhere
Read the tale of the silken ladder —
And Rukhla did not know of this.
Perhaps she thought of it herself.
She'd had enough
And wove herself a ladder,
Then descended to the street
To meet her student friend.
Instead of running far away,
They dearly kissed, they're
Kids of course, with
Passion by the gate.
And the Jew, as if possessed,
Comes running with an axe!
Such grief! Grief to you,
Old mother, you no longer have a son,
He's sprawled out in the street,
Murdered by the Jew,
Grief to you, dear mother.
And the Jewish maiden...
Whence comes the sudden power
In the girl's arms?
She grabs the axe
And plows the blade so deep
The blunt end
Sinks inside her father's chest.

Such sensation came to pass
In the famous town of Vilna.
People wondered long,
Where did that girl hide,
The little Jewish viper
Who took the life of her own father?
The poor dear late at night
Drowned herself in Viliya[418] waters,
Because they found her in Zakret
And that is where they buried her.
The wretched countess,
Having lost her child, lived on.
To Rome, they say, she made her way
And found someplace to stay,
And, they say,
Got married to some poor marquis.
Perhaps, they lie, because of course,
That is why they're people.
They'll not forget the widow,
They'll condemn her too.

Kos-Aral, End of September — December 1848

417 *Zakret* — A park in Vilnius on the Neris River. It is known today as Vingis Park, the city's largest.
418 *Viliya* — Slavic name for Lithuania's Neris River.

A black cloud hid
A cloud of white.[419]
From beyond the Lyman
Advanced Tatars with the Turks.
From Polissia creeps the gentry,
And a preacher's son, the Hetman,
Presses from the Dnipro —
Stupid Samoylovych.[420]
Along with Romodan.[421] Like a flock
Of jackdaws, they blanketed Ukraine
To peck away at will.
And you, Chyhyryn!
And you, old Doroshenko,[422]
Zaporizhian brother!
Are you ill or do you fear
To rise against the foe?
"I fear not, my otamans,
But feel sorry for Ukraine, —
And Doroshenko wept
Like a little child!
We'll not disperse the evil force,
I'll not rise again!..
Take my hetman's symbols, sirs,
Send them to the Muscovite,
Let Moscow know
That Doroshenko serves no longer
As hetman in this world.
And I, my Zaporizhian brothers,
Will don a cassock
And head for Mezhyhir
To bow before the Savior."
All the bells rang out,
A cannon opened fire.
Dnipro warriors
Stood with Muscovites
In two long rows
That stretched a mile —
Between the rows
They passed the symbols...
You've had your fill, Petro,
Of drinking water
From the Tiasmyn.[423]
Go, Petro, and pray to God at Mezhyhir.
They did not let the Hetman in,
They spied him in his cassock.
He was shackled,
Sent to Sosnytsia,
And from Sosnytsia to Yaropolche[424]
To live out his final years.
This is what it came to,
Zaporizhian brother!

Above the town of Chyhyryn
The sun peeked through a cloud,
Tatars hauled off with the Turks
For their uluses.[425]
The Polacks with Czarniecki,[426]
With their evil Stefan,

419 *Black cloud, white cloud* — Symbolic depiction of enemy forces in Ukraine.

420 *Ivan Samoylovych Samiylovych* (?-1690) — Pro-Russian Hetman of Left-Bank Ukraine (1672-87).

421 *Romodan* — Reference to Russian General Grigori Grigorovich Romodanovsky (?-1682). He participated in the 1654 Council of Pereyaslav that resulted in the loss of Ukrainian independence to Russia.

422 *Petro Dorofeyevych Doroshenko (1627-98)* — Hetman of Right-Bank Ukraine (1665-72). He briefly united both banks, but lost to Polish and Russian forces and to Kozak leaders instigated by them. He resigned in favor of Samiylovych.

423 *Tiasmyn* — A right tributary of the Dnipro River that runs through Chyhyryn.

424 *Sosnytsia and Yaropolche* — Hetman Doroshenko lived in the Northern Ukrainian town of Sosnytsia after giving up his command. He was then given the village of Yaropolche (today's Yaropolets) west of Moscow. His grave and a chapel above it are still well-maintained.

425 *Ulus* — *Nation* or *people* in various Mongolic and Turkic languages. Here it means settlements.

426 *Stefan Czarniecki (1599-1665)* — Polish general, nobleman and national hero. He fought numerous battles in Ukraine.

Set God's church on fire.
In Subotiv, they nicely
Burned the bones
Of Bohdan and Tymosh,[427]
And blithely went back home to Poland,
As if they'd done some good.
On a Sunday morning,
The Muscovites with Romodan
Went with the preacher's son along
The Romodan Road.[428]

Like a captured eagle
Without wings or freedom,
The famous Doroshenko
Tired of sitting in captivity
And simply died of boredom.
He got sick of dragging chains.
They forgot the famous Hetman
In his own Ukraine.
Only you, the holy Rostovsky,[429]
Recalled your great friend
While praying in your dungeon,
And saw to the construction of a
Chapel on the hetman's grave,
And you prayed to God
For the Hetman's soul,
And held a requiem for Petro.
And even now each blessed year,
When the day arrives,
They go to Yaropolche
To say prayers
At the Hetman's grave.

Kos-Aral, End of September — December 1848

Kyiv-Mezhyhirsky Monastery, 1843

427 *Bohdan and Tymosh* — Reference to Hetman Bohdan Khmelnytsky and his son Tymosh. The Hetman's estate was located in Subotiv.

428 *Romodan Road* — An old trade route through Ukraine's left bank. It was a major thoroughfare from Russia to Crimea.

429 *Rostovsky* — Reference to Danylo Savych Tuptal (1651-1709), known as St. Dimitriy Rostovsky, the metropolitan of Rostov near Moscow. He was of Ukrainian origin.

Recall me, brother
As you leave your mistress late at night
Not to sleep, but just to wander.
When boredom is your guest
And spends the night with you,
Count on me, my friend,
For a bit of consolation.
Then recall your happy friend
Who's in a desert past a sea,
To find out how he deals with grief.
How he hid his thoughts, his
Feeble heart, and how he walks about,
Saying prayers to the Lord,
As he recalls Ukraine and you,
My friend;
At times he'll be dejected —
Not much, of course,
But just a bit. Outside, you see,
A feast is nigh...
It's hard, my friend and brother,
To rejoice alone in a desert far away.
Tomorrow morn,
Bells throughout Ukraine will peal;
Tomorrow morning folks will
Bow their heads in churches...
That same morning in the desert,
A hungry beast will wail,
Sand and snow will sweep
Across the barracks I call home,
Driven by a chilly cyclone.
That is how I'll spend
The holy day!
What to do? That is why
There's trouble, to struggle
With that trouble.
And you, my only friend,
If you must be sad,
Read this note
And know, that life on earth
Is only tough in deserts and in exile;
Yet they live there, poorly to be sure,
But what am I to do?
Death would be an answer. But hope,
My friend, dies not.

Kos-Aral, December 24, 1848

Like a verst[430] traversed in autumn
By chumaks in the steppe,
So too my years elapse.
But I'm indifferent.
I embellish books
And persist on filling them with poems.
I amuse my foolish head,
And thus I forge my chains
(Should these gentlemen find out).
For all I care,
They could stage my crucifixion,
But I'll not rest without my poems.
I've embellished two long years,
And in goodly measure,
I'll soon begin a third.

Raim, January — April 1849

430 See glossary or fn. 215

SOTNYK[431]

In Ohlav...[432] Is anyone aware of
Ohlav and its homes so white?
Just a bit! An explanation is required
Lest grief turn into laughter.
From Boryspil[433] it's not far,
And it quite resembles Boryspil.
There's a little row of poplars
Standing neatly by the common,
As if the girls of Ohlav
Went to tend a flock of sheep.
And stopped. This, by now,
Was long ago —
A beanstalk, it so happened,
Trailed up a pole from
A woven fence,
And a glass-paned window
Opened to the summer garden.
And the house, you see, behind the
Woven fence was the sotnyk's house.
The sotnyk was a wealthy man,
And with him grew a child,
Someone's bastard on God's graces.
Or perhaps the aging Kozak
Simply took an
Orphan daughter as his child
To care for like a blossom
In his cozy corner.
His son (the sotnyk had been married,
But his wife passed on), the son
He sent to Kyiv to study at a seminary.
Himself he waited for Nastusia,
A foster child, in fact,
To fit in as his own.
Not to match her with his son,
But the old man had a hankering
To play the fool himself.
So that none may know of it,
He did not seek advice.
He just mulled it over by himself...
And the ladies... the devil only knows!
They already laughed at him!
They sense this matter with their noses.

. . . .

Sitting by his house
The sotnyk thinks his thoughts,
And Nastusia flies around the garden
Like a little bird.
She'll sit beside him,
Kiss his hand,
And muss his
Gray and fearsome mustache, —
The old man she caresses
Like a little child, of course.
But that's not the old man's thing,
It's something else he wants.
His aging body yearns
Caresses of a sinful kind!..
The old sotnyk runs his fingers
Through Nastusia's hair,
Braiding it together like
Two thick dangling vipers.
He'll then undo them,
Thrice wrapping hair
Around her neck!..
And she, my little sweetie,
Has no inkling of it all.
She plays beside the oven nook,
Like a kitten with an aging tomcat...

---

431 *Sotnyk* — Commander of 100 men in many Slavic languages. In Ukraine it was a rank equivalent to captain.

432 *Ohlav* — A town near Kyiv that Shevchenko visited before being exiled. Shevchenko is believed to have heard a story there similar to the theme of this poem. Ohlav today is the village of Hoholiv.

433 *Boryspil* — A town outside of Kyiv. Today it is home to Ukraine's largest airport.

S[OTNYK]

Leave me be, you crazy girl.
Just take a look, you've
Ruffled all your braids,
Just like a mermaid in the sea…
Why don't you ever weave the ribbons
That your auntie brought?..

N[ASTUSIA]

If you'd let me go to dances,
I'd weave the ribbons in my hair,
I'd slip on yellow shoes,
I'd wear a nice red skirt,
And trim my hair with periwinkle…

S[OTNYK]

Hold on, hold on, plain-haired girl!
You silly thing, where would you get periwinkle
To trim your pretty hair?

N[ASTUSIA]

By the woven fence! There's
Such a green patch growing there,
With cross-shaped flowers of blue!
Sky-blue has blossomed too…

S[OTNYK]

You'll not be a maiden long.

N[ASTUSIA]

Is it that I'll die?

S[OTNYK]

I had a dream last autumn
When we were grafting grafts…
If they take… I dreamed,
If they take, then you'll
Get married in the autumn.

N[ASTUSIA]

Get a grip!!
I'll break those grafts of yours…

S[OTNYK]

And when the periwinkle blossoms…

N[ASTUSIA]
Then I'll pull the periwinkle too.

S[OTNYK]
But from marriage you'll not run!

N[ASTUSIA]
But no, I'll run, I'll run and cry as well.

(She cries.)

S[OTNYK]
You're so silly, Nastia, as I see it,
You can't bear much laughter...
Don't you see, I'm joking.
Just go get the fiddle.
You'll dance to end your sorrow,
And I'll play all the tunes...

N[ASTUSIA]
Okay, daddy.

(She darts happily toward the house)

S[OTNYK]
No, I need to wait a while.
That's the way it is!
But here's what, brother:
Years don't wait. Years fly by,
And yet this notion, like a cursed specter,
Clings tightly to my heart...
And you've brought the fiddle?
What tune shall we strike up with you?

N[ASTUSIA]
Ah, no, wait, do not play just yet.
Because I will not dance until
I gather periwinkle and trim
My hair with flowers. Be right back.

She goes not far, picks periwinkle, trims her hair and sings.
And the sotnyk tunes the fiddle.

S[OTNYK]
One's already broken.
Stand by, I'll break another…

N[ASTUSIA]
(She returns adorned and singing.)
"If I had wings, a falcon's wings,
I'd fly to find my sweetheart,
To find my mate for life.
I'd fly into a forest,
Into a verdant grove,
I'd fly, a dark-browed beauty,
Beyond the quiet Danube."

Meanwhile, as she sings, a young man enters the garden wearing a straw hat, a short blue jacket, green pantaloons, with a sack slung over his back and a whip in his hand.

PETRO
The best to you this day! God sustain us!

N[ASTUSIA]
Daddy! Daddy! It's Petro! Petro! He's come down from Kyiv!

S[OTNYK]
Well, I can't believe my eyes and ears. Freely, or not freely?

P[ETRO]
Freely dad, and now a theologian…

S[OTNYK]
Wow!

N[ASTUSIA]
A theologian?! How scary!

S[OTNYK]
Silly girl, what's to fear?!

(Approaches his son, makes the sign of the cross and kisses him.)

May God bless you, my child! Nastusia! Show him in and feed him, because he may not have had his lunch yet.

P[ETRO]
Indeed, that's right.

(He goes with Nastusia into the living room.)

S[OTNYK]

(Alone)

Such a child, such a son
God has granted me!
Already he's a theologian.
There's a reason, a wise reason.
(He ponders.) For what?
For what I think? To be a priest,
And if he wishes otherwise,
He can choose the Sich.[434]
The kid won't perish there.
I should go inside the house…
And another thing:
The theologian needs a duty,
So he does not squander time at home,
So that while he's on his break,
He can teach Nastusia
God's commandments,
So there's no need to hire the cantor,
Like I did for my late wife.
Unless she knows them,
Father Tom, I know, won't marry us.
I'll go tell my son,
Lest it slip my mind…

(He goes inside the house)

To live, indeed to live, praising God,
And loving children,
But if not,
There's a need to fool oneself,
And for an aging codger
To marry such a child!
Get a grip, don't marry,
For she will die,
And you will be a
Gray old laughing stock
In the confines of your home,
You'll forever curse that wedding,
You'll cry, and not a soul will
Wipe your tears. Don't marry!
It's not at all appropriate!
Look: paradise surrounds you
With children, just like blossoms,
Why think of killing them,
Those youngsters?
But no, my old man preens himself,
It's disgusting to behold!
And from the theologian
Nastusia learns the Ten Commandments.
Take a look: they're in the garden
For a walk.
They both stroll about,
Like a pair of darlings.
And the old man's not at home,
So they're free to play.
Look: over there, beside the poplar,
They've stopped to gaze
At one another.
That's how blessed angels
Look at God,
Just as they behold each other.
And Petro then asks:

P[ETRO]

Why, Nastusia, is it
That you really do not read?

N[ASTUSIA]

What am I, some school kid? I don't want to, and that's that.

---

434 See glossary or fn. 37

P[ETRO]
Learn this day but one commandment,
a small one, say, the fifth.

N[ASTUSIA]
Neither fifth nor sixth, I want none of them.

P[ETRO]
If you don't know, the priest will never marry you!

N[ASTUSIA]
I don't care, let him wed me not.

P[ETRO]
And with me?

N[ASTUSIA]
And with you, let him... Ah, no, let him marry us!..

P[ETRO]
So read, or...

N[ASTUSIA]
Or what ever will you do?

P[ETRO]
I'll kiss you, just you see!

N[ASTUSIA]
If you wish, kiss all you want, but I'm not going to read!

P[ETRO]
(He kisses her and says)
Here's one for you! Here is two!

The sotnyk then peers through the fence, goes inside
and betrays no sign of what he's seen.

N[ASTUSIA]
(Resists)
Enough already, stop! Father soon will come,
I really must start reading.

P[ETRO]

Ah! Now read!

S[OTNYK]

(Exits the house)

Children, enough studying already. Isn't it time to eat?

P[etro] and N[astusia] go silently inside.

S[OTNYK]

(Alone)

They've learned, to say the least!
Some child! No, Nastusia,
I've cared for you,
And it will, my dear, be different now!
She won't read unless
He gives a hundred kisses!
A seminarian at that!
You've got taste, you dirty dog.
I'll drill you good, but not like
At the seminary!.. With a rod instead!
So there's no trace of you at home!
You'll not perish, the world is big!
Just look, his mug is like a dog's!
There you have a theologian!
Stealing from his father!
Okay, young man!
How wicked people have become!..
What's going on inside?
Again, you know, my kids are reading...
Need to chase them off.

There are such fathers in this world,
What need have they for children?
To offend the Lord.
But show respect and honor, children,
Because it's your gray-haired father!
Your wise father! It's good for
Happy orphans not to have such fathers
For they'll not sin against them.

NASTUSIA

(Runs crying from the house)

He won't permit a proper meal,
And hounds him back to Kyiv.
O my God all merciful,
What am I to do?
I'll wander off *(Peers into house.)*
He's set his sights!
Ugh! He's so angry!
But he won't hit...
Come what may, but I'll
Wander with Petro to Kyiv!
I'll not be afraid,
I'll wander off at midnight.
And if a witch should scare me?
No, she'll not frighten me. *(Peers again.)*
My poor sweetheart!
In a sack he packs his books and
Takes his hat. Farewell, my dear,
My sweetheart!.. In the evening?..
Beyond the village gate? I'll be there!
I'll be there early! Here, catch!
(Throws a flower over the fence.)
Do you hear! Wait!

The sotnyk enters. Nastusia sings.

"Come not, bore not, woo not,
Do not court me, I won't go,
So drop your expectations."

S[OTNYK]
She's indifferent! As if she did not know!
She's hopping like a magpie.
Nastusia! Why is it you don't cry?
After all, Petro has left.

N[ASTUSIA]
Look, such sorrow!
So cry, if you're so sorry…

S[OTNYK]
I care not.

N[ASTUSIA]
I care
Even less, he's not mine.
And each commandment I now know,
Every single one of them!

S[OTNYK]
All?

N[ASTUSIA]
Yes, your very vocal Father Thomas
Can hear confession right this minute!

S[OTNYK]
And we'll marry then on Sunday?

N[ASTUSIA]
Yes, that'right! We've not prepared yet for communion;
When we're prepared — no sooner.

S[OTNYK]
(He kisses her)
My gray-winged dove!
You're my sweetie!..

(He dances and sings along)

"In a foursome late at night
I was walking in the peas,
Walking late at night,
I lost my necklace in those peas."

N[ASTUSIA]
Enough about that necklace. Go, hurry up to Father Thomas to consult. That's what's what!

S[OTNYK]
Right, right, my blossom! I'll run quickly, and you, my dear, stay here, take a quiet walk and adorn yourself. But don't wait for me, because I'll need to stay for vespers.

(Kisses and goes)

N[ASTUSIA]
Fine, fine, I'll not wait.

I won't wait, I won't,
I'll don a peasant coat,
I'll don a pretty necklace,
And give chase to Petro.

We'll embrace, we'll kiss, hold hands and go to Kyiv with each other. I need to wear some flowers, — for what may be the last time, because he said that we would marry in the town of Brovary.

(Adorns herself and sings)

"I'll go along the shore and meadow,
And I'll meet a man not meant for me.
Greetings, greetings my good friend!
We shared good love, but shared no destiny.
We loved, but did not marry,
And all that's left is heartbreak."

What a song I have recalled! Enough, it's lousy! I'll just run faster. Farewell, my lofty poplars and my cross-shaped periwinkle.

(She leaves)

Going home quite late at night
Is the drunken sotnyk, and as he walks
He babbles gladly to himself:
— Let all people know of us!
Though I'm gray and stooped,
But we!.. heh! heh! But we are married.
But we!.. — He crawled
Into the house with effort
And lay quietly to sleep,
So as not to wake, you see, Nastusia
Or to cause disgrace.
The last song of mass resounded,
People now go home —
Nastusia's not among them,
There's no sign of her!
They barely woke the sotnyk up
And told him: this and that!
The poor guy crossed himself,
Saddles up his finest horse
And gallops off to Kyiv. In Brovary
His young Nastusia dances,
Duly married!
My sotnyk came back home,
Three days, three nights he did not rise,
Telling not a soul,
Nor complaining either.

. . . .
. . . .

Man earns and worries,
Knowing not
That in old age
He'll lose his mind
And will neglect it all.
So it is now with my fool,
The aging sotnyk.
He's chased away his children,
And though his wealth remains
He can't share it with another.
And thus alone he scatters it,
He squanders it,
Spending not a coin
To bring kindness to another.
He's a lesson for good people,
Reduced to sighing
Under heavy blankets in a frigid house
Without a soul to light a fire
Or to sweep the floor...
Reduced to walk and wander
In a dump, until an owl
Beneath an eave
Hoots in through a window,
And a hireling will not
Throw a blanket
On a cold stiff corpse,
And will steal the cupboard key
Stashed behind his belt...

Such grief
Befell the sotnyk.
Not a year had passed since
Nastusia had departed,
And already in the garden
Not a thing remained,
Just roaming pigs and calves...
And the periwinkle! The
Cross-shaped periwinkle!
Trampled near the fence
It's now parched and withered!
And the lonely sotnyk,
Bloated, filthy in his sheepskin coat,
Paces by his barn.
Uncovered haystacks,
Rooms unpainted,
Beams undusted,
Cattle gone,
All the servants left the home,
Except a shabby hireling,
And she's a bully
To the aging lord... Serves you right:
Don't chase away your children,
You aging gray-haired fool!
The drunken sotnyk lived not long
And his wealth was spent.
Another summer graced the world,
And in autumn on the street,
The sotnyk was found slain!

Or perhaps the poor wretch died
Simply walking from the tavern?
No one cared to ask.
Good people even took
His leggings, and
In a meadow nicely buried him,
But did not place
A cross above him.
One even feels for him. He had wealth,
He had kids and kin,
But none will place a cross from him.
The sotnyk died,
His rooms decayed, collapsed,
And all was lost and wasted,
Except a little row of poplars
Standing neatly by the common,
As if the girls of Ohlav
Went to tend a flock of sheep.

Raim, January — April 1849

How am I to worry,
How am I to trouble people,
I'll just go away forever,
And what will be, will be.
I'll find my fortune, I'll get married,
And if I don't, I'll drown,
But I'll sell myself to none.
I went away forever,
But fortune hid from me;
Good people did not trade in liberty,
But still, without a trade they cast me
Into distant bondage…
So that potent herbs of freedom
Would not grow amid our field.

Raim, January — April 1849

Why should I get married?
Why should I be wed?
I, the youngster, would
Be mocked by Kozaks.
He wed, they'll say,
Unclothed and hungry,
And the fool destroyed
His budding freedom.
That's true. But what to do?
Teach me, people,
Should I serve you as a hireling?
Is that the proper way?
No, I won't graze or drive another's cattle,
I won't respect an in-law mother
In a stranger's house.
I'll sport a sky-blue coat
On a jet black horse with Kozaks.
I'll find a dark-browed maiden
In the steppe beside a valley —
I'll find a lofty mound
In this Ukraine of ours.
At the wedding friends will dance,
They'll bring out guns,
Roll in a cannon.
When they lift their friend
Into his home,
Muzzle loaders will resound,
Hackbuts[435] will reverberate.

---

[435] *Hackbut* — An early muzzle-loading rifle. Term derived from the Dutch *haakbus,* meaning hook gun. Also called an arquebus.

When they lay the otaman
In his home to sleep,
A cannon, like a mother,
Will boom a lullaby.

It will roar and thunder
For more than just an hour.
And it will spread the glory
All throughout Ukraine.

Raim, January — April 1849

Gray geese honked in
The valley by the pond;
Throughout the village
Spread renown
About the local widow.
Not so much renown as gossip,
That a Kozak from the Sich,
Came to see her in her home.
"They had dinner in the parlor,
Drinking mead and wine;
In the bedroom on the bed
Both laid down to rest."
The renown did not expire,
It was not in vain.
The widow bore a son by Lent.
She fed the child,

Had him schooled.
Receiving him from school,
She bought a horse,
And having bought a horse,
She sewed a silken saddle,
And gilding it with gold,
She dressed him
In a crimson coat,
Then placed him on the horse...
"Enemies, behold!
Look!" And she led the horse
Around the village.
And steered it to the Kozak unit;
She sent him to the army...
And took a pilgrimage herself,
To join the nuns in Kyiv.

Raim, January — April 1849

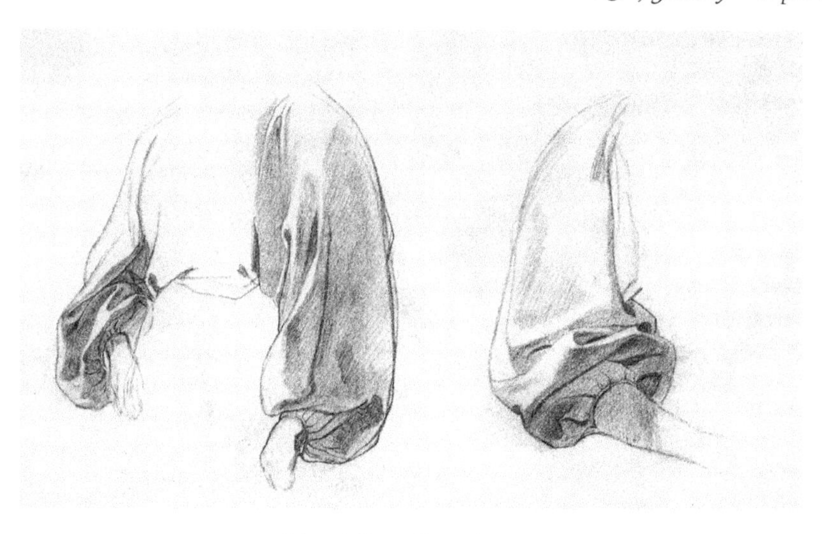

Woman's Blouse Sleeve, 1841-42

"Should it so happen
That you come
To rule among us,
Then you'd know, dear fellow,
Just what to call
Your young unlucky unwed mothers.
But you blather like the devil,
Thinking — 'We're it!
We'll show the people
These unfortunates,
We'll teach self-respect
To evil lordlings!'
It's not worth the effort!
While villages exist,
And while they're ruled by lords,
Happy unwed mothers
Will loaf in taverns
With some soldiers,
Worry not, my brother."
"Good, — I say. — But listen
Lordlings, nonetheless, to this one,
This last and tiny tale.

Girls raked the meadow,
Young guys stacked the hay.
They glanced, you know, up at the sun,
Talking nonsense, 'cause
They're boys, of course.
The girls, like magpies,
Chattered often by the well, and
Frolicked in the valley.
The prettiest in the village went
A while ago and took along a pitcher;
And the foreman searches not,
As if he does not see. This evil foreman's
Not a novice, but a sly old dog,
Experienced at that.
From the valley something screamed,
The young guys ran to help.
And there a raving lordling,
Still an adolescent,
Has created such a scene.
He's raping the poor girl.
The wretched girl screams.
The boys run to her,
But do not help,
Because they fear the lord.
But one, the youngest, looked around
And pierced the lordling
With a pitchfork, as if he were a frog.
The scoundrel groaned and croaked.
They discussed,
Sending word of it to town;
The court converged, they looked,
Then the judges all got good and drunk.
They bound the youngster,
Locked him up...
And that was that.

By the main road in a field
Stands a tavern in a willow's shade,
And sitting by the tavern
Is a group of shackled convicts.
The wretches are allowed some rest
And a drink of water.
They sit around, they talk,
A few of them doze off.
Then three troikas with
A wedding party took the road
Down from a hill.
And they stopped, of course,
Beside the tavern
To let the horses rest,
And the bridesmaids
Joined in, singing.
They got up,
The bride got up,
And took a quart of vodka
And shared it with a guard
And a wretched convict.
She looks, gazes...
God! O dear God!
Her only and her doomed avenger
Is among the shackled convicts —
He carries from Ukraine
His chains and fetters to Siberia...

And you'll stay here in luxury,
And will neither know nor hear
His daily lamentation.
She did not share a drink
With her sanctified avenger,
Nor did she even say hello,
She merely looked at him...
And nothing more.

The wedding party hit the road.
Behind them convicts
Clanged their shackles.
There was not a person to be seen
Or heard beside the tavern,
An empty place with just the barmaid;
Dust spread in the field around it.
Then twilight.
Life's not long, nor is the day.
At the manor
There was dancing, there was music —
Till the midnight hour.
They went to make the bed
With dowry linen from the storeroom,
But the bride had softly
Left the house and vanished.
They searched all over, looked till dawn,
But did not find a trace.
Where'd she go?
Where? She wandered to Siberia with the
Wretched convict... And that's that.

Raim, January — April 1849

Roads leading to that country
Are overgrown with thorns,
Perhaps I've left it,
Left it evermore.
Am I perhaps not ever destined
To go home again?
Am I perhaps to read
These verses by myself?
My dear God!
It's so hard for me to live!
I have a heart that's big —
But no one I can share it with!
You've not granted me kind fate,
A youthful destiny!
Not ever have You granted it,
Never! Never!
Nor did You grant my youthful heart
Any union with a girl's!
My youthful days, my youthful nights
Slipped away devoid of joy!
They simply passed in foreign lands.
Not a soul was found
With whom to share the heart.
And now I haven't anyone
With whom to even talk!..
It's hard, dear God,
To bear these verses all alone.
And not to share
With anyone, not to say a sacred word,
Not to cheer a needy soul,
And not to chide an evil man.
And to die!.. O Lord!
Let me see at least that broken people,
Let me see Ukraine!

Raim, January — April 1849

In the valley bloomed
A guelder rose,
Which seemed to smile
Like a little girl.
It was pleasant, oh so pleasant.
A bird was cheered,
It chirped a song.
A maiden in a coat of white
Heard the song,
Descending from her sparkling home
To stroll about the valley meadow.
Coming out to meet her
In that verdant meadow
Was a youthful Kozak;
He kisses her and greets her,
And they walk along the valley,
And they sing a pretty song.
They came beneath the guelder rose
Like a pair of children,
And then sat down to kiss.

What sort of Eden
Do we ask of God?
Eden pulses in our hearts,
And we with blinders
Rush to church, —
That's not the paradise we want.
I'd speak the truth,
But what's the use?
It would hurt me,
And for priests and people
It would make no difference.

Raim, January — April 1849

In our paradise on earth
There's nothing nicer
Than a youthful mother with her little babe.
At times I look,
Amazed with wonder, and sadness
Grips the soul; I feel sorry for her,
I worry and I pray for her,
As if it were before an icon
Of the Holy Mother,
Who brought our God into this world…

Now for her it's pleasant,
Living is a pleasure.
She wakes at night
To guard her treasure,
And awaits the light
To see her child again,
To express her love in words.
"It's mine! Mine!"
She gazes at the child,
Prays to God for it,
And strolls along the street
Much prouder than the empress.
To show, you see, her treasure
To the village people. "Just look!
Mine is better than all others!"
And by chance a person glances.
She's happy, joyous, God Almighty!
She takes her Ivan home.
It seems to her the village
Spent the day gazing but at him,
That beside her wonder,
There was nothing else at all.
She's happy!..
Years go by.
Children slowly grow,
And having grown they leave
For work, to join the Muscovites.
And you, poor dear, remain.
No one's left with you at home.
You're short of clothes
To hide your old and naked body

And there's no wood to heat
Your home come winter.
And you're too sick to stand
To even start that fire.
In your chilly dwelling
You pray for them, your children.

And you,
Great martyr!
You pass by villages at night,
Crying as you go.
And as you walk through
Steppes and fields,
You hide your son from sight.
Because at times a bird will see
And chirp the news to all:
"There goes an unwed mother
With her bastard to the market."

O unlucky girl! What happened
To your beauty that so amazed
The people? Gone. No more!
It was taken by your child,
Driven from your home,
And you went past the village gate,
As if taken from a cross.
Beggars shun you like a leper.
But your child is tiny,
It has yet to crawl.
Only someday will it play
And pronounce that pleasing word,
Mama. The great and sweetest word!
You'll rejoice; you'll tell your child
The truth about the evil lord,
And you'll be happy. But not for long.
Though not full grown,
The child will go to guide a blind man
And will leave you crippled
At a crossroads to be harassed by dogs,
And moreover you'll be cursed.
Because you bore your child here on earth.
And because you dearly loved that child.
And, poor dear,
You'll love it till the day you die,
Among the dogs out in the cold,
Beneath a fence somewhere.

Raim, January — April 1849

Children boasted
Of the clothes they got
As they played with colored eggs
Amid some straw
Against the sun on Easter.
An embroidered shirt
Was sewn for one.
This one got a ribbon
And they bought a band for that one.
Someone got a sheepskin cap,
Another got some horsehide boots.
Just an orphan sits without a gift
Of nice new Easter clothes,
And she hides her little hands

Inside her baggy sleeves.
"My mommy bought this."
"This my daddy made."
"And this embroidery was stitched
By my godmother for me."
"And I dined with the priest," —
Said the orphan girl.

Raim, January — April 1849

Children of M. I. Keykuatov, 1847

Whether I was working, playing
Or praying to the Lord,
I always thought of him
And something frightened me.
I was young and foolish, —
I always looked with expectation
For a sign of our betrothal…
I did not expect that I, the fool,
Would be taken
For a fool by him,
And my heart was hurt,
And seemed to know
That this would be,
But did not know
Just what to say.
And if it spoke,
I'd not have loved,
Perhaps I'd not have
Frequented the grove and well,
But indeed I went

To frolic night and day…
In vain I went, and now remain,
Remain forever as a spinster maiden;
It's hard to face old age,
Staying home with mama.
And not to ever have a home
That I can call my own!
Even now, be it work or rest,
I always think of him,
And do not know myself
What it is I'm thinking!
Why did I go into that grove?
Why did I love him for so long,
Why did I love so much!

Raim, January — April 1849

At times an old man does not know
The reason he's rejoicing,
It simply seems he's young again,
So he sings a song… as best he can.
Hope before him rises
Like a sacred angel,
And a star, his youth,
Hovers merrily above him.
What's happened that the old man
Should so suddenly be happy?
Because, you see, the old man
Thought of helping out another.
And how, just how to do that?
Living's good for him, whose
Soul and spirit learn to
Love what's decent!
There's often bliss
Adorned with periwinkle.
And so, at times, the blessed sun
Will peek into a dreary pit,
And in that dreary pit
Some bright green grass will grow.

Raim, January — April 1849

It seems indeed I need to write
A missive to myself,
To say everything completely,
All that's needed or is not.
You'll otherwise await in vain
The blessed truth
And sacred text from some other person.
Indeed, I've no one to expect them from.
The time is nigh, it seems:
It's nearly now the tenth long summer
Since I gave the people my *Kobzar*,
But it seems their lips are sewn,
No one even barks at me or snarls,
As if I don't exist.
It's not praise I seek, dear public!
Perhaps, I'll do without it.
I await instead advice and counsel!
I'll likely wait in vain
And from soldiers' ranks will transfer
Straight into the grave!
O my dear God,
How my heart at times grew faint!
How I yearned for anyone to
Say at least a learned word;
So I could know,
For whom I write and why.
Why is it that I love Ukraine?
Is she worth the sacred fire?..
For while I age because of this,
I still don't know just what I do.

Time is sacred, I'll not trade it,
Which is why I write,
And at times a whiskered aging Kozak
Strikes this sinner's fancy,
With his freedom
Mounted on a jet-black horse!
More of freedom I know not,
Though because of it I waste away
In a distant foreign land.
Was this the work of destiny?
Did my mother not say prayers to God
Before she gave me birth? Thus —
I'm like an angry serpent dying,
Trampled in the steppe
And impatient for the sun to set.
That is how I suffer now,
Awaiting death out in the steppe,
But why, by God, I do not know!
But still, I love my vast Ukraine,
Though I'm alone because of her
(Because, you see, I've found no mate)
And have reached the brink of ruin.

No matter, comrade, worry not!
Chain yourself with tempered steel,
Pray in earnest to the Lord,
And disregard the public!
It's just a cabbagehead.
But then, good brother, use your wits,
No fool, it's yours alone to ponder.

Raim, January — April 1849

On every road and everywhere
We're people proud and foolish,
But we boast of soaring
O'er the land and sea,
And that we're all kings
From palaces to prisons,
Though we're despots to ourselves —
Such kings sit on the throne
And in captivity,
All with good intentions
With reason glowing freely
Like a beacon on the blue, blue sea
Or… on the sea of life.
Thus reason as a beacon
Glows within our boney shack.
We just fan its flame
And sing indifferently to ourselves,
Be the hour clement or inclement.
Eagles, darling gray-wings,
Lest you've dreamed of evil,
For just a bit, for just an hour.
And there, beneath a tavern bench
You'll cool off in its shade.
That celestial fire has dimmed,
And in the boney shack,
Snorting pigs now wallow
As if it were a mud bath.
It's good they forge good shackles
And deny the hands a knife or shot glass,
Or you'd drink in grief at dawn
And would later cry in sorrow,
Cursing mom and dad and those
Who served as godparents.
And then the knife — and suilline blood
Would flow like tar,
From all your piggie livers,
And then...

Raim, January — April 1849

I'm not sorry, may you know,
For my dear and golden
Fate in youth;
But sadness sometimes
Shrouds the soul,
So much it makes me cry.
More so when I see a village boy.
He seems broken from a branch,
Dressed in ragged burlap,
Sitting by a fence alone.
He, it seems, is I,
And his youth my own.
To me it seems that youngster
Won't ever witness freedom,
Freedom oh so sacred.
That his best years will be futile,
They'll all fly by in vain,
That he'll not know
Where he should go
Upon this world
So broad and free.
And he'll become a hireling,
Then someday,
So he'll not cry or worry,
So he may have a place to stay,
They'll hand him to the Muscovites.

Raim, January — April 1849

. . . .

Together we once grew,
And as kids we loved each other.
Our mothers watched us,
Saying they will someday marry us.
They guessed wrong.
The old folks died ahead of time,
And we as youngsters parted,
To never meet again.
I was carried far and wide
Fettered and unfettered.
In old age, I came back home, but barely.
The once happy village
Seemed to me, an old man,
To be dark and mute,
Like I am in old age.
In that needy village
One can see, or so it seems to me,
That nothing grew and nothing rotted,
It's just like it once was.
The valley, field and the poplars
Plus a willow by the well.
It leaned over like the lonely sadness
Of confinement in a distant land.
A pond, a little dam, and by the grove
A windmill with its beating wings.
And a verdant oak, like a Kozak,
Steps out from the grove to dance
Beneath the hill. Upon that hill's
A somber garden, and in that garden,
In its shade, my old folks lie
As if in Eden.
The oaken crosses are now tilted,
Inscriptions scrubbed by rain…
But Saturn's[436] smooth erasures
Are not the work of rain alone,
Nor are words his only object…
May my old folks rest in peace with saints…
"Is that wee Oksana
Still among the living?" —
I softly ask my brother. "Which?"
"The little curly one
That used to play with us.
Why, my brother, are you worried?"
"I'm not worried. That wee Oksana
Wandered off with soldiers,

---

436 *Saturn* — Roman god of agriculture, harvests and time.

Then vanished.
True, a year went by and she returned,
But what of it? With a bastard she returned
Unwed and shorn of hair.
She sat, at times,
Beneath a fence, calling like a cuckoo,
Shouting sometimes,
Singing softly now and then,
And undoing phantom braids.
Again she disappeared,
Gone insane and ruined,
No one knows her destination.
And what a girl she was,
Yes, yes, she was a beauty!
And not poor, but God had given
Her no fortune..."
Or perhaps He did, but someone stole it,
And deceived the sacred Lord.

Raim, January — April 1849

Ready! We set the sail,
And launched aboard a
Good-sized boat
Onto waves of blue,
Plying through Syr Darya's sedge.
Farewell, impoverished Kos-Aral.[437]
You diverted my accursed boredom
For two long and lonely years.
Thank you, friend. You can boast
That even you were found by people,
Who knew just what to do with you.
Farewell, my friend! Neither praise,
Nor shame will I invent
About your desert sands;
I know not if I'll recall the boredom
When I reach another land!

Underway from Kos-Aral to Raim, End of September 1849

Chikita-Aral Island, 1849

[437] *Kos-Aral* — An island in Kazakhstan's Aral Sea, where Shevchenko served on a military scouting mission during portions of 1848-49. The island has since been attached to the mainland. The Syr Darya River once emptied into the Aral Sea, but dried up because of Soviet irrigation projects.

In small measure in the autumn
We bear resemblance to God's image,
Not all of us, of course, but a few at least.
The steep ravine,
Like a swarthy naked gypsy,
Lies asleep or dead within the forest.
Along the valley
And along its broad expanse
A tumbleweed from grasslands
Rushes like a ruddy lamb
To drink some water in the stream.
But the stream grabbed hold of it
And took it to the mighty Dnipr',
And the Dnipr' took it to the sea,
Which bore the wisp
And cast it off in foreign lands.

And you'll feel sorry
For the little wisp.
You'll wander worried
Through the valley forest.
The forest whispers, willows
In the gulley lean beside the road,
Then thoughts beset the soul
And tears roll down the cheeks.

One yearns to make confession
To relieve the heart,
One yearns... dear God!
How one yearns to live,
To live and love Your truth,
And to embrace the whole wide world!

Blessed are you, friend and brother,
If you have a home.
Blessed in that home are you
If you've someone to converse with.
Be that someone just a baby,
It will guess your happy thoughts...
God Himself converses through
The baby's pristine lips.

And for you, my forlorn and
Only friend,[438] for you
There's lonely grief
In a distant foreign land.
Who's to strike up conversation,
Who will greet or merely glance at you?..
Sprawling like a lifeless corpse around you
Is a withered desert,
Forsaken by the Lord.

Raim, September — Early October 1849

I count the days and nights in bondage
And forget the count.
O Lord, how hard the days go by.
And among them flow the years,
Drifting quietly,
Seizing good and evil!
They take, returning nothing evermore!
And do not plead, because the prayer
Will be lost on God.

So the fourth year passes
Slowly, softly,
And I now begin to scribble
My fourth booklet in captivity, —
In blood and tears
I'll scribble of my grief abroad,
For there's no place on earth
Where spoken words
Can ever, ever tell someone of grief.

438 *Only friend* — Shevchenko's reference to himself.

There are no words in distant bondage!
There are no words, there are no tears,
What exists is nothing.
Even God Almighty
Can't be found beside you!
There's not a thing to look at,
Not a soul to talk with.
You have no will to live,
Yet you must live alone.
I must, I must, but why?
To not lose the soul?
It's not worth the grief.
Here's why I must live on earth,
And drag my chains in bondage!
Perhaps I'll see Ukraine again...
Perhaps I'll share my words and tears
With verdant groves!
With twilit meadows!
Though I have no kin in all Ukraine,
Nonetheless, the people in this alien land
Can't compare with those at home!
In happy villages I would frolic
All along the Dnipro,
And I'd sing my sad and quiet thoughts.
Let me live, let me look,
O my dearest God!
Upon the lush green meadows,
Upon the burial mounds!
If You grant me not my wish,
Then deliver to Ukraine my tears;
For I, O God!
I am dying for her!
It will perhaps be easier
To rest in foreign lands,
If I'm recalled from time to time
Back in my Ukraine!
Deliver, my dear God!
Or send the soul a bit of hope...
Because I'll do nothing, nothing
With this poor head of mine,
Because my heart turns cold
When I think, perhaps,
They'll bury me
In a foreign land, — and inter
My thoughts with me...
And no one in Ukraine
Will ever mention me!

Or quietly across the years perhaps,
What I scribbled with my tears
Will someday reach Ukraine...
And it may fall like dew
Upon the earth
To reach a true young heart
With gently rolling tears!
And that youth will nod his head,
And will cry with me,
And perhaps O Lord, will
Recall me in his prayers to You!

What shall be will be.
Swim a stream or ford it.
Even if I'm crucified!
Despite it all,
I'll scribble quietly
Upon these pale sheets.

Orenburg, January — April 1850

We sang, we parted[439]
With not a word or tear.
Will we meet again?
Will we ever sing?
Perhaps... But where? Which words?
Which song?
Not here, and not these words, for sure!
And what we'll sing won't be the same!

Our songs here were not happy
For this was not a happy place,
Though we lived somehow
And shared at least our sadness,
Remembering that happy land,
And the mighty Dnipro's plunging banks,
And our youthful sorrow!
And that young and sinful paradise!

Orenburg, January — April 1850

My mother did not pray for me,
Nor did she deeply bow in church;
She rather swaddled me
As she sang some songs:
"May he grow, may he be healthy!"
And I, praise God, grew up,
But to no avail.
Better that I'd not been born,
Better I'd been drowned
Than I should live in bondage
And give the Lord offense.

What I asked of God was little,
Not too much, just a tiny home,
A single home within a grove
Beside a pair of poplars,
And for my luckless, sweet Oksana;[440]
So we could both together
Watch the mighty Dnipro from a hill,
To watch the valleys,
All the golden meadows,
And the soaring mounds;
To look, to think, to guess,
When were they all raised?
Whom did people bury there?
So we could sing serenely
That sad and ancient ballad
About that knight, the hetman,
Whom Poles once roasted on a fire.
From the hill we'd then descend;
Above the Dnipro in a shady grove,
Till twilight we would dance,
Till God's world would fall asleep,
Till the evening star would join
The moon to rise above the hill,
And a mist would shroud the meadow.
We'd look, we'd pray,
And conversing, we'd have supper
In our tiny home.

You, our only God, grant
Gardens in your paradise to lords,
You grant them lofty mansions.
But greedy paunchy lords, O God,
Spit upon your paradise
And do not let us watch
From a poor and tiny home.

All I asked for in that paradise
Was a tiny home, and still I ask for it,
To die along the Dnipro
Upon at least a tiny hill.

Orenburg, January — April 1850

---

439 *We* — Possible reference to the departure in 1850 of several of Shevchenko's close friends from Orenburg.

440 *Oksana* — Reference to Oksana Stepanivna Kovalenko (1817–?), an orphan, village neighbor and childhood friend of Shevchenko.

PETEY

A Poem

In a hamlet were some gentry,
A not too wealthy lord and Mrs.
Their little daughter grew,
And flourished with the years.
A general courted her,
For she was awfully beautiful
And he was awfully rich.
God's good fortune
Blessed the humble hamlet,
For they implored the King of heaven!
They took and dressed her nicely,
Wed her on a Sunday,
Dubbed her as a general's wife
And had a team of horses
Drive her to Kyiv.

In the hamlet was
A bastard, a small and ugly swineherd
By the name of Petey;
As a portion of the lady's dowry,
He went with her, luckless, to
The general's village
To herd pigs, of course.

At the general's,
Ball came after ball,
And following the general's wife
Was a goodly horde of lords and lordlings.
At night, the general's wife began to cry.
"Mother has destroyed my life.
In vain will all my youth and beauty
Wither in this mansion."
"You cry, dear soul?" — "Who, me?
No, I'm not crying..." — "You know, Manya,
The Armenians are in town,
Buy yourself a shawl, my dear."
"I don't need a shawl."
"Don't torment your heart!
Buy it, dear!
Don't hurt my heart as well.
Come spring, you and I will go to Paris,
Or the village,
As you wish, my sweetheart."
Gently, gently winter passed,
Toward the general's wife crept trouble,
And settled in her very heart.
In spring, they made the village visit.
The village reeled with banquets,
But the general's wife just cries and cries,
Though the general does not see
What every villager has seen.

She left the courtyard out of boredom
And took a pensive walk
Past the village gate,
And there she saw a little boy
Grazing lambs amid the stubble.
"Oh woe, oh woe is me,
What am I to do on earth?
Is that you, Petey?" — "Indeed, it's I."
"Come to me, we'll live
Like we did once at the hamlet,
Yes, we lived, we lived." — She leaned,
Looked at Petey,
And did not take her eyes off him.
Her girlhood and maidenhood
Were spent alone,
Then they ruined her
And sold her to the general!
As one, they drank away the money...
Then she sobbed and sobbed.
"Let's take a walk, my dear!
Let's go, Petey, to the orchard,
To the mansion."
"But who here will keep watch?
Who will graze my lambs?
"Whoever wants to!" —
And she led him to the mansion.
She then groomed him in the mansion,
Dressed him, and felt pleased.

Let her rejoice,
May her heart be warmed by hope,
And from that seed will sprout
Rows of wheat or tare.
For what he's doing we know not,
He will tell us nothing. Had mommy
Knowledge of your grief, would she have
Let the general take her only child?
No, she wouldn't...
But then, I do not know...
For there is every kind of mother.

Days slip slowly by,
Petey goes to school
And comes from school,
He walks with books and grows.
She seems younger,
And the general is delighted,
Because, you see, together
They have done this blessed deed.

They gave Pete his freedom,
In winter sent him to Kyiv,
Enrolling him in school,
And there they taught him quite a bit.
Petey, now a lordling,
Came from Kyiv
Known as Peter,
With locks down to his shoulders,
A black mustache on his lip,
And also...
But this can wait,
By-and-by we'll tell the story
Of the dreams that came to Peter.
But what dreams now came to
The general's dark-browed wife?
That's the story we will tell.

Beneath the image
Of the Blessed Virgin
Burns an icon lamp.
Bowing deeply, crying, struggling...
She poured impure and fiery tears.
She begged the Blessed Virgin,
That She may... that She may
Save her. That She not let her go insane,
For she, the wretch,
Was smitten by her Petey.
It's hard on her!
On a young and sinless soul.
But what to do?
Her strength ran out,
The dear completely lost her senses.
How is she to spend these
Sacred years of youth?
They'll not, of course, return!
Do as you please, but trouble
As they say, must be hurdled,
Or it will get the best of you.
The general's wife failed the hurdle,
Because the young gal wished to live.
Would have wished... The kasha [441] is
Quite thick, but that
Kasha is not ours,
Ours is saltless cornmeal,
Eat as best you can.

"Petey! O my only friend!
My heart! My son!
Save me! Save me! Save me!
O Mother of God!
Free my soul!" — She cried,
Then cursed her mother,
Cursed her father
And everything on earth.
And her only child, Petey,
Danced most guiltlessly
Around the orchard
And softly hummed some aria.
Nothing more did Petey see.

---

441 *Kasha* — A type of porridge in Eastern Europe usually made from buckwheat.

And what to do
The wretch herself knows not.
Either hide beneath the waves,
Or, at least, to bash her head
Against a wall…
"I'll go to pray in Kyiv.
Prayer may perhaps
Drive away the devil…
O! My Petey!
Prayer won't redeem me,
I'll go drown in the Dnipro."

Pray to God, young girls,
Pray to God that mother
Won't give you up as well
For a general, for a mansion,
Just selling you away like that.
Love, my children, in your spring.
There are many you can love on earth
And do so selflessly. Love will
Dwell within a hut,
Sacred, pure and innocent.
And it will keep your blessed peace,
Even in the grave. What then is to be
Of her excellency, the lady?
What will you do with yourself,
With all your godly beauty?
Who will guard your inner peace,
Stolen by your Petey?
Perhaps only the Archangel?
Now even he will not protect her.
I'm afraid and fear to say
What exactly looms before you…

She went to Kyiv, prayed,
Going even to Pochayiv.[442]
The miraculous image did not help,
Nor did sacred power.
You even wept, you prayed —
And then gave up.
Coming back, you brought with you
In your heart an angry serpent
And a dash of poison in a vial.

Returning from the pilgrimage,
For three days she had no food
Nor a drop to drink. And three
Long nights she did not sleep;
Her hazel eyes began to droop,
Her lips were parched and dry;
Walking late at night,
She whispered something, laughing.
For a week she roamed like that,
Then prepared the poison to
Slake the general's thirst,
And went to bed,
Having done the deed.
"I'll now inter the old guy,
And I'll greet the young one,
Then I'll live, I'll live
And love my sweetheart, Petey," —
She thought or said out loud.
She yearned to sleep,
But did not sleep.
She awaited dawn, but feared
The light of God's next day.

In early morning church bells tolled
For the general's soul;
People spoke of something dire,
As they went to pay respects.
There's a buzz, and people
From all over come,
Whispering hints of poison.
They await the judges,
And for a minute all grew silent.
They arrived; take out their knives
And cut the general open
To find venom in his gut.
Dumbfounded people swear an oath.

442 See glossary or fn. 119

Sworn in, the court then asks:
"Now tell us, Christians, who
Has poisoned him?" They drone,
Sounding like a dampened bell.
Then they loudly roar,
"The lady! Yes, the lady!"

Then Petey walks out on the porch
To speak to all the people.
He says: "I did it, I gave
The general poison, and you
Know not a thing!" —
They seized young Petey,
And took him into town in chains.

They tortured him not long
In jail and in court, then in due course
They forged good shackles,
And cut his locks for added measure;
Thus attired, Petey crossed himself
And schlepped his shackles
The entire distance to Siberia...

Orenburg, January — April 23, 1850

It seems to me, though I don't know,
That people do not really die,
But just crawl into
A swine or a thing akin, and
Live, to wallow in the mud
Like they wallowed once in sin.
Indeed, it's so. I'm indifferent
Toward the gray and simple wretches,
The Lord too has forgotten them.
So there's nothing here
For me to further bash or scorn!
But the rest??
Does the boor not
Feed himself in pens for lard?
Perhaps, it's so?
A lot of good they did on earth,
Spilling streams of tears
And a sea of blood.
People know just whom they feed
And who it is they tend.
What say you then:
Did they fill a bloody sea
For glory or themselves?
No, for us! They set the
World on fire for us, the wretches!
Until they placed them in a pen.
If not for that, a swineherd
Would have grazed them in a pasture.
The damned! The damned!
Where's your glory?? It's all in words!
Where's your gold, your palaces?
Where is your enormous power?
In sepulchers, in sepulchers, whitewashed[443]
All by tyrants, those same ones
Who ruled when you were wild creatures
And then turned into pigs!..
Where are you?
O you great and sacred martyr?[444]
You, the Omnipresent,
Are hovering among us

443 *Whitewashed* — Reference to Matthew Chapter 23, Verse 27, "Woe unto you, scribes and Pharisees, hypocrites! for ye are like unto whited sepulchers, which indeed appear beautiful outward, but are within full of dead men's bones, and of all uncleanness."

444 *Sacred martyr* — Reference to Mikhail Yuryevich Lermontov (1814-41), an influential Russian writer, poet and painter.

As a blessed angel.
You, dear friend,
Will speak so ever softly...
Of love, misfortune, grief,
Or of God, the sea and people's blood
Spilled all for naught
By distinguished tyrants.
You'll shed heavy tears before us,
And we will cry as well...
The poet's living soul is sacred,
It lives in sacred verses,
And as we read them we revive
And hear God amid the heavens.

Thank you, my impoverished friend![445]
You, I know, have shared
The only mite you had...
With God, my brother,
You have earned much more!
You have sent to me in bondage
Verses of our poet...
You opened me the doors to freedom!
Thank you, friend! Though I'll
Read but little... I'll revive...
I'll welcome hope into my heart,
I'll softly, softly sing
And will speak of God as God.

Orenburg, January — April 23, 1850

If you, gentlemen,[446] but knew,
Where people cry their lives away,
You'd compose no elegies,
Nor praise the Lord in vain
As you mock our tears.
I know not why
They say a cottage
Is a quiet paradise.
I suffered once in such a home.
There my tears were shed,
Indeed my very first; I know not,
Is there under God any cruel evil
That would not dwell within that home?
Yet they call that home a paradise!

I call it not a paradise,
That cottage in a grove
Above the pristine pond
Along the village edge.
There my mother swaddled me,
Singing as she swaddled,
Easing all her tedium through
Her little child... In that grove,
Within that hut, in paradise,
I witnessed hell itself...
Bondage, crushing labor,
And they leave no time to pray.
That's where poverty and drudgery
Sent my mother, still quite young,
To an early grave.
There, my father, crying with his children
(And we were small and bare)
Could not bear the cruel fate,
And also died in servitude!..
And we dispersed among the people
Like a horde of mice. I to school —
To carry water for the students.
My brothers bore the yoke of serfdom,
Until their heads were shorn![447]
And my sisters! Sisters!

---

445 *My brother* — Reference to Shevchenko's friend Mykhailo Matviyovych Lazarevsky, who responded to the poet's request for a copy of Lermontov's works. Shevchenko received them in Orenburg toward the end of 1849.

446 *Gentlemen* — Reference to writers who confused the superficial appearance of a village with life in it.

447 *Head shorn* — Reference to the crew cut given to military draftees.

Woe be unto you,
My young and precious doves,
For whom do you exist on earth?
You grew as hirelings of strangers,
And as hirelings will your braids
Turn gray, and as hirelings,
Sisters, you will die!

It feels awful to recall
That cottage at the village edge!
Such, our Lord, are deeds
That we commit in this, our paradise,
Upon Your righteous earth!
We created hell in paradise,
And beg You for another.
With our brothers we live quietly,
We plow with them the fields,
Which we sprinkle with our tears.
And perhaps, there's also…
No, I do not know, it just seems…
You Yourself…
(For without Your will, O God,
We'd not languish naked in
This paradise.) Or You Yourself,
Perhaps, our Father, laugh
At us in heaven, and consult
With lords on ways to rule the world!
For look, there a verdant grove reclines,
A pond, just like a painting,
Peers out through that grove,
And all along the pond
Willows softly bathe their
Greenery… Paradise, correct?
Then look and ask!
What goes on there in that paradise!
Joy and praise, of course!
To You, the sacred and the only
For Your wondrous deeds?
There you have it. Not!
Praise for none, but rather blood,
And tears, and blasphemy,
Blasphemy of everything!
No, no, there's nothing sacred
On this earth…
It seems to me that even You
Have now been cursed by people!

Orenburg, January — April 23, 1850

At times it happens in captivity
That I recall my distant past,
I look, I look to boast of something,
That I too really lived,
And I too once truly praised the Lord!
I look, I look… O God,
How I'd wish to recollect
If but any single thing!
But I stumbled on a thing so horrid
That I fell asleep
Not praying to the Lord!..
So here's the dream that came to me…
Having dozed off like a pig,
A nightmare can occur, of course...
It seems I was still little,
Grazing lambs beside a mound;
I look, the mound appeared to open,
And from it seemed to come a Kozak,
A gray-haired wretch,
Who came toward me... I cowered
Like a puppy pressed against a fence, —
Small, of course, and frightened.
He seems to lift me in his arms
And take me to the mound,
And the deep dark mound seemed
To open even wider.
I look, all inside are Kozaks:
Some are headless, some are armless,
Some seem cut off at the knees, —
The boys just lie around,

Like in a cozy house.
"Look, child, these are Kozaks,
(He seems to say to me), —
Lofty mounds dot all Ukraine,
And each, look closely child,
Is like the one you see.
They're stuffed,
Stuffed together
With our noble corpse;
This is liberty asleep!
It lay down in glory,
It lay down together
With all of us, the Kozaks!
See how glory lies —
As if swaddled!..
Here there is no lord,
We lived in freedom all as equals!
We died as equals for our freedom,
And we'll all arise as well,
God only knows, however, when.
Look, my child!
Look very closely — I'll
Share with you the reasons
Why our Ukraine expired,
Why I too lie among them
In this burial mound.
When you're grown,
You'll tell the people, son.
Listen up, my child." And then
I dreamed my lambs were grazing
In a field of rye,
And the overseer comes a running,
Beats me hard, and it seems,
The cursed man, strips me of my
Peasant coat. It still hurts,
When I recall that dream.
And when I recall the Kozak
In the mound, I still don't know,
If it was so,
Or if it was a ghost of sorts.
This is what that Kozak told me...

"I don't know how Poles today
Live with their free brothers.
But we consorted just like brothers!
Until Sigismund the Third[448]
And his accursed Latin priests
Drove a wedge between us.
That's the woe that hit us all!

In the name of Christ the Lord
And His blessed Mother,
The Poles brought war to us!
God's sacred holy cities!
Defiled by rabid Latin priests!
Kozak land was set ablaze
And blood, my son, was spilled,
Then mounds and mounds
Arose like mountains,
On this, my son, our land!

I lived out on a hamlet, with [*illegible*].
I was old and feeble.
I sent at least a herd of horses
To the transport unit.
A cannon, two wagons filled
With muskets, millet, wheat
That I acquired;
Those small goods I gave away
To my dear Ukraine...
Plus three sons of mine.
"I thought, as a sinner before God,
May at least that meager portion
Take my place to guard our land,
God's church, and people,
While I stay home to pray."
Because I, my son, became too ill
To rise and raise my arms
Against our enemy!

With me, listen up, remained
My orderly Danylo, I of course,

---

448 *Sigismund III Vasa (1566-1632)* — King of Poland from 1587-1632. Supported the Union of Brest, which split Ukraine into rival Orthodox and Catholic churches. The latter remains the dominant faith in Western Ukraine.

And Prisia, my dear daughter!
She had just begun to grow,
And ripen like a sweet red cherry!..
For a sin, a heavy and perhaps,
A grievous sin, the Holy Sovereign
Did not let my aging eyes
Enjoy the pleasure of
My little child!..

Latin priests did not walk
In villages, but
Were driven by the people
From one place to another,
That's the way it was!
Somehow they, the cursed,
Were carried to my hamlet.
With them came a rabid entourage
And dragoons in tow...
Permit me, O dear God, whenever!
To gaze upon Your world
From the confines of this mound. —
I'll roast the nobles on a fire!
They, they — do not fear, my son! —
They, the Latin priests, all drunk,
Took my daughter to the house,
And I saw them lock it.
And to the barn
Went drunken servants
To sleep on piles of straw.
Dragoons as well.
Danylo gathered straw with me
That we scattered on the porch
And simply set the barn on fire...
The cursed ones won't rise again
To torment Kozak children.
Each one burned to death!
And with the damned
Burned my poor and little Prisia!
And I... Upon the ruins with me
Danylo placed a cross,
Then we prayed and cried...
We then hauled ourselves
On horseback to the Kozak camp,
Found each of my three sons,
And in due course,
We all came here to rest!..
. . . .
How we fought, how we died
Why we stacked our heads
Within these burial mounds?
You'll live, perhaps you'll know,
Dear boy, for glory loudly shouts
About those heads of ours...
Or perhaps among the people,
The righteous and unhappy ballad
About the mounds and us,
Wanders through the villages
With beggar-bards of God..."

Orenburg, January — April 23, 1850

I delight my aging eyes with
Your supple figure and
Flawless youthful beauty.
I look at times, I look,
And it's wondrous,
How I'll pray before you,
As I'd pray before a saint.
Then, I, an old man,
Feel sorry for your Godly beauty.
Whither will you go with it?
Who on earth will rise to be
Your sacred guardian?
Who will be your champion?
Who will fend off human evil
In a trying hour?
Who will warm a heart so pure

With the flame of love, just who?
You're an orphan, you have no one,
But the righteous Lord.
Pray, my dear, I'll pray with you.
A prophetic something
Now looks into my eyes, and I no longer
Pray to God, nor do I gaze at you.
I had a dream: you're now a mother.
Not in velvet, not in manors
Does your hungry child live…
You wither, and the days fly by,
Taking with them all that's good.
They've carried hope away as well,
And you are left on earth alone;
With you was a single treasure —
Your child, as it grew,
Until its down turned into feathers.
Then you were left old,
Alone and feeble.
And in the name of Christ,
You extend your aging hands
To beg people, hostile people,
Beside heavy bolted doors.

Thus I delight my aging eyes at times
With you, my youthful dear.
I gaze at times, I gaze
Upon your supple figure,
And say a quiet prayer to God for you.
You too should pray, because
Your fortune or misfortune, dear,
Has not yet come from heaven.

Orenburg, January — April 23, 1850

Fires burn, music plays,
The singer soars and wails;
Like fine expensive diamonds
Youthful eyes all glisten;
Joy and hope fill happy eyes,
Eyes contented, young and pure.
All are boisterous, laughing,
Everyone is dancing.
Only I, as if accursed,
Look and cry in secret.
Why do I cry? Perhaps,
It's sad that my youth
Passed over like a storm,
Leaving me without a love.

Orenburg, January — April 23, 1850

Is it misfortune and captivity,
Or the fleeting years,
That rent the soul apart?
Or did I never even live with it,
Having lived in muck with people,
Thus mucking up a wholesome soul?..
And people!
(People flippantly, of course)
Call it sacred, young, and pure,
And also something else… Foes!!
And cruel! Cruel! It is you who stole it
And buried in a filthy swamp my clean,
My precious diamond,
My once sacred soul!
And you laugh! Unchristians!
Was it not amongst you, the foul,
That I so befouled myself
That it can't be known
If ever I was clean,
Because you took me in

From holy heaven — and taught me
How to write foul verses.
On the path you placed a heavy stone...[449]
And dashed against it...
Fearing God!
My small, my poor
Once righteous heart!
I now go forward with no road,
Without a beaten path... and you!
You wonder that I stumble,
That I curse my fate and you,
Crying heavy tears, and, like you...
I shun my needy soul,
My sullied sinful soul!

Orenburg, January — April 23, 1850

I squander on the devil's father
Paper, quills, and days!
And at times I weep,
Much too much indeed.
Not for having seen the world
Or what happens in it,
But rather, getting drunk at times,
The gray old man sheds tears —
For he, you see, is orphaned.

Orenburg, January — April 23, 1850

I still dream: beneath a hill
Among the willows by the water
Stands a whitewashed cottage.
Even now, it seems,
A gray old man sits beside the house
Playing with his nice,
His curly little grandchild.
I still dream
That the happy, laughing mother
Gives the child and gramps
A kiss, three happy kisses even,
Takes the child in her arms,
Feeds, and carries it to bed.
Grandpa sits and smiles,
Saying gently to himself:
"Where's that grief?
Those sorrows and the enemies?"
Then quietly, having crossed himself,
The old man says, *Our Father.*
The sun shines through the willows,
And silently grows dim.
The day is done and all's at rest.
The gray old man went in the house
To rest himself as well.

Orenburg, January — April 23, 1850

[449] *Placed a heavy stone* — Reference to Zechariah Chapter 12, Verse 3, "And in that day will I make Jerusalem a burdensome stone for all people: all that burden themselves with it shall be cut in pieces, though all the people of the earth be gathered together against it."

SOLDIER'S WELL[450]

A Poem
To Y. Kukharenko[451]
In Memory of May 7, 1857[452]

Not in Ukraine, but faraway
Past the Urals, past the Ilek River,[453]
A surviving branded convict
Told me this about a well,
A well dug by a soldier.
And being sad I wrote it down,
Adding just a bit of rhythm,
To scrawl a cheap and trifling poem
(Plagiarized, of course)
In remembrance of you,
My earnest friend, my only!

I

After the great winter,
Under Catherine the Empress,
A soldier dug a well;
And how he dug it, we'll say later,
But you keep notes, it won't
Hurt to write this down.
For this is not a fable, but the truth,
Non-fiction, if you will.

Write like this. There was a well,
No, not a well, a village.
Write, long ago amid the orchards,
By a valley, there was in our Ukraine
A village blessed by God.
In that village lived a widow,
And the widow had
A growing daughter and a little boy.
For a rich man to have kids is good,
To praise the Lord in luxury!
But that's not for a needy widow,
Because she almost perished
From all the grief they caused her.
She thought of entering a convent,
Or to take her life, to drown.
But she felt sorry for her little children,
Of course, a mother, say no more,
Or perhaps a son-in-law was expected,
Because Katie had grown up
(The widow's daughter was named Katie).
Should she live her years in maidenhood?
Bat the eyelashes in vain?
For having been an orphan?
Beauty, though, is beauty!
O my dear God! She's so calm, hardworking,
Neat and diligent. An orphan, see,
Yet splendid in all ways.
At times she peered out from the hut,

---

450 *Soldier's Well* — First version of this poem was written in 1847.

451 *Yakiv Herasymovych Kukharenko (1800-62)* — Ukrainian writer, ethnographer and general of the Black Sea Kozak Host. Shevchenko met him in 1840 and supported his literary efforts.

452 *May 7, 1857* — Having received a supportive letter that day from Kukharenko, Shevchenko was inspired to write a second version of the *Soldier's Well*.

453 See glossary or fn. 360

Like a blossom from the dew,
Like the sun through breaking clouds.
Standing there at times,
I'd turn cold, inanimate.
Neither punishments,
My son, nor torture,
Shackles nor the years,
Have exhausted all those strengths...
And so I'll die!
Thus I'll perish. Because look:
Death is something I expect,
But I cry much like a child,
When I recall Kateryna. Listen, son,
My only friend! Listen well,
Take notes, and if God leads you
To Ukraine, tell people there, my son,
That with your eyes you saw the devil.

II

So, you see, that maiden grew.
And a hardworking orphan
(Because orphans everywhere are lazy)
Grew up as a hireling,
Like a father's son.
And that poor orphan
With a tad of this, a bit of that
Earned some cash,
Got some clothes, an overcoat,
And out of nowhere,
Bought a little house and orchard;
He thanked good people
For their bread and salt,
For an education, and whoosh,
He made a hasty beeline
To the widow's daughter
To get some wedding scarves.
They did not haggle with the matchmakers,
As it so happens with the wealthy;
The priest too did not negotiate
(Itself a miracle to people's disbelief),
And he wed them on a weekday
For a mere three kopas,
Simply, without pomp.
And here, my friend,
And here is where the trouble started!

III

Pokrova's Feast[454] had passed, it seems,
As I ventured from the Don, and again
(Because I'd twice already
Sent the girl go-betweens
To get some wedding scarves)
I considered yet another try.
With the chumaks, with the oxen
I lumbered to the Sunday wedding
Of the widow's daughter.
Lost! All that's good was lost!
Not a shred remained.
I too was lost, not in a bar,
But on a *rack*. In a lifetime, son,
Every person sees some evil,
But that kind, my friend,
That kind they've not ever seen,
Not even at a distance,
Like I, an evil man, had seen.

Meanwhile, the widow's eyes
Had dried. The old woman
Rested surely with her son
And son-in-law,
As if sheltered by God's door,
Merely watching Kateryna,
Her very precious child.
I went to drink my soul away
With drunkards in a tavern!
And drank it away.
I sold my soul,
My soul and body too,
The body to a tormentor,
And the soul!..

---

454 *Pokrova's Feast* — Feast of Saint Mary the Protectress. It is celebrated on October 14th (October 1st according to the Gregorian Calendar).

O my dear God!
There's such desire to live on earth,
But nay! One must learn,
One must learn from childhood
How to live on earth,
Otherwise they'll beat you,
And very hard at that!..
I don't know, my friend,
If the evil was the devil's work?
Had I taken ill?
Or was I driven toward it
By a vicious fate?
To this day I don't yet know,
I do not know a thing.
I only know I'm sober.
Because, my son, I've drunk
No wine, no mead, no booze.
And that's what happened.
Father died and mother too,
Strangers buried them...
And I, like the accursed Judas,
Spurned by God and people,
Lurk around and hide,
And it reached the point one night,
That I, having crept to Maksym's house,
(Because they called the
Widow's son-in-law Maksym)
And set the place on fire.
The house burned down.
The cursed soul, though,
Did not burn. My soul!
My friend, my brother!
It did not burn, but stayed,
And smoldered, still it smolders!
When will it go out?
When will it finally rest?
The good Lord only knows.

IV

Kateryna died
Of fright.
And Maksym gazed upon
The ruins and ashes.
Nothing could be done!
The wind just whistles
In the flue and chimney.
What on earth to do?
And what is he to start?
Having crossed himself
And pondered,
He again worked as a hireling
To feed his hungry misery.
The widow stayed, though not alone,
But rather with her strapping son;
In autumn she prepared to wed him.
When suddenly! An order
From the mother-empress,
From the capital itself,
Came to shave young heads.
It was the first decree
To come from Muscovy to us.
Because in our Ukraine, it happened,
That Kozaks volunteered,
And they recruited pikesmen,
Also volunteers. In the village
They convened a council
To determine whom to shave.
The council counseled
And they chose
The widow's lazy son,
Deeming him an SOB,
And securing him
With wooden shackles,
They rode him to the draft board.
Such are things that happen
In this world! That, my son,
Is justice for the common people.
We still have the same, I think,
In Ukraine today.
And there won't be any other
Among a captive people.

V

The great winter came next year.
Ravines till Pentecost
Were tinted white with snow;

That is when Ochakiv[455]
Was taken by the Muscovites.
But first in Zaporizhia,
They ruined the Kozak Sich.[456]
The brotherhood dispersed.
And how special the
Zaporizhians were —
Not before or after
Did such people live.
Maksym as well was driven
To Ochakiv.
He was wounded there
And discharged to Ukraine.
His right leg was shot, you see,
Or perhaps the left,...
It was none of my concern back then.
Again the vicious viper
Imbibed within the heart;
It coiled itself three times around.
Like Herod. What to do here?
I can't handle it.
And Maksym the cripple
Is not hindered;
He hobbles on his crutches,
With no inkling of my hate.
On blessed Sundays
He dons his service uniform,
Pins a cross and medal,
Weaves a braid
And even sprinkles it with flour.
I've yet to fathom,
Why did Muscovites weave braids
Like girls, and waste sacred flour?
For fun, I think, just to do it!
Thus Maksym on Sundays,
Dresses grandly like a general
And hobbles off to church.
He stands beside the choir
And with the cantor sings along,
And he even reads the Acts.
He learned to read
Among the soldiers.
He was uncertain,
This Maksym, my brother.
But diligent, hard-working,
Quiet too, and kind...
You had a man
Who gave offense to none,
Not with deeds,
Not with words.
"Fortune and misfortune,
All, — he said, — was granted
By Almighty God,
And by no one else."
That Maksym, my son,
Was the purest man on earth.
And I! And I!.. It won't come out.
My child!
I murdered him! Just wait,
I'll rest a bit.
Only then.

VI

So you say,
You saw a well,
The soldier's, from
Which people still draw water,
And a cross, the Lord's, you say,
Still stands beside the road
Upon an open field.
And did people there
Not tell you anything?..
They've died out
Those people, my witnesses,
And righteous people!
And I still suffer in this world
And will always suffer.
Listen, here's how Satan

---

455 *Ochakiv* — A town in Ukraine's southern region of Kherson that Russia captured from the Turks in December 1788.

456 See glossary or fn. 37

Leads our soul astray.
If there's no awareness,
Or return to God,
He'll sink his claws
Into the heart.
So listen up, my son,
About Maksym the righteous…
It so happened that
He never rested.
And on Sundays or some holiday,
He'd take the Holy Psalter in his hands
And read it in the orchard.
In the orchard in the shade
Is where they buried Kateryna.
Thus in the orchard
He would read the Psalter
For her soul's repose,
Then softly, to himself,
He sang prayers from a requiem.
He then remembered in his prayers
His in-law mother, her son, their health
And once again felt happy.
"God grants all, — he told himself, —
Years must all be lived."
That's the kind of righteous man
That lived here in this world.
And on weekdays, he won't
Just sit around the house,
He'll poke around the yard instead,
"Gotta work —
He'll say at times in soldier-talk,[457] —
Or you'll put on weight
Just lying 'round the house."
And so he took a spade and shovel,
Went into the field
And began to dig a well.
"May it be, — he says. — People will
Someday drink water from this well.
And say prayers to the Lord
For my sinful soul."
He went into a field
Some distance from the road,
Then climbed into a valley
Where he dug a deep, deep well.
(Not all alone; good people
Came for work bees
To help him dig the well.)
He topped it off with logs
And in the field beside the road
He placed a towering cross…
Throughout the field's expanse
It could be spotted from afar.
This way, you see,
It would be known that
There's a well beside the road,
So others might come and drink,
And say a prayer to God
For the man who dug it.

VII

You see now
What it's coming to.
That I intend to kill
Maksym, the blessed man.
That's right! And for what?
For that, which Cain killed
His righteous brother
In the sunny light of Eden.

Was it on a Sunday,
Or some holiday?
Listen up, my son,
Here's how the cursed Satan teaches.
"Let's go, — I say, — Ulasovych,
To see that well of yours."
"Good, — he says, — let's go
Drink its pristine water."
And we both went off,

[457] *Soldier-talk* — The language of Ukrainian men was often corrupted by Russian due to prolonged service in the czarist army. In the 18th century, Russian military service lasted a lifetime. In 1793, the term was reduced to 25 years. It was further lowered to 12 years in 1855.

Taking with us rope and pail,
We then come up to the well,
And first I looked if it was deep.
"Ulasovych, — I say —
Draw the water, if you would,
I know not how it's done."
He leaned,
Then lowered the bucket down the well;
And I… I grabbed him by the legs,
And threw the blessed Maksym
Down the well…
It was my doing, son!
Such a deed in our Ukraine
Had never been committed.
And will never be repeated
In this world or ours, my brother!
All around are people,
But only I'm a cursed devil!

VIII

In a week they pulled Maksym
From the well he dug
And in the valley buried him.
The people built a goodly chapel
And the well they dubbed
The Soldier's,
There you have the story,
An inhuman story,
Of the Soldier's Well.

And I went with the haidamaks,
And landed in Siberia.
(For this was once Siberia.)
And here I perish, like a dog,
Like Judas! Pray for me to God,
My son, in our most glorious Ukraine,
In that happy, happy land.
Won't my burden ease?

Novopetrovsk Fortress, May 16, 1857

Sketch of 'The Tale,' 1843

NEOPHYTES[458]

A Poem

Thus saith the Lord,
keep ye judgment, and do justice:
for my salvation is near to come,
and my righteousness to be revealed.

Isaiah 56: Verse 1

To M. S. Shchepkin[459]
In Remembrance of December 24, 1857

Lover of the muses and of graces,
Awaiting you, I gently weep
And my melancholy thought
I deliver to your soul.

O great wizard,
My great friend,
Kindly welcome
My meek orphan!
If you do; this poor
Gray child will swim
With you across the Lethe.[460]
And will someday fall to earth
In a fiery tear
To become a parable
For tormenters of the people,
For emerging tyrants.

I've long since sat in bondage,
Like a thief in jail,
Gazing at a road and field,
And upon a raven perched
Atop a graveyard cross.
Nothing more is seen from prison.
Thank God I see even that.
Christened folks still live,
Pray to God and die,
And in the graveyard
On the side, there stands
A lofty cross painted in bright gold.
Not someone poor perhaps
Who's buried there?
And portrayed: the Son of God
Crucified upon the cross for us.
Thanks to all the wealthy orphans
For putting up a cross. And I...
Such is my humble fate!
I sit and always look from prison
Upon that lofty cross.
I look, I look, I pray:
My grief, my simple grief,
Subsides a bit
Like a child that's been fed.
And the prison seems expanded.
The heart sings, it cries, revives
And asks you, O God,
And all Your saints and righteous,
What did that saint, that Nazarene,

---

458 *Neophytes* — Early Christians, or recent converts to a belief.

459 *Mykhailo (Mikhail) Shchepkin (1788-1863)* — Renowned Ukrainian and Russian actor. A close friend of Shevchenko and also a former serf. December 24, 1857 is the day the Shchepkin arrived in Nizhny Novgorod from Moscow to welcome Shevchenko back from a decade in exile.

460 *Lethe* — In Greek mythology, the river of forgetfulness in Hades. The dead had to drink from it to forget their life on earth.

That only Son of God,
Of the chosen Mary,
Ever do to them? And why did they
Torment Him, a saint,
And tie His hands in knots?
And crown His honest head with thorns?
And lead Him out with thieves
Atop Golgotha's hill;
And suspend Him flanked by them —
For what? Nothing's said not even by
The gray Supreme Creator
Nor His saints —
Accomplices, Apologists,
Mute castrati!

Blessed among all women,
Is the saintly righteous Mother
Of the Holy Son on earth.
Permit not death in bondage,
Nor loss in vain of fleeting years!
O joy of the afflicted! Send,
Send a holy word to me,
A new and righteous voice of truth!
And with sacred reason,
Revive the word, enlighten it!
And I'll relate the woe
Of how a mother cried entire rivers
And a sea of bloody tears,
As did You as well. And took into
Her living soul the unseen world
Of your Son, The Crucified!..
You're God's Mother here on earth!
You shed every drop to the
Very limit of a mother's tears.
I cry, and as cry I pray, send,
Grant a needy soul the power,
So it may speak with fire,
So the word ignites in flame,
To warm the hearts of people.
And may it spread across Ukraine,
May that word be sanctified,
May it be God's censer,
Censer of the truth. Amen.

I

Not in our land, beloved by God
Not under rule of czars or hetmans
But on idolatrous Roman land
Did this lawlessness transpire.
Perhaps under Decius the emperor?
Or under Nero's stewardship?
Exactly I can't say.
Let's say under Nero.
Russia
Then did not exist,
When a little girl grew in Italy.
With her beauty,
Her blessed pristine beauty,
She blossomed like a lily.
Her mother gazed at her
And was younger for it.
She searched out people for the girl.
And succeeded.
Then, having prayed to Hymen[461]
In her happy gynaeceum,[462]
She took her daughter
To another happy dwelling.
Soon, that good girl became a mother:
She bore a child, a son.
She prayed to her Penates[463]
And left goodly sacrifice
In Juno's lofty Capitol.[464]
She prevailed upon its priests
To have her first-born
Blessed by sacred idols.
Day and night a sacred fire

---

461 *Hymen* — Greek and Roman god of weddings.
462 *Gynaeceum* — The part of a dwelling used by women.
463 *Penates* — Domestic or household gods in Roman mythology.
464 *Juno's Capitol* — Temple of the god Juno on Rome's Capitoline Hill.

Burns before Penates.
The mother's joyful:
Her son is growing like Alcides[465]
He grows, hetaeras[466] woo him,
Lighting lamps
Before the image of fair Venus.

II

A star was rising then
Above the town of Bethlehem.
The universal star of love, of sacred truth,
And of its word, had risen!
And it brought peace and joy
To people on this earth. Pharisees
And all despicable Judea shuddered,
Hissing like a snake in mud.
And they crucified with thieves
The Son of God incarnate
Upon Golgotha's hill.
And they slept, the butchers,
Drunk with blood, Your holy blood.
And You arose from death,
The word arose,
And the word of truth was carried
Throughout the captive world
By all of Your apostles.

III

That's when her Alcides,
The young hetaeras too,
And the drunken half-goat[467]
All stripped nicely by the Appian way,
Got drunk nicer,
And paid homage to Priapus.[468]
Suddenly!.. Saint Peter comes along
On his way to preach in Rome,
And he went into the grove
To get a drink of water
And a bit of rest. "Bless you!"
Said the tired disciple,
And he blessed the orgy.
With a brief, quiet, decent word
He heralded a newfound word,
Of love, of truth and good,
The greatest good on earth,
Brotherly love, that is.
And that sated, drunk and naked Faun,
Your son, Alcides, and the hetarias —
All, all fell to the ground before Saint Peter.
And this apostle they then took
For dinner at their thermae...

IV

In the thermae there's an orgy.
Amphoras smoke,
Chambers blaze with gold and purple.
Girls nearly naked
Stand before the goddess Cypris[469]
And sweetly sing a song.
A joyous feast has been prepared.
The guests sprawl out on couches.
Laughter! Clamor!
Hetarias ushered in the graybeard guest.
And from lips of the apostle
The word poured forth
Like precious unction.
The orgy faded. And the priestess
Of the goddess Cypris,
Of the orgy's empress,
Bowed her forehead with respect
For Apostle Peter. She arose,
And all rose with her,

---

465 *Alcides* — Another name for Hercules, a mythological hero noted for his strength.

466 *Hetaera* — Ancient Greek word for unwed, independent and educated women. The term later came to mean a type of highly skilled prostitute.

467 *Pan* — The god of nature in Greek mythology.

468 *Priapus* — Roman god of carnal pleasure. Noted for his large permanent erection.

469 *Cypris* — Another name for Venus, the Roman goddess of love, beauty and sexuality.

Following the apostle
Into catacombs. And with them
Went your only son, Alcides,
With his teacher,
The sanctified apostle.
And you left your home quite happily
For the road beside the grove
To await your son, Alcides. No, he's gone.
Not ever to return. You'll pray alone
To your Penates, you'll dine alone at home.
No, not to dine, but rather weep,
To weep and curse your fate,
And cursing to go gray. And grief!
Like a leper
You will die alone!

V

Head down upon a cross
They crucified that saint,
The Apostle Peter.
And the neophytes they sent
To Syracuse in chains. And your son
Alcides, your only son,
Your only family, only love,
Rots in bondage and in shackles.
And you, most sorrowful, know not,
Where he languishes and withers!
You go to find him in Siberia,
Or to Scythia, rather… And you…
Are you the only? Mother of God!
Shelter us, protect us!
There's not a family, not a home,
Not a brother or a sister
That walks and does not weep,
Or is not tortured in a prison,
Or is not drilled in far off-lands
In British or in Gallic legions.
O Nero! O cruel Nero!
God's justice, righteous and abrupt
Will condemn you in mid-stride.
Holy martyrs will then fly and swim
From every corner of the world.
All children of sacred liberty.
They'll appear in chains
Around your bier,
Your funeral bier. And…
Will forgive you.
They're brothers and they're Christians,
But you're a dog! A cannibal!
A rabid tyrant!

VI

The vaults and dungeons
Teem with slaves in Syracuse.
And Medusa[470] sleeps inebriated
With beggars in a tavern.
Any minute she'll awake…
With your blood, your tyrants' blood,
She'll stage a drunken bout.

The mother sought
Her child all over.
Not finding him she sailed on to Syracuse.
And there the poor dear found him
Shackled in a dungeon.
And she had to sit beside the prison.
To await, to await her son,
Like waiting for the Lord in heaven,
Until they drove him shackled to
Sweep the city boulevard.

There's a holiday in Rome, meanwhile.
A major holiday!
From all corners of the empire,
A crush of people,
Governors, praetorians, senators,

---

470 *Medusa* — In Greek mythology, a dreadful female creature with snakes instead of hair. Those who looked at her were turned to stone. Some scholars believe Shevchenko meant Megaira, one of the mythological Furies. The name means envious anger. Furies pursued heinous criminals and drove them mad. The text refers to bloody revenge against tyrants.

Priests and lictors[471] stand
Beside the Capitol. They sing a hymn
In concert, breathing smoke from censers
And amphora. Caesar comes himself
With his entourage in tow.
Caesar's now a cast bronze statue
That they carry up in front.

VII

This uncertain holiday
Was contrived by nobles, by patricians
And Caesar's clever senate.
They, you see, praised Caesar
In every sort of manner,
Till it became repugnant
For them to praise the fool,
So they decided at a council
To simply call the emperor Jupiter himself.
And they wrote to every governor
Throughout the Roman empire: like this —
Caesar's god. Superior to god!
And they had a sculptor
Cast Caesar out of bronze.
To that they added, nota bene,
That this Caesar will show mercy.
The humble, like birds
That flock in nesting grounds,
Made a pilgrimage to Rome.
From Syracuse the poor wretch sailed
To plead with Caesar and with god.
Was she the only one? My God!
They came by thousands
All in tears, from near and far.
Woe to you!
Who is it that you came to beg?
Your tears are meant for whom?
For whom your tear-drenched hopes?
Woe, you blind and eyeless slaves!
Will a butcher pardon anyone?
Pray but to a single God,
Pray for truth on earth,
And to no one else on earth
Should you bow your heads.
All is lies — kings and pontiffs....

VIII

Yesterday, before the Emperor Nero,
Before the newest Jupiter,
Senators and patricians prayed,
And yesterday god's grace
Blissfully poured forth.
One got money, one got rank,
One a lease on Palestine,
Even bastards got some crumbs.
For others they bestowed as wives
Their concubines, used a tad, however.
No matter, just so she lay under Caesar.
They took into their harem
A sister from another. Again, no matter.
That's why he is god,
And beneath him we should lay
Our sisters, to say nothing of ourselves.
Praetorians said a prayer,
Praetorians got an order,
To do anything they wished,
And we will pardon all.
And you, plebian-buckwheat farmers,
You too prayed,
But no one pardons you.
They know not very well
How to pardon you.

IX

Finally on the third day
They let people pray for Christians.
You came, you prayed,
And the idol in its mercy
Deigned to transfer Christians
From Syracuse to Rome in chains.
You're glad, and again

471 *Lictor* — A special Roman civil servant and attendant, who guarded magistrates that had the right and power to command.

You happily beseech your idol.
But this idol, this new Jupiter;
Just watch the feast that
He'll be staging in the Coliseum.
Meanwhile, go and meet your son.
Just don't rejoice too much, poor dear.
You don't yet know this
New and kindly god.
For now, Alcides' mother
Went with other mothers
For a meeting with him,
And to welcome
Saints upon the shore.
You went, indeed,
Nearly singing,
Praising and exalting:
"Jupiter, yes, Jupiter!
It's not a pity
To call him by his name.
And I, a fool, went to plead
With Jupiter in Athens.
A fool, nothing more!"
And quietly she prayed
To the deity, to Caesar.
And she went above the swamp
That overlooks the Tiber.
And along the Tiber past a grove
Comes a longboat or a galley.
They bring your son upon that galley
With neophytes in chains.
What's more, your son
Is shackled to the mast —
Not a novice neophyte,
An apostle rather
For the living word of Christ.
Such is he. Do you hear?
Your martyr sings
In chains.

"To our Lord we'll sing
A psalm that's new
And in an honest congregation,
With a heart not evil
We'll sing praises to new glory.
With timbrels and psalteries[472]
We'll praise the goodness of our God,
And how He smites unrighteous people
And how He helps the righteous.
The blessed in their glory
And in quiet chambers
Praise, acclaim and celebrate
The name of God above.
In their hands are righteous swords
Sharpened on both edges[473]
To bring vengeance to the pagans
And enlightenment to people.
They'll bind in chains of iron
All insatiate kings,
With handcuffs they'll secure
The infamous.
The unrighteous they'll condemn
With their righteous justice,
And eternal glory will arise,
Glory to the blessed."

X

You stood upon the shore
Like a dismal cliff.
Not listening, not crying,
But singing *Hallelujah*
For the Christian mothers.
Like bells, the chains of
Neophytes rang out.
And your son, your only one!
The new apostle
Crossed himself, proclaiming:
"Pray, my brothers! Say prayers

472 *Timbrels and psalteries* — Ancient musical instruments

473 *Sharpened on both edges* — Reference to Hebrews Chapter 4, Verse 12, "For the word of God is quick, and powerful, and sharper than any twoedged sword, piercing even to the dividing asunder of soul and spirit, and of the joints and marrow, and is a discerner of the thoughts and intents of the heart."

For the evil tyrant.
Recall him in your prayers.
Do not, my brothers,
Bow before his pride.
Prayer is to God.
Let the tyrant rage on earth,
Let him kill the prophet,
Let him hang us all upon a cross;
Grandchildren conceived already
Will someday grow as well.
Avengers they are not,
But rather holy warriors of Christ!
Without fire, without knives,
Strategists of God will rise.
Then by thousands
And by tens of thousands,
Pagans all will flee the saints.
Pray, my brothers."
They prayed,
Prayed before a cross,
The shackled neophytes
Prayed joyfully. Praise!
Be praised, young souls!
Be praised, O blessed knights!
Praise forevermore.

XI

The galley sailed into Rome.
A week goes by. The drunken Caesar,
Having coiffed himself as Zeus,
Puts on a jubilee for Zeus.
Rome rejoices. They carry past the idol
Carts of incense, carts of myrrh,
Driving Christians group by group
Toward the Coliseum. Blood gushed out
Like in a slaughterhouse. Rome rejoices!
Gladiator and patrician, drunk alike,
Besotted by the blood and smoke.
Rome drinks away the ruins of glory.
It holds a funeral feast for Scipiones.[474]
Cruel, cruel, loathsome elder.
Indulge in all your harems. Beyond the sea
A sacred star is rising. They'll kill you not
By sacred righteous thunder. They'll slay you
With a knife that's dull,
Or kill you like a dog
With the blunt end of an axe.

XII

The arena roars a second day.
Its golden Lydian[475] sand
Is smeared with purplish red,
Turned to mud with blood.
And the Nazarenes of Syracuse
Have not yet stepped
Inside the Coliseum.
On the third day, they as well
Were led into the slaughterhouse
By guards with swords unsheathed.
The arena roared just like a beast.
And into the arena proudly stepped your son,
With a psalm upon his lips.
And the drunken Caesar
Cackled like a madman.
Then a leopard from a cellar
Pounced onto the stage,
He took a step, he looked...
And holy blood began to gush.
A storm rolled across the Coliseum,
Quickly dying out. Where were you?
Where did you hide? Why did you
Not hurl yourself upon your sainted Caesar?
Because he was defended
Three rows deep by lictors,
All surrounding Zeus.
Behind your holy Jupiter
They closed an iron gate.
You remained outside all alone and lonely.
What can you do? "Grief! Grief!
O vicious grief of mine!

474 *Scipiones* — An influential patrician family in the Roman Republic.
475 *Lydia* — A Roman province in Asia Minor known for gold deposits.

You're my bitter destiny! What will
I do without him?
Whom will I now lean upon?.."
The wretch then looked around,
And against a wall,
Against a wall, she bashed her aging head,
Falling like dead weight
Beneath the iron gate.

XIII

By evening, the spectacle was over,
Holy Caesar and his lictors
Disappeared inside the thermae.
The Coliseum was deserted
With no Caesar and no Romans
And alone it seemed to weep.
The Coliseum darkly looms in Rome
Like a hill amid a field.
Gently, gently blows the wind
From the Tiber,[476] from Albano[477]
O'er the city of Rome.
Above the darkened Coliseum
Floats a round-faced moon.
Then upon night's bosom
The world primordial lay to rest.
Only we your sinful children, Adam,
Do not rest until the grave
In this, the paradise we lost.
Like dogs we gnaw each other
For a smelly bone,
And hold in raw contempt as well,
You, our idle forebear!

XIV

She rested some,
The old and beaten mother.
The power of night
Revived her vital power.
She rose, whispering something
As she walked around
The bolted gate.
Did she not softly curse
Revered and holy Caesar?
Perhaps, indeed.
She stole quietly to the gate,
Listened, smiled,
And murmured something,
Just a word.
Then silently she sat
And worried by the gate.
Soon it swung wide open.
And on carts, on chariots
From the Coliseum,
From the slaughterhouse,
They brought out sacred bodies;
And took them to the Tiber.
With bodies of the sacred dead
They fed the Tiber's fish
For the table of the very emperor.
The mother rose, looked around,
Grabbed her beaten head,
Then like a gloomy apparition,
Quietly, without a word
She followed all the carts
To the Tiber River.
And the gray-eyed Scythians,
The drivers, slaves of slaves
Thought that Morok's[478] sister
Came from hell to escort
Romans into hell.
They dumped the bodies in the water
And with their carts returned to Rome.
You alone remained along the river.
You watched the rings spread over him,
Above your righteous son!
You watched until no living trace

---

[476] *Tiber* — River that flows through Rome.

[477] *Albano* — A town near Rome.

[478] *Morok* — Mythological ruler of the underworld. Unverified notations attribute the deity to Scythian or Norse mythology.

Was left upon the water.
You smiled, then wept bitterly
And dreadfully
And for the first time prayed
To the One who died for us.
And you were saved
By Mary's Son, who was nailed
To the cross. And His living words
You took into your living soul.
Then into palaces and public squares
You brought the word of truth
From the true and living God.

Nizhny Novgorod, December 8, 1857

Encolpion, 1859

HOLY FOOL[479]

In the days of sergeant-czar,[480]
Corporal Gavrilovych the Armless[481]
And assistant drunkard Longarm[482]
Were the rulers of Ukraine.
A lot of good they did.
These satraps dressed in livery
Stripped a lot of people.
Especially the closely-cropped Havrylych
With his wickedly wicked
And lively little corporal,[483]
Who so drilled the people
That the sergeant was himself amazed
With the drill and all…
But "the favored always stood by
Their loyal corporals."
And we just watched, kept quiet,
And scratched our heads in silence.
Dumb and abject slaves!
Czarist footstools, lackeys
Of the drunken corporal!
You, informers, pharisees,
Decked out in lacy livery,
You're not the ones
To stand for sacred truth and freedom!
You learned to crucify,
Not to love your brother!
O vain and cursed clan,
When will you die out?
How long must we await
Our Washington
With a new and righteous law?
Our wait indeed won't be in vain.

In days of yore,
Havrylych bent not hundreds of you,
But millions of
Polans, Dulibs and Derevlians.[484]
The satrap-corporal
Handed you, my sainted Kyivans
And your tidy women,
As servants to his drunken wardens.
And you're indifferent.
But found among you was an oddball,
Some obtuse original,[485]
Who slapped the corporal in the mug,
In a church no less,
But it could have merely been a dog.
Oh yes, oh yes indeed!
Among a million swineherds
Emerged a single Kozak,
Who put the realm on notice —
He slapped the satrap in the mug.
And as the corporal mends,
You — holy fools —
Have declared the sacred knight
To be himself a holy fool.

---

479 *Holy Fool* — An oddball such as a beggar or madman who challenges authority, promotes truth and faith, and has the gift of prophecy.

480 *Sergeant Czar* — Reference to Nicholas I.

481 *Gavrilovych the Armless* — Dmitri Gavrilovich Bibikov (1792-1870), Russian political leader, and military governor of Kyiv, Podiliya and Volyn. Lost his arm in the Patriotic War of 1812.

482 *Assistant drunkard Longarm* — Nikolai Andreievich Dolgorukov (1792-1847), Russian governor-general of Chernihiv, Kharkiv and Poltava. His surname means Longarm.

483 *Lively little corporal* — Nikolai Yevarestovich Pisaryov (1806-84), Bibikov's office manager. Shevchenko referred to him as an ingenious bribe-taker.

484 *Polans, Dulibs and Derevlians* — Slavic tribes of Kyivan Rus. Polans lived around Kyiv, Dulibs in Volyn and the Derevlians along the Prypiat and Teteriv Rivers, right-bank tributaries of the Dnipro.

485 *Obtuse original* — Functionary M. Matveev. In his diary entry of July 19, 1857, Shevchenko refers to an incident, when Pisaryov was slapped in the face by a subordinate during mass in a Vologda church. Matveev was sentenced to hard labor. In the poem, it is Bibikov who gets slapped.

And your former sergeant, Sardanapalus,[486]
Sent a saint to suffer torture,
And toward the beaten satrap,
"He remained forever merciful."

Nothing more transpired.
They took the drama
Past secluded murky alleyways
And tossed it in a dump, and I…
O my bright star!
You lead me out of prison,
Out of bondage,
Right into the little dump of Nicholas,[487]
And you shine, you blaze above him
With an unseen, sacred, procreative fire,
And from the dung,
Like a pillar facing me,
Rise all his godless deeds…
Godless czar! Evildoer!
Cruel oppressor of the truth!
What evil have you wrought on earth?
And You, All Seeing Eye,
Did You look from up above
When they drove prisoners
Chained and holy
By the hundreds to Siberia,
When they tortured, hanged and crucified?..
And You knew nothing?
And You watched them
Without going blind?
Eye! Eye! You don't see so very deeply!
You sleep inside an icon case, and czars…
To hell with them, the evil czars!
May chains fill all their nightmares.
And I'll fly to Siberia, past Baikal;
I'll peer inside of hills,
Inside abysmal caves and pits so deep
They have no bottom, and you,
Champions of sacred liberty —
From darkness, stench and bondage
I'll lead you row by row into the world
To display your chains to czars and people.

Nizhny Novgorod, December 8, 1857

DESTINY

You did not deceive me,
You became a friend, a brother
And a sister to this hapless wretch.
You took me, a little child, by the hand
And led this boy to school
For an education with a drunken cantor.
"Learn, my dear,
You'll be someone someday,"— you said.
So I listened, studied

486 *Sardanapalus (668-627 BC)* — Said to be the last Assyrian king. According to legend, a self-indulgent ruler who burned himself, his concubines and treasures when his besieged capital was flooded amid a rebel uprising.

487 See glossary or fn. 347

And I learned.
But you lied. What did we amount to?
All in vain! We did not deceive each other,
We simply forged ahead. There's not
A hint of lies between us.
Let's go, my destiny!
My needy, uncorrupted friend!
Let's move ahead, ahead is glory.
And glory's my commandment.

Nizhny Novgorod, February 9, 1858

MUSE

And you, the pure, the holy,
You, Phoebus's young sister.[488]
You held me by the hem
And took me far afield.
And on a mound amid a field,
Like freedom's broad expanse,
You cloaked me in mist of gray.
You sang, you rocked me,
And you worked your magic...
And I... O my little sorceress!
Everywhere you helped me,
Everywhere you cared for me.
In the steppe, in the vacant steppe,
In distant bondage,
You glowed and gloried
Like a blossom in a field!
You flew pure and sacred
From a filthy barrack
And soared with wings of gold,
Singing high above me...
As if to lift a soul
With a dash of vital water.
I live, and you, my star,
My sacred counselor,
Glow above me
With your godlike beauty!
You're my youthful destiny!
Don't abandon me.
In the nighttime, in the daytime,
In the evening and at early morn,
Stay with me and teach,
Teach me how to tell the truth
With lips that do not lie.
Help me live my prayers
To the very end.
And when I die, my blessed!
You're my mother! Lay your
Son into a coffin,
And shed at least a single tear
In your eternal eyes.

Nizhny Novgorod, February 9, 1858

[488] *Phoebus* — The name used by Roman poets to refer to Apollo, the Greek god of light, prophecy and poetry, music, and healing; twin brother of Artemis.

FAME

And you, floozy, barmaid,
Drunken harlot!
Where was it that you tarried
With a tyrant and your charms?
Did you hand them out on credit
To the robber at Versailles? [489]
Did you entice another
When you were bored and tipsy?
Just snuggle up to me,
We'll make the best of it,
And oh so nicely we'll embrace.
Then, my gorgeous lady,
We'll quietly exchange a joke,
A peck, and we'll marry one another.
Because I still swagger after you.
Though you put on airs
With assorted drunken Caesars,
You lurched around in taverns,
Especially with
That Nicholas [490] in Sevastopol, —
That's all the same to me.
For me, my fate,
Let me gaze at you,
Let me hold you close,
To be snug beneath your wing,
Sleeping sweetly in the shade.

Nizhny Novgorod, February 9, 1858

THE WITCH [491]

I pray, again I hope,
Again I pour out tears,
And share the burden of my muse
With the silent walls.
Respond, O silent ones,
Lament with me
The falsehoods of humanity
And an awful fate.
Respond!
And perhaps hard luck,
So ever wary, will take your lead,
To respond as well and deign
To smile upon us.
It will square us with misfortune,
And will thank us kindly.
It'll cry, pray,
Then lay quietly to sleep.
The meek man will dream
Of decent people, love,
And goodness. He'll rise
At dawn delighted
And forget again his trouble.
In bondage he'll see paradise,
He'll see liberty
And all-embracing love.

Near the Feast of Nicholas, [492]
Gypsies, tattered, nearly naked,
Walked at night along Bendery road.
And walking…

---

489 *Robber at Versailles* — Reference to Emperor Napoleon III (1808-73), who replaced the Second French republic with authoritarian rule.

490 See glossary or fn. 347

491 *The Witch* — Shevchenko reworked his earlier poem of the same name after returning from exile.

492 *Feast of Nicholas* — St. Nicholas Day, December 19th on the Julian Calendar.

They were free, of course, and sang.
Onward, onward, then they stopped.
They pitched a tent beside the road,
Lit a giant fire,
Gathered 'round it,
Some with shish-kabobs,
Some to merely sit,
Each, though, free as once were Kozaks.
They sit, they doze.
And behind the tent amid the steppe,
A young wife sings, sounding like
A drunken woman
Coming from a wedding.

> "In a home of newlyweds
> The couple went to sleep,
> The bride then dreamed
> Her mother went berserk,
> That her husband's father married,
> And her own had drowned.
> And... hoo..."

The gypsies laugh and listen:
"And how'd those people get here?
They're probably
From beyond the Dniester.
For all around is steppe...
A ghost! A ghost!"
The gypsies shouted,
Clutching one another.
And that which sang
Appeared before them...
Fear and sorrow!
Some person shivered in a patchy coat,
Blood from bitter frost
Beaded on the hands and feet; it caked,
And burrs entangled in her lengthy braids
Tussled with her skirt!..
She stood, then sat
Beside the fire, and warmed her hands
Upon the very flames.
"Well, okay,
A wretch got married!" —
She seemed to whisper to herself.
And she smiled very dreadfully.
What's this? It's not a ghost.
It's my mother and my sister.
It's my witch, so you may know.

GYPSIES
Where ya from, young wife?

WITCH
Who, me?

(Sings)

"When I was still a youthful wife,
They kissed me in the face,
But when I turned into a plain old hag,
If they'd kiss me, I'd be glad."

GYPSY
A songstress, not half bad!
To get one just like her,
With a bear as well...

WITCH

I sing,
Regardless if I sit or dance.
I always sing, I always sing,
I've forgotten how to talk…
I once spoke quite well.

GYPSY

Where were you? Did ya go astray?

WITCH

Who, me? Or you?

(Whispers)

Just hush, hush.
There, you see, the master sleeps with me.
The fire's out, the moon is rising,
A werewolf grazes in the valley…

(Smiling)

At the wedding fete I'd gotten drunk,
And for the girl it did not work…
It's those damned lords
That do such things to maidens…
Yet another must be married off,
I'll go, because without me
They'll not even know
How to place a body in a grave.

GYPSIES

Don't go, poor dear, remain with us,
Life with us, by God, is good.

WITCH

And have you any children?..

GYPSIES

None.

WITCH

Whom then do you feed?
Whom do you lay down to sleep?
Who is it that you rock at night?
When you rest and when you wake,
Who is in your prayers? Oh, children!
Always children! Always children!
I know not where to hide from them.
Where'er I go, they're right behind,
They'll someday devour me…

GYPSIES
Don't cry, poor dear, don't worry:
We've neither children nor their wailing...

WITCH
May as well just leap
From a hill into the water...

She then cried and cried.
The gypsies wondered silently,
Until they fell asleep,
Each dropping where they were.
But she was sleepless and unworried,
She sat and stuck her feet
Into the heated ashes;
A waning moon rose o'er a mound,
And seemed to peek inside the tent,
Until obscured by clouds.

Why does the rich, the gray
And well-fed man not sleep?
Why does the poor old
Orphan stay awake?
One ponders how
To quickly build his mansions.
The other thinks of how to pay
For tolling of his funeral bell.
One old man will rest forever
In a splendid coffin,
The other will get by
Beneath a fence somewhere.
And both shall rest without a care.
Of the poor they'll
Make no mention,
And the other they will curse.

An old gypsy sits a dozing
With a pipe beside the fire,
He gazes at the stray,
Caring not about a funeral bell.

GYPSY
Why not lay, and why not rest?
Look, the morning star is rising.

WITCH
I looked, now you look.

GYPSY
Come morning we'll move on,
We'll leave you,
If you don't wake up...

WITCH
I won't wake up!
Now I'll never wake,
I'll just perish anywhere
In a patch of weeds...

(Sings quietly)

"O grove, O shady grove,
O the quiet Danube,
I'll frolic in the grove,
In the Danube I will swim.
I'll unwind amid green algae…
I'll bring along perhaps
At least a crippled child!.."
Whatever, just so long as it can walk,
And knows enough
To curse its mother.
There… there… do you see?
A cat winks on the mound,
Come to me… Kitty, kitty…
The lousy creature isn't coming!
Or else, I'd give you drink
From my sparkling well…

(Sings)

"There's kutia [493] in the corner,
And children in the oven nook.
She begot them, she produced them,
And has no place to put them.
To drown them?
Smother them?
Or to sell them to a Jew for blood,
And drink away the cash?"

What, do our people treat you well?
Just sit closer, here. That's just it!
And you don't know…
That I was in Wallachia! [494]
When I remember, I'll relate it.
In Bendery [495] I bore twins.
I rocked their cradle in white Iasi, [496]
Bathed them in the Danube
Swaddled them in Turkey,
And brought them home —
All the way to Kyiv.
And at home,
Without incense, without holy water,
I had them christened for three coins,
And drank away three others.
I got drunk, I got drunk!
And drunk I still remain!...
And now I'll never rest.
For now I fear not even God
And feel no public shame.
If I could find those kids somewhere!
Don't you know,
If there's perhaps a war in Turkey?

GYPSY

Once there was, now there's not,
The oldest officer has died.

WITCH

And I thought there was, even now…
But now it seems there's none.
So listen up, I'll tell you,
Who it is I'm looking for.
I seek little Natalie…
And my son Ivan.
My little daughter Natalie…
And I seek the lord,

---

[493] *Kutia* — A wheat pudding traditionally served in Ukraine on Christmas Eve. It is made of ground poppy seeds, wheat berries, honey, nuts and sometimes raisins.

[494] *Wallachia* — A principality between the Danube and southern Carpathians founded in the 14th century.

[495] *Bendery* — A Wallachian city in what today is Moldova. It was captured by Russia from the Ottomans during the Russo-Turkish War.

[496] See glossary or fn. 225

That Herod, you know what?
Hold on. I now recall.
I was young and had no inkling,
I strolled throughout the orchard grove,
Adorned with flowers, proud.
And that Herod eyed me!..
In my dreams I did not know
That I was just a serf,
Or I'd have drowned myself,
For that would have been simpler.
So he eyed me,
And takes me in the chambers,
Cuts my hair just like a boy,
And takes me with him on a trip.
In Bendery we arrived.
We stayed with soldiers in their quarters,
And the soldiers fought the Turk
Past the Danube River.
There God gave me twins,
Just before the Savior's Feast.
And he abandoned me,
He did not let me in the house,
Nor did the cursed Lucifer
Even glance at his own children!
With the bastards I returned
Through steppes, through thorns,
And shorn, back to my Ukraine.
Whatever. In villages
I asked for roads to Kyiv…
And how the people laughed at me!!
I nearly drowned myself,
But felt sorry for the little twins.
In fits and starts I weaved my way
To my native land… I rested,
Waiting until evening,
And went into the village,
Because, you see, I did not want
A soul to know.
To my house I crept.
It's dark inside, my father's out
Or perhaps he's gone to sleep.
I barely tread and walk inside the house.
And something's moaning as if dying, —
It's my father.
There's no one there to fold his hands
Or to sign the cross. O damned
And wicked children,
What do you contrive on earth!..
I was frightened,
The home reeked as if deserted,
So in the shed I hid the twins,
Then rushed into the house,
And he was barely breathing.
Me to him: "Daddy!
My daddy! It is I that's come."
I grabbed his arms.
"It's I," I say. And to me he whispers:
"I forgive. I forgive."
That is all I heard.
I collapsed, it seems. And slept.
If only I had slept forever!
At midnight I awoke —
Like in a hole and in the house.
And father grips my hand.
I scream, "Daddy! Daddy!"
But he's already cold as ice…
I twisted hard to free my hand.
So, gypsy!
If your daughter was a bitch like that.
What would you do?

GYPSY

I don't know, by God!

WITCH

Oh, be quiet, or I'll forget.
I'll later not recall.
The kids, you see,
I fed and hid them in a crib.
And I lined a cap with oakum,
That was in the morning,

So none would know that I was shorn.
I tidied up and walked around
While people in the yard
Started working on the coffin.
They finished, laid him in,
Carried, and then buried him…
And I, alone, like a blade of field grass,
Remained here in this world…
There were children,
But they did not remain.

"I walked across the valley
Bringing water back,
Alone I baked a wedding loaf,
I gave away my daughter's hand,
And married off my son!..
And… hoo…"

GYPSY
Don't whimper, 'cause you'll wake them all!

WITCH
Do I whimper, crazy man?

GYPSY
Well, okay, okay, what's next?
Tell me more…

WITCH
What's it worth to you?
Will you make some grits tomorrow?
I'll bring the corn…

I remember! I remember!
To his bed he took his daughter…
He turned his son into a lackey…
The people drove me from the house…
I remember.
With beggars under windows
I provoked the dogs.
And the bastard twins
I carried on my back.
So they'd get accustomed…
Until he himself returned.
I threw myself at him,
Forgetting all the evil.
He greeted me, the Lucifer,
Blessed the children
And took them to the chambers…
My blossoms grow!
And they grew up. He gave our son, Ivan,
To some lady as a lackey. And Natalia…
Are all you gypsies now asleep?

GYPSY
All asleep.

WITCH
So my word they may not hear.
It will be awful.
And you, my aging friend,
Will be frightened when I say it…
Is it all the same to you?
Little Natalie! His child!
Herod the perverse!..
Destroyed!... And me, you see,
He sends for prayers to Kyiv.
And I, the fool, went and prayed…

No, I prayed in vain, my gypsy.
Does any kind of god
Exist among your people?
He is not among us…
He's been stolen by the lords
And hidden in a lacquer box.

Coming back from Kyiv —
The rooms are closed.
He took Natalie
And went somewhere with her…
Do you hear?
The damned one sheared his child.
I flew to find him in Wallachia.
And I search.
Like an owl I fly above ravines.
I seek children, little children,
Little Natalie! No, no, no, no!
I seek the lord. Him I'll tear apart!..
Take me, gypsy, with you,
I'll lead the bear,
And when I find the tyrant,
I'll sic the bear on him.
Begone, the damned!..
No, I'll not sic the bear.
I'll gnaw him all myself…
Do you hear?
We'll marry, sweetheart,
I am still a maiden.
I've married off my son,
And my daughter will remain as is.
We prowl beneath the fences
Till people find me dead. Did you see?
My lovely son Ivan is there…
Ooow, it's cold!
Lend me money,
I'll buy a fancy necklace,
And I'll hang you with it.
Myself I'll then head home…
Look, a mouse, a mouse,
Taking little mice to Kyiv.
You'll not get them there,
You'll drown them
On the way somewhere!
Or the lord will seize them!..
Will I find my children,
Or will I simply perish?

She then fell silent, as if sleeping.
The gypsies all began to rise,
Taking down their tent,
Preparing for the road ahead,
And they hit it. They rode the steppe.
And she, the luckless wretch,
Got up without a word
And said a silent prayer to God,
Then hobbled off to catch
The gypsies. And quietly,
Very quietly she sang:

"People talk of Judgment Day,
But that day will never come,
For I've been judged already
By people in this world."

And from beyond the Dniester
The gypsies traveled to Volyn
And also to Ukraine.

They passed village after village,
They walked around the towns,
And the stray they led along
Like an apparition.
She sang, she danced,
She did not eat or drink…
Through villages she walked,
Walked like death with gypsies,
Then coming to her senses,
She began to eat and drink,
And to hide behind the tents,
And say prayers unto God.
Old Mariula did this to her,
Giving her some herb to drink,
And so it passed.
She then taught her how to heal,
And what derives from what;

Which herbs,
And where to look for them.
How to dry them, how to brew them…
Mariula taught her every, everything.
And she learned,
Saying prayers unto God.
Summer passed, a second came
And then a third;
To Ukraine at last they came…
Did she feel any sorrow?
She bowed at Mariula's feet
For all the lessons taught,
She said farewell to all the gypsies,
And said prayers unto God;
She then went home,
To her own land.
"I'll be back — she said — I'll
See my son and daughter."
It was not to be. The lord returned,
Having left Natalia
In the land of Muscovy.
And you searched for her
Beyond the Dniester.
And the son, your young Ivan,
They handed to the army
Because you taught him
No respect for lords.
Whom can you now lean on?
There's no one!..
Lean on people, wretch,
People will receive you.

Upon return the lord took ill,
He's now moaning and expiring.
She gathered herbs
And went to treat him in the mansion,
To help and not to curse.
She did not help the sick man,
Because they did not let her.
When he died,
She prayed to God for him.
She lived a saintly life,
Teaching girls not to love the lords,
And not to shun the people.
"Or God will punish you,
And what's worse, so will people.
People have their pride, they're fake,
And judge by their own justice."
Thus she taught,
And healed the sick.
And with the poor she shared
The only crumbs she had.
People good and wise
Knew her very well.
But they called her, nonetheless,
An unwed mother and a witch.

Nizhny Novgorod, March 6, 1858

I count the days and nights in bondage,[497]
And forget the count.
O Lord, how hard the days go by.
And among them flow the years,
Softly drifting,
Taking with them good and evil!
They take, returning nothing evermore!
And do not plead, because your prayer
Will be lost on God.

Three years sadly followed others
Through murky swamps and weeds.
They took a lot from my dim shed
And washed it softly out to sea.
The sea swallowed quietly
Not some gold or silver —

[497] Shevchenko wrote a very similar poem in 1850.

But my years, my goodness,
Boredom, pain,
And unseen tablets[498]
Written with an unseen pen.

Let the years of bondage
Drift amid the weeds
Of putrid swamps. And I!
Such is my commandment!
I'll sit a bit and frolic,
I'll watch the steppe, the sea,
I'll recall a thing or two, and sing,
Then I'll begin to scribble
In my little book. I'm off.

St. Petersburg, 1858

DREAM

To Marko Vovchok[499]

She reaped wheat in serfdom,
Weariness set in; it's not for rest
That she hobbled to the sheaves,
But to feed her son, her Ivan.
The child cried, swaddled
In the shade behind a sheaf.
She unwrapped him,
Fed and pampered him.
Sitting by her son she dozed,
Then dreamed. She dreamed
Her Ivan to be handsome, rich,
Not alone, but married
To a freewoman, because, you see,
He himself is not a serf, but free;
They're on a happy field of their own,
Reaping wheat that is their own,
And their children bring them lunch.
The wretch then smiled, awoke —
There's nothing...
She glanced quickly at her son,
Took him, swaddled him again,
And to keep at bay the *overseer,*
She went to reap
Another three-score sheaves.

St. Petersburg, November 22, 1858

---

498 *Unseen tablets* — Tablet with sacred text. Used here as a figurative allusion to the poet's own life.
499 *Marko Vovchok (1833-1907)* — Pen name of Maria Oleksandrivna Markovych, a Ukrainian writer.

I'm not unwell, knock on wood,
But the eye sees something,
And the heart is yearning too.
It hurts, it hurts, it does not rest,
Like a child unfed.
You await perhaps a dark
And wicked hour? Don't await well-being,
Don't bank on hopes for freedom —
It sleeps: put to sleep by Nicholas.
To awaken feeble freedom,
The world, society must temper axe heads,
Then finely sharpen blades,
And begin at last to waken.
If not, the wretch will sleep
Until God's day of Final Judgment!
And nobles will assuage,
Building palaces and churches,
They'll love their drunken czar,
And will glorify the byzantine.
Beyond that, nothing more.

St. Petersburg, November 22, 1858

IMITATION OF PSALM XI

My dear God, how few
Saintly people remain upon this world.
Each forges for another
Shackles in the heart.
Yet with honeyed words upon their lips
They kiss, bide time, and ask,
Will their brother soon be carried
In a coffin from a gathering
To a graveyard?
But You, our only Lord,
Will seal the evil lips
And hold the haughty tongue that says:
"We're not vanity!
We'll exalt for all to marvel at
Our wisdom and our tongue…
And where's the lord who would forbid
Our thoughts and speech?"
"I'll resurrect! —
That Lord will tell you, —
I'll resurrect today! For their sake,
For my shackled people,
For the poor, the destitute… I'll exalt
Those mute and lowly slaves!
And beside them as a sentry
I will place the word.
And your thoughts and speech will wither
Just like trampled grass."
Your lofty words, O Lord,
Resemble silver, forged, struck,
And seven times refined by fire in a furnace.
Spread Your holy words
All throughout the world.
And Your little, poor and lowly children
Will believe Your wonders here on earth!

St. Petersburg, February 15, 1859

TO MARKO VOVCHOK[500]

In Remembrance of January 24, 1859

Not long ago,
I wandered past the Ural River
And beseeched the Lord
That our truth not vanish,
That our word not die; and succeeded.
The Lord delivered you to us,
A gentle prophet and a witness
To the deeds of cruel, voracious people.
My light!
You're my sacred star!
You're my youthful vigor!
Shine on me,
Warm, revive my heart
For it is bare, beaten, poor and hungry.
I'll revive, and from the coffin where it lies,
I'll return free thought to freedom...
And the muse of liberty...
O destiny! Our prophet!
O my daughter!
I'll call the muse your own.

St. Petersburg, February 15, 1859

ISAIAH. CHAPTER 35

Imitation

O arid field, O barren earth
Rejoice, rejoice with florid grain!
Bloom with lilies, blossom!
You'll grow green and blossom
Like the Jordan's sacred verdant banks!
Carmel's[501] honor and righteous glory
Of the range in Lebanon[502]
Will drape you with a holy vestment
Sewn with golden thread by masters,
And lined with decency and freedom.
Then sightless, unenlightened people
Will see wonders of the Lord.

And tired captive hands will rest,
So too will knees confined in chains!
Rejoice, O needy souls,
Do not fear the wonder, —
It's God that judges, freeing
You, the languishing and poor.
And rendering justice to the evil!

When the sacred truth
Descends to earth, O Lord,
For at least an hour's rest,
The blind will see,
The lame will bolt like chamois.[503]
Lips of mutes will open;
The word will surge like water,
And arid desert wilds
Will burgeon,
Washed by healing water;
Joyous rivers will spring forth,
Lakes will all be ringed by groves,
Alive with happy birds.

---

500 See fn. 499

501 *Carmel* — A mountain ridge in Palestine and Biblical symbol of beauty and fertility.

502 *Range in Lebanon* — Mountain range in Northern Palestine.

503 *Chamois* — A very agile goat-antelope (*Rupicapra rupicapra*) in European mountains.

Steppes and lakes will come to life,
Sacred roads will spread,
Roads not bound by markers,
But free and broad in all directions;
Masters will not find those roads,
But slaves will congregate
Upon them happily and joyously,
Without hue and cry.
And the desert masters
Will be happy villages.

St. Petersburg, March 25, 1859

N. N.

A lily just like you
Once blossomed on the Jordan.
It made the Holy Word incarnate
And spread it 'round the earth.
If you too, O Dniester blossom...
No, no! God forbid! They'd crucify.
They'd lead you shackled to Siberia.
And you, my unprotected blossom...
I'll not say it...
O Lord, send her, grant to her
A happy paradise!
Grant her fortune in this world
And give her nothing else.
Don't take her in the spring
To your celestial paradise, please don't,
But leave Your beauty undisturbed
To be marveled at on earth.

St. Petersburg, April 19, 1859

THE SLAVE[504]

A Poem

DEDICATION

O my youthful thoughts —
My gloomy children,
You too have abandoned me!..
There's no one left to warm my void,...
I remain, but not an orphan,
But with you, my youthful paradise,
My serenity, my morning star,
My only pristine thought. You hover...
As you did with Numa[505]
And the nymph Egeria,[506]
Thus, you too, my star,
Twinkle high above me,
As if to talk,
To smile... I look —
I see nothing...
I awaken — the heart cries,
And eyes begin to weep.
Thank you, little star!
My hazy day
Is passing; it's now twilight,
And already the uncertain reaper
Holds his unhoned scythe
Above the head...
He'll mow without a word,
And then — a chilly wind will
Scatter my trace too... All is fleeting!..
O young star, you'll recall perhaps
My muse poured out in tears,
And you'll say: "I loved him in this
World, and I'll love him in the next..."
O my peaceful world,
O my evening star!
I'll drift along beside you
And will beseech the Lord for you!

That one roams beyond the seas,
He rambles o'er the world,
Seeking fate and fortune —
They're nowhere to be found...
It seems they died;
And that one chases destiny
Using all his might...
He nearly, nearly overtakes it —
Then ka-boom into the grave!
Another wretch has neither home
Nor field, just a sack, and from
That sack peeks fortune
Like a little babe; but he curses it,
Condemns it, and pawns it for a
Quarter liter — No, he won't
Abandon it!
Like a burr, he grasps
His patched lapels,
Collecting spikes of grain
Upon a foreign field.
Over there are sheaves,
Over yonder — stacks.
And in a mansion thither,
Sits a wretch,
As if he were at home.
Such is this thing called destiny,
Do not bother searching for it:
Whom it covets it will find,
It will find them in the cradle.

This all happened long ago
When the Hetmanate yet ruled,
When villages still gloried
In the happy land of our Ukraine,

---

504 *The Slave* — This poem is a rewrite of Shevchenko's 1845 verse entitled *The Blind Man.*

505 *Numa Pompilius (753-673 BC)* — Legendary second king of Rome. Successor to Romulus.

506 *Egeria* — A nymph in early Rome. Divine consort and counselor of Numa Pompilius.

When an aging Kozak
With his two young children
Led a righteous life.
So it was around midday, a Sunday,
It was even Pentecost,
That an aging Kozak in a bright white shirt
Sat beside a house, a bandura in his hands.
"This way, and that way!" —
Reflects and says the old man. —
It should be, says he,
But it's somewhat of a pity.
But it needs to be; for two-three years
Let him wander through the world,
On his own he'll search for his,
Just as I once searched. Yaryna!
Where's Stepan?" —
"There he is, he's standing
By the fence, as if he was embedded."
"But I don't see! Just come right here;
Go now, both of you!..
Alright, kids, try this!" —
And he hit the strings.
The old man plays, while Yaryna
Gaily dances with Stepan!
The old man plays, he sings along,
Tapping with his feet:

"If I'd encounter double trouble,
And my husband's mom was calm,
If my husband was a young man,
Who did not love another."
"Oh hop, click, click!
With a pair of bright red shoes
And a trio of musicians, —
I'd love my husband
Till the day I die.
O hop, he came to see her,
Built a house, and they got married,
He lit a fire in the oven
And cooked a meal for dinner."
"Hey, kids, like this, kids!"
And the oldster raised himself.
See him thump and see him hit it —
He even danced with arms akimbo.
"Is it so or is it not,
Some parsnip grew a lot.
Cut some parsley
For the broth —
Oh how tasty it will be,
Yes it's so, indeed it's so
That a Kozak once got married,
But he left his room
He left his home
And took off for the valley."

"No, it's not the same,
My former strength is all worn out,
I'm tired... it's your doing
To have stirred me up,
Oh, confound you!
What's the toll of time?
No, I'm no longer fit,
It's all passed me by.
The only dancing left
They say, is to get piece of bread
And to make some lunch.
Just sit. Stepan, you were little when
They killed your father, Ivan, during
Rule of the Aristocrats;
You had yet to crawl..." —
"So I'm not a son, dad,
I'm a stranger to you?"
"Why no, you're not a stranger,
Just hold on.
Then your mother died,
And you were left alone;
And I tell the late Maryna,
My wife: "So, — I say, —
We'll take him as a child?"
Namely you. 'Good,' —
Says the late Maryna, —
Why not take him?' — We took you
Then we paired you with Yaryna,
The two of you together...
And here's what's left to do.
You're of age,

Yaryna is maturing.
Need to find some people
And get a few things done.
What say you?" — "I don't know,
Because I thought that..."
"That Yaryna is your sister?
She's not.
Quite simply, love each other
And God be with you at your wedding.
Meanwhile, you need to look
How others live;
If they plow,
If they sow on unplowed fields
And simply take the harvest,
Then winnow grain unthrashed.
How they grind, and how they eat —
All that must be known.
So here's the plan, my partner:
For a year or two
You need to work for others;
Then we'll see what comes.
Because he who knows
Not how to earn
Will know not how to live.
What do you think, my man?
And if you want to know, my son,
Where best to deal with trouble,
You should live upon the Sich,
And if the Lord will help you out,
You'll get your fill of every bread.
I ate my share,
And still feel stuffed when I recall it!
If you acquire it, you'll bring it,
If you lose it, you'll still live,
My good son! You'll learn, at least,
Of Kozak customs
And you'll see the world.
It won't be like the seminary,
Instead with fellow Kozaks,
You'll read a living alphabet.
Like a young man
You will pray to God,
You won't mumble like a monk.
Thus, my son, having prayed to God,
We'll saddle up the dun
Then you'll hit the road!
Let's just go and have some lunch.
Did you, Yaryna, fix us something?
So it is, my son..."
"It's ready, daddy!" — Yaryna
Answered from the house.
Neither eating, neither drinking,
Nor is there any heartbeat,
The eyes don't see, the head feels nothing.
It's not a piece of bread,
But a ladle that he reaches for;
Yaryna watches and laughs quietly:
"What's come over him?
Neither food, nor drink,
There's nothing that he wants!
Has he fallen sick?
Brother Stepan! What ails you?" —
Yaryna asks. The old one is indifferent,
As if he does not hear.
"To reap, or not to reap,
There's still a need to sow, —
The old man speaks,
It looks like to himself. —
Let's all get up, perhaps I'll mosey over
For the evening service.
And you, Stepan, will go to sleep,
Because you'll need rise come morning
To saddle up the horse."

"O Stepan, my dearie!
Why is it that you cry?
Smile, look,
Oh, don't you see I weep as well?
He's mad at God knows whom
And doesn't talk to me.
I'll run away, by God,
I'll hide amid the weeds.
Say something, my Stepan!
Perhaps you're really ill?
I'll get some herbs,
I'll run to call the seer,

Perhaps it's from the evil eye?"
"No, Yaryna, my dear heart,
O my glowing blossom!
O Yaryna, I'm not a brother to you!
Tomorrow I'll leave you and father,
And I'll perish
In a foreign land somewhere.
And you won't mention me,
You'll just forget your brother..."
"Be sensible! By God, it is
The evil eye.
Not a sister! Who then am I?
O my God, my world,
What is to be done?.. Father's gone,
He's taken ill, and may yet even die!..
O my God! And he's indifferent,
Looking like he's laughing.
Stepan, my dear!
Don't you know that dad and I
Will not last without you?"
"No, Yaryna, I won't leave you,
I'll just go not far away.
I'll return next year
And then come to you
With matchmakers,
Requesting wedding scarves.
You'll offer them?"
"Enough talk of wedding elders!
He has the nerve to joke!" "It's no joke,
So help me God, Yaryna..." —
"So it's true you'll go away
From me and father in the morning?..
No, you're joking.
Tell me, please, Stepan!
Am I truly not a sister?"
"No, my love!
My dear heart!" — "O my God,
Why did I not know?
I would not have loved you
Nor would I have kissed you.
Oh, oh, what shame! Go away from me.
Let me go! See, how good he is!
Just let me go! By God, I'll cry."
And Yaryna burst out crying
Like a little child.
And through her tears she said:
"He'll leave! He'll leave!"

Stepan leaned just like a sycamore
Beside the water.
Earnest Kozak tears
Boiled in his heart!
They burned like hell...
In turns Yaryna
Curses, pleads, falls silent... looks,
And wails again!

Twilight caught them unawares.
The father came upon
The sister and the brother,
Embracing as if bound together.

Daylight dawned, and Yaryna's
Not asleep — but crying.
Stepan is at the well
Already watering his horse.
And she ran to the well
Supposedly for water...
Meanwhile, from the shed,
The old man brings
A Zaporizhian weapon.
He looks, rejoices,
And tries it out for size... as if
The oldster was rejuvenated!
And he wept... "My weapon!
O my golden weapon!
My youthful years,
My youthful strength!
Perform, my faithful weapon,
For valor that's still young!
Perform for him as earnestly,
As you did for me!"

From the well they both returned,
Stepan saddles up the horse, his friend,
And dons a Kozak overcoat.

Standing on the doorstep,
Yaryna hands the weapon;
His sword is serpent-like,
His spear a sharpened rod,
And across his back he slung
A gun that measured seven palms.
She fainted at the sight;
And the old man cried
When he saw atop the horse
A rider that was such a fine young lad.
Yaryna takes the reins to lead the horse
And cries along the way.
The father walks beside,
And instructs his son.
How to function in the army,
How to honor his superiors,
To respect the brotherhood,
And not hole up in camp.
"May God protect you!" —
Said the old man,
Stopping at the village edge,
And the three of them
Together all began to cry.
Stepan shouted, then dust
Rose up along the road.
"Do not linger,
Come back soon, my son!.." —
Said the aging man.
Yaryna leaned just
Like a valley spruce.
Yaryna did not say a word,
She merely wipes her tears,
And looks on down the road.
Something flickers in the dust
Then vanishes again.
It seems a hat across the field.
It rolls, it's silhouetted…
It vanishes… and like a gnat
It barely… barely… glimmers,
Then it disappeared. Yaryna
Stood there for a long, long time
To see if through the dust
Perhaps the insect won't return.
It did not — it vanished! Yaryna,
Weeping yet again,
Slowly went back home.

Days pass by, the summer passes,
The season turns to autumn, yellowed
Leaves are rustling; the old father
Sits beside the house
Not unlike a dead man;
Illness grips Yaryna,
His only child wants to leave him;
With whom to live what years are left?
With whom to cap his life?
He recalled his young Stepan,
He recalled his feeble age,
He recalled and cried, that's what
The old gray orphan did.

"All on earth is in Your hands.
Your will is universal!
May Your will be done,
Such is my fate!" —
Said the old man quietly
As he prayed to God
Beside the house;
He then withdrew to
Stroll about the garden.

Spring adorns the earth with
Primrose, rue and periwinkle;
Like a girl in a verdant grove.
And the sun rose higher in the sky,
It stopped, and eyed the earth
As would a fiancé his bride.
And Yaryna left the house
To take a look at God's good world,
But she barely walked…
She'll smile, she'll go and stop,
Look around and wonder
Oh so quietly and dearly,
As if born just yesterday…
And the raging anguish…
In her very heart it stirred.

And set the earth on fire.
Yaryna wilted like a
Blade of grass mowed over;
Tears rolled forth like
A flower's morning dew.
The old father stood beside her,
Leaning over like an oak.

Yaryna was restored to health.
People go to pray in Kyiv and Pochayiv
And she comes along.

In the great Kyiv
She prayed to all the saints;
She took Communion thrice
At the Mezhyhirsky Savior.
In Pochayiv at the sacred monastery
She wept and prayed
That her Stepan, his fate,
Would at least appear
To her in dreams!..
No dreams. She returned.
White winter once again had
Whitened everything.
After winter came God's
Spring and greenery.
Yaryna left the house
To wonder at the world,
And not to beg the sacred Lord,
But to ask a seer about Stepan
In a manner quite discreet.

The seer saw,
Conjured up the evil eye,
Then molded fate and marriage
From melted wax on water.
"There, you see, a saddled horse
That stomps its foot
Beneath a Kozak;
And walking there's a grandpa
With a beard down to his knees.
That means money.
If the Kozak thought to scare
The elder;
Yes, he scares him
Then hides behind a mound,
Counts the money,
And again the Kozak goes,
Acting like a beggar,
Out of fear, you see,
So that Poles or Tatars
Don't confront him."
Thus Yaryna left
And went back home quite happy.

It's a third, a fourth,
And now a fifth year that has passed,
Not a short year.
And Stepan remains away, away.
In the valley past the hill
The little way and footpath
To the seer is now
Overgrown with grass.
Still no sign of him.
And the luckless one undoes her braid
To become a nun,
The old father falls
And pleads beside her,
To wait a year, a summer,
Until Saint Peter's or at least
The Pentecost. They waited, and
Nicely decked the house,
Then dressed in bright white shirts,
They sat beside the house unhappily
Like a pair of orphans.
There they sat, they grieved,
And listened... something's playing
On the street, it's like a kobza
And it seems there's singing.

DUMA[507]

"Early Sunday morning
The azure sea rolled on,
Comrades of the Kozak chief
Requested at a council:
"Give your blessing, otaman,
To launch the baidaks,[508]
To frolic past the Isle of Tender,[510]
And to find the Turk."
They launched the chaikas[509]
And baidaks,
Equipping them with cannons,
And then set sail
From the Dnipro's mouth.
In the darkness of the night
Upon the azure sea,
Just beyond the Tender,
They began to sink
And perish.
One boat sinks,
Another bobs,
A Kozak waved his hand, shouting loudly
To his brethren from an azure wave:
"May God help you, brothers!"
And in that azure wave he sinks,
And perishes.
Just three ill-fated chaikas
Weren't sunk beneath the sea,
Among them the otaman's, thank God,
And that of Stepan, the young orphan.
The sea, instead, drove them
Without rudder to captivity
In the land of Turks and Muslims.
Then the Turkish janissaries
Caught the orphan Stepan,
A Kozak duly registered,
And they caught the youthful otaman.
They opened fire with cannons,
Forging shackles,
Throwing captives into harsh captivity.
O our Mezhyhirsky Savior,
Our miraculous savior!
Don't let even fiercest enemies
Fall into the land of Turks,
Into such harsh and hard captivity.
The shackles are three heavy poods,[511]
And otamans get four.
They never see nor know
God's light of day,
They break up rocks
Beneath the ground,
And croak like dogs
Without the sacrament of confession.
In this captivity the orphan Stepan
Thought about his faraway Ukraine,
About his old and unrelated father,
About his jet-black horse,
And Yaryna, his unrelated sister.
He cries, he weeps,
He lifts his hands to God,
Then breaks his chains
And runs for liberty, for freedom…
The Turkish janissaries
Caught him
On the third of many fields,
They tied him to a stake,
And burned away his eyes,
Using glowing iron rods,
Then they fastened him
With shackles,
Threw him in a dungeon,
And sealed it up
With bricks."

---

507 *Duma* — An epic poem sung in recitative style by kobzars, blind Ukrainian itinerant musicians.
508 See glossary or fn. 191
509 See glossary or fn. 189
510 See glossary or fn. 190
511 See glossary or fn. 193

A kobzar still quite young
Stood and sang about a captive.
Behind the fence Yaryna listened,
And not hearing how it ends, she fell.
"O Stepan! My dear Stepan! —
She screamed and wept. —
My dear Stepan, my little sweetheart,
Where is it that you tarried?
Daddy! Come here, daddy!
Come and take a look."
The old man comes, he gazes,
And recognizes not his own Stepan,
That's what shackles did to him.
"O my hapless son, my child!
Where on earth have you been suffering,
My one and only son?"

The old one cries, he weeps,
And Stepan the blind one cries
With his sightless eyes,
As if he'd seen the sun.
They take him by the arms,
And lead him to the house,
And Yaryna greets him,
As if he really was her brother.
She washed his head,
And washed his feet.
And sat him by the table,
Dressed in a thin white shirt.
She fed him, filled his glass,
And laid him in a room to sleep...
Then softly left the house with father.

In a week and with no matchmakers
The old man gave Stepan
Yaryna's hand in marriage.
And Yaryna stayed at home.
"No, my father, there's no need,
There's no need, Yaryna, —
Stepan says. — I perished,
Forever I have perished.
Why waste your youthful years
Living with a cripple? Yaryna!
People will make fun,
And the sacred Lord will punish
And will banish fortune
From this happy home
To a stranger's field.
No, Yaryna, God won't leave you,
You will find a mate,
And I'll go to Zaporizhia.
I won't die there,
They will feed me" — "No, Stepan,
You're my child,
And the Lord will leave you,
If ever you abandon us."
"Stay, my dear Stepan!
If you do not wish to marry,
We'll be who we are. I'm your sister,
You're my brother,
And the both of us are children
Of our aged father.
Don't leave us, O my dearest Stevie,
Don't leave us once again.
You'll not leave us?.." —
"No, Yaryna..."
And Stepan remained;
The old man exulted like a youngster,
And even grabbed a kobza;
He so wished to whirl and dance
Using all his might...
He couldn't pull it off...
Beside the house
All three sat down.

"Tell us now, Stepan,
About your great misfortune.
Because I too once sauntered
In a Turkish prison."
"And I, already blind,
Was released with comrades.
To go again into the world,
The group of comrades took me
As they headed for the Sich,
Cutting through the Balkans,
Walking on free legs

Toward our dear Ukraine;
And on the placid Danube
We were met by Kozak brothers
Who turned us toward the Sich.[512]
And as they cried they told us
How the Sich was ruined,
How the Muscovites took gold,
Silver and the candlesticks
From Our Lady the Protectress;
How the Kozaks fled at night
To start a new encampment
By the Danube's quiet waters.
How the empress
Walked with Scraggly[513]
Through the city of Kyiv,
And reduced the Mezhyhirsky Savior
To a flaming ruin.[514]
How she sailed the Dnipro
In a golden galleon,
To watch that fire spread
With a subtle, quiet smile.
And how they divvied up the
Zaporizhian steppe,
And enslaved the people
For nobles in Ukraine.
How Kyrylo and his officers
Dusted wigs with powder,
Then licked slippers of the empress
Like a bunch of dogs.
That's the way it was, dad! I'm lucky
That I have no eyes,
That I don't see the world or know
What's happening in it.
Poles were here, seizing all,
Drinking up the blood!..
And Muscovites forged chains
To bind God's lovely world!
That's the way it is! It's hard, dad,
To leave your home
And beg a Turkish infidel
Just to be a neighbor.
Now, they say, Holowaty[515]
In Slobozia[516] gathers those left over
And exhorts the boys to Kuban.[517]
Godspeed to him,
And what comes of it —
The good Lord only knows:
We'll hear what people say about it."
Thus the two of them
Conversed every day till midnight,
As Yaryna kept the house
And pleaded with the saints.
They responded to the pleas.
On a Sunday after Lent
She married her blind man.
This all came to pass
In this world of ours,
My darling girls,
My rosy blossoms.
Thus it was.
My youngsters both got married.
Perhaps, it should not

---

512 *Sich* — Reference to the Trans-Danube Sich (1776-1828), established after Russia destroyed the Zaporizhian Sich in 1775.

513 *Scraggly* — Grigori Alexandrovich Potemkin (1739-91), senior Russian political and military leader. He advised Catherine II to destroy the Kozak Sich. Kozaks called him Scraggly Greg (Hryts Nechesa) because he wore a wig.

514 *Flaming ruin* — A fire at Kyiv's Mezhyhirsky Monastery occurred on the eve of Catherine's departure from the city during a trip to Crimea. She was accompanied by Potemkin. Rumor circulated that she ordered the fire.

515 *Antin Holowaty (1744-97)* — Ukrainian military leader. He helped organize the Black Sea Kozaks and resettled them from the Dniester to the Kuban.

516 *Slobozia* — A city in today's Moldova on the Dniester River.

517 *Kuban* — A region of today's Southern Russia between the Black Sea, the Caucasus and the Volga. It was once heavily populated by Ukrainians.

Be this way,
But what am I to do,
If that is how it happened?
A year has passed already,
Followed by a second.
Yaryna dances 'round
The garden with her loving spouse.
The old father
Sits beside the house
With his little grandson,
And teaches him the proper way
To salute a Kozak.

St. Petersburg, February 5 — April 28, 1859

My dear God, again there's trouble!..
It was so pleasant, it was quiet;
We sought to break the chains
That have bound our slaves.
And suddenly!.. The blood
Of peasants runs again!
Tyrants in their glory
Are gnawing yet again
Like dogs that hunger for a bone.

St. Petersburg, April — May 1859

To Fedir Ivanovych Chernenko[518]
In Remembrance of September 22, 1859[519]

Daisies blossom on a hill,
A Kozak walks the valley
And he asks of sorrow,
Where does fortune revel?

With the rich in taverns?
In the steppe with chumaks?
Or is it freely carried by the wind
Across a field and broad expanse? —

Not there, no, not there,
My friend and brother,
It's with a girl
In a stranger's home,
In a wedding scarf
That's hidden in a brand new chest.

Lykhvyn, June 7, 1859

---

518 *Fedir Ivanovych Chernenko (1818–76)* — Military engineer and architect. Shevchenko's friend who hosted meetings of St. Petersburg's Ukrainian community. Chernenko was custodian of the poet's library after his death.

519 *September 22, 1859* — The dedication came after the poem was written. The occasion is unknown.

I have, I have two lovely eyes,
But to gaze at, mama, I have no one.
I have no one, dear, to gaze at!

I have, I have two lovely arms…
But no one, mama, to embrace,
I've no one to embrace, my dearest!

I have, I have two lovely feet,
But not a soul to dance with, mama,
I've no one, dearest, I can dance with!

Pyriatyn, June 10, 1859

TO MY SISTER[520]

Passing poor unhappy
Villages along the Dnipro banks,
I thought, where will I find refuge,
Where on earth am I to live?
Then I dream a dream: I look,
Standing in a garden
On a hilltop decked with flowers,
Like a girl, is a single cottage.
The Dnipro stretches wide!
The Old Man glistens all ablaze!
I look, and in a darkened orchard,
Beneath a cherry in the shade,
Is my only sister! A saintly martyr!
She rests as if in Paradise
And from beyond the Dnipro
The poor dear waits for me.
It seems to her, a boat emerges
From a wave, drifts…
Then in a wave the boat submerges.
"My brother! My good fortune!"
We then awoke. You…
In serfdom, I in bondage!..
Thus you and I were fated
Yet as children to tread a thorny field!
Pray, my sister! If we live,
God will help us cross.

Cherkasy, July 20, 1859

I had a thought once in my silly head, —
Woe is me!
How am I to live on earth?
To praise the Lord and people?
Like a rotten log in muck,
To lie, grow old, decay,
To die without a trace
Upon a plundered land.
Oh woe! Oh woe is me!
Where on earth am I to hide?
Each day the Pilates crucify,
And torment the meek
With frost or flames.

Cherkasy, July 21, 1859

520 *Sister* — Yaryna Hryhorivna Boyko (1816-65). Like all of Shevchenko's relatives, she remained a serf.

If you, the drunken Bohdan,
Were to look at Pereyaslav[521] now!
If you'd see the castle ruins!
You'd get plastered! Really plastered!
O wise all-exalted Kozak father!..
You'd get sloshed in a smelly
Jewish home, or you'd drown in slop
Beside a bog for pigs.

Amen to you, great statesman!
Great and glorious! But not very…
Had you not been born on earth
Or if you'd gotten plastered
In the cradle…
I would not be bathing you,
The ultra-glorious, in slop. Amen.

Pereyaslav, August 18, 1859

In Judea long ago,
In the time of Herod's reign,
Zion and Mount Zion
Were defiled by Roman legions.
And with the King,
With that selfsame Herod,
Lictors stood inside and on the threshold,
And the king…
An autocratic tyrant!
He licked the lictor's boot,
So that he would lend him
Half a dinar, maybe more;
To purchase this or that;
And that one shakes his pocket,
Takes out money, doesn't count it,
Then hands it over
As if to please a beggar.
And the drunken Herod drinks again!
Then suddenly, not in Nazareth itself,
But in a nearby cave,
Maria bore a son,
And with the infant went to Bethlehem…
A postman runs from Bethlehem
And says: "King!
Such and such has happened!
Thistle, broom[522] and cockle
Are growing in the wheat!
David's cursed tribe has appeared among us!
Cut it down before it grows.
"Well, then, — states the drunken Herod, —
Mow down little children
All throughout the kingdom;
Otherwise the villains
Will not let us rule."
The postman, knock on wood, was drunk,
And passed the order to the senate

521 See glossary or fn. 204

522 *Broom — A* Mediterranean shrub in the pea family. It has bright yellow flowers. Considered an invasive species.

To slaughter little children
In Bethlehem alone.
Save us,
O great and righteous Youngster
From the drunken king and ruler!
You were saved from even worse
By Your all-righteous Mother.
Where are we to get this Mother?
Our hearts are stripped and bare!
We're slaves with cockades on our foreheads!
Lackeys all adorned in gold...
We're but stockings, we're but waste
From the grist of his exalted majesty.
That's all.

St. Petersburg, October 24, 1859

MARIA

A Poem

Rejoice, for you restored those conceived in shame.
Akathist to the Blessed Mother of God. Ikos 10[523]

O my shining Paradise,
All my hope I place in You,
And on Your mercy, Mother.
O sacred power of the saints,
Immaculate and Blessed!
I pray, I cry, I weep:
Behold them, Most Immaculate,
The robbed, unseeing slaves.
Give them power of
Your Son, the martyr,
To bear their chains
To the very utmost limit.
You, most worthy and renowned!
I plead! Queen of earth and heaven!
Relieve their wailing, send
A blessed end, O All Merciful!
And I, without resentment,
Will then sing about the blooming
Of impoverished villages,
And with a calm and joyous psalm
I'll praise Your sacred destiny.

523 *Ikos* — A short composition during an Akathist, or hymn dedicated to Christ, the Blessed Virgin or a saint, in an Orthodox church service.

But today, with crying, tears and sorrow
Of a poor and needy soul —
I present my one last mite.

At Joseph's, at the carpenter's
Or at the sacred cooper's
Is where Maria grew,
She grew there as a servant.
It was family. The poor dear
Thus matured, she grew and grew
Into a maiden...
She blossomed as a rosy flower
In another's poor and humble home,
In a quiet sacred paradise.
The carpenter watched his servant
As if she were his child,
And would at times
Lay down his adze and plane
Just to gaze at her; an hour
Would fly by and he would not
Even blink, thinking all the while:
"She has no family!
Nor has she any home,
She's all alone!.. Unless...
Is death behind my back?.."
And she just stands beneath a fence,
Spinning bright white wool
For his festive cloak,
Or she leads a goat and lovely kid to shore
To graze them, give them water.
Even though it's far. She so loved
The broad Tiberias,[524]
That peaceful godly pond,
And was so glad she laughed, glad
That Joseph, sitting, uttered nothing;
He did not forbid, he did not keep
Her from the pond. She went, laughing,
And the wretch just sat and sat
Not taking plane in hand...
The goat eats and drinks its fill.
And the girl stands beside a grove,
As if planted in the ground,
And looks sadly and unhappily
At that expansive godly pond,
And said: — Tiberias!
Expansive king of ponds!
Tell me, my advisor!
What fate awaits me
And the aging Joseph? O fate! —
And she leaned just like
A valley poplar bending in the wind. —
I'll become for him a child.
My young shoulders
Will support his aging back."
She cast her gaze around
So that sparks flew from her eyes.
And from her youthful shoulders
A patched and ragged chiton
Slipped gently to the floor.
No one will behold
Such godly beauty ever!
But misfortune mocked the
Beauty with a stroke
Of prickly thorns.
Such hard luck!
She went along the water
With a quiet gait.
She found burdock by the shore,
Picked the burdock,
And used it like a little hat
To protect her rueful, sacred head!
She then vanished in a shady grove.
O our world that never sets!
O You, purest of the women!
O exquisite fragrant lily!
In which groves? In which groves,

[524] *Tiberias* — Another name for the Sea of Galilee.

In which unfamiliar caverns do You hide
From the swelter of the blaze
That melts the heart without a flame,
And will burst and drown
Your sacred thoughts?
Nowhere! The fire's ignited! It has spread.
Too bad, power will be lost in vain.
That unquenching raging fire
Will reach the blood and bones,
And You, exhausted, will need
To pass through hellish fire!
Your future prophesies already,
It's peeking in Your eyes. Don't look!
Dry the one prophetic tear!
Adorn Your maiden's head
With lilies and bountiful red poppies.
Then fall asleep beneath a maple's shade,
Before things come to pass.

In the evening, like that star,
Maria leaves the grove bedecked.
Remote and lofty, Mount Tabor
Shines, it seems, with blinding
Gold and silver. Maria smiled
As she turned her gentle eyes toward Tabor.
From the grove she led the goat and kid,
And began to sing:
"Paradise, O paradise!
O you shady grove!
Will I, dear God, a maiden,
Get my fill of dancing
In Your paradise?"
She fell silent.
She looked sadly all around,
Took the goat in hand
And went happily to the
Humble coopers' hamlet.
Along the way, the dear
Rocked, amused and swung
The kid as if it were a babe in arms,
Gently pressing it against her bosom,
Kissing it as well. Like a little kitten,
The kid did not resist or bleat
But played and cuddled in the bosom.
For some two miles with the kid
She nearly, nearly danced
And tired not at all. From the fence
The old man sadly peered,
Long awaiting his child's return.
He met and greeted her,
Saying quietly:
"Where was it that you lingered, dear,
Here on God's good earth?
Let's go inside so you may rest,
And we'll dine together
With a young and joyful guest,
Let's go my daughter." — "Who?
Who's this guest?" "From Nazareth
He came to rest with us." —
He adds: "Early yesterday, God's grace
Was shed on old Elizabeth.
She bore — he says — a child, a son.
And old Zachary named him John...
That's the news, you see!"
The guest, clothed in a
Single bright white chiton,
Left the tent pristine and barefoot,
Shining like a painted picture.
And then, standing grandly
At the threshold,
He bowed and softly hailed Maria.
She, the dear, felt odd and strange.
The guest stood and truly seemed to shine.
Maria looked at him and shuddered.
She clung to her old Joseph
Like a frightened child,
Then with a seeming glance
She bid the youthful guest
A welcome in the tent.
From the well she brought fresh water,
And for supper served them
Cheese and goat milk.
Herself she neither ate nor drank.
Instead she nestled in a corner,
Marveling and looking
At the unfamiliar guest

And listening as he spoke.
His holy words fell upon Maria's heart,
And the heart then froze and burned.

"In Judea, spoke the guest,
What is seen today
Was never seen before. Rabbis,
Rabbis of a splendid word,
Are being sown upon a virgin field!
They'll grow, and then we'll reap,
And in our granary we'll amass
Holy golden grain.
I go among the people
To herald the Messiah!"
And Maria said her prayers
In this apostle's presence.
In the hearth
A fire flickers gently,
As righteous Joseph sits and thinks...
The evening star up in the heavens
Has begun to brightly glow.
Maria stood, took a pitcher
And went to draw some water.
The guest went after, and
Caught up with Maria in the little valley...
In the cool before the sunrise
They accompanied the Herald
To Tiberias's very shore. And pleased,
So very pleased, they returned back home.
Maria waits for him,
While her youthful cheeks,
Her eyes and lips very clearly wither.
"You're not the same,
The same, Maria, you are not!
Our lily, our fair beauty! —
Joseph said. — Something strange,
My daughter, has occurred to you!
Let's go, Maria, we'll get married,
Or else... — This he did not say:
They'll kill you in the street. —
And we'll hide in our oasis."
And Maria hastened to get ready
Crying, weeping bitterly.

And thus they go along,
The old man lugging on his back
A brand new little pail.
It could be sold to buy
A kerchief for the maiden
And to cover wedding costs.
O righteous, wealthy elder!
Grace comes not from Zion,
It was heralded instead
From your peaceful home.
Had you not presented
Your worthy hand to the Immaculate,
We'd still be dying poorer than
The poorest slave. Oh grief!
Oh the heavy torment
Weighing on the soul!
No sorrow, wretches, do I feel for you,
The blind and lowly souls,
I feel it for those who see
An axe and hammer up above
And fashion chains anew.
They'll kill and butcher you,
O murderers, and they'll lead
Their dogs to drink from
A bloody well.
Where is
That strange and evil guest?
He should come at least to see
The glorious and most glorious
Wedding, that despoiled wedding!
No word, not a word
From him or the Messiah,
But people are awaiting something,
Something quite uncertain. Maria!
What do You, the hapless,
Await and will await from God
And also from His people? Nothing,
Even that apostle You should not expect.
An impoverished carpenter
Leads You married
To his humble home.
Pray, be thankful he did not abandon You,
That at a crossroads he did not expel You.

Or else with bricks
They would have killed You —
Had he not hidden and protected You!
People in Jerusalem quietly conversed
About decapitation in Tiberias,
Or did they talk instead about
The crucifixion of some man
Who presaged the Messiah.
"Him!" Maria said,
And went off happily to Nazareth.
And he rejoices that his servant
Carried in Her womb the righteous
Soul of the Man crucified for freedom.

Thus they walk along,
And then arrive at home. They
Live in wedlock, but not happily.
The carpenter on the porch
Crafts a sturdy cradle.
And she, the most Immaculate Maria,
Sits beside the window
Gazing at the field
As she sews a little shirt —
For someone new?
"Is the master home? —
Some yelled outside. — A direct decree
From Caesar, that you today,
This very minute!
That you go into the town
Of Bethlehem to be counted in the census."
And that someone vanished,
That heavy voice was lost.
Just the echo lingered in the valley.

Maria started right away
To bake a batch of flat-cakes.
She baked them, put them gently
In a sack and set out with
The old man to the town of Bethlehem.
"O holy power! Save me, my dear God"
That was all she said.
Both sadly walk along.
The needy pair drives the
Goat and kid ahead,
Because at home there's none
With whom they could be left.
And perhaps along the way
God may send a child; and lo
There's milk for the poor dear Mother.
A goat, grazing, treads along;
In a row behind it
Walk the Mother and the father,
And slowly, quietly they begin to talk.
"The high priest Simeon,[525] —
Said Joseph, —
Told me this prophetic word:
The sacred law!
That of Abraham and Moses!
Will be renewed by Essene statesmen.[526]
He says, I'll not die
Until I see Messiah! '
My Maria, do You hear?
The Messiah's coming!" —
"He's already come,
And we're seen Messiah!" —
Spoke Maria.

Joseph found
A flat-cake in the sack,
He hands it to Maria, saying:
"Here, you must sustain yourself,
My child, lest anything transpire."
Bethlehem is not nearby.
They then sat nicely by the road
For lunch. Thus they sit,
And the righteous sun rolls swiftly down.
And look! It's hidden, and the field
Has dimmed. Then a wondrous wonder!
Such a wonder no one ever saw or heard of.

---

525 *Simeon* — Biblical figure described in Luke, Chapter 2 as a just and devout man who was first to recognize Jesus as the Messiah.

526 *Essenes* — An ascetic Jewish sect that flourished from the 2nd century BC to the 1st century AD.

The holy carpenter even shuddered.
A comet from the east has risen,
A fiery comet above the
Very town of Bethlehem.
It has lit the steppes and hills.
Maria did not rise upon the road,
But bore instead a Son.
The lone Child that
Saved us all from torment!
The Most Holy, innocent,
It was crucified for us, the evil.
Nearby shepherds drove
A flock of sheep and saw them.
The poor Dear and Child they
Sheltered in their cave,
And the humble shepherds
Named the babe Emmanuel.

Before sunrise in the early, early morn!
People gathered at the
Square in Bethlehem
And whispered,
That something quite uncertain
Is to happen to Judeans.
The crowd buzzes then falls silent.
"O people! People! —
Some shepherd runs and shouts. —
The prophecy of Jeremiah and Isaiah
Has finally been fulfilled! Fulfilled!
Among us, the shepherds,
The Messiah was born yesterday!"
A cry swept across the square
In Bethlehem:
"The Messiah! Jesus! Hosanna!"
And the crowd dispersed.
In an hour,
Maybe two, a decree
Came from Jerusalem and a legion too,
And it came from Herod.
What then transpired was unheard of
And never seen before.
Swaddled children yet asleep,
Mothers warmed their baths,
But they warmed for naught:
They did not bathe their children!
The soldiers rinsed their knives
In the righteous blood of children!
That's what came to pass
In this world of ours!
Look, O mothers!
What kings and tyrants do!

Maria with her child
Did not even hide.
Glory be to you, shepherds
And poor people, that you
Welcomed and you hid from Herod
Our most Holy Savior. You gave Him
Food and drink, a sheepskin coat and
Clothing for the road,
And you added, my poor dears,
A milk-producing ass.
And through secret byways
Late at night you led
The wretched Dear and Child
To the Memphis road.
And the comet, the fiery comet
Shined like the sun above,
And watched the ass
That carried into Egypt
The meek Maria
And the new-born Savior.

If an empress in this world
Sat even once upon an ass,
The empress's renown
And the outstanding ass's fame
Would spread around the world.
This one carried the true and living God.
Some poor Copt wished to purchase
You, poor dear, from Joseph,
But you went and died: Was the road
Perhaps a bit too much for you?

The Child, swaddled by fate
And bathed in Nile water,

Calmly sleeps beneath a willow.
Among the reeds, the righteous Mother cries
As she weaves a cradle from those reeds.
And Joseph sought to build a house of cane
To have a roof at night at least.
Like owls beyond the Nile, sphinxes
Watch it all with their dead
And dreadful eyes.
Behind them in a row
Stand pyramids on naked sand,
Like sentries of the pharaohs,
And they seem to tell the pharaohs
That God's justice rises here on earth,
And the pharaohs should beware.

Maria was hired by a Copt
To spin for him some wool.
And Holy Joseph grazed the herd,
To earn money for a goat
So the Child could have milk.
A year goes by. In his little shed
Beside the house,
The righteous holy cooper
Has no inkling,
And joins a cask and barrel
As he hums along. And You?
You don't cry, You do not sing,
You ponder, think and guess,
How to teach and set
Your Holy Son upon a sacred path,
And how to spare Him from all evils?
Guide Him 'round the storms of life?

Another year went by. A goat
Grazes by the house; the Child
And a little kid are playing on the porch.
And the Mother sits beside the house,
Spinning wool from a loaded spindle.
And the old man, cane in hand,
Walks softly by the fence:
He carried tubs to sell in town.
For him a honey biscuit,
For her a simple scarf,
He carries leather for himself
To make a pair of shoes.
He rests and says:
"Do not worry daughter.
King Herod is no more.
He ate something in the evening,
He ate so much he croaked,
That is what they told me.
Let's go, — he says, — into our grove,
Into our little paradise!
Let's go home, my child."
"Let's go," she said, and went
Down to the Nile to wash her Son
Some shirts for the road back home.
The goat grazed with its kid,
And Joseph sitting by the house
Amused his little Son until
The Mother at the river
Cleaned those little shirts.
Then inside the house, he
Flexed the leather on his shoes
For the road ahead. They set off
Before the sun had risen,
With a sack across each back,
And the Child they carried
In a cradle held by both.
One way or another,
They finally made it home.
May no one witness such a sight.
Bliss! A quiet grove amid a field,
That grove their only fortune!
How it thrived cannot be known.
The home and every,
Everything was plundered.
In a ruin they spent the night.
In the valley to the well Maria
Quickly rushed.
The sacred fair-faced guest
Had met her there before.
Thorny thistle, weeds and nettle
Had grown beside the well.
Maria! Woe be unto you!
Pray, pray, my Dear!

Shield Your sacred power...
Shield it with perseverance,
Temper it with bloody tears!..
In that well the wretched Dear
Came very near to drowning.
What grief that would have been
For us the slaves redeemed!
As the Child grew it would
Not have had its Mother,
And we'd still not know
Truth upon this earth!
Sacred liberty! She recovered,
Smiled hard and heavy,
Then broke down in tears.
Her holy tears poured
And dried upon the well-curb.
The poor Dear's load felt lighter.

Elizabeth,
The aging widow with her youthful son,
Lived in Nazareth,
Indeed with little John. She was a distant
Relative of theirs. In the early morn,
The hapless Mary fed and dressed her Child,
Then following her saint,
She went to Nazareth to the widow
To ask for work and be a neighbor!

The Child grew
And played with John, the widow's son.
He grew a lot already.
They played together in the street,
And there they found two sticks.
They brought them home
So their mothers would have kindling.
Little common children! They walk,
They're happy, hale;
They're a pleasure to behold!
The Child, yet small, took
The second stick from John —
John was playing horse with it —
He made a little cross and took it home
To show, you see, that he too is a craftsman.
Past the gate Maria met the children,
And fainted, falling like dead weight
When she saw that little cross and gallows.
"Evil! A bad and evil man!
He, my child, taught you how to make this!
Leave it! Leave it!"
And He, innocent and small,
Threw the holy little gallows,
And crying for the first time,
Poured boyish tears upon
His Mother's bosom.
The poor Dear seemed relieved.
She took Him, led Him to the shade,
Kissed Him there amid an orchard
Near some brush,
And fed Him with a cookie,
A fresh-baked little cookie.
The Child cuddled, played a bit,
And lay dozing on Her lap.
Thus the Child sleeps just like
An angel up in Paradise.
And the Mother gazes
On Her only Child,
Crying oh so softly;
The Angel sleeps,
Let nothing wake Him up.
But one thing she neglected.
A drop like scalding water
Fell on Him like fire,
And the Child awoke.
Maria quickly wiped her tears,
Laughing so He would not see.
But the poor Dear was not able
To trick her little Son.
The Child saw and cried.

The widow
Earned or maybe borrowed
Half a kopa[527] for a primer.

---

527 See glossary or fn. 137

She would herself have taught,
But alas she was illiterate.
She took the boy and led
Him off to school, to a school
Run by Essenians. She herself took
Care of Him, and by herself
She taught Him decency and wisdom.
Johnny, a widow's son indeed, took
After Him and both together
Went to school and studied.
He never played with other children,
Nor ever did He run;
Alone, all by Himself He would sit
At times amid the weeds and
Carve a barrel stave. He thus helped
His father in his sacred toil.
Sometime after He turned seven —
The little boy was quite a craftsman —
The old man rested in a corner,
Wondering about his Son,
And what sort of master He'll become!
What sort of person He'll become!
Having grabbed some pails and bowls,
The father, Mother and the Child,
Went to market
In the very city of Jerusalem.
Though far, they could fetch a better price.
So they came, spread out.
The father and the Mother sit
And sell their goods.
But where's the Child?
It ran off somewhere.
The Mother searches,
Crying. Not a sound
Of where He may have gone.
A synagogue she entered to ask mercy
Of the Lord most merciful,
So Her Son would be recovered.
Then look, among the rabbis is a Child,
Her little Boy is sitting, innocent,
Learning how to live on earth,
How to love the people,
To stand up for the truth!
And to die for it!
Without truth there's woe!
"Woe to you, teacher-prelates!"
The Pharisees and scribes
Were astonished at His words.
Beyond description was the Mother's joy.
The Messiah, God Himself,
She had seen on earth.
They sold their wares,
Prayed in the temple to the Lord
And happily took the road
Back home in the cooler nighttime air.

They grew
And learned together, developing
As Holy Children. The Holy Mothers
Shared delight in their little Children.
From school the two
Explored a thorny path.
They prophesied God's words,
And truth upon the earth,
Though they were doomed to die for
Freedom, sacred freedom!

John went off into the desert,
And Yours to preach among the people.
And You too followed Him,
The righteous Son You bore.
You left Your Holy Joseph
In an old and foreign hut!
You went to wander beneath fences
Until, until You reached Golgotha.
Because everywhere
The Son was followed
By the Holy Mother —
She thus heard and saw
His words, His deeds,
And swooned, trembling silently with joy
When she watched Her Son.
And He would sit at times,
Resting on the Mount of Olives.
Proudly stretched below
Was the city of Jerusalem,

The Israeli prelate
Shining like a golden byssus![528]
A golden Roman commoner!
An hour, two go by, He'll not rise
Nor look His Mother's way,
And She'll cry, looking
At the capital of Judea.
And She'll cry, going quietly
To the valley well for water.
She'll bring fresh water,
And wash the tired holy feet,
And She'll let Him drink,
She'll blow away the dust
That settled on his chiton,
She'll patch a hole then return to sit
Beneath a fig tree's shade.
She sits and watches, O Most Holy!
How that mournful Son reposes.
And running up quite suddenly
Are children from the city.
Blessed children loved Him.
In the streets they traced His steps,
And at times the little ones
Would run to Him
Upon the Mount of Olives.
And they ran up. "O saints!
Immaculates!" — He said,
When He saw the children.
He kissed and greeted them,
And with a blessing
Played with them just like a youngster,
Donning a burnoose.
Then happily with His children
He descended to Jerusalem
To spread new tidings,
To bring the word of truth
To all the wicked people!
To the word they paid no heed!
Him they crucified!
As they led Him to the cross,
You stood with little children,
Watching at a crossroads.
Peasants, brethren, and His students,
Were terrified and fled.
"Let Him pass! Let Him pass!
He'll lead you that way too!"
She told the little children.
Then like a corpse
She collapsed upon the ground.
Crucified —
Your only Child!
And You, having rested by a fence,
Kept going on to Nazareth!
Strangers long ago
Had the widow buried
In another's borrowed coffin.
And John was butchered in a prison.
And Your Joseph is no more.
And You, like an aching finger,
Remain alone and lonely.
Such is your patchy fortune, Dear!
His brethren and disciples,
Weak impoverished souls,
Did not submit to tyrants' torture,
But hid and then dispersed,
And You were forced to gather them…
Thus it was somehow
They gathered 'round You late at night
To mourn Your only Son.
And You, are great among all women!
Their dejection and their fear,
You dispersed like chaff
With your fiery holy word!
You instilled Your holy spirit
In their impoverished souls! Glory!
Glory be to You, Maria!
What was sacred lifted hearts of men.
They dispersed throughout the world,
And in the name of Your dear Son,
Your mournful only Child,

528 *Byssus* — A fine and valuable ancient linen cloth.

They carried truth and love
To the world's every corner.
But You died grieving
In the weeds beneath a fence of hunger.
Amen.

Monks then donned on You a purple robe.
They crowned You like an empress...
And like Your Son,
Those killers crucified You too,
And on You, the pure, they spat;
They crucified the Good, and You,
Like gold within that crucible,
Revived within the human soul,
Within a small and shackled soul,
Within a poor and mournful soul.

St. Petersburg, November 11, 1859

Holy Family, 1858

IMITATION TO EDWARD SOWA[529]

In honor of my wife
To evoke my one and only,
I will plant beside the house
An apple and a pear tree!

God willing, they will grow.
My wife between those
Trees will sit with children
In the shade.

And I will pick the pears
And hand them to the children...
With my one and only,
I will quietly converse.

"Back then, my sweetheart,
When we married, these are
The trees I planted...
I'm happy!" — "And I, my mate,
Am happy with you!"

St. Petersburg, November 19, 1859

IMITATION OF EZEKIEL

Chapter 19

Lament, O Prophet, Son of God!
For princes, nobles
And these kings. And say:
"Why, cubs, did the bitch, your mother,
Copulate with lions?
And bring you, the evil, forth?
And multiply your cursed breed?
Then you, the sharp-toothed cubs,
Turned into roaring lions! People!
You, the rabid, devour gentle
Righteous children!
Like a kite that snares
A hen amid the weeds,
Picking at it, ripping it. And people...
People see, but do not speak.
There's a wild cub! Vicious!
They ambush it and take it captive.
Then having bound it well in tethers
The people carried it to Egypt —
For drudgery. And the vicious mother!
She bore another raving rabid creature.
It was a tyrant that devoured towns and all.
The earth shook, it trembled from
The roaring of your savage offspring.
This one too was bound by people.
With a bit they closed his jaws
And in Babylon they locked
Him deep down in a dungeon.
So the snarling of the tyrant prelate,
Of the czar insatiate, could not
Be heard on earth...
The days of lawlessness
And wickedness will pass,
Indeed they're slowly passing.
But lion cubs don't know that,
They merely grow like willows

529 *Sowa* — Antoni Sowa, pseudonym of Polish writer Edward Witold Zeligowksi (1816-64). Exiled to Orenburg for Polish revolutionary activity. Shevchenko's pen pal during their respective exiles. Both later met in St. Petersburg.

In a shady grove. On their roots
They place their hopes,
Roots already rotten,
Wormy, small and scanty. A wind gust
From the field will then bend and break it.
And your evil license will be bathed,
Bathed in its own blood.

Great lamentation,
Not the snarls of lions,
Is what people will then hear.
Among people,
That lament, the tyrant's crying,
Plaintive, long and ugly,
Will become a parable."

St. Petersburg, December 6, 1859

HOSEA, CHAPTER 14

An Imitation

You'll die, you'll perish, O Ukraine,
A trace will not be left on earth,
Though you once gloried
In luxury and goodness.
O Ukraine!
My land so dear and innocent!
Why are you so punished,
Punished harshly by the Lord?
He inflicts a total ruin,
For Bohdan, for rabid Peter,
And those evil lords...
He'll punish, killing truly, imperceptibly;
For it was long that the Long-indulgent
Watched your sinful womb in silence,
Then finally said in anger:
"I will claim your beauty, your adornment,
You will crucify yourself.
You'll be killed in malice by your full-fledged sons,
And those conceived in evil will die and perish
In the womb, like chicks not incubated by a hen!..
I'll fill the towns and fields with crying,
The sound of mothers crying.
So that the earth defiled may realize
That I'm the Ruler, I see all.
Be resurrected, mother! Go home,
Go back to your parlor; rest,
For you've grown too weary,
Bearing all the sins of sons.

Having rested, mournful one, speak out,
Reveal to your evil progeny,
That they, the wicked, all shall perish,
That their deceit, dishonor and dishonesty
Are carved into the souls of people
With a flaming bloody sword;
That there shall be the din of unrelenting punishment,
That no good czar, their gentle drunken master,
Will be there to save them,
He'll not give them food or drink,
He won't provide a bareback horse
To allow for their escape;
You'll not run and you'll not hide;
Truth and retribution will find you in all places;
You'll be abruptly ambushed by the people,
They will catch you, they won't try you,
They'll tightly shackle you,
They'll lead you to the village
And make a spectacle of you,
Then on a cross without a czar or hangman,
They'll rend, cut and crucify you,
And your blood, you dogs,
They'll give to dogs to drink…
And add,
Add this word for them without a parable:
"With your impious hands,
You — tell them — have created
Your own hope;
And proclaim the czar to be our God,
The czar to be our hope."
No, not that. Here is what you tell them:
"The gods are lying,
Those idols found in foreign palaces.
Tell them that again the truth will flourish,
It will inspire, summon, and collect
Not the old, not the ancient word defiled,
It will spread instead among the people
A new word with a shout,
And it will save the cheated people
From the czarist favor…"

St. Petersburg, December 25, 1859

A lovely dark-browed lass
Carried beer up from the cellar.
And I glanced, I looked —
And even leaned...
Who will drink the beer she carries?
Why is she walking barefoot?
God Almighty! It's Your power
And it does You harm.

St. Petersburg, January 15, 1860

Oak forest — shady grove!...
Thrice yearly you are clad...
You have yourself a wealthy father.
He first wraps you
In a gown of lavish green —
He marvels to himself
At his shady grove...
Gazing at his daughter,
So very dear and young,
He takes her and envelops
Her in a cloak of gold,
Then proceeds to wrap her
In a veil of white —
He then lays himself to sleep,
Weary from his worries.

St. Petersburg, January 15, 1860

Tree, 1846

IMITATION TO THE SERBIAN

Matchmakers converged,
Behind them came the groom:
Inside the house they went
For conversation with the father;
And from the young
And dark-browed groom
I gladly take his horse —
I lead it to the well.
The horse is weary,
Its hooves unshod and shattered,
Its ornate saddle
Broken and uncovered.
"Tell me, horse, to whom
Did you so hurry?"
"We wandered through the night
To some dark-browed girl."
"Will you, horse, be drinking
Water from our well?
Will the dark-browed girl
Be a bride this year?"

St. Petersburg, May 4, 1860

A PRAYER

Send the czars, the universal tavern keepers,
Ducats, dollars
And forged shackles.

Grant Your power
To the working heads and hands
Upon this plundered earth.

For me, my God, grant me
Love on earth, that heartfelt paradise,
And grant me nothing more!

St. Petersburg, May 24, 1860

Bind the czars, the bloody tavern keepers,
With shackles forged in fire,
Then lay bricks to seal them deep within a vault.

Grant Your power, O Most Merciful,
To toiling people
On their plundered land.

And the pure of heart?
Place Your angels at their side,
So they may guard their purity.

For me, O Lord,
Grant the love of truth on earth,
And send an honest friend!

St. Petersburg, May 25, 1860

Stay the evil instigators,
Don't bind them in forged shackles,
Don't lay bricks to seal them deep within a vault.

But show and help
Creative righteous hands
And grant them sacred power!

And the pure of heart?
Place Your angels at their side,
And guard their purity.

And to all on earth together,
Grant us unanimity
And the love of brotherhood.

St. Petersburg, May 27, 1860

Sometime ago in days of yore,
Numa Pompilius,[530] the Roman king,
A meek and gentle ruler,
Grew weary writing laws,
And took a pleasant break
To get a bit of rest.
And to ponder as he rested,
How to fashion shackles
For his fellow Romans.
He took a supple
Year-old willow switch
And began to weave a noose,
For someone's neck perhaps.
He spied a girl, however,
All adorned in flowers,
Sleeping in a maple's shade…
To such a beauty,
Such a goddess
Even dryads[531] can't compare!
Egeria[532] herself,
Cursed her fate
And in a grove she hanged herself.
And Numa the astute,
Marvels at the girl and flowers,
Then ponders: "What other kind of
Chain is there yet to weave?"

St. Petersburg, May 28, 1859

To greedy eyes
And earthly gods — the czars,
Grant plows and ships,
All goods on earth,
And psalms of admiration.
This to petty gods.

To working minds,
To working hands
Grant fallow fields to plow,
To think, to sow without delay
And to reap what has been sown.
This to working hands.

To the humble and kindhearted
To the saints of peace,
O Creator of the earth and heavens!
On this world grant them many years;
In the next… grant Paradise.

All on earth is not for us,
It's for those gods — the czars!
The plows, the ships,
All goods on earth.
My dear!.. and to us —
To us grant love among all people.

St. Petersburg, May 31, 1860

530 *Numa Pompilius (753-673 BC)* — Legendary second king of Rome. Successor to Romulus.
531 *Dryads* — Tree nymphs in ancient mythology.
532 *Egeria* — A nymph in early Rome. Divine consort and counselor of Numa Pompilius.

IMPROVISATIONS ON "THE LAY OF IHOR'S HOST"[533]

YAROSLAVNA'S LAMENT[534]

Early morning in Putyvl-burg[535]
Yaroslavna sings and weeps,
Mourning like a cuckoo,
Adding words to grief.
"I'll fly, — she says, — just like a cuckoo
With a widowed seagull,
Above the Don I'll fly
And wet my beaver cuff
In the Kayala River.[536]
And on the body,
On the prince's pale withered body,
I'll wash away encrusted blood,
I'll dress his deep and heavy wounds..."

Early on the ramparts of Putyvl
Yaroslavna sobs and cries:
"O my wind, my precious sail,
My master light and fleet!
Why do you shoot upon your mighty wing
The arrows of the khan,
Aimed at my dear warriors,
At my prince, my gentle love?
There's ample sky, blue sea and earth.
Sway the freighted ships at sea.
But you, ferocious one... Woe! Woe!
You've stolen all my joy,
And dispersed it in the grassy steppe."

Early in Putyvl-burg,
Yaroslavna mourns and sobs and cries
She says: "Old and mighty,
O broad Dnipr', O great river!

---

533 *The Lay of Ihor's Host* — An ancient epic poem about the failed 12th century raid of Prince Ihor against the Polovtsians.

534 *Yaroslavna* — The wife of Ihor, Prince of Novhorod-Siversky and daughter of Yaroslav Osmomysl, the Prince of Halych (Galicia).

535 *Putyvl* — A town in the Novhorod-Siversky princedom.

536 *Kayala River* — A river mentioned in the chronicles where Prince Ihor lost a 12th century battle to the Polovtsians.

You sliced through lofty cliffs,
Flowing to the land of the Polovtsian,[537]
You carried longboats
Filled with Sviatoslav's contingent
Against Polovtsians and Kobiak!..[538]
O my glorious Slavutych![539]
Bring me back my dearest love,
So I may joyfully prepare his bed,
And not send tears into the sea,
Tears won't fill the sea."

Yaroslavna cries and cries
In Putyvl at the rampart gate.
The sacred sun had risen.
She says: "The sacred sun's
Brought joy to earth
To the people and the soil,
But it's not dispelled
My longing and unease.
O sacred, fiery master!
You've scorched the steppes and meadows,
You've scorched the prince and all his forces,
Scorch me in my loneliness!
Or send no warmth and shine no light...
If my dear love is dead... I will perish too!"

St. Petersburg, June 4, 1860

Early morning in Putyvl-burg
Yaroslavna mourns and cries.
"I'll fly, — she says, — just like a cuckoo,
I'll fly above the Danube!
I'll wet my beaver cuff
In the Kayala River...
And I'll cleanse his sturdy princely body

537 *Polovtsians* — Nomadic warriors on the Eurasian steppe that first attacked Ukraine in the mid-11th century and many times after. Also known as the Cumans.

538 *Kobiak* — 12th century Polovtsian ruler and military commander who staged attacks on Rus. Captured by Kyivan Prince Sviatoslav ca. 1184.

539 *Slavutych* — Ancient name for the Dnipro River.

Of encrusted blood...
I'll dress deep wounds of my true love..."

In Putyvl-burg,
Yaroslavna cries and cries
And says:
"O my wind, my precious sail, my master!
Why do you blow and carry
On your gentle wing
The arrows of the khan?"

St. Petersburg, September 14, 1860

From predawn till evening,
And from evening until daybreak,
The tempered arrow flies,
The sabre clangs on helmets,
Seasoned lances whizz
Across the steppe on an unfamiliar field
In the land of the Polovtsians.

The black earth is plowed,
Plowed and raked by hooves;
The ground is sown with bones,
And with blood it's showered.
Sprouting on that Polovtsian field
Is grief and longing
For the land of Rus.[540]

What clamors there,
Bidding well at dawn?
It's that Ihor[541] pivoting his army
To help Vsevolod[542] the auroch.[543]

They fought a day,
They fought a second,
And on the third at noon
Ihor's banners drooped.
And thus the brothers parted
On Kayala's shore; because there was
A shortage of the wine called blood!..
The courageous Rusych[544] warriors
Finished off that feast,
Gave their partners drink,
Then set forth themselves
Toward the land of Rus.
The grass, crying, swayed and spread,
Tall trees bowed as well...
Bending worried to the ground!

St. Petersburg, July 6, 1860

540 *Rus* — Ukraine's historical name. A millennium ago, the Rus Empire included parts of what today is Belarus and European Russia.

541 *Ihor (1151-1201)* — Prince of Novhorod-Siversky and Chernihiv. Hero of *The Lay of Ihor's Host,* an ancient epic poem about his failed raid against the Polovtsians.

542 *Vsevolod (?-1196)* — Prince of Kursk and Trubchevsk. Prince Ihor's brother.

543 See glossary or fn. 374

544 *Rusych* — Adjectival form of Rus.

The great man in a haircloth died.[545]
Cry not, orphans, cry not, widows,
And come morning, you, Askochensky,[546]
Use the grave tone[547] to lament.
And Khomiakov,[548] coveter of Rus,
Lover of the fatherland and Moscow,
Lament the one who fought the skirt.[549]

And confess your sins, O *Russkaya Beseda,*[550]
In a single voice.
And weep! And weep!

St. Petersburg, June 17, 1860

THE NUN'S HYMN

Strike, thunder, strike this house,
The house of God, where we all perish,
Where we offend you, God,
And as we do so, we still sing,
Hallelujah!

If not for You, we'd fall in love,
Have desire and marry,
And we'd raise some children,
Teaching them to sing,
Hallelujah!

You duped us, the poor.
We, cheated wretches,
Cheated You ourselves
And, whimpering, we sang:
Hallelujah!

You shore our hair as nuns,
But we're just maidens...
We dance, we sing,
And as we sing, we do proclaim,
Hallelujah!

St. Petersburg, June 20, 1860

545 *Man in a haircloth* — Grigori Petrovich Postnikov, Orthodox Metropolitan of St. Petersburg and Novgorod (1784-1860). Considered by critics as a reactionary opponent of science and a free press.

546 *Viktor Ipatiyovich Askochensky (1813-79)* — Russian journalist, historian, editor and publisher of the reactionary magazine, *Domashnaya beseda.*

547 *Grave tone* — One of eight tones or modes used in Byzantine church music.

548 *Alexei Stepanovich Khomiakov (1804-60)* — Russian poet and Slavophile. Shevchenko too was a Slavophile, but rejected its Russian version. He believed Russian Slavophiles used the movement to advance Russian interests at the expense of other Slavic peoples.

549 *Fought the skirt* — Writer and activist Alexander Herzen called Grigori a skirt fighter when the Metropolitan protested a magazine article that included a drawing of women's clothing with designs that looked like crosses.

550 *Russkaya Beseda* — Russian Slavophile magazine in Moscow in the late 1850s.

By a Dnipro inlet
Stands a sycamore
Between a fir and willow
With a crimson guelder rose.

The Dnipro rakes and rakes the shore,
Washing roots beneath the sycamore.
The old one stands, but leans,
Saddened like a Kozak.

One without a fortune, without kin,
Without a faithful wife,
And with neither wife nor hope
He'll grow gray alone!

The sycamore then says: "I'll lean
And in the Dnipro I will bathe."
The Kozak says: "I'll roam
And find myself a sweetheart."

The guelder rose and fir
With the supple willow sing,
Like little girls
Near a grove.

All dressed up, adorned,
Engaged to fortune,
They have not a single care,
They merely weave about and sing.

St. Petersburg, June 24, 1860

Together they grew up, matured;
They ceased to laugh and play.
As if they truly parted!..
Soon they reunited. Married;
Quietly and happily,
They reached the tomb
With heart and soul still innocent.
Though they lived with people!

Bless us too, all-giving God!
Grant that we thus grow and prosper,
That we so wed
And reach the great beyond
Without strife on life's hard road.
And to take no crying, wailing
Nor any gnashing of the teeth —
But love eternal and exquisite
Into that placid other world.

St. Petersburg, June 25, 1860

O bright light! O gentle light!
Light unfettered and so free!
Why, O brother light
Have you been bound and bricked
In your warm and decent home
(A sage deceived).
Enclosed in crimson mantles
And beaten with a crucifix?

But not to death! Rise up!
And shine above us,
Enlighten!.. We'll rip leggings, brother,
From the crimson mantles,
We'll puff on pipes from censers,
With icons we'll heat stoves,
And with an aspergillum,[551] brother,
We'll sweep a new house clean!

St. Petersburg, June 27, 1860

551 *Aspergillum* — A brush for sprinkling holy water.

TO LYKERA[552]

In Remembrance of August 5, 1860[553]

O my dear beloved! My friend!
They'll not believe our faith
Unless there is a cross,
They'll not believe our faith
Unless there is a priest.
Slaves, ailing bondsmen!
Asleep, like pigs in muck
In their own captivity! O my friend,
My dear beloved! Do not cross
Yourself, give nothing and pray
To no one on this earth!
People will tell lies,
The Byzantine Sabaoth
Will deceive as well!
God will not deceive,
He'll not punish or show mercy:
We are not His slaves — we're people!
My dear beloved! Smile, my friend,
And grant your free and sacred soul
And your unfettered hand to me.
He will help us step by step,
He will help us bear the evil
And to bury wicked pettiness
In a quiet happy home.

Strelna, August 5, 1860

TO M. Y. MAKAROV[554]

In Remembrance of September 14[555]

The periwinkle blossomed,
Growing green it crept and spread;
But a predawn frost
Stole into the little garden.
It trampled cheery flowers,
It beat them… Froze them…
For the periwinkle there's regret
And so too for the frost.

St. Petersburg, September 14, 1860

552 *Lykera Ivaniva Polusmakova (1840-1917)* — Shevchenko's fiancée and former Ukrainian serf brought to St. Petersburg by her owner. The engagement fell through and she later married a barber. Upon his death in 1904, Polusmakova moved to Kaniv, where Shevchenko is buried, and frequently visited his grave.

553 *August 5, 1860* — Shevchenko that day was denied permission by Polusmakova's guardian to take her to St. Petersburg on a shopping trip. Since they were not married, the guardian considered such a trip improper.

554 *Mykola Yakovych Makarov (1828-92)* — A St. Petersburg journalist and functionary from Ukraine with close ties to the local Ukrainian community.

555 *September 14* — The significance of the date is unknown, but is thought to be connected to his breakup with Polusmakova. Shevchenko may have recognized that Makarov's opposition to the engagement with her was correct.

Archimedes and Galileo
Never saw a drop of wine.
Unction flowed into the
Abbot's belly!
And you, forerunners divine,
Spread throughout the world
And brought a scrap of bread
To all impoverished kings.
Rye sown by the kings
Will be beaten down.
But people will arise.
Kings yet unconceived will die…
And on lands revived
There will be no foe, no rival,
There will be instead
A son, a mother,
And there will be people on the earth.

St. Petersburg, September 24, 1860

L.

I'll build a house and room,
I'll plant a little garden-paradise.
I'll sit about and stroll
In my blissful nook.
I'll be resting in the garden
All alone and lonely,
I'll dream of little children,
Of a happy mother,
And a vivid dream from long ago
Will come to me again!.. And you!..
No, I will not rest, for you'll
Be in the dream. And quietly
By stealth you'll sneak into my
Little Eden. You'll wreak havoc…
You'll set my lonely paradise afire.

St. Petersburg, September 24, 1860

I don't complain of God,
I complain of no one.
I fool myself, a fool,
And even sing along.
I plow my fallow field —
A meager field indeed!
Then I sow the word.
A fine harvest it will someday yield.
But I deceive! Myself, in fact,
Myself and no one else, it seems?

Be plowed, my field,
In the valley, on the hill!
Be sown, dark field,
With the light of freedom.
Be plowed, ripen,
Spread across the field!
And be sown with wholesome rye,
Be watered with good fortune!
Spread in all directions,
O field-desiatyna![556]
Be sown, O field, not with words,
But wisdom!
People will turn out to reap the rye…
A joyful harvest!..
Ripen, spread, O needy field!!!

Do I deceive myself not yet again
With my good chimeric word?
I do! For it's better to deceive oneself,
Than to live the truth beside a foe
And complain of God in vain!

St. Petersburg, October 5, 1860

SAUL

In quiescent China,
In Egypt dim and dark,
In our land,
And above the Indus
And Euphrates,
A shepherd long ago,
On his field so free,
Would freely tend his flock
In his paradise.
He had no care or inkling,
He grazed his flock,
He milked it, sheared it,
Singing as he worked…
But then the devil brings a king
Bearing laws, swords, hangmen,
Princes and dark slaves.
They crept up at night,
Seized the flocks upon the field;
They took it all, the shepherds,
All their tents, their meager shelters,
All their goods, their little children,
A sister, and a wife,
Corrupting and defiling everything,
Inflicting drudgery and toil
Upon those defiled, the feeble
And weak-hearted.
Day by day went by.
Slaves were silent,
Kings were born, they grew
And piled bricks for Babylons.
Magi, monks and bonzes
(Like our reverends, it seems)
Stuffed themselves in temples and pagodas,
Like boars for
The sausages and lard of kings.
And kings built for themselves
Alters, shrines and temples.
Silent slaves bowed down.

---

556 *Desiatyna* — A Russian imperial measure of land equivalent to 2.69 acres or 1.09 hectares.

Poor Jews grew envious,
That they hadn't even had a minor king
And lacked an altar made
Of even dung briquettes.
They then asked old Samuel,
That he find a king, wherever,
Just so that he gave them one.
Thus the wise clairvoyant,
Having pondered, took holy oil,
Then took that brawny Saul
From his goats and pigs
And anointed him as king.
Saul, *no fool was he,*
Took himself a goodly harem
And began to rule.
Shepherds looked and marveled
At the new recruit,
And said they too were no one's fool.
Look at what an autocrat
We solicited from God. Saul then
Grabs the city, grabs the village,
Takes the girl, takes the lamb,
Builds palaces of cedar,
Altars forged of gold,
And doles out favors
To his most submissive naked subjects.
In a long and crimson robe
He walked about his palace;
This narrow-minded fellow walked,
Until, alone within his harem,
The wretched Saul went mad.

A council soon convened.
"Gentlemen of this august circle!
What are we to do? Our wise king,
The autocrat and ruler,
This wretched man went mad.
Gentlemen! Are we now to treat him?
Or find instead a king more hearty?"
Upon deliberation,
The saddened shepherds left
The council of the wise.
In the new and cedar palace
The king won't sleep,
Won't eat, drink or even whisper.
But on the floor, instead, the almighty ruler
Rips his mantle to make leggings,
And seems to flex his sandals,
Then ties the leggings, dons the sandals
And within the cedar walls
Asks about the father of a baby ass.
He takes his scepter and plays
It like a little pipe.
Shepherds,
Benjamin's descendants,[557]
Gave a lamb to the retainers,
So they'd be allowed to sing
Upon the royal porch.
Saul's gray-bearded, hairy, paunchy
Kinfolk roared,
And they even brought a zither player,
Some shepherd by the name of David.
"King Saul went, he went, —
The shepherd sang, — to war..."
Saul came to his senses,
Then through and through,
Just like a Muscovite,
He cusses out his hairy kin.
And he nearly killed
That zither player, David.
If he knew what evil would ensue
From that wicked David,
Then, like a snake,
He would have trampled him,
And wiped the serpent's drooling venom.
With plows or shares
We'll now not till the cursed field,
It's overgrown with thorns. Woe! Woe!
People on the earth diminish,
Kings grow tall and mighty.

St. Petersburg, October 13, 1860

---

557 *Benjamin's descendants* — Reference to one of the 12 tribes of Israel and their descendants. Saul was among them.

Days of youth have passed,
Cold winds buffet hope.
Winter! In a chilly home
You sit alone
With no one for a quiet chat,
Nor anyone for consolation.
No one, not a soul is there!
Sit alone, till hope deceives
And mocks a fool...
It binds the eyes with frost,
And disperses prideful thoughts,
Like a snowflake in the steppe!
Sit alone off in a corner.
Await no spring or sacred fortune!
It will never dawn again
To make your garden green,
To revive your hope!
Nor will it come
To free your thoughts of freedom...
Sit and don't await a thing!..

St. Petersburg, October 18, 1860

The sexton's daughter of Nemyriv
Embroiders with a golden thread a kerchief.
And rocks a tiny Muscovite,
A little baby boy.

The sexton's daughter of Nemyriv
Scorned a lot of people...
But secretly she welcomed
A roguish Muscovite!

The sexton's daughter of Nemyriv...
From a decent family...
Awaits the roguish soldier
As he comes back from a mission.

St. Petersburg, October 18, 1860

Though they do not beat a soul asleep,
They do not let a laggard rest.
As for you, O bitch![558]
We ourselves, our grandkids,
And people in our land will curse you,
Nay, they will not curse,
They'll simply spit at
All the pups
That you whelped and weaned.
O my grief! My grief!
O my sorrow, O my pain!
Will you ever pass? Or
Will czars with slavish ministers,
Sic their dogs on you, my raging pain!
They'll not succeed. And people softly
With no sort of angry evil
Will lead the czar to an executioner.

St. Petersburg, October 20, 1860

Here and everywhere — it's bad all over.
A wretched soul rose early,
Wove but little, then
Rested once again.
And freedom watched his soul.
"Awake, — she says. — Weep, poor dear!
The sun won't rise. Darkness, darkness!
And there's no justice on the earth!"
Idle freedom fooled the minor soul.
The sun approaches,
Drawing daylight in its wake.
And already all those stiff-backs,
All those czars are stirring…
And justice will be done on earth.

St. Petersburg, October 30, 1860

558 *Bitch* — Reference to Russian Empress Alexandra Feodorovna, the wife of Czar Nicholas I. She died on October 20, 1861, the day the poem was written. She gave birth to seven children.

O people! Wretched people!
What use have you for czars?
What use have you for huntsmen?
You're people, after all, not dogs!
At night there's ice, and fog,
And snow, and cold.
And quietly beneath a bridge
To a place unknown,
The Neva carried quietly
A slender slab of ice.
And I, indeed at night,
Walk, and as I walk I cough.
I look: like lambs,
A group of ragged girls go by,
And an old man (a wretched invalid)
Leans after them, he hobbles,
As if rounding up a stranger's cattle
Into a holding pen.
Where's the light!?
And where's the truth!? Woe! Woe!
They drive the naked and unfed
(To pay their last respects),
They drive the girls,[559]
Like a flock, to the mother
Of some bastards.
Will there be a judgment!
Will there be a penalty!
For czars and princes here on earth?
There should be, for the sun will rise
And scorch the earth defiled.

St. Petersburg, November 4, 1860

If there was someone I could sit with
To eat some bread, to share a word,
Then be life as it may,
It would be easier to live.
Alas! There's no one.
The world is vast!

With many people on the earth...
But I'll come to die alone
In a cold, lopsided house
Or beneath a fence somewhere.
Or... No. I must get married,
If even with the devil's sister!
For I'll go mad of loneliness.
Wheat and rye were sown
Upon a fertile field,
They'll be reaped by people
Who will someday say:
"He was killed somewhere,
The wretch, in a foreign land..."
Oh woe, oh woe is me!

St. Petersburg, November 4, 1860

The day goes by, the night goes by.
You clasp your head,
You wonder, why cometh not
The apostle of the truth and reason!

St. Petersburg, November 5, 1860

---

559 *Drive the girls* — Shevchenko witnessed a group of girls in St. Petersburg being led to the Saints Peter and Paul Cathedral, where the body of Empress Alexandra lay in repose.

Water from beneath a sycamore
Flows down along a valley.
Proudly up above it
Stands a guelder rose.
The little guelder rose takes pride,
The sycamore rejuvenates,
And growing green around them
Are willow trees and osiers.

Past the grove flows water
Along the hillside edge.
Amid the sedge splash ducklings.
Toward them swims the duck
With the drake beside her,
She snatches duckweed,
Conversing with her little children.

Water flows along a garden.
The water then becomes a pond.
A maiden came
To fetch some water,
And fetching it she sang.
From the house come mom and dad
To stroll about the garden,
And to discuss, whom should
They name as son-in-law?

St. Petersburg, November 7, 1860

It somehow came to me at night
Walking by the Neva...
I walked along and to myself
I pondered: "What if, — I thought, — if
Slaves refused to bend...
Then these defiled palaces
Would not be standing by the Neva!
There'd be a sister!
There would be a brother!
But alas... there's nothing now.
No demigod or even God.
Huntsmen with their petty huntsmen rule,
And we, the witty kennel keepers,
Feed the hounds and cry.
So it was at night,
That with myself I nicely pondered,
Walking by the Neva.
I can't quite make out
A kitten blinking from the other side,
From a pit, it seems.
It's really two lamps burning
By the gate of the apostles.[560]
I came about, crossed myself
With a holy crucifix, spat three times
And began again to ponder
What I pondered first.

St. Petersburg, November 13, 1860

560 *Gate of the Apostles* — The Nevsky Gate to the Petropavlovsky Fortress, which was converted into a high security prison. Shevchenko referred to political prisoners who passed through the gate as apostles.

There were wars and army feuds:
The Galagans, Kisils
And Kochubey-Nahays — [561]
Of such ilk there was a lot.
All has passed, but not yet vanished.
Woodworms still remain: they gnaw,
Devour and decay the ancient [oak]...
But lovingly and quietly,
Greenery and [shoots]
Are pushing from the roots.
And when they grow; even with no ax
There will be roars and groans,
A Kozak with no horse will pounce,
He'll smash the throne, rip the mantle,
And your idol, human woodworms,
He will crush,
Nannies and master servants
Of a foreign fatherland!
Your sacred idol will not last,
Nor either will you last, —
Weeds and nettles —
Nothing more above your corpse will grow.
Foul manure will build in heaps —
The wind will wear away those heaps.
And we, not rich, not poor,
Will freely pray to God.

St. Petersburg, November 26, 1860

N. T. [562]

O great martyr, O my friend!
You're foolish and unwise!
In a happy paradise you grew,
Amid pink flowers you blossomed,
Yet you never saw that lovely Eden,
You never looked, because you
Cared not to behold God's day,
Its bright and vital light!
Your eyes were blind, unseeing,
Your heart remained unmoved;
You slept days, you slept nights.
Things around you happened,
They grew, they bloomed and blossomed,
And brought glory to the Lord Creator.
And you, my friend, just slept and slept,
Taking pride in maidenhood,
Waiting, waiting for a suitor,
Sheltering your chastity.
And how you feared adulterous sin.
But the might of Saturn moves and moves,
And weaves the righteous sin
Into a graying braid,
But you seem not to notice:
You remain a maiden;
You pray, you sleep,
And offend God's Mother
With your wicked humbleness.
Awaken, friend, rise up
Look around,
Scorn that girlish glory
And with a heart sincere and guileless
Go astray, my dear, if only once in life.

St. Petersburg, December 2, 1860

561 *Galagans, Kisils and Kochubey-Nahays* — Ukrainian landowers or magnates who served foreign interests.

562 *Nadia Vasylivna Tarnovska (?-1891)* — A friend of Shevchenko whom he met in the Ukrainian village of Kachanivka in 1843. They were godparents at a baptism in 1845 for the child of a deacon.

We met, we married, bonded,
Rejuvenated, grew.
Around our home we planted
An orchard and a grove.
We took pride, like princes.
The children played,
They grew and they matured…
Soldiers stole the girls,
The boys were drafted by the Muscovites,
And it seems we parted,
As if we never married —
As if we never bonded.

St. Petersburg, December 5, 1860

My friend and I
Wandered through the labyrinth
Of Petropolis[563] — darkness, darkness…
"Let's go my friend, into the pyramid,[564]
We'll light a candle there." We entered.
We brought myrrh and unction.
And a tidy priest of Isis,[565]
A black-haired cavalier,
Humbly shook our hands,
And the choir sang with the manic fervor
Of a priest or lackey:
In Judea there was once a king named Saul.
Then the choir belted out Bortniansky:[566]
O grief, my grief! O great grief of mine!

St. Petersburg, Second Half of September — December 1860

Should we, my humble friend,
My wretched neighbor,
Not take leave
Of writing useless poems,
And equip instead our wagons
For a distant journey;
We'll mosey over, partner,
To the other world, to God, for rest.
We're worn out and weary,
But we've gained some wisdom,
So we've had our fill! Let us sleep,
Let's go to rest into the house…
A happy house, so you may know!..
But let's not go, not yet,
It's early, friend, it's early —
We'll stroll about, sit around
We'll look upon this world…
We will, my fortune, look…
See, how broad,
How high, how happy,
Bright and deep it is…
We'll walk about, my star…
We'll ascend a mountain,

---

563 *Petropolis* — Reference to St. Petersburg. Petropolis in Greek means the city of Peter. Shevchenko here equates a Russian Orthodox church service with Egyptian pagan ritual.

564 *Pyramid* — Reference to the Saints Peter and Paul Cathedral in St. Petersburg, where Russian czars were buried, just as the pyramids were the graves of pharaohs.

565 *Isis* — Ancient Egyptian goddess, who personified the pharoah's throne and power.

566 *Dmytro Stepanovych Bortniansky (1751-1825)* — A Ukrainian and Russian composer who also wrote church music.

We'll rest, and meanwhile,
Your sister stars,
Eternal in the firmament,
Will drift above and shine.
We'll wait, my sister,
O my sacred mate!
And with lips unsullied
We will pray to God,
And we'll quietly embark
Upon our lengthy journey —
Above the boundless turbid Lethe.
Bless me, friend, with hallowed fame.

February 14

But there's still this, that and the other...
Frankly — let's go for a favor
Straight to Aesculapius[567] —
Might he not deceive Charon and
The Spinner Parca?..[568]
Then, while the wise old man contrived,
We'd recline, create an epic verse,
Soar far and wide above the earth,
And we'd weave hexameters
That we'd serve the
Attic mice for breakfast.
We'd then sing in prose,
With notes, of course,
Not just randomly...
My friend,
My devout companion!
Before the fire grows cold,
It's best that we see Charon —
We'll swim the boundless, turbid Lethe,
We'll carry hallowed fame across —
Young and endless.
Or to hell with her, my friend,
I can do without her —
And if I'm well
Then in a grove, a primeval grove
Above the Phlegethon itself
Or perhaps the Styx, in Paradise,
As if it were the mighty Dnipro,
I'll set up a little home, and plant
An orchard 'round it;
You'll float over to the shade,
And there I'll seat you like a beauty.
We'll recall the Dnipro and Ukraine,
The happy villages in groves,
The lofty mounds upon the steppes —
And cheerfully we'll sing...

St. Petersburg, February 15, 1861

567 *Aesculapius* — The Greek god of medicine and healing.

568 *Parca* — Singular of Parcae, the three personifications of destiny in Roman mythology. The first spun it, the second measured it, and the third cut it.

DUBIA[569]

I'm down, it's hard — what am I to do?...
Pray to God? There's no inclination!
Not gladly, oh by God,
I'd not gladly worry,
But woe has struck, and I'm an orphan.
There's none on earth to lend advice,
There's none with whom
To share my cursed sorrow,
None to hug you as a mother,
None to ask, "What is your pain?"
The grove is green — but what is that to me,
If the green adorns an alien land!
People shun me like a stranger,
And should they greet me —
They cause sorrow, nonetheless!
They carouse and drink;
Fortune cares for them,
But it's eluded me. They mock me:
"You see, a laggard frolics here among us."
Laggard?.. Why?..
Because he's in a foreign land!
Carouse and mock —
Fortune is your mother,
But I've no place to stand among you.
I'm in a dowdy peasant coat,
You are wealthy lords,
But mock me not that I'm an orphan!
The time will come, when I'll not die —
Among you, the lords, is my misfortune, —
I'll fly; I'll see my dear Ukraine:
She is my beloved, my mother,
Sisters standing —
Lofty mounds amid the steppe
Beside the road...
There's my destiny,
There's God's dear and loving world.

I worry not, but do not sleep...
At times till midnight,
All the while,
Your dark and brilliant eyes aglow.
They seem to softly say:
"Do you, my friend, seek paradise?
It's here with me, it's in my heart."
But there is no heart,
Nor was there ever,
Just a piece of flesh...
Why ever have you blossomed
So lavishly and beautifully?
I worry not, but I, at times,
Don't sleep until the break of dawn,
A thought nipping all the while
About a way to live,
So that eyes like yours
Would never touch the heart.

569 Two poems often associated with Shevchenko are of dubious origin and cannot be confirmed as his. Experts believe he may have written the first in 1837 in St. Petersburg along with other early poetry. It was discovered between handwritten copies of Shevchenko's known verses made by someone unknown. The second is attributed to him by Ukrainian-Russian writer and ethnographer Oleksandr Afanasyev-Chuzhbynsky, who wrote it down in his recollections. Chuzbynsky claims the verse was written in Kyiv in 1846. While it recalls Shevchenko's style, some of the word usage is not considered characteristic of him, leading others to dispute the attribution.

GLOSSARY

ALTA RIVER — A tributary of the Trubailo, which drains into the Dnipro on Ukraine's left bank.

AUROCH — An extinct ancestor *(Bos primigenius)* of domestic cattle known for its large size and strength.

BAIDAK — Large sea-going boat used by Zaporizhian Kozaks.

BANDURA — Ukraine's national musical instrument. It typically has between 30 and 68 strings.

BANDURIST — A musician who plays the bandura.

BENDERY — A Wallachian city in what today is Moldova. It was captured by Russia from the Ottomans during the Russo-Turkish War.

BRAID, COVERED — The braid in Ukrainian culture is a symbol of maidenhood. Covering it was a sign of disgrace for bearing a child out of wedlock.

BROVARY — An old Ukrainian town, now a suburb of Kyiv.

CARIHRAD — Variation on Czarhorod, the former Ukrainian name for Istanbul (Carigrad in other Slavic languages). Derived from the words czar (Caesar) and hrad (city).

CHAIKA — A dugout boat with sails and oars used in battle by Zaporizhian Kozaks.

CHALIY, SAVA *(?-1741)* — A Kozak officer who participated in the haidamak uprising against Poland but switched sides. He was executed by haidamak rebels.

CHUMAK — A merchant and trader who carted goods to and from Ukraine before railroads. The chumaks were venerated in Ukrainian folklore and culture.

CHYHYRYN (CHYHRYN) — A city in Central Ukraine that was the country's capital during the Kozak Hetmanate.

CREW CUT — Short haircut given military draftees. Shevchenko's shorthand for forced military service.

DNIPRO — The Ukrainian name for the river commonly translated into English from Russian as Dnieper.

DUMA — An epic poem sung in recitative style by kobzars, blind Ukrainian itinerant musicians.

FASTIV — A town near Kyiv that was a center of the anti-Polish uprising of the early 18th century.

GONTA, IVAN *(?-1768)* — One of the leaders of the 1768 haidamak rebellion. He was captured by a Russian unit, which handed him to the Poles. After brutal torture, his body parts were nailed to gallows in 14 towns.

GREG (SONG) — Reference to *Oy ne khody Hrytsju*, a Ukrainian folk song. An American adaptation, *Yes, My Darling Daughter* was a hit in the early 1940s with performances by Dinah Shore, Benny Goodman, Glenn Miller and others.

GUELDER ROSE — A tall flowering shrub that produces bright red berries. It is a national symbol of Ukraine and is mentioned throughout Shevchenko's poetry, Ukrainian folklore, art and culture. Also known as the snowball tree or European cranberrybush (*viburnum opulus*).

HAIDAMAKS — Participants in bloody 18th century Kozak and peasant rebellions against Polish nobility, Jesuits, Ukrainian Catholics and Jews. The main haidamak uprisings occurred in 1734, 1750 and 1768.

HAIR, SHORN — A way to mark thieves or witches. A shorn head also meant a military crew-cut.

HETMANATE — The Ukrainian Kozak state from the mid-17th to the mid-18th centuries.

HETMAN — The title of the top Ukrainian Kozak leader.

HLUKHIV — The capital of the Kozak Hetmanate. It was located near Russia according to Czar Peter's order to watch Kozak movements following destruction of the previous capital, Baturyn, in 1709.

HOPAK — The Ukrainian national dance. It is characterized by acrobatic jumping and spinning.

IASI — A city in Romania.

ILEK RIVER — A tributary of the Ural River in Kazakhstan and Russia's Orenburg Oblast.

IRON MAX — Translator's rendering of Maksym Zalizniak (ca. 1740-?), leader of the 1768 haidamak rebellion. The root word of his surname is derived from the Ukrainian word for iron. He was captured by a Russian unit and sentenced to life at hard labor in Siberia. Russia feared the rebellion's spread.

JACKDAW — A type of crow.

KHMELNYTSKY, BOHDAN (ca. 1595-1657) — Hetman of Ukraine who signed the controversial Pereyaslav Treaty with Russia, which led to the loss of Ukrainian independence.

KHORTYTSIA — One of the largest Dnipro River islands and former stronghold of the Zaporizhian Kozaks.

KOBZA — A Ukrainian instrument similar to a lute.

KOBZAR — An itinerant Ukrainian bard, often blind, who sang religious songs and national epics. Kobzars accompanied themselves with a kobza.

KOPA — A unit of measure that equaled 60 of certain items such as boards or sheaves of wheat. In monetary terms, 50 kopeck coins equaled one kopa.

KOPECK — A small coin roughly equivalent to a penny.

KOS-ARAL — An island in Kazakhstan's Aral Sea where Shevchenko served on a military scouting mission from September 26, 1848 through the end of January 1849. The island has since been attached to the mainland. The Syr Darya River once emptied into the Aral Sea, but dried up because of Soviet irrigation projects.

KOZAK — The Ukrainian transliteration of Cossack. It generally refers to Zaporizhian Kozaks, a powerful military force from the 16th to the 18th centuries, consisting mostly of Ukrainians seeking to escape serfdom. Zaporizhians were forcibly disbanded by Russian Empress Catherine.

LYMAN — The Dnipro River estuary.

MAKOVIY'S — An Eastern Christian feast on August 1 that celebrates the seven Jewish Maccabean martyrs, who died protecting their faith in one God from imposition of paganism.

MAZEPA, IVAN (1639-1709) — Ukrainian hetman who sided with Sweden against Russia in the pivotal Battle of Poltava during the Great Northern War. Many Ukrainians consider him a generous patron of the arts and hero who fought for Ukraine's independence. His image is on the ten hryvna banknote of independent Ukraine. Russia denounces Mazepa as a traitor.

MEADOW, THE GREAT UKRAINIAN (VELYKIY LUH) — Grassy lowland that stretched along the left bank of the Dnipro. It ran near the Zaporizhian Sich, the Kozak island stronghold in the Dnipro Rapids. The Rapids and Meadow were largely submerged during the Soviet period by hydroelectric dams.

MEZHYHIRSKY SAVIOR — Church at the Mezhyhirsky Monastery in Kyiv. It was destroyed in 1934 by Bolsheviks. The area was turned into a closed resort for Communist Party elites. President Viktor Yanukovych claimed it as a presidential estate.

MOUNDS — Shevchenko uses the image of the burial mound throughout *The Kobzar*. It connotes not only the place where ancestors rest, but also a symbol of Ukrainian historical and cultural continuity.

MUSCOVITE (МОСКАЛЬ) — Term for a soldier and also a pejorative Ukrainian term for a Russian. Both connotations are used in the poem *Kateryna*. Elsewhere in *The Kobzar*, it mostly refers to soldiers.

NALYVAIKO, SEVERIN *(?-1597)* — A Kozak otaman and leader of a rebellion against Poland from 1594-96. His full name was Pavlo-Semeriy (Severin) Kravchenko-Nalyvaiko.

NANKEEN — A red silk burial cloth imported from China. Russia later produced such fabric from cotton.

NICHOLAS I, CZAR (1796-1855) — Russian autocrat who personally forbade Shevchenko to write or draw during his decade-long internal exile.

NYMPH — In Ukrainian mythology, a river spirit that preys on the unsuspecting, whom they tickle to death.

OTAMAN — A Kozak leader.

OWL — Shevchenko frequently used the image of the owl to convey gloom and despair.

PALIY, SEMEN (ca. 1645-1710), historic name of Semen Pylypovych Hurko, a colonel and hero of an uprising against Polish nobility in Right-Bank Ukraine. Also a veteran of wars against Crimean Tatars and Ottoman Turks. Hetman Ivan Mazepa considered Paliy to be a social radical, feared his popularity and arrested him. Czar Peter exiled Paliy to Siberia, but released him after Mazepa sided with Sweden. Paliy fought on Russia's side at Poltava.

PEREYASLAV — A town in Central Ukraine that Shevchenko considered important for several historic reasons dating to the times of Kyivan Rus. In 1654, it was the place where Hetman Bohdan Khmelnytsky signed the controversial Pereyaslav Treaty with Russia that led to the loss of Ukrainian independence.

POCHAYIV — A large Orthodox Monastery in the Ternopil Region of Western Ukraine.

POLTAVA — A city in Eastern Ukraine and site of the 1709 Battle of Poltava, where Peter the Great defeated Sweden's Karl XII. The pivotal battle marked Russia's rise as a great power.

POOD — An old unit of weight used in Belarus, Russia and Ukraine. It equaled 36.11 pounds or 16.38 kilograms.

SAFARIK, PAVEL JOZEF *(1797-1861)* — Slovak and Czech poet, linguist. He opposed Russia as leader of Slavic peoples, promoting instead Pan-Slavism that treated all Slavs as equals. His father was a Protestant clergyman.

SCUTARI — Today's Uskudar, a suburb of Istanbul on the Anatolian side of the Bosporus.

SICH — Fortified Kozak stronghold on an island in the Dnipro rapids near the modern city of Zaporizhia. Russian Empress Catherine II ordered its destruction in 1775.

SOUL TAX — A Russian imperial tax introduced by Peter I and levied on each man in a household based on a census. Because a census was infrequent, many widows were forced to pay for dead husbands.

SUBOTIV — Central Ukrainian village where Hetman Bohdan Khmelnytsky's estate was located.

TENDER — A cape on the Black Sea near the Dnipro delta. It was once an island.

THIRD ROOSTERS — A cock can crow at any hour, but in Ukrainian, those that do so at midnight are referred to as first roosters. Second roosters are heard at two o'clock. Third roosters mark the end of night when evil spirits must disappear.

TRIASYLO, TARAS – A 17th century Kozak hetman. He is known by the surname of Triasylo, i.e. the one who jolts or shakes others. Dates of birth and death unknown.

UMAN REGION — The area around the central Ukrainian city of Uman on the right bank of the Dnipro.

UNIATE — A Ukrainian who converted from Orthodoxy to Catholicism following the Union of Brest in 1596. Sometimes used as a derogatory term.

VERST — An old Eastern Slavic unit of length equal to approximately 3500 feet or 1.06 kilometers.

VOLYN — A region of Northwestern Ukraine.

YELLOW WATERS (ZHOVTI VODY) — Site of a 1648 battle near the Zhovti Vody River in which Kozaks defeated Polish troops.

ZAPORIZHIANS — Ukrainian Kozaks who lived beyond the Dnipro River rapids in Central Ukraine.

ZAPORIZHIA — The territory of the Ukrainian Kozak state. Its fortified capital, the Zaporizhian Sich, was located on Khortytsia Island in the Dnipro River rapids.

TITLES IN ENGLISH

(Poems not titled by Shevchenko are listed in italics by first lines)

TITLES IN UKRAINIAN

(Poems not titled by Shevchenko are listed in italics by their first lines)

Peter Fedynsky gained translating experience as an international broadcaster with the Ukrainian Service at the Voice of America. During his 34-year career at VOA, Fedynsky hosted a Rock and Roll program transmitted to Soviet Ukraine, wrote a radio series in English on the theory and practice of democracy, and also served for more than 11 years as anchor of *Window on America,* a weekly TV news magazine in Ukrainian that was the first U.S. Government television program to go on the air overseas. Fedynsky culminated his career in broadcast journalism as VOA Moscow bureau chief and New York TV correspondent. He also translated documents for the U.S. State Department and served as a simultaneous interpreter at high-level meetings between U.S. and Ukrainian officials. In addition, he was a Ukrainian and Russian-speaking guide on two U.S. Information Agency exhibits in Russia, Ukraine, Lithuania and Armenia.

Fedynsky in Shevchenko's Jail Cell
Orenburg, Russia, May 2010

Fedynsky was born in Ashland, Pennsylvania to post-war Ukrainian immigrants and grew up in Cleveland, Ohio, where he was active in the local Ukrainian community as a scout leader and human rights activist. He was a German major at Ohio's Bowling Green State University, having spent his sophomore year abroad at the University of Salzburg, Austria.

Dear Reader,

Thank you for purchasing this book.

We at Glagoslav Publications are glad to welcome you, and hope that you find our books to be a source of knowledge and inspiration.

We want to show the beauty and depth of the Slavic region to everyone looking to expand their horizon and learn something new about different cultures, different people, and we believe that with this book we have managed to do just that.

Now that you've got to know us, we want to get to know you. We value communication with our readers and want to hear from you! We offer several options:

- Join our Book Club on Goodreads, Library Thing and Shelfari, and receive special offers and information about our giveaways;
- Share your opinion about our books on Amazon, Barnes & Noble, Waterstones and other bookstores;
- Join us on Facebook and Twitter for updates on our publications and news about our authors;
- Visit our site www.glagoslav.com to check out our Catalogue and subscribe to our Newsletter.

Glagoslav Publications is getting ready to release a new collection and planning some interesting surprises — stay with us to find out!

Glagoslav Publications
Office 36, 88-90 Hatton Garden
EC1N 8PN London, UK
Tel: + 44 (0) 20 32 86 99 82
Email: contact@glagoslav.com

Lightning Source UK Ltd.
Milton Keynes UK
UKHW011832120721
387068UK00001B/99